DELACORTE WORLD HISTORY

VOLUME V

The Greeks and the Persians

FROM THE SIXTH TO
THE FOURTH CENTURIES

The Greeks and the Persians

FROM THE SIXTH TO THE FOURTH CENTURIES

EDITOR

Hermann Bengtson

CONTRIBUTORS

HERMANN BENGTSON
EDDA BRESCIANI
WERNER CASKEL
MAURICE MEULEAU
MORTON SMITH

TRANSLATED BY
John Conway

DELACORTE PRESS

NEW YORK

Contents

EDITOR'S INTRODUCTION xi

1 The Persian Empire and the Greeks ca. 520 B.C. 1

2 The Fall of Tyranny in Athens and
the Reforms of Cleisthenes 26

3 The Ionian Rebellion and the Persian Wars
to the Battle of Marathon 37

4 Xerxes' Preparations for War, and His Expedition 47

5 The Founding of the Delian-Attic Maritime
League: The Rise of Athenian-Spartan Rivalry 69

6 Pericles and Athenian Democracy 82

7 Cultural and Intellectual Life in
the Age of Pericles 111

8 The Peloponnesian War (431–404 B.C.) 154

9 The Greeks of the West in the Fifth Century B.C. 195

10 Sparta's Hegemony and the Corinthian War
(404–386 B.C.) 201

CONTENTS

11 The Decline of Greek Independence and the Idea
    of the General Peace (386–362 B.C.)   215

12 The Greeks of the West in the Fourth Century B.C. 240

13 Greek Culture in the Fourth Century B.C.   250

14 The Rise of Macedonia under King Philip II
    (359–336 B.C.)   280

15 Alexander and the Conquest of the Persian Empire
    (336–323 B.C.)   303

16 Egypt and the Persian Empire   333
        by EDDA BRESCIANI
        Translated from the Italian by Phyllis Johnson

17 Mesopotamia Under Persian Rule   354
        by MAURICE MEULEAU
        *Translated from the French by
        Robert F. Tannenbaum*

18 Palestinian Judaism in the Persian Period   386
        by MORTON SMITH

19 Syria Under the Persians   402

20 Arabia   409
        by WERNER CASKEL

    CONCLUSION   421

    NOTES   425

    BIBLIOGRAPHY   439

    INDEX   451

    NOTE ON EDITOR AND CONTRIBUTORS   479

Illustrations

[*between pages 242 and 243*]

1. Archer-bodyguard of Darius I
2. Achaemenian cylinder seals
3. Head of ibex, Achaemenian period
4. Throne hall at Persepolis
5. Reliefs on stairway at Persepolis
6. Relief panels from stairway at Persepolis
7. Darius and Xerxes: relief from Persepolis
8. Face of bull-man from Persepolis
9. Fifth-century Persian gold drinking horn
10. Bust of Themistocles
11. Sixth-century amphorae
12. Speaker's platform on the Pnyx
13. Bust of Euripides
14. Greek drinking vessel, c. 470
15. Fifth-century Greek chalice
16. Fifth-century Athenian vase
17. East frieze of Parthenon
18. Fragment of treaty between Athens and Hermione
19. West pediment, temple of Zeus at Olympia
20. The Acropolis
21. The Parthenon
22. Temple of Nike on Acropolis
23. Theatre at Epidaurus
24. The Erechtheum on Acropolis
25. Head of a maenad, late fifth century
26. Temple of Apollo at Delphi

27. Temple of Poseidon at Paestum
28. Temple of Concord at Acragas
29. Bust of Plato
30. Stele of Ampharete, c. 405
31. Alexander the Great
32. Mosaic from Pompei showing the Battle of Issus
33. Egyptian naophorous statue of Henat
34. Egyptian naophorous statue of Psamtik-sa-Neith
35. Falcon: Egyptian faience hieroglyph
36. Kneeling man: Egyptian hieroglyph
37. Temple of the Moon at Marib, Arabia

Acknowledgments

The publishers wish to thank the following for providing illustrations for this volume:
The American School of Classical Studies at Athens, Institute for Advanced Studies, Princeton, figures 11, 12, 18; Art Reference Bureau, Ancram, New York, figures 29, 32; The British Museum, London, figure 2; The Cairo Museum, Cairo, figure 34; Foto Alinari, Rome, figures 13, 31, 33; Foto Marburg, Marburg, Lahn, Germany, figures 1, 23, 24, 27; German Archaeological Institute, Rome, figure 10; Greek National Tourist Office, New York, figures 20, 21; Hirmer Verlag, Munich, figures 17, 26, 28; Holle Verlag, Baden-Baden, Germany, figures 19, 22, 30; The Metropolitan Museum of Art, New York, figures 3, 9, 14, 15, 16, 25; The Metropolitan Museum of Art, The Carnarvon Collection, Gift of Edward S. Harkness, 1926, figures 35, 36; The Oriental Institute, The University of Chicago, Chicago, figures 5, 6, 8; Wendell Phillips, The American Foundation for the Study of Man, Honolulu, figure 37; Dr. Erich F. Schmidt, The Oriental Institute, The University of Chicago, Chicago, figures 4, 7.

Maps

The Persian Empire c. 500 B.C.   17
Classical Greece and the Aegean   31
Battle of Salamis   58
Greece on the Eve of the Peloponnesian War   163
Southern Italy and Sicily, Fifth Century B.C.   198
Battle of Leuktra   228
The Empire of Alexander the Great   324
Arabia c. 500 B.C.   413

Editor's Introduction

Any attempt to present the history of the Greeks and the Persians, from Darius I to Alexander, immediately faces a serious difficulty: the problem of sources. A few Old Persian inscriptions and some meager details derived from Greek traditions constitute the inadequate source materials for a history of the Persian Empire and for an estimate of its role in world history.

It is quite otherwise with the history of the Greeks. There are many literary and epigraphic materials still in existence that allow the historian to re-create the essential features of the political and cultural life of this most gifted of all peoples of ancient times. Many gaps still remain, of course, particularly the nearly fifty-year span between 479 and 431 B.C.—the so-called Pentecontaetia—for which there is a lamentable dearth of original sources. Even in recent years, intensive work by many scholars has been unable to alter matters here.

In general, however, thanks mainly to the ancient Greek historians themselves, with Herodotus and Thucydides heading the list, the history of the Greek people can be adequately set forth, and the great figures of Greek history can be brought once more to life.

In this volume I have refrained, for various reasons, from drawing historical parallels, especially contemporary ones. Many will suggest themselves of their own accord to the interested reader.

In order to present the history and culture of a few important areas at the edges of the Mediterranean world, certain chapters written by specialists in their subjects have been added to this volume. They round off the total picture of the age, and will reward the attentive reader.

HERMANN BENGTSON

Tuebingen, 1964

DELACORTE WORLD HISTORY

VOLUME V

The Greeks and the Persians

FROM THE SIXTH TO
THE FOURTH CENTURIES

1

The Persian Empire and the Greeks ca. 520 B.C.

Beginning with the year 550 B.C., when the elder Cyrus founded the Achaemenid Empire, the history of the ancient world is increasingly dominated by the threat of expanding Persian power. From 547 on, Persia's pressure on her neighbors continued without abatement for nearly seventy years. Even after the failure of Xerxes' great invasion of Greece itself at Salamis in 480, Persian pressure on the Greeks did not cease. Not until the Peace of Callias in 449–448 was an unstable equilibrium achieved, and this lasted only a few decades. Then, with Persia's intervention in the Peloponnesian War on the side of Sparta (412), a new period of Persian hegemony began, culminating in the King's Peace of the year 386, limiting the Greeks' freedom of action.

It was only with the rise of Macedonia under King Philip II (359–336) that a genuine counterweight to the power of the Persian Empire appeared on the western side of the Aegean. A few years later the campaigns of Alexander the Great, Philip's son and heir, finally overthrew the Empire of the Achaemenids. Alexander himself took the place of the last Persian King, Darius III Codomannus, and for a time a fusion of the Macedonian and Iranian peoples seemed in prospect. But its realization was frustrated by Alexander's early death (323). In the fighting among Alexander's successors (Diadochi), conservative Macedonianism triumphed. Nevertheless,

the indigenous Iranian culture did not disappear. It was revived politically in the third century B.C. in a struggle against
the Seleucids, when the traditions of the Achaemenid Empire
were given new life by the Parthian Arsacid Empire. Founded
in 248–247 (?) B.C., the Parthian Empire rapidly became
an adversary not to be despised—as the Seleucids and then the
Romans (Battle of Carrhae, 53 B.C.) were to discover to their
cost.

The clash between the world of Rome and the world of
Iran was greatly intensified after the appearance, in A.D. 226,
of the New Persian, or Sassanian, Empire. From then on, the
later history of the ancient world was largely based on the
confrontation of the two empires, the Roman and the New
Persian, until the rule of the Sassanids collapsed before the
onslaught of the Arabs in the battle of Nehavend (A.D. 642).

This confrontation of two separate and opposed civilizations—Iranian and Western—over a period of more than a
thousand years was accompanied, naturally, by a great many
intellectual and artistic crosscurrents flowing between the
peoples involved. It is common knowledge that the Greeks
made an outstanding contribution to the building of the
Achaemenid Empire. There were Greek physicians, scholars
and architects at the Persian court; the role played by Greek
mercenaries in the Persian army can hardly be overestimated.
The Parthians themselves were abundantly aware of the importance of Greek culture, particularly since between their
empire and that of the Achaemenids not only the Empire of
the Seleucids had intervened, but also the Empire of Alexander, under which Greek culture had spread as far as Iran
and northern India. Without Alexander there would probably
have been no Greek world culture; without Hellenism, no
Imperium Romanum, for in the civilization of the Roman
Empire the Hellenistic contributions were of fundamental importance. They were no less important in preparing the way
for the eventual victory of Christianity in communities stretch-
ing from Ireland to India.

The question must be raised whether and to what extent it
is justifiable to regard the history of antiquity as determined

by the conflict between Greco-Roman culture and that of Iran. Ernst Kornemann's answer is, yes. Nevertheless, impressive as is the structure of his argument, doubts still remain. These doubts are based not only on the well-known torpidity of the Persian Empire at decisive moments in her history, but also on a comparison of the Greek culture of the fifth and fourth centuries B.C. with the intellectual life of the Persian Empire during the same period. With all due respect given to the achievements of the Persians in monumental architecture, in the entire far-flung empire there is to be found nothing even approximately comparable in artistic content to the magnificent edifices of the Age of Pericles. Finally, Persian culture offered nothing to equal the free play of the Greek spirit in philosophy, drama, and historiography, although for many decades the gates of cultural contact were wide open on both sides.

It is significant, for instance, that it is to Herodotus that we owe a description of the Persian Empire unexcelled even to this day. The Persian inscriptions, important as their data may be for us, are on the order of ancient Near Eastern rulers' decrees, set forth for the glorification of the Great King. In the Greek world the individual was allowed to develop in the field of politics and intellectual life according to his inclinations and abilities. But of the Achaemenid Empire, beyond the names of the Great Kings, we know only those of a few of their closest collaborators and friends—and even those come to us for the most part through Greek history or tradition.

Though the Persian Empire, after Darius I (552–486), presented a concentration of political power such as had never existed before in the history of the ancient world, the fact cannot be overlooked that little Greece possessed an intellectual life of incomparably higher significance. Hellenism gave the fifth and fourth centuries before Christ their intellectual stamp. In these centuries were laid the foundations of Western intellectual life, certainly not without non-Greek influences, but nonetheless in essence the product of the intellectual achievements of the Greeks themselves.

The empire of the Persians, which in the political sphere

3

could not be taken lightly, nevertheless appeared to the Greeks
—despite innumerable contacts in peace and war—as something entirely foreign. The Persian wars seemed to diminish
rather than increase the Greeks' understanding of their eastern
neighbors. If we did not possess the work of Herodotus, not
only the political but also the intellectual background of the
great Hellenic-Persian conflict would be a closed book to us.
What was lacking among the Greeks, with few exceptions, was
a real understanding of the individual character of the Persian
race and of the Achaemenid Empire. No serious effort was
made on the Greek side to examine the sustaining forces of
Persian civilization that held the empire and its peoples together. To the Greeks, the Persians—or, as they usually called
them, the Medes—were and remained barbarians. In the unquestioned authority of the Great King over his subjects, the
Greeks saw the dreariest despotism; in the loyalty of Persian
vassals to the hereditary ruling house they saw blind obedience. They felt no need for a deeper understanding of the life
of the Persian subject himself. Despite manifold contacts in
trade and in intellectual life, Greeks and Persians lived next
to each other without spiritual contact, and this for over two
full centuries.

In the final analysis this is the reason that we know so little
about the Persians. Since this state of affairs is not likely to
change materially in the future, we must reconcile ourselves
to the fact that we cannot do justice to the Persians in the same
way as we can to the Greeks, who have left to us such an
abundance of historical evidence.

The Medes themselves, who formed a large part of the empire of the Elder Cyrus, first appeared on the stage of world
history in the year 612 B.C. In that year, Nineveh, the
capital of the once proud Assyrian Empire, sank into ruins
before the onslaught of the armies of the Chaldeans (Neo-
Babylonians) and the Medes from the Zagros Mountains of
Iran. The event marked the end of an epoch in Near Eastern
history.

For centuries, all the nations of the Near East, from Armenia and Eastern Anatolia to Egypt, had lived in terror of the Assyrians. The Assyrian armies had been considered invincible. No city could withstand their siege machines. No nation could hold out against them. Now the Near East was to be temporarily dominated by four great, separate powers instead of one: the Neo-Babylonian Empire, Egypt, Lydia, and Media. Of these, the Median Empire proved to be the most powerful. In less than two years after the fall of Nineveh, Cyaxares the Mede seized the last, ephemeral Assyrian kingdom, the domain of Assur-uballit in Harran, between the upper Tigris and Euphrates rivers; the Medes from then on ruled northern Mesopotamia, coming into contact with its age-old cities and advanced culture.

Advancing then across Armenia to Cappadocia, the Medes threatened the Kingdom of Lydia. The armies of the two powers collided in battle on the Halys River in eastern Anatolia, and the treaty that followed marked the river as the new boundary between Lydians and Medes (585). The first empire established by Iranians had reached its limit.

Cyaxares' successor, Ishtuwegu—Herodotus calls him Astyages—appears to have been content with this. A weak personality, his long reign (585–550) shows no urge for further conquests. But ruling at this time in Anshan, a region of Persis, was a vassal prince of the Median king, a certain Cambyses of the House of the Achaemenids. Enjoying the best of relations with Astyages, he became the latter's son-in-law, and from his marriage to the Median Princess Mandane issued a son, Cyrus, who succeeded his father at Pasargadae in 559.

It was Cyrus who for the first time brought the Persians to the head of the Iranian family of nations.

With Cyrus' revolt in 550 against the domination of the Medes began the ascent of the Persians under the rule of the Achaemenids. But the overthrow of the hegemony of the Median king was not synonymous with a suppression of the Medes. The noble families of the Medes had their full share in all the new ruler's successes and in all the honors. It is not by chance that Greek tradition mentions the Medes and the Persians in one breath, and that in Greek the word "Mede" is synonymous with "Persian." The expansion that followed represented the unfolding of a dual Iranian nation under the purposeful leadership of Cyrus, who passed even into Greek tradition as the shining model of a Persian ruler. Almost two centuries later, the Athenian Xenophon depicted the figure of the young Cyrus in bright colors in his *Cyropaedia*, an ancient *Mirror for Princes* which, then and since, has found many readers and many literary imitators.

Like his predecessor, Cyaxares the Mede, Cyrus turned first against the Lydians, this time with decided success. Gaining a victory at Pteria, his Persians pursued the Lydian army under Croesus as far as western Asia Minor. There, on the "Field of Cyrus," Persian arms again proved superior to the Lydian, and after a siege that is said to have lasted only fourteen days, Sardis, the Lydian capital, and its supposedly impregnable citadel fell into the hands of the Persians, and the Lydian King Croesus was taken prisoner (547).

The fall of Croesus, who had been connected by many friendly ties to the Greek world, marked a new epoch in the relations between Greece and Persia. With it began the direct contact between the Hellenes and the Persians that was never again to be broken off during the history of the two peoples.

The Greek communities on the western coast of Asia Minor had been subjects and supporters of the Lydian king, whose rule had not weighed heavily on them, especially since the Lydians had been eagerly receptive to Greek culture. The Lydian royal house had always been conscious of the great importance of its Hellenic cities, and the Greeks themselves had adopted the Lydian invention of coinage, the introduction of which gave the economy of the Mediterranean area a new foundation.

The Greeks of Ionia and their importance were not unknown to Cyrus. Before the decisive passage at arms he had approached them diplomatically, but only Miletus had seen fit to place itself openly on his side. After the fall of Sardis, the Milesians received a Persian treaty of friendship and alliance —the first of a long series of Greco-Persian treaties—whereas all the other Greeks of Asia Minor were put under the direct

6

rule of the Persian satraps. Some of the Greek cities, moreover, had to be subdued by Cyrus' general, Harpagus, having refused to open their gates to the Persians. Sparta attempted to intervene by dispatching an embassy calling on Cyrus not to attack them, but to no avail.

A revolt was raised by the Lydian Pactolus; the Persians broke it, but now adopted another tone. They secured their hold on the country by means of occupation forces and military colonies, and in the cities entrusted the government to partisans of Persia, who for their part found their position bolstered by foreign rule. As a result, it did not long remain hidden from the Ionians that Persian rule, with its satraps and garrisons, was much more oppressive and unpleasant than that of the Lydian kings, who had always given special consideration to the Greek cities in their realm. The Greek idea and the Persian idea of the state, it became clear, were as incompatible as fire and water.

A great power after the conquest of Lydia, Persia became a world power within eight years, as Cyrus proceeded to subjugate the Iranian east as far as the borders of India and finally seized the Neo-Babylonian Empire of the Chaldeans.

With its numerous cities and its age-old temple culture, Babylonia must have held an irresistible attraction for Cyrus' Persians, similar to that which Mesopotamia under the Seleucids later held for the Parthians. Although Babylonia was in decline politically under its last king, Nabonidus, it was still the commercial center of the Near East, its trade extending to all the parts of the region as far as Ionia. The military strength of the country was, however, no longer at its previous high level, and King Nabonidus had been unfortunate in his behavior toward the powerful priesthood of the god Marduk in Babylon. So the Persian king had an easy time defeating the Chaldeans. Within a few months Cyrus' general, the governor of Gutium—a Babylonian, Gubaru, or Gobryas, as our Greek sources call him—made his entry into Babylon and the struggle was ended. Sixteen days later Cyrus himself followed, on October 29, 539, and the victor issued a massive pronouncement in which he did not fail to point out his own good re-

7

lationship with the gods of the country, Bel-Marduk and Nabu. Syria and Phoenicia, former Babylonian possessions, soon hastened to pay reverence to their new master, and with their adhesion the Persian Empire had reached the sea and had at its disposal the fleets of all the Phoenician maritime cities on the Mediterranean. To reassure his new subjects and make clear the religious tolerance of the Achaemenids, Cyrus decreed from Ecbatana the reconstruction of the Temple of Jerusalem (538), an act that assured him for all time the gratitude of the Jewish people.

The Neo-Babylonian Empire and its adjacent lands were now united in a personal union with the crown of Persia. From now on, Cyrus was not only King of the Medes and the Persians but also King of *Babilu û Êbir-nâri*—"King of Babylonia and the Land Beyond the River," namely, the Euphrates. His power, however, lasted less than eight years longer. The founder of the Persian Empire met his end in 530, in battle with the Massagetes—the "Saka with the pointed caps"—who, emerging from the steppes between the Caspian and Aral Seas, had again and again pressed upon the open flank of the empire's northeastern border.

The great conqueror was succeeded by his eldest son, Cambyses (530–522), named after Cyrus' own father. He first avenged Cyrus' death at the hands of the Massagetes and then, in 525, set forth on the conquest of Egypt, the last ancient imperial civilization then remaining in the Near East. And here again we find a Persian Great King in league with Greeks. Polycrates, the tyrant of Samos, is said to have concluded an alliance with Cambyses and to have placed a part of his fleet at the Persian's disposal for the campaign against Egypt. There the Persian found the Egyptians unable to offer serious resistance and victory was quick. Psammetichus III, the last native Pharaoh, was at first allowed to continue as a vassal prince; then, after rebelling, was put to death.

Only in Cambyses' attempt to subjugate the Greeks of Cyrenaica and in his expedition against Nubia did the Persian king fail to realize his ambitions.

Ancient tradition portrays the figure of Cambyses at this

point in dark colors. He is pictured not only as the author of the murder of his younger brother, Bardiya—or Smerdis—but also as a wholly intolerant and ruthless tyrant in his attitude to the gods of the Nile Valley. Be that as it may, after a three-year stay in Egypt, he received the news of the revolt at home of Gaumata—the "false Smerdis"—and returned to Syria only to die there, a natural death, and not suicide, as had been formerly assumed.

Already, however, the revolt of Gaumata had plunged the empire into chaos. In his rebellion, Gaumata, himself a Magus, had relied for support above all on the powerful priestly caste, which was attempting through him to obtain control of the empire. A series of especially popular measures, among them a three-year remission of taxes, won the masses to his side, while the influence of the nobility was in every respect curtailed. It is difficult to overestimate the importance of these changes on the internal structure of the Persian Empire. Without any doubt, they signified a quite decided turning away from the old tradition of an omnipotent military aristocracy that had obtained under Cyrus.

The revolt, therefore, very soon called counterforces into play. Darius, son of Hystaspes, the satrap of Parthia, descended from a collateral line of the Achaemenids, acted in company with six Persian nobles; he resolved upon the destruction of Gaumata, and in a few weeks, at a castle in the vicinity of Ecbatana, the Magus was struck down by Darius. He is said to have ruled only two months in all.

The coronation of Darius in Pasargadae and his marriage to Atossa, the daughter of Cyrus, were followed by difficult times. Both Elam and Babylonia were shaken by dangerous revolts which quickly spread to the Iranian heartland. In Media, Fravartish—Phraortes in Greek—a member of the old Median royal house of Deïocids, took the regnal name of Khshathrita and attempted to restore the Median Empire. Parthia and Hyrcania joined him and even Armenia fell away from Darius. In the great monumental inscriptions on the rocky wall of Behistun, Darius himself has left us a detailed account of his struggles with the rebels and his victories over them.

Apparently they constituted such a multitude of powerful opponents, supported in part by the populations of their provinces, that today it seems like a miracle that Darius in little over a year got the upper hand. (His express testimony to this effect there seems no reason to doubt.) But by the end of 521 Arakha in Babylonia had been suppressed and with him the last of the insurgents—the "liar kings" as Darius called them. The struggles were ended and the Persian Empire lay at the victor's feet.

Much has been written about the imperial organization set up by Darius. Since Eduard Meyer's description of the empire of the Achaemenids as a state possessing a high level of civilization, historians have increasingly arrived at a very positive evaluation of the achievements of the first Achaemenid rulers. These achievements seem all the greater when one takes into account the great distances within this gigantic empire, a factor that would have created enormous obstacles to any organized imperial administration.

The reorganization of the empire by Darius was probably completed in the years between 518 and 514. It was certainly the result of a comprehensive plan formed and executed point by point by Darius himself, with the aid of his collaborators and confidants. Viewed as a whole it appears to have been a flexible compromise between a feudal and a centralized state. Its foundation was the personal loyalty felt by the Great King toward his subjects and, in return, their feeling of unconditional fealty to him. The leading role in the empire was awarded to the Persians. From their ranks the satraps and the commanders of the imperial armies were appointed. The other nations, with the exception of the Medes, had to be content with essentially subordinate functions.

From the Old Persian inscriptions—above all, the royal inscriptions of Behistun, Naksh-i-Rustam, Persepolis, and Susa—and also from Greek sources, particularly Herodotus (III, 89ff.), one gathers that Darius undertook to redivide his enormous empire by organizing the entire clumsy mass of provinces into satrapies. (In the inscriptions they are called "Lands.") Over each of these "provinces" a governor was placed whose official title was "satrap." Satrap (in Old Persian, *khshathrapavan*) roughly meant "protector of the kingdom," a title that possibly had its origin in the original Median Empire. There had also been satraps under Cyrus, but they had been great feudal lords probably ruling over vast territories. Darius made these old feudal satrapies smaller, and in principle placed them all on the same legal basis. All the satrapies were obliged to pay tribute to the Great King; without tribute it was not possible to govern in the East; Darius was only extending a principle that had formerly been applied by the Assyrians.

In considering the list of satrapies set up by Darius it must be noted that, even during his reign, certain changes took place which we can follow in detail only with great difficulty. According to the inscription of Behistun, the earliest of the great royal inscriptions, there were the following satrapies:

(1) Persis, (2) Huza (Elam), (3) Babairu (Babylon), (4) Athura (Assyria), (5) Arabaya (the North Arabian Jezireh), (6) Mudraya (Egypt), (7) the satrapy on the sea (southern Asia Minor), (8) Sardis, (9) Yauna (Ionia), (10) Mada (Media), (11) Armina (Armenia), (12) Cappadocia, (13) Parthia, (14) Zranka (Drangiana), (15) Haraiwa (Aria), (16) Huwarazmiya (Chorasmia), (17) Bactria, (18) Sogdiana, (19) Gandhara, (20) Saka (the land of the Scythians), (21) Tatagus (Sattagydia), (22) Harahuwati (Arachosia), (23) Maka (location doubtful).

To these provinces of the early period a few others were later added, above all Putiya (Libya), Kusiya (Nubia), and, after Darius' campaign against the Scythians, Skudra (Thrace) as well.

Of the tributes paid, Babylonia—which, according to Herodotus, was the most productive province of the entire empire—delivered a total tribute valued at a thousand silver talents. This sum was paid in precious metals in the form of vessels, fine garments, and humpbacked cattle (in which the province was especially rich) intended for the provisioning of the Great King's court and army. Egypt's total contribution is estimated by Herodotus at seven hundred silver talents. The

11

land of the Nile delivered grain and cattle primarily; whether the total figure included the profits of the Lake Moeris fishery is a disputed question. The latter, in any case, brought the Great King a considerable income. For the rest, numerous other satrapies had to provide horses, which were of great importance for the imperial army.

The tributes themselves were delivered to the central treasuries in the royal residences, for the empire could be administered only by means of a bureaucracy trained in detail and using a uniform language. At the head of this bureaucracy stood the *hazarapatish,* or "chiliarch," who as Chief of the Great King's Bodyguard had risen to become Grand Vizier of the Empire. This high dignitary, "the first after the King," was, next to the sovereign, the actual ruler of the empire. An interesting impression of the treasuries is conveyed to us by the American excavations in Persepolis; here the treasury (*ganzaka*) has been rediscovered, and with it several thousand clay tablets in the Elamite language, showing provision delivery accounts which afford us a lively insight into the functioning of the local administration.

The use of Elamite in Persepolis is a special case, of course, explained by the location of Elam, with its age-old culture, nearby on the Persian Gulf. The language of the Royal Chancellery itself and of the entire administration of the empire was Aramaic, and in a particular form: Imperial Aramaic. Documents in this idiom are found even in the most remote parts of the Achaemenid Empire, in Elephantine in Upper Egypt as well as at Sardis and in India. Imperial Aramaic is known even from the Bible, where it occurs in some chapters of the Book of Ezra.

This language, without exception, had to be used by scribes for whom it was not the mother tongue. But this was outweighed by the fact that with it the entire enormous empire possessed a uniform language of administration. In addition the letters of its alphabet, which had been borrowed from the Phoenician script, were much easier to commit to pliable writing material (leather and papyrus) than was the cuneiform writing, which remained basically a monument script.

12

Whether Darius introduced a new cuneiform writing of his own in his monument inscriptions is highly questionable. At any rate he refrained, for good reasons, from using one for the business of government.

Even the best administration is worth little if it does not succeed in bringing its orders in minimum time to its subordinate offices. For the transmission of information there was in the Achaemenid Empire an excellently organized postal system that probably was a continuation of a similar arrangement made by the Assyrians. Across Asia there stretched a series of highways by which the residences of the Great King —Susa, Persepolis, Ecbatana—were kept in touch with the other parts of the empire. The best-known is the so-called Royal Road described by Herodotus. On this highway one could get from Sardis in Lydia through Cappadocia to the upper Euphrates and thence to the Tigris. Through the passes of the Zagros Mountains—the exact route is not precisely known—the King's Highway reached the palace at Susa. By frequent changes of horse and messenger, even great distances could be covered in minimum time—up to two hundred miles in a single day—so that a message from Susa to Sardis was en route no more than seven days. This Achaemenid postal system was taken as a model by Alexander and his successors, and even the *cursus publicus* of the Romans is linked indirectly with this system.

Undoubtedly the Persian imperial administration also had its dark side. In all the satrapies the Great King had his confidential agents, who, in popular parlance, were called the "eyes" and "ears" of the king, resembling the *missi dominici* of Charlemagne. The function of these men was to report to their master on everything of note that they saw or experienced. Since their place was directly under the Great King, they had as a rule uneasy relations with the satraps and the local authorities, for this truly oriental system of spying on one's fellows was only too apt to undermine the morale and the zeal of other officials.

Economically the regions of the Achaemenid Empire stood on quite varying levels. Whereas coinage existed in Asia

13

Minor and Babylonia, and to some extent probably also in Egypt, the other provinces of the empire remained mainly at the level of a simple, primitive economy. Darius, who was uncommonly gifted in economic affairs, brought about a certain change in this regard through the introduction of an imperial coinage. A gold coin, the daric, with a gold content of 8.42 grams, was introduced; this was half the weight of the Phocaean stater, a coin of the Ionian Greeks that had wide currency in trade. Its weight was also one sixtieth of that of the Babylonian mina. So the daric stood in a fixed relationship to the two most important monetary systems within the empire—a relationship we cannot assume to have come about by mere chance.

In addition to the gold daric, on which the Great King was portrayed as a kneeling archer—among the Greeks the coin was popularly known as the *toxotes* or bowman—there was also one of silver weighing 14.9 grams, which was called *shiklu* in Babylonian and *siglos* in Greek, the Biblical *shekel*.

Darius, of course, like his successors, carried his financial reforms only halfway. Like all Persian kings he did a great deal of hoarding of precious metals, storing them in the treasuries of the royal residences without deriving the smallest use from them. In fact, it is likely that many of the economic difficulties of the Persian Empire can be traced to this short-sighted policy of hoarding. Nevertheless, even in the fourth century B.C. the Persian kings always had sufficient money on hand to pay for foreign mercenaries, especially Greeks. The parallel to Byzantium suggests itself—an empire that stayed alive largely by judicious use of its financial power.

The power and the glory of the Persian world-empire found its most conspicuous expression in the edifices of the Achaemenids. The earlier rulers, Cyrus I, for example had resided in Pasargadae. Here there still stands the grave of the Elder Cyrus, restored by Alexander the Great. In strong contrast to the very simple construction of this tomb are the magnificent buildings of Darius and Xerxes in Persepolis, which was actually called "Persai." As one surveys the wide field of ruins today is visible even now, beneath the rubble, the ordering hand of the architect. Persepolis, the "City of Persia" as the Greeks called it, was not actually a city but a palace. Here is to be found, before the grandiose backdrop of the rocks of Kuh-i-Rahmat, an entire complex of imposing, mutually harmonious edifices: the Apadana (audience hall) of Darius, the palace of Darius, the palace of Xerxes, the Council Hall, the Hall of the Hundred Columns, the Harem (which today serves as the expedition headquarters) and the Treasury. All these buildings were adorned with splendid reliefs. The figures appearing on them, from the Great King down to the last soldier and tribute bearer, are executed with the greatest care, their clothing and arms rendered with such exactness that we can identify at once each one's national origin. Especially famous is the relief from the Hall of the Hundred Columns: the Great King, sitting on a raised throne, is being approached by a dignitary who covers his mouth with his hand. Today in the East it is still considered polite not to offend a superior with one's breath. (This has nothing to do with the Persian obeisance to royalty, called by the Greeks *proskynesis*.) The execution of the reliefs is in part reminiscent of Assyrian models; for the rest, however, the buildings were erected with the assistance of the numerous, varied peoples of the empire. In the inscription of Darius on the palace at Susa, for instance, appear not only Babylonians and Assyrians but also Ionians and Carians from Asia Minor. At the foot of a royal relief of Darius in Persepolis, two heads by Greek artists have been immortalized in sketches scratched on the rock.

Not inferior in monumental character to the great buildings in Persepolis are the royal graves that stand not far from the palace in the rocky wall of Naksh-i-Rustam, and the towering cliff relief of Behistun at the "Gate of Asia." The relief of Behistun, fashioned after Oriental models, shows Darius as the victor over the "false Bardiya" and the "liar kings." Over the scene hovers Ahuramazda, extending to the Great King the ring, symbol of sovereign power.

One of the first to attempt to transcribe the trilingual inscription in Babylonian, Old Persian, and Elamite on the steep cliff wall was the German scholar and traveler Carsten

Niebuhr. The glaring sunlight and the great distance of the observer from his subject presented him with extraordinary difficulties, quite apart from the fact that at the time, in 1766, the cuneiform script had not yet been deciphered. The decipherment was accomplished early in 1802 by a young high-school teacher, Grotefend, in Hanover.

As to who was the creator of these buildings and reliefs, tradition is silent. The men were masters of their work, above all, those architects who originated the plan of the palace in Persepolis. Was it perhaps some Eastern Greek master who, with a fine feeling for space and the impressive setting, created here an unforgettable masterpiece? We do not know. At any rate, in the plan of the building, massiveness and decorative detail are united with a disciplined feeling for space that does not overwhelm, but wholly serves the utilitarian purpose of the edifice. Such buildings are, in any case, a mirror of the best traditions of Persian civilization, which received many foreign impulses yet created something peculiarly and characteristically its own.

In Darius' own inscriptions a breath can still be felt of the spirit of that great administrator and commander in chief. The great inscription of Behistun is, of course, primarily a historical document. Darius' ethics are more clearly attested to in the epitaph of Naksh-i-Rustam. In it, Darius extols the favor of Ahuramazda:

> By the favor of Ahuramazda I am such that I am a friend of what is right and am not a friend of what is evil. It is not my pleasure that the poor man endure injustice at the hands of the mighty; neither is it my pleasure that the man of high station endure injustice for the sake of the lowly. What is right is my pleasure.
>
> So far as my body has the strength, I am considered as a warrior, a good warrior. When to my reason it appears doubtful whom I should regard as a friend and whom as an enemy, then I think first of his good deeds in deciding whether it is an enemy or a friend that I have before me.
>
> Skilled am I of hand and foot. Considered as a horseman, I am a good horseman; as an archer, I am a good archer, on

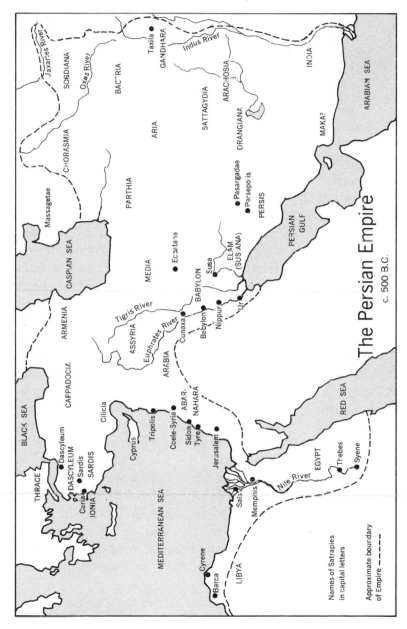

The Persian Empire

c. 500 B.C.

Names of Satrapies
in capital letters

Approximate boundary
of Empire ─────

foot as well as on horseback. As a spear-thrower, I am a good spear-thrower, on foot as well as on horseback. As to the abilities with which Ahuramazda has arrayed me—and I have had the strength to use them through the grace of Ahuramazda —what I have accomplished I have wrought with these abilities that Ahuramazda has conferred on me.

There is no reason to doubt the faith of Darius. His confession, at the end of a long and illustrious life, is at once proud and humble; Darius is a king who is fully conscious of his high dignity. What he has created rests upon a firm foundation, trust in Ahuramazda, who has taken the Great King into his keeping.

The actual religious faith of the ancient Persians is a subject on which it is very difficult to speak. We know so little of their religion that every statement must remain more or less questionable. We do know that over it there shone the great name of the prophet Zarathustra, but when precisely he lived is still a matter of dispute. Was it at the turn of the seventh to the sixth century B.C.? Or does he date from a much earlier time? Were the Achaemenids themselves Zoroastrians at all? The so-called *daiva* inscription of Xerxes, a foundation inscription at Persepolis, seems to support the view that they were: in particular the occurrence of the expression *rtavan* gives credence to such a view, and a connection has been seen between it and the Zoroastrian concept of *rtm,* which signifies a divine system of salvation.

Be that as it may, the Persian people worshiped divinities without images under the open sky, and two of these divinities in the time of Herodotus, Mithras and Anahita, are known to us. Finally, a role that we can scarcely reconstruct was played by the Magi, with whose brand of religion the fire cult was connected, and who also occupied an important position in political life.

Darius was one of the great builders of the Persian Empire. It was he who gave the empire its definite character. Nevertheless, we cannot ignore the dark shadows that developed even in Darius' day—shadows that grew deeper the longer the empire existed. Without any doubt, the Persian concept of the sovereign and his relation to his subjects was quite incompatible with the Western and, in particular, with the Greek ideal of freedom. For the Great King, all his subjects, irrespective of station or origin, were in the final analysis his slaves; and it is certainly not by chance that not a single one of the aides of Darius stands out clearly in the Persian tradition. In addition, the life of the Great King was lived in conscious isolation from his people; even the great and powerful had to view him from afar in audiences. Obviously no ruler of the world can completely renounce power, but the important thing for most of us is that, when it is used, it should not be used for its own sake, but for the fulfillment of a moral idea. We are therefore horrified when we learn in what an inhuman way Darius had the "liar kings" mutilated, and how maliciously he had Oroetes, a satrap of Sardis, eliminated.

Of course, Darius regarded himself, after the death of Cambyses, as the legitimate successor of the Achaemenids. But whether he was the only Persian who could rightfully assert this claim remains open to doubt. In general, Darius, in his propagandistic inscriptions, probably makes things rather too easy for himself by finding the truth and the right always on his side, and falsehood and injustice always on the side of his enemies. Zarathustra had conceived of the struggle of truth against falsehood as being the unrelenting struggle of faith against its adversaries—a very dangerous conception. Darius took this idea, applied it to politics, and followed it throughout his career, thus in the last analysis making justice the right of the stronger. What the reasons were that led the Achaemenids to their toleration of foreign and alien religions —an almost incomprehensible point of view for that time— we do not know. Did Cyrus and Darius really seek by it to divert their subject peoples from political life and make renunciation of political power bearable for them by granting them all imaginable freedom in the field of religion? Was this the reason for their extraordinary tolerance? To this question we find no answer. Religious freedom did not satisfy the Greeks, as is shown by the Ionian revolt which shook the Persian Empire at a critical time (500–499 to 494).

19

Actually, despite the varied beliefs of its multitude of peoples, the Persian Empire was a centralized state ruled by the will of the Great King. It was quite another thing with the Greek world, which presented a picture of extreme fragmentation. At that time the Greek world extended from the Aegean to Spain and from southern Russia to Egypt and Libya. But it was, apart from Hellas, the mother country, essentially an extension that can be represented on a map by single points and not by frontiers. At many places on the shores of the Mediterranean there were Greek settlements, but they were in a variety of ways turned inward on themselves and lacked common ties. Even in Hellas itself, the many Greek city-states, the *poleis,* existed side by side in disunity. There was not even a great common idea, a Hellenic national feeling; this began to take shape only on the eve of the great Persian War. To be sure, every four years the flower of Greek youth assembled from all parts of Hellas and the Greek colonies for the sacred festivities in Olympia; and in the list of victors there appear, besides the Greeks of the mother country, also the names of many Greeks from southern Italy and Sicily. But this did nothing at all to alter the state of political fragmentation that existed. Certainly, in addition to an accepted common descent from a mythical ancestor, there were other elements among the Hellenes that created a bond between the Greeks of the various cities, in particular the pan-Hellenic pantheon as unfolded in the epics of Homer. But alongside the Homeric gods there was also an abundance of local divinities, with each city and each tribe venerating its own. In this age in fact, in Sicily and Greece proper, the tyrants were at work building great temples to give such local gods worthy homes. There was not even a common literary language to act as a unifying cultural factor; Attic Greek became a vehicle for local Athenian literature only in the course of the fifth century, and its employment for all Greek literature began later still.

Nevertheless, the heart of Hellenism continued to be the Greek mother country, and here Sparta occupied the leading position. With the conquest of the fertile Messenian lands and the enslavement of the luckless Messenians, Sparta had become the first state of the Peloponnese. This position the Spartan leaders had been able to strengthen still further through a calculated policy of alliances. As a result, from 550 on, Sparta, the state of the Lacedaemonians, was at the head of the so-called Peloponnesian League, an alliance that, with the notable exception of Argos, included the entire Peloponnese. Argos and Sparta were and had been bitter enemies for a long time, the issue being the possession of the fertile district of Cynuria, an object of bitter struggles in the past and destined to remain so during the decades to come. (Battle of Sepeia, 494). As against Sparta and the Peloponnesian League, however, all the other city-states of the Greek mother country were of secondary significance.

Among them the maritime states of Athens, Corinth and Aegina were easily the most important. Corinth's location on the isthmus gave it an advantage over the other two cities, and it also possessed a number of colonies on the Ionian Sea and in the northern Aegean which were in close dependence on their mother city. The most important of these colonies were the rich islands of Corcyra (Corfu), the city of Dyrrhachium (Durazzo), and Apollonia and Potidaea on the peninsula of Chalcidice.

Athens at that time was ruled by tyrants of the House of the Peisistratids, then represented by Peisistratus' two sons, Hippias and Hipparchus. Their father had laid the foundation for Athenian sea power. Under his rule not only had the island of Salamis—bone of contention between Athens and Megara —passed into Athenian hands once and for all, but also control of the Dardanelles, the strait between Europe and Asia through which the Black Sea grain ships had to pass on their way to Athens. Here an important strong point had been secured for Athens many years before: the city of Sigeum, which had become Athenian under Solon. In addition to these possessions, the tyrant Peisistratus had secured valuable holdings north of Thasos in the interior of Thrace, in particular the gold mines of Mount Pangaeum, from whose output Peisistratus used to pay his foreign mercenaries. Later, once the Persians had es-

21

tablished themselves on the European side of the Hellespont and Darius had waged his Scythian campaign (513–512), these possessions were drawn into the Persian orbit, and it is possible that the loss of these rich sources of income helped to bring about the fall of the tyranny in Athens.

In Greece proper all the Greeks lived according to their own laws. All states were autonomous; they did not recognize foreign masters. With the Greeks of Asia Minor it was quite otherwise. The Greek cities from the Propontis (Sea of Marmora) to Lydia were under the dominion of Persian satraps. Even though their independent municipal life was, as a rule, not infringed upon by the Persians, still the Persians in many cities had helped tyrants to attain power, and these tyrants were accustomed to rely on Persian arms. Nevertheless, the cultural life of Ionia was not substantially affected by the course of political events. In Miletus, Anaximander and Hecataeus still lived, of whom the latter was prominent as a geographer and historian, a forerunner of Herodotus. In Ephesus we find Heraclitus, "the obscure," and the iambic poet Hipponax. The latter, however, was unable to stay in his native city and had to emigrate to Clazomenae. Samos was the birthplace of Pythagoras, who found a new place for his many-sided spirit in southern Italy. His achievements as a mathematician form the beginnings of Greece's science of mathematics. His work as a statesman was done in Croton, in Italy. There his adherents united around him to form a league of their own. Through his teachings—in particular the idea of the migration of souls and the prohibition against eating meat —he made a profound impression on his contemporaries, as well as on the later world of the Roman Caesars. His ideas were closely bound up with those of the Orphics, a religio-mystical movement that in those days won many adherents.

A political event of special importance was the fall in 522 of the tyranny of Polycrates of Samos. The then satrap of Sardis, Oroetes, had been able to lure the tyrant onto the mainland of Asia Minor and there have him killed. Maeander, the private secretary of Polycrates, ruled Samos for a short time, but the Persians soon brought Polycrates' brother Syloson back to the island, where he took the reins of government as a Persian vassal. Samos was thus incorporated into the Persian empire, and the first step taken toward domination of the Aegean.

Meanwhile the Greek cities on the Black Sea had so far remained untouched by the expansion of the Persian Empire. This situation changed—probably in 513–512 B.C.—when Darius set out on his Scythian campaign. The aim of this costly expedition is difficult to determine now. The Scythians, bursting forth out of the steppes between the Aral Sea and the Caspian Sea, had again and again threatened the open northeastern flank of the empire. Was it Darius' aim now, by an attack from the west, from the direction of the lower Danube, to fall upon them in their rear? In so doing, did he—as Eduard Meyer suspected—confuse the Don with the Jaxartes and thus considerably underestimate the vast distances that had to be traversed? We do not know. This much is certain: the expedition was carefully prepared and was carried out as a combined action in which Ionian contingents also participated. The Ionian architect Mandrocles bridged the Bosporus, whereby Europe and Asia were linked for the first time, and over this bridge Darius' land army advanced through Thrace to the lower Danube and thence, over a second bridge, into the steppes of Bessarabia.

The Scythians, however, would not let themselves be brought to battle, so the Persians were finally forced to turn back. It is not likely that Darius crossed the Dniester or any of the other great southern Russian rivers. Despite this, the undertaking was not a complete failure. From then on Thrace belonged to the Persian Empire as a European bridgehead, and with it went the overlordship of the Greek communities on the western shore of the Black Sea. The Persian colossus had now approached another step closer to the Greek mother country.

For the Greeks in the west, also, dark storm clouds were approaching. The native peoples of Italy were stirring, and in addition there was an increase in the political pressure of the Etruscans, who were dominant not only in northern Italy but also in Campania. The wealthy trading city of Cyme (Cumae) would have been lost had it not found in the figure of Aristodemus a capable commander, who later rose to become tyrant of the city. Cyme is certainly only one example of the plight of the Greeks of southern Italy. They were also troubled by dissensions among themselves. The sharpest kind of animosity, for instance, existed between Croton and Sybaris. A treaty recently found at Olympia shows that the Sybarites even allied themselves with the "Serdaeans." (Are we to identify these with the Sardinians?) But the alliance did not prevent the overthrow of Sybaris by fellow Greeks. In 511–510 the city fell before the attacks of the Crotonians, Sybaris was completely destroyed, and the waters of the Crathis were diverted over its ruins. Italian archaeologists believe that they have now rediscovered the site of the ancient city.

In the Greek cities of Sicily, meanwhile, tyranny was everywhere advancing as the sixth century drew to a close. This was true of Zancle, Himera, Selinus, Acragas, Gela, Leontini. Even Syracuse, one of the largest of the Sicilian Greek cities, was almost paralyzed by internal party struggles. Tyrannical rule triumphed in Gela under Cleander and, after his murder, under his brother Hippocrates. In Sicily, Hippocrates subjugated the neighboring native Sicels and also the cities of Callipolis, Naxos, and Leontini. Syracuse maintained its independence only at the cost of great effort and trouble and the cession of Camarina, a subject city.

By 540, all western Hellenism, exposed to the double pressure of the Etruscans and the Carthaginians (sea battle off the Corsican city of Alalia, about 540), was in danger of falling under foreign domination. Despite armed conflict with the Etruscans, however, Greek commerce continued to thrive. One reason for this was that the quality of the work of Greek artisans was quite unequaled. This is shown by the many rich archaeological finds of Greek vases in Etruscan graves and the discovery of single pieces like the enormous and beautifully decorated bronze mixing bowl unearthed deep in the interior of present-day France, at Vix near Châtillon-sur-Seine. It is to be assumed that this particular piece found its way there via Massilia, (Marseilles), the Phocaean settlement not far from the mouth of the Rhône (600 B.C.). Spina, at the mouth of the Po, an important harbor of the Etruscans, was another city that maintained ties with Greece, although its period of prosperity came later, in the second half of the fifth century.

Keeping pace with the expansion of the Greek *polis* as far as Egypt (Naucratis), southern Russia, and Spain was the expansion of Greek civilization and Greek intellectual life. Greek science and philosophy were equally at home in Ionia and southern Italy. Even small and unimportant cities like Elea (Velia) harbored within their walls significant thinkers (such as Zeno of Elea), and their teachings were, like the pan-Hellenic pantheon, a possession of the entire world of Hellenism. Split up politically into an almost incalculable number of autonomous city-states (*poleis*), the Greek world was nevertheless united, by the spirit of its thinkers and philosophers, in an intellectual macrocosm in which each individual member unfolded a rich life of his own. Wherever one looks, one sees the kind of fresh life which sprang from the variety of the Greek spirit.

2

The Fall of the Tyranny in Athens and the Reforms of Cleisthenes

In Athens, in 561 B.C., a new age had begun with the rule of the tyrant Peisistratus. It was Peisistratus who strengthened Athens' foreign policy and showed its citizens the way to new goals. The existence of such a tyranny was, to be sure, irreconcilable with the Athenians' feeling for liberty; it was no accident therefore that Peisistratus was twice expelled from Athens. But he returned each time, and died a natural death in 528/527. In the meantime he had adorned the city with magnificent edifices; indeed the period of his rule and that of his house was in general one of extraordinary artistic creativity. It need only be recalled that under Peisistratus the first and decisive step was taken in the development of classical tragedy, when in 534 an Athenian, Thespis of Icaria, placed opposite the tragic chorus a single "respondent" (*hypokrites*). Even though it was a long way from this to the classical drama of the century following, a start had been made, and in a manner that was as inspired as it was simple.

After Peisistratus' death, his sons followed the course he had laid down in internal and foreign policy, though the regimes of the tyrants of Greece were everywhere in difficulties. Lygdamis of Naxos, a friend and ally of the House of the Peisistratids, was forced to retire before the power of the

Spartans, and with the overthrow of Polycrates of Samos (522) another stalwart among the tyrants had fallen.

Added to this was the continuing expansion of the Persian Empire which, after Darius' campaign against the Scythians, had engulfed not only Thrace but also the possessions of the Peisistratids on the northern coast of the Aegean.

Of the two sons of Peisistratus who succeeded him in Athens, Hipparchus, the younger, was the more striking personality, but found in his brother Hippias the necessary support for his artistic and literary inclinations. Both brothers embraced with fervor the mystic religious movements of their age. They were adherents of the secret teachings of the Orphics, and of Hippias it is reported that he had an especially good knowledge of the oracles, whose influence was at that time felt everywhere. When Onomacritus, the Athenian interpreter of oracles, was discovered to have falsified an oracle, Hippias banished him even though he was his close friend. It must not be forgotten in this connection that in political affairs, too, the oracles were of great importance. On their advice political undertakings were launched or abandoned.

Hipparchus himself was friendly to the poets, for whom he made a home at his court in Athens. Thus there lived in Athens Lasus of Hermione and Pratinas of Phlius (the latter perhaps at a later date). On the hermae along the Attic highways there appeared epigrams by Hipparchus that long remained in the memory of later generations.

Not all Athens' citizens had remained in the country during the period of the tyranny. The powerful family of the Alcmaeonids in particular had preferred to eat the bread of exile. It is possible, however, that this did not happen till 525, for there is evidence that the Alcmaeonid Cleisthenes was archon during the tyranny. This evidence, however, is based on a fragment of an inscription that is capable of more than one interpretation.

First to meet the fate that was hovering over all the tyrants was Hipparchus. He perished under the daggers of the conspirators Harmodius and Aristogeiton, as he was organizing a pan-Athenaic festival procession. The motive for his assassination was not political but personal: Hipparchus on an earlier occasion had insulted Harmodius. Whether political or not, the deed shook the rule of the House of the Peisistratids to its foundations. Hippias began to resort to an unqualified rule of force. He fortified the hill of Munychia so as to have free access to the sea, and the citizens were disarmed. An attempt by the Alcmaeonids to overthrow the tyranny ended in failure at Leipsyhydrion; the exiles were forced to evacuate the castle they had occupied.

But the Alcmaeonids would not give up. They appealed to the Delphic oracle, whose priests were obligated to them, whereupon the oracle called upon the Spartans to dissolve their bonds of friendship with Hippias and put an end to tyranny on the soil of Attica. This Delphic command led to a bitter exchange of views among the Spartans, but finally it was decided that Sparta, as the leading power among the Greeks, must bow to the will of the Delphic oracle. First a surprise attack was attempted, but the Spartan forces, faced with the combined power of Hippias and his allies the Thessalians, proved too weak. Sparta was now compelled to mobilize the forces of the Peloponnesian League. This time the Thessalian cavalry was no match for the Spartan hoplites, and Hippias, who had retreated to the Acropolis, capitulated after being given assurance of free withdrawal (510). He took ship for Sigeum, where he ruled thereafter as a Persian vassal prince. Thus ended the Attic tyranny, after a rule of more than fifty years.

Like the Peisistratid Hippias, the younger Miltiades, too, had become a subject of the Persian Great King. After having assumed the government of the Thracian Chersonese for his brother Stesagoras—the elder Miltiades had colonized the peninsula by agreement with Peisistratus—he joined Darius' campaign against the Scythians, as did the other Greek tyrants in Asia Minor and the cities of the Propontis. It was Miltiades who advised the Greek tyrants to tear down the bridge that had been built across the lower Danube, in order to leave the army of Darius to its fate on the Bessarabian steppes. Although his advice was not followed, it is clear that this was the reason why Miltiades had to leave the Chersonese. Not until Ionia was in full rebellion did he return, and then only for a few years (499/498–493).

After the expulsion of Hippias, the Alcmaeonids emerged in Athens as the saviors of the city. Preeminent among them was Cleisthenes, son of Megacles, whose name is so strongly linked with the history of Athens.

What was to happen in Athens, now that the tyranny had been overthrown? Could the nobility maintain their predominance? Were they, in fact, capable of mastering the many problems in the fields of politics, economics, and intellectual life that faced the city? In addition there was the frightening recollection of the period when the nobility, with their wide family ramifications, had been responsible for the internal strife that had helped Peisistratus to make his way to power.

It was a tribute to the political insight of Cleisthenes that he refrained from reestablishing the old order. Instead, with the assent of the Athenian people (whether as archon, as *nomothetes*—i.e., lawgiver—or in some other official capacity, is not known) he created the foundations of a new Athenian state whose guardian principle was *isonomia:* the equality of citizens before the law. Whereas the nobility (the *eupatridai*), with their powerful following, had until now determined the destinies of Athens, this was now fundamentally changed. By means of a new apportionment of the Attic people Cleisthenes tore asunder the old family alliances and thereby deprived them of their political significance. The old *phylae* (tribes) continued to exist only as cultic associations.

Cleisthenes divided the territory of Attica, including the city of Athens, into three "zones": the city (*asty*), the coast (*paralia*), and the interior (*mesogeia*). These three "zones" were in turn divided each into ten individual parts, the "thirds" (*trittyes*). Individual "thirds," one from each of the three different zones, were joined together to form new tribes (*phylae*). Contiguous location of the "thirds" was not sought

29

after; the new territorial tribes are said to have been constituted by the drawing of lots. They were named after Attic
heroes. From now on the Attic citizen was named according
to which of these new tribes he belonged to.

The new division was constructed so artificially that it is
hardly possible to imagine a contemporary model for it. It
can only have sprung from the brain of a man who wanted to
achieve his political goal at any cost; and this goal was the
creation of the Attic nation. Henceforth the nation appears as
a single body, divided into ten tribes, thirty "thirds," and about
one hundred communities (*demoi*). Without this revolutionary
act of Cleisthenes the great age of Athenian history that followed would have been unthinkable. Cleisthenes unquestionably deserves the title of one of the principal architects of
Athenian democracy.

Connected with the reform of the tribes was the reorganization of the Athenian army. Each of the ten tribes had to provide a contingent of infantry for the army. At the head of the
tribe's levy was a *strategos* (general), and at the head of the
entire army a polemarch, who as late as the battle of Marathon
was still the real commander of the Athenian army.

Cleisthenes created, as an executive body, a council of five
hundred members, which took the place of the Solonic Council of the Four Hundred. Each of the ten tribes provided fifty
members, and of these fifty each community (*deme*) within
the tribe provided a number of councillors corresponding to
its population. For the sake of efficiency the council (*boule*)
was divided into ten sections according to tribes, and each
tribe had charge of the affairs of the council for a tenth part
of the year. Without question, Cleisthenes was very skillful in
the way he constituted the council. Here, for the first time in
the history of Athens, the idea of representation of the people
in the executive was realized, and that in a manner that was
as effective as it was novel.

In order to prevent, once and for all, a return of tyranny,
Cleisthenes created the institution of ostracism. Once a year
in the popular assembly of the citizens (*ekklesia*) the question
was raised whether or not there was to be an ostracism. If the

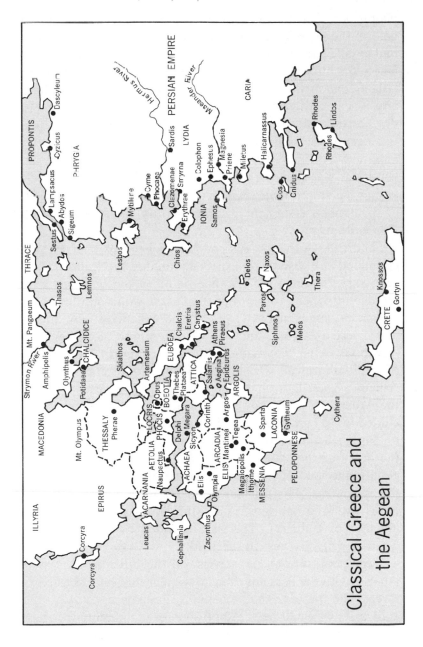

Classical Greece and the Aegean

people voted in the affirmative, a kind of reverse election was held in the near future, in which at least six thousand citizens had to take part to give the vote legal effect. The citizen against whom the highest number of ballots had been cast had to leave Athens and Attica for ten years, without, however, suffering any loss in terms of property. Amazingly, the first ostracism did not take place until the year 487. In other words, for a full twenty years the Attic *demos* did not feel threatened by any new tyranny. The view held by some scholars—that ostracism was first introduced then rather than twenty years earlier—is improbable; it breaks down, moreover, in the face of an express statement to the contrary by Aristotle in his *Constitution of Athens* (Ch. 22, par. 1).

So drastic were the reforms of Cleisthenes that they encountered stiff resistance, especially among the Eupatrids. His adversary Isagoras, for instance, induced the Spartans to intervene in Athens (508); but the *demos* would not let its new powers be snatched away from it. The Athenians took up arms and invested Isagoras and the Spartan King Cleomenes in the Acropolis. After they had capitulated, in return for assurance of free withdrawal, Cleisthenes and his followers returned to Athens. When a fresh intervention by the Spartans loomed, the Athenians—certainly at the instance of Cleisthenes—concluded in 507 an alliance with Artaphernes, the Persian satrap of Sardis, a move, however, which proved unnecessary, for the army of the Peloponnesian League, which had little inclination to fight the Athenians, virtually dissolved in 506, and the Athenians, allegedly on the same day, won decisive victories over the Spartans' allies, the Boeotians and the Chalcidians (of Euboea). The state founded by Cleisthenes had weathered its first test in the field.

Very doubtful and dangerous, on the other hand, was the alliance with the Persians. It is no wonder that once the Spartan threat had passed, the Athenians quickly disavowed their emissaries who had been responsible for concluding the treaty.

Cleisthenes' end is not known. In his reforms he had set up for himself an imperishable monument. In the old aristocratic council of the Areopagus, in the *boule* of the five hundred, created by Cleisthenes himself, in the popular assembly, and, not least, in the various administrative offices, the Athenian citizen could find the opportunity for political activity to fit his inclinations and capabilities. To be sure, the archons con tinued to be chosen from among the members of the highest tax class, the *Pentakosiomedimnoi*.* Moreover, the only citizens allowed to become members of the Areopagus were those who had been archons—and of those only archons who had administered their office without objection being raised against them. But what did these restrictions matter as against the fact that participation in the council and the popular assembly was now open to many thousands of Attic citizens? If Cleisthenes' constitution had had a chance to become firmly established, there would surely have been formed, over a period of years, a political ruling class, as well as that broad mass of politically experienced citizens which is indispensable to any well-run state. Nor would this have been the only good result. The general interest in public affairs and the common good would inevitably have risen as more and more citizens took part in public service.

In marked contrast to Cleisthenes' bold innovations in the field of politics was his conservative attitude toward all matters touching religious tradition. Cleisthenes allowed the four old Ionian tribal *phylae* to continue—the Hopletes, Argadeis, Geleontes, and Aigikoreis—as they had cultic functions, and likewise the old sacred *trittyes* (which had nothing to do with the newly created local *trittyes*), the phratries, and the priesthoods. It would have been a grave mistake to infringe upon these age-old institutions, and Cleisthenes carefully avoided this. Genuine statesman that he was, however, he was able to separate the political element from the religious, placing the former on a firm basis that proved capable of sustaining it as long as an independent Attic state continued to exist.

The Athenian *isonomia* created by Cleisthenes was an iso-

---

* Those possessing land that produced annually 500 measures (*medimnoi*) of grain.

33

lated phenomenon in Greece. No matter where one looked, there was no state with a similar constitution; everywhere the aristocracy was in command. Furthermore Sparta, as the foremost power of the Peloponnesian League, was militarily far superior to all the other Greek states. Whether the Peloponnesian League was also in a position to solve other and greater tasks outside Greece remained for the time being an open question. Sparta hitherto had in the main refused to undertake overseas expeditions or, if it had undertaken them, had done so halfheartedly, as, for example, the one against Polycrates of Samos.

Earlier views of Greek history tended to reflect the nationalistic ideas of the nineteenth century. Scholars, seeing in the Greek world a national and cultural unity, spoke of the Greek nation as they were accustomed to speak of the German or the Italian nation—an approach that today should be regarded as outmoded. It is, above all, the merit of Hans Erich Stier's *Grundlagen und Sinn der griechischen Geschichte (Foundations and Meaning of Greek History;* Stuttgart, 1945) to have pointed out the fundamental differences between ancient and modern forms of national consciousness.

In point of fact, the Hellenic world of the period around 500 B.C. had real unity only in the field of religion. Although countless minor deities were worshiped locally, all Hellenes were united—largely through the influence of Homer and his epic poems—in the recognition and cultic veneration of the pantheon of Olympian gods. With the exception of this spiritual bond, however, there was little else that the Greeks had in common. Although the poems of Homer were read everywhere, no universal Greek literary language existed. Each Greek used the dialect of his city or his tribe, and it can well be imagined that communication between, say, a Lacedaemonian and a Thessalian was sometimes difficult. Only on the perimeter of the foreign world surrounding Greece—in the colonial areas in Asia Minor, Italy, southern Russia, everywhere that Greeks lived side by side with foreign peoples—were the Hellenes conscious of their national and cultural individuality.

34

It is certainly no accident that the idea of "Panhellenes" occurs in the poetry of Archilochus (fr. 52). (The context is interesting; the poet is speaking of the "misery of all Greece," and by this he means all the penurious souls who, like Archilochus himself, took part in the colonization of Thasos, an event that took place about the middle of the seventh century.) The same concept is found earlier in Hesiod; in his catalogues, "Hellen" is the *heros eponymos* of all the Greeks.

In glaring contrast to this unity on the ideal plane, however, stood the hard realities of political life. Each polis, even the smallest, jealously guarded its autonomy; not one was prepared to renounce it in favor of another and larger state. For this reason every attempt at the formation of a major power proved impossible; when one state concluded an alliance with another, it did not surrender one iota of its sovereignty. Moreover, the individual communities were frequently at odds with each other and were involved in numerous and often protracted feuds. Thus for decades Athens fought with Aegina for supremacy in the Saronic Gulf, Sparta struggled bitterly with Argos over the fertile region of Cynuria, and the quarrel between Croton and Sybaris in southern Italy led eventually to the wiping out of the latter city.

A certain pan-Hellenic prestige was enjoyed by the oracle of the Delphic Apollo. The extensive connections of the Delphic priesthood in all the regions settled by Greeks, and even beyond, made it possible for the Pythia to issue to those who sought its counsel oracular utterances that, particularly in politics, often decisively tipped the scales. Of course the language of the Delphic oracle, like that of all oracles of ancient and modern times, was deliberately obscure, and not of itself intelligible to everyone. One need only recall the oracle that the Pythia gave to the mighty Lydian King Croesus, when he embarked on war against the Persians: "When you cross the Halys, you will destroy a great empire." (In fact he destroyed his own.) But trust in Apollo remained quite unshaken, until the Persians drew near.

For a foreigner, political conditions in Hellas were difficult to understand; he saw a world of city-states both bound by friendships and split by numerous enmities. It seemed next to impossible that the Greeks could ever forget the things that divided them in order to turn to greater, to a certain degree national, tasks. There was no generally recognized hegemonial power. If a foreign power were to succeed, by blandishments and threats, in subjecting a part of the Greek world, the remainder, it was thought, would inevitably have to follow, and the freedom of the whole country would be lost. Then, at the turn of the century (500–499), an event took place that revealed, like a flash of lightning, the real condition of the Greek world on both sides of the Aegean. This was the Ionian rebellion, the prelude to the Persian Wars.

3

The Ionian Rebellion and the Persian Wars to the Battle of Marathon

The history of the Persian Wars is known exclusively from Greek sources, above all through the historical work of Herodotus. Persian tradition, if it ever existed in written form, has not been preserved. What this means can only be fully realized if one recalls the grave distortion that resulted from the absence of a Punic tradition of the great conflict between Rome and Carthage.

Herodotus (born before 480, died before 424 B.C.) wrote in the time of Pericles, a full generation after Marathon and Salamis. But Herodotus used good sources, oral accounts above all, and as a rule there is no reason whatever to mistrust him. In addition Herodotus knew at first hand extensive parts of the Persian Empire. He had been in Egypt and Babylonia, and it is very likely that he spent some time in Scythia in southern Russia. His own experience, coupled with his unrivaled gift for narration, made Herodotus the first historian of the Western world worthy of the name.

That he had certain weaknesses cannot, of course, be overlooked. In his view of the Persian Wars he was unduly influenced by the greatness of Periclean Athens, and the result naturally was an exaggeration of the Athenian role in the war.

Moreover, he often took a partisan attitude toward the leading personalities among the Greeks, a failing that can no more be overlooked than can the vast exaggerations in his statistics. Scholars, on technical grounds, have long since held the latter to be erroneous. More difficult to judge is his habit of attributing historic decisions, even far-reaching ones, to purely personal motives on the part of the men involved. Here it is necessary to exercise strict critical judgment, although it can hardly be denied that in some cases Herodotus may have been on the right track.

For example, there is the Ionian revolt (500/499–494), whose immediate and underlying causes are not clear to us. Herodotus tells us that the Ionian revolt grew out of the personal difficulties of Aristagoras, acting tyrant of Miletus. Aristagoras, we are told, had persuaded the Persian satrap of Sardis, Artaphernes, to make a joint campaign against the island of Naxos. But the enterprise failed, and since Aristagoras feared that he would be called to account by the Great King, he is said to have realized that his only salvation lay in a revolt by the Ionians. Moreover he was encouraged in the undertaking, we are told, by a secret message from his father-in-law, the tyrant Histiaeus, then languishing in Susa. So Herodotus tells the story in Book V, Chapter 35, of his *History*. Aristagoras, it appears, abdicated as tyrant of Miletus, and was followed in his example by many other tyrants of Ionian cities. Thereafter the defection from the Persians spread rapidly over the whole of Ionia. For the first time the foundations of the great Persian empire were shaken by a large-scale rebellion in an important border province, and scholars have repeatedly tried to find convincing reasons for the strength of this movement in Ionia. Of one thing there can be no doubt: Aristagoras could never have ventured on the rebellion if he had not been certain that popular sentiment in Ionia was on his side.

Nevertheless, the question still remains: Should the rebellion be attributed primarily to economic or nationalistic causes, or to a combination of the two? As far as the economy is concerned, there is no doubt that Ionian commerce had suffered one blow after another. Naucratis, the important Greek colony in Egypt, had been weakened by the Persian occupation of that country under Cambyses (525); moreover, ever since Darius' Scythian campaign (513–512?), the Persians had been in control of the Dardanelles and the Bosporus, thus effectively blocking the Black Sea commerce of the Greeks. Finally, after the downfall of Phocaean trade in the western Mediterranean, the Ionians had been watching with mounting anxiety the rise of the power and commerce of the Carthaginians and the Etruscans. Indeed when Sybaris, which had such close ties of friendship with Miletus, was destroyed by its envious neighbor, Croton (511–510), the Milesians are said to have shorn their heads in sorrow.

But these developments, so unfavorable for Ionian trade, are not in themselves enough to explain the rebellion. No people will plunge into the uncertainties of war—and war with a great world power at that—unless they are impelled by motives that stand far above mere economic considerations. The decisive motive here was the Ionian Greeks' love of freedom. Only a Hellene could know what it meant to have the accustomed autonomy of his city constantly violated by the arbitrary interference of the Persian satraps, and to see the vital decisions concerning his community made, not by the free citizenry, but by tyrants installed and maintained by the Persians. Is it not significant that Aristagoras, after abdicating as tyrant, should have immediately proclaimed *isonomia* —the equality of all citizens before the law? This principle had first been put forth by Cleisthenes in Athens; and now the power of this idea could be seen at work in Ionia. One does not have to be immersed in nineteenth-century ideas of nationalism to recognize that what was at stake here were the basic interests of the Ionian Greeks, which everyone, nobility and *demos* alike, was ready to defend.

The rebellion, without the help of the mother country, was far too weak to hold out, with any prospect of success, against the far superior power of the Persian Empire. For this reason Aristagoras, in the winter of 500–499 (or 499–498) set out for Greece. The success of his mission, however, fell considerably below his expectations. Only Athens and Eretria promised to send naval contingents to join their Ionian brothers. The Athenian desire to protect its possessions near the Dardanelles, Lemnos and Imbros, may have played a part in this decision. Even at that time Athens was already dependent on the import of south Russian grain, and had never reconciled itself to Persian control of the straits. Sparta's rejection of Aristagoras' request, on the other hand, was a serious matter. The Lacedaemonians' aversion to overseas expeditions was well known, and added to this was the imminent conflict with Argos (see p. 73).

The Ionians opened the war with a campaign against the Lydian capital of Sardis. The city was laid waste by fire and sword, but the Ionians were unable to take the acropolis, to which the satrap had withdrawn with the Persian garrison. With the burning of Sardis, not only the Greek cities on the Propontis and the Bosporus joined the movement, but also the Carians and the Lycians. Even the Cypriotes threw off the Persian yoke. Out of small beginnings had grown a great conflagration whose flames rose high from the Bosporus to Cyprus. The rebellion threatened important communications arteries of the Persian Empire. The satrapy of Thrace was entirely cut off.

In the countermeasures taken by the Persians an overall plan is evident. First they succeeded in recapturing Cyprus. The last rebellious city on the island, Soli, capitulated in the spring of 496. On the Hellespont and in Caria the Persians also made gains. Gradually the net drew ever tighter around Miletus, the center of the rebellion. After a conference in the Panionion, the Ionian Confederacy's shrine (which has been rediscovered by German archaeologists), the Ionians decided to seek a decision at sea. Nine Ionian cities sent their contingents to the Confederate fleet, which assembled off the island of Lade just off Miletus. (As a result of the accretion of the alluvial deposits of the Maeander River, Lade has long since been connected with the mainland.)

Unfortunately, discipline among the Ionians was not all it should have been. As leader of the Confederate fleet, Dionysius of Phocaea did not succeed in establishing his authority, and in addition he had made himself hated by his severity on maneuvers. During the decisive conflict the contingents of Samos and Lesbos deserted the Greek ranks, and despite all the exertions of the Chian contingent and the personal courage of Dionysius—who himself took no less than three Persian ships—the battle was lost (495). The following year Miletus fell. The city was destroyed by the Persians and its inhabitants deported to the land of the lower Tigris. At a later date, Ionian and Carian names appear on Darius' inscription at Susa in the listing of the artisans who worked on the construction of the Imperial Palace; perhaps they had been deported into the interior of the Persian Empire in the aftermath of the ill-fated rebellion.

The outcome of the Ionian rebellion had demonstrated to all the world the power of the Persian Empire. Planned collaboration between the army and the fleet—the latter based primarily on the Phoenician maritime cities—had finally enabled the Persian command to crush the Ionians. There is no reason, however, to disparage the conduct of the Ionians. Resistance to the power of Persia had primarily been carried on by those communities which from time immemorial had united around the Panionion, the Ionian League's shrine on Mount Mycale. Here the cities had held joint war councils and had individually contributed ships, armed men, and probably also considerable sums of money to the cause. A common coin had been minted, the Ionian rebellion coinage, made of electrum. The outcome of the war had, of course, cut off these hopeful beginnings. The rule of the Persian satraps returned, and the tribute was renewed; but henceforth the Persians avoided pushing things too far. At the suggestion of Artaphernes, the Greek cities were obliged to conclude treaties with each other providing for the settlement of legal disputes, a most salutary measure in view of the incessant conflicts among them. In addition the land was resurveyed and registered in cadastres, probably in order to tax it more equitably.

Aristagoras did not live to see the end of the revolt; in 496 he had been killed in battle in a war against the predatory

Edones of Thrace. A similar fate befell his father-in-law, Histiaeus: he was captured as a pirate and crucified in 493. Histiaeus is a rather inscrutable personality. He betrayed the trust of Darius without being able thereby to win the trust of his own countrymen. In general the Ionian leaders appear in an ambiguous light. The most appealing among them seems to have been Dionysius of Phocaea, who succeeded in escaping by ship to the West, to Sicily.

The Athenians had already recalled their small supporting force from Ionia in 498. This measure in all probability is to be attributed to political rather than military reasons. The young Athenian state, which had just been placed upon a new footing by Cleisthenes, was a rather unstable creation that reacted to all influences with extraordinary sensitivity. What little is known of Athens' internal development around the turn of the century suggests that it had reached a point where the conflict for political leadership had become acute. Two political groups were involved, the Alcmaeonids, with their supporters, and the adherents of tyranny, neither of whom seems to have held in principle any enmity toward the Persians. An event that occurred in the year 496, when the Ionian revolt had entered its decisive stage, throws some light on the political trends in the city in that year. A certain Hipparchus, son of Charmus, was elected archon. This man was at least close to the Peisistratids, if not actually related to them. Nevertheless, in the summer of 494, when Miletus fell, there appeared on the Athenian stage a tragedy by Phrynichus that had as its subject the fate of the Ionian city. The Athenians, on whom the destruction of wealthy and cultivated Miletus had made a deep impression, fined the poet for reminding them of their misfortunes. It has been supposed that the supporter of Phrynichus was the Lycomid, Themistocles, the brilliant victor of Salamis, who was elected to the office of archon in 493–492 B.C. Even then Themistocles must have had a significant political following among his fellow citizens, but the return of Miltiades of the Philaid clan from his possessions in the Thracian Chersonese again forced Themistocles into the background. Still, with the fortifying of the Piraeus,

Themistocles, as archon, had begun a work whose significance was only fully recognized by later generations. As for Miltiades, he was brought to trial on a politically inspired charge of tyranny in the Chersonese, but was acquitted.

Once the Ionian revolt had been suppressed, the Persians under Mardonius proceeded to reestablish their rule in the satrapy of Thrace on the other side of the Hellespont. Mardonius, son-in-law of Darius, substantially carried out this task, but a part of the Persian fleet was lost as a result of storms off Mt. Athos on the Chalcidice, and the land army suffered severe attacks from the predatory Brygae. The rich island of Thasos had also submitted to the Persians (probably fearing the loss of its gold mines on the mainland). Thus the Persians had been able to restore their supremacy in the northern Aegean (492). Darius certainly had not pursued more ambitious goals than these. Herodotus is in error when he says that this Persian campaign was in reality directed against Hellas, and that only the Persian losses had prevented its execution. So, too, are those modern historians (G. Busolt, Eduard Meyer) who have merely echoed what Herodotus wrote.

Herodotus also reports that in 491 the Persian Great King sent envoys to Hellas to demand earth and water, the symbols of submission, from the Greeks. Numerous states, among them the rich island of Aegina, had let themselves be intimidated and had submitted to Darius. In Athens and Sparta, on the other hand, the envoys were put to death. This version, however, hardly seems plausible. It need only be recalled that Athens, ever since its participation in the Ionian revolt, had been in a state of war with the Persians. Why then should the Great King have sent envoys there? In the summer of 490 the Persian fleet in Cilicia put out to sea. It was under the command of Datis and the younger Artaphernes. It carried land troops, infantry, and cavalry, certainly not more than 25,000 armed men in all, but well equipped. Also on board was Hippias, the former tyrant of Athens. As to the purpose of this expedition, Herodotus (VI, 94) says that the Great King had dispatched it, first, to punish the Athenians for taking part in the Ionian revolt, second, because the Peisistratids had urged the King to undertake the enterprise, and third, to subjugate all the Greek cities that had refused to recognize Persian suzerainty. To the reasons given by Herodotus there is nothing to be added, for to the discerning observer it will be clear that without the subjugation of the Greek mother country, Persian rule in the Cyclades, Thrace, and Ionia itself would have stood on the most unstable footing.

The Persians were in no great hurry with their expedition. The fleet's first stop, in the year 500, was at Naxos, where the inhabitants were punished for their earlier resistance. The Persians had forgiven nothing and forgotten nothing. To Delos and the shrine of the Delian Apollo, on the other hand, the Persians showed the greatest respect, Datis presenting to Apollo a costly votive offering. The Persians then turned to the island of Euboea. Carystus was annexed by force, and so, after a six-day siege, was Eretria, which had supported its Ionian brothers with an auxiliary force. The city's temples were set in flames and the inhabitants deported to the interior of the Persian Empire.

The Athenians probably thought that the Persians would land at the Bay of Phalerum to the south of their city, but instead the invaders chose the plain of Marathon, perhaps on the advice of Hippias. Peisistratus, too, had been put ashore at Marathon when he returned after his exile from Athens. Were there supporters of the tyrants waiting to receive his son? After a sharp debate, the Athenian Popular Assembly, on the counsel of Miltiades, decided to send its forces out from the city to go and meet the Persians. This decision was an extraordinarily bold one; if it failed, the city would be lost for certain, since it was not equipped to withstand a long siege. (The question of whether Athens was walled at the time is still in dispute.) The command was in the hands of the polemarch Callimachus, who, however, relied entirely on Miltiades, the most eminent of the ten Attic *strategoi*. The 10,000 Athenians were joined by 1,000 men from the allied city of Plataea. A Spartan auxiliary force arrived one day too late; the Spartans excused themselves on the grounds that they were forbidden to take the field before the full moon, and this explanation may have been the simple truth.

The course of the battle of Marathon, which took place about the beginning of September, 490, may never be fully clarified. We may, however, proceed on the obvious assumption that the Persians were numerically superior, and that this feeling of superiority therefore caused them repeatedly to offer battle to the Athenians. It was Miltiades again who persuaded the polemarch to take up the challenge. That the Persians, however, and not the Athenians were the attackers is also clear from the fact that Miltiades, according to Herodotus, adjusted the length of the Athenian battle line to that of the Persians. The Persians, in short, stood in readiness while the Athenians were still regrouping. There is little plausibility in the view that the encounter was actually a rear-guard action of the Persians (F. Schachermeyr). While the Athenian hoplites on the wings maintained the upper hand—primarily because of their better arms and training—the Greek center was at first forced to give ground. But then the victorious left and right wings wheeled inward and the victory was won. Success was not total for the reason that the Persians succeeded in reembarking a great part of their army aboard their ships, only seven of which were lost. Of the fallen there were 6,400 Persians and 192 Athenians, among the latter the polemarch Callimachus. Nothing is said about the Persian cavalry in the battle; it appears not to have been committed, or perhaps it was numerically too insignificant to mention.

Linked to the battle of Marathon is the story of the shield-signal. As the Persian fleet headed to sea, the Athenians noticed the repeated blinking of a shield reflecting the sun inland, and they suspected that somebody was signaling to the Persians. The shield-signal is in all probability a historical fact; a connection has been made between it and the Alcmaeonids. But there is no compelling proof to support this interpretation. Herodotus expressly defends the Alcmaeonids against the charge of treason; but whether he is justified in this is open to question. On the other hand, the story of the runner from Marathon who, having brought news of the victory to Athens

45

(*nenikekamen:* "We have been victorious!"), collapsed and died on the spot is mere legend.

Despite Marathon the Persians had not given up their plan of punishing Athens. The fleet rounded the southern tip of Attica and appeared in the Bay of Phalerum. But Miltiades had anticipated this move, and after a forced march, the Athenian army had reached the city and was encamped at the Gymnasium of Cynosarges when the fleet appeared. Thereupon the Persians sailed back to Asia.

The victory at Marathon was of enormous significance for the Athenians and for the Greeks in general. It had shown that the Greek hoplites, when properly committed to action, were superior to the Persians. Greek leadership, combining cool deliberation with hard-hitting resolution in the hour of decision, had also been proved superior. Miltiades was well acquainted with the Persians; he understood their tactics, and was able to anticipate the Persian surprise attack on Athens after the battle. For the Persians, the losses were of little significance; the course of the campaign had, however, shown them that nothing was to be accomplished through minor expeditions; that careful planning and major preparations were required if the Greeks were to be brought to their knees. As for the Greeks, the success at Marathon strengthened their will to resist to the last their overwhelming adversary.

4

Xerxes' Preparations for War, and His Expedition

In the spring of 489 B.C. Miltiades, whose prestige in Athens had now reached its zenith, induced his fellow citizens to undertake an expedition against the islands of the Aegean. Most of the islands had submitted to the Persians, and it did not seem a difficult matter to ravage them on the pretext of "Medism." The enterprise, however, failed before the walls of Paros, where Miltiades was wounded. The fleet had to return home, its purpose unaccomplished. The result was that charges were brought against Miltiades, whom his opponents accused of deceiving the people. He was sentenced to pay a fine of fifty talents, and died shortly afterward of the wound he had received before Paros.

This abortive enterprise of Miltiades is revealing in many ways. Despite the superiority of the Persian fleet, the Athenians had dared to send an expedition against the Cyclades; the attempt, undertaken without adequate naval strength, had proved to be premature. The view of Herodotus, that the undertaking is to be attributed to Miltiades' personal motives, is as incorrect as is Berve's assumption that the voyage was a private enterprise of Miltiades. How could Miltiades even have thought that he would be able to hold his own in the Aegean against the preponderant force of the Persian Empire?

The fall of Miltiades cleared the way for a greater man, Themistocles, from the deme of Phrearrioi, who from now until his banishment in 471 was to be the dominant figure in Athenian politics. In the years following the battle of Marathon a series of upheavals took place in Athens, but because of the gaps in our historical records there is little of a definite nature that can be said about this period. An event worthy of note was the introduction of the practice of selecting the archons by casting lots. Up to this time the nine Attic archons had been elected, but in 487 the procedure was changed, and thereafter they were chosen by lot from among 500 candidates who had been preelected by the individual communities (demes) in accordance with their population. Without question, the new procedure promoted the democratization of the supreme office in the Athenian state. Moreover, from now on the members of the second tax class, the knights (*hippeis*), were admitted to the office of archon, a move that was necessary in order to be able to muster the 500 candidates.

How greatly the internal political struggle in Athens had intensified is shown by the number of ostracisms in the decade between Marathon and the campaign of Xerxes. First to go into banishment, in 488–487, was Hipparchus, son of Charmus; he was followed by Megacles, the son of Hippocrates and leader of the Alcmaeonids, and finally, in 483–482, by Aristides. All these men stood in the way of Themistocles' plans, and it is not too daring to assume that Themistocles, with the support of his political followers, was responsible for all three expulsions.

Immediately after Marathon the Persian Empire had commenced new military preparations. Darius, however, as a result of a revolt in Egypt and internal unrest in Babylonia, was forced to abandon the idea of a new expedition. His successor Xerxes (486–465/464), on the other hand, dug a canal through the eastern peninsula of the Chalcidice in 483 in order to avoid another shipwreck like that off Mt. Athos in 492. Traces of this canal, incidentally, have been rediscovered as a result of modern soil research operations.

This enterprise could no more be concealed from the Greeks than could the great military preparations that were being undertaken throughout the entire Persian Empire. Nor was there any lack of activity in Greece. On the advice of Themistocles, Athens was planning a very considerable increase in its navy. The projected number of 200 triremes, which would have made Athens by far the greatest naval power in Hellas, was not actually achieved before the Persian return. On a motion of Themistocles the necessary funds were raised by diverting the surpluses from the rents of the mines in Laurium, ordinarily distributed among the individual citizens, to the building of the fleet. About ten years before, Thasos had built a fleet in a similar manner, but had shrunk from a conflict with the approaching Persians out of concern for its possessions on the Thracian coast, and had then fallen under the Great King.

All these preparations, however, were by no means sufficient to provide an effective defense against the imminent Persian attack. Of crucial importance was the attitude of Sparta, the strongest military power among the Greeks. Sparta was closely allied with Athens; it had, for instance, thrown its influence into the scales when Athens was in conflict with neighboring Aegina.

But there were a good many states in Hellas that had no interest in a war of common defense, whether because they did not feel themselves threatened by the Persians or because they had, openly or secretly, placed themselves on the side of the Persians. Thus the Aleuadae, the princes of Thessaly, were on friendly terms with the Persians, while Argos, sworn enemy of the Spartans in the Peloponnese, and recently humbled by them in the battle of Sepeia (494), had a secret understanding with the Persians. Other states, like Achaea in the northern Peloponnese, cared for nothing but their own peaceful, provincial existence. Nor was much help to be expected from outside Greece proper. The Greeks of Sicily were threatened by Xerxes' alliance with the Carthaginians. From southern Italy only Phayllus of Croton, with a trireme, came to the aid of the Greeks of the mother country. The Hellenes of Ionia, Cyprus, and Cyrene were under the dominion of the Persians and were compelled to place their contingents at the disposal of the Great King.

49

In the fall of 481, after a prior consultation in Sparta, the ambassadors from all the Greek states that had refused earth and water, the symbols of submission, to the Persian King assembled on the Isthmus of Corinth. There they bound themselves in an alliance, Sparta and Athens at their head. A general public peace was proclaimed for all Hellas. Feuds were to cease, exiles were recalled. Greeks who joined the Persians without being forced to do so were threatened with destruction; a tenth of their possessions was to fall to the Delphic Apollo. Though the Greek Isthmian League comprised only a part of the Hellenes of Greece proper, it was still significant as a first indication of Greek national feeling.

A resolution to stand against the Persians at all costs was not, of course, felt by all Hellenes to the same degree. Among the poems of Theognis—though undoubtedly not from the pen of the poet himself—there occur these lines: "May Zeus and may the other gods protect the city [Megara] and may Apollo grant us just speech and just thoughts. We want to make music, to drink and chat and not fear the War of the Medes—that is better. In united harmony of mind and without care, we want to celebrate merry feasts and keep far from us the miseries of age and death." Whoever thought and spoke thus obviously did not consider the approaching "War of the Medes" as an affair of the Greek nation, but only as a most unpleasant interruption in everyday life.

Voices such as these in Greece were by no means isolated. Far more ominous, however, in this decisive hour, was the role of the Delphic oracle. It is quite clear that, ever since the fall of Croesus (547), the Delphic priests had been completely convinced of the Persians' invincibility; their minds were dominated by the thought that against the myriads of the Persian land army and the far superior Persian fleet all resistance was hopeless. It is not by chance, then, that the oracles spoken on the eve of the great war breathe a mood of undisguised pessimism. To the Greeks seeking counsel, downfall and destruction are prophesied. The Argives and the Cretans were advised to stay out of the war (as if any real neutrality would have been possible in such a conflict!). Finally, the Athenians were counseled by the oracle to flee to the ends of the earth. In a wooden wall (said the oracle) lay their only hope; by this, it would appear, was meant the wooden palisade walls of the Acropolis, and not the fleet, as Themistocles interpreted the oracle.

In contrast to this Greek disunity, the Persian preparations were most imposing. At this time the Persian Empire, highly organized as it was, had attained the peak of its efficiency, and the Great King's summons was everywhere obeyed. All the satrapies, from India to Egypt, sent their contingents to the army. The fleet consisted of ships and seamen primarily from Phoenicia, Egypt, Ionia, and Caria. The huge army was assembled at Sardis, and in the spring of 480 crossed the Hellespont over two pontoon bridges built by the Greek Harpalus. Herodotus has given us an impressive description of the different national contingents assembled from the great empire: the Indians in cotton garments, the Caspians in their furs, the black Ethiopians in leopard and lion skins, Arabs in loose-fitting burnooses, and the Persians and Medes in loose-sleeved coats and pointed fur caps, armed with short spears, bows, and wicker shields, with the short sword, the *akinakes,* at their right hip. Xerxes mustered his army in Doriscus on the Strymon. The size of his army (so the story goes) was determined by crowding 10,000 men together in a narrow space and drawing a circle around them. A wall was then built on the circle, and successive lots of 10,000 warriors were brought into the walled area until all had been counted.

Whether or not this account of Herodotus' is based on fact, the figures he gives for the Persian army are much too high and again are hardly credible. How could an army have been fed and supplied if it consisted of no less than 1,700,000 combatants plus 80,000 cavalry and 20,000 riding on camels or in chariots? Even the figures given by later writers—800,000 men according to Ephorus and Ctesias, 700,000 according to others—are still much too high. Eduard Meyer, with his sober sense of fact, has estimated the number of warriors at a maximum of 100,000; General E. von Fischer puts the figure at only 50,000. These figures are certainly much closer to

51

reality. The fleet, according to Aeschylus, numbered 1,207 vessels, but this figure may include even the smallest boats.

What were Xerxes' goals in launching this campaign? Without question, this was an undertaking planned on a large scale and well in advance, which is proved, among other things, by the alliance with the Carthaginians, to whom was assigned the role of tying down the forces of the Western Greeks. Xerxes' aim can only have been the subjugation of all of Greece, probably even of the whole of the Greek-populated Western world. The view occasionally advanced by Orientalists, such as A. T. Olmstead, that the campaign was a mere border war of the Persian King, is basically absurd. The thorough preparation and the quantity of resources committed are sufficient in themselves to refute this interpretation.

At the congress on the Isthmus the Greeks had resolved to accede to the request of the Thessalians and send a force of 10,000 hoplites to the northern border of Thessaly, with orders to hold the Tempe Pass and thereby form a first line of defense against the Persian army advancing from Macedonia. The Greek force was transported by ship to Halus in Thessaly, whence it marched to the Vale of Tempe. This position, however, proved difficult to hold. It could easily be circumvented by way of a pass in the district of Perrhaebia; besides, Persian landings in the Greeks' rear would have to be reckoned with. To the great disappointment of the Thessalians, the Greeks therefore evacuated the position at the Tempe Pass and, shortly afterward, the whole of Thessaly.

Strangely enough, Xerxes did not exploit the Greek withdrawal. Although he must have had knowledge of the altered situation, he had his army make a detour involving a ten days' march. He moved westward around the massif of Olympus and here for the first time entered Greek territory. The Greeks now resolved to await the Persians at Thermopylae, the gateway to central Greece. The narrowness of the pass might make it possible for limited forces to hold a far larger army and delay it for some time. The core of the Greek force consisted of 4,100 Peloponnesians, among them only 300 Spartans and 1,000 Lacedaemonians; in addition there were 700 Thespians,

400 Thebans, and besides these some contingents of Phocians and Locrians of Opus. In command was the Spartan King Leonidas.

While an attempt was being made to hold the pass at Thermopylae the fleet was to be disposed at Cape Artemisium, the northern tip of the island of Euboea. The supreme commander of the fleet was the Spartan Eurybiades, and of a total of 270 triremes, only 147 had been provided by the Athenians. Nevertheless the soul of the naval leadership was the Athenian Themistocles. He it was who had originated the plan that the Greeks were now to attempt to translate into reality at Thermopylae and at Artemisium. Leonidas' contingent was to delay the Persian army until the Greek fleet had succeeded in inflicting a decisive defeat on the Persians. Defensive action on land coupled with an offensive at sea: this was the basic Greek plan.

The land battle at Thermopylae and the sea battle off Artemisium, which took place at the beginning of August, 480, show clearly how well this plan actually worked. The inner strategic relationships have been clarified primarily through the research of August Koester. On both sides communications were maintained between the forces on land and those at sea; the operations on water and on land complemented each other as in a chess game.

Persian naval reconnaissance made first contact with Greek warships off the little island of Skiathos. Three Greek triremes, placed here as an outpost, turned and fled at the Persians' approach, but were overtaken. Only one ship, an Athenian, was able to escape to the north; its crew went ashore in Thessaly and fought its way home. To make secure the advance of the main body of their army, the Persians erected a naval beacon on the so-called Lephtari Rock between Skiathos and Cape Sepias. Fortunately for the Greeks a mighty storm arose from the north. It lasted three days and caused great damage among the Persian fleet, numerous ships being dashed to pieces on the rocky coast of the Magnesia Peninsula. In addition, fifteen Persian ships inadvertently sailed into the ranks of the Greeks and were captured.

How did matters stand, meanwhile, at Thermopylae? While the storm was blowing, Xerxes camped with his army in the plain of Trachis, completely inactive. Of course, there would have been little sense in giving battle before the fleet had announced its readiness. Besides, the Persians had sent a squadron of 200 ships eastward around the elongated island of Euboea. Its mission was to block the channel between the southern part of the island and the mainland, so that the Greek fleet would be caught in a box. The Greeks, however, got word of this undertaking through a Greek deserter from the Persian ranks, Scyllias of Scione.

Thermopylae as a whole consists of three narrow defiles between the present-day villages of Antheli and Molos. Thermopylae proper—it is named after the hot springs—is the middle pass, situated between the western and the eastern defiles. The pass at this point was only about fifteen meters wide (half a plethron) and could be held with little effort by a small body of soldiers under good leadership. (Today, of course, as a result of the alluvial deposits of the Spercheius, the shape of the landscape has been considerably altered.) Earlier scholars were of the opinion that the position of the Greeks was strengthened by the so-called Phocian Wall, which was pictured as running in a north-south direction. The investigations of Spyros Marinatos, however, have shown that the Phocian Wall almost certainly ran instead from west to east, in other words parallel to the defiles.

For three days the Persians, in a frontal assault, tried in vain to force a passage through the defile, but the Greeks, arrayed by Leonidas in a flexible defense, proved superior in equipment and training. Meanwhile the Persians had received word of a path leading around the Greek position. Led by a native guide, Ephialtes, they marched over the mountains and into the rear of the Greeks, after overrunning a Phocian contingent that had been placed to guard the path.

With the loss of the most important heights south and west of Thermopylae, Leonidas and his loyal troops were all but encircled. In this situation, the Spartan King allowed the bulk of his army to withdraw, covering their retreat with Spartans,

Thespians, and Thebans. He was still able to send word to the leaders of the fleet that his position had been surrounded; his task was now to hold out until the fleet had succeeded in withdrawing to the south through the waterway of the Euripus, which was in some places only about fifteen meters wide. This, however, could be done only after disengagement from the Persian naval forces, and certainly not before nightfall. In the meantime Leonidas with the remainder of his men—in all, about one thousand combatants—was forced back upon a hill, now called Hill II, on which today the Leonidas Monument stands, and where a great number of arrowheads have been found, testimonials of the battle. The embattled Greeks finally succumbed to the superior Persian forces, the Thebans alone laying down their arms. Leonidas, after proving his qualities as a military leader, fell bravely in battle. Xerxes later had his head cut off and the headless body nailed to a cross. But Leonidas had achieved his goal; Xerxes' army had been delayed while the Greek fleet made an orderly withdrawal through the straits of the Euripus.

This happened on the evening of the third day of the naval battle off Artemisium. The Greeks had drawn up their ships in a line between the island of Argyronesi and Cape Cephala on Euboea, and despite every effort the Persians had not been able to break through it. Losses were of course high on both sides. With the news of the fall of Thermopylae it was immediately recognized that the fleet's position at Artemisium was untenable. Under cover of darkness therefore it disengaged from the enemy and moved back into the Saronic Gulf. Themistocles had ordered signs to be placed on the coastal cliffs calling upon the Ionians and Carians fighting on the Persian side to desert to the Greeks or, if this proved impossible, to display no particular zeal in battle. This early example of psychological warfare becomes even more understandable when it is recalled that in the naval battle off Artemisium a Carian leader on the Greek side, Heracleides of Mylasa, had made a substantial contribution to the Greek success in that engagement with a new naval tactic.

The battles of Thermopylae and Artemisium were, of

55

course, a Persian rather than a Greek success. Though the Persians had suffered considerable losses, the goal of their combined operations on sea and land had been achieved: central Greece had been opened up to them. There was little further resistance to the Persian steamroller. Most of the city-states in central Greece submitted, and Delphi openly joined the Persians, thus saving the treasures of its shrine from plunder. In Athens a resolution was passed to remove the noncombatants—women and children—to safety in Troezen, Aegina, and Salamis, and to have all men capable of bearing arms put aboard the ships, on which, it was believed, rested the salvation not only of the city but of all Greece.

According to a Greek inscription which was very recently found in Troezen and has attracted a great deal of attention, the decision to leave Athens had been taken well before this time, certainly before the battles of Thermopylae and Artemisium. However, this historical evidence, seems, for psychological and other reasons, most dubious. How could one expect Leonidas and his soldiers to fight to the last man at Thermopylae while in Athens everyone was preparing to flee? The inscription, moreover, directly contradicts Herodotus, whom there is no reason at all to mistrust on this point. Allegedly a decree initiated on a motion by Themistocles, the inscription is obviously a later work not deserving of credence; it cannot be dated earlier than about the middle of the fourth century B.C.

Meanwhile a wall had been erected across the Isthmus of Corinth in order to give the defenders the necessary support. The Greek fleet was concentrated in the Gulf of Salamis, and on it reposed the hopes of all Greeks who were unwilling to bow to the Persians. Athens itself fell into Persian hands; only on the Acropolis was there some weak resistance. Trusting in the oracle that had been given by the Delphic Apollo concerning the "wooden walls," a small band sought to defend themselves behind the wooden palisades of the Acropolis. The Persians set the fortification afire with flaming arrows, and the hapless defenders were massacred. It seems certain that the Greeks were at odds about committing their precious fleet to battle; it is even possible that the Spartan admiral, Eury-biades, decided to withdraw to the Isthmus. It is out of the question, however, that any of the Hellenes were at that time thinking of flight. Whatever the situation, Themistocles, it seems, had to use strong language. He is said to have threatened to sail the Athenian triremes to the far west if the Greeks refused to offer battle in the Straits of Salamis.

The Persians, too, were willing to seek a decision at sea, since a breakthrough at the Isthmus appeared to be both too difficult and, after the experience at Thermopylae, much too costly. Nevertheless many weeks passed before the Persian fleet left the beach at Phalerum and made preparations to challenge the Greeks to battle in the waters between Attica and the island of Salamis (see map no. 3). Once again, a pro-found distaste for the battle is said to have swept the Greeks, which brought Themistocles to dispatch a false message se-cretly to the Persians, urging that they attack as soon as pos-sible because the Greeks were resolved on flight. Whether or not this story is true, the Persians quickly made their neces-sary dispositions, landing a contingent of soldiers on the island of Psyttaleia with orders to take shipwrecked Greeks prisoner. The Persian fleet, entering the Straits of Salamis from the east, sealed off egress from the Gulf in that direction, while the Egyptian naval contingent was ordered to sail southward around the island of Salamis to seal off the access to the Straits from the west. These dispositions were well thought-out; and since the strategy recalls the orders of the Persian leaders at the battle off Cape Artemisium, there is no reason not to regard them as historical fact.

The 300 or so Greek warships at Salamis were certainly confronted with a stronger enemy, but the superiority of the Persians cannot have been as great as is stated in the ancient sources. The Persian fleet—its right wing formed by the Phoenicians, experienced sea fighters, its left wing by the Ionians—lay facing south between the islands of Hagios, Georgios, and Psyttaleia. The Greeks—the Athenians on their right wing, the Aeginetans forming their left—lay with the prows of their vessels facing north.

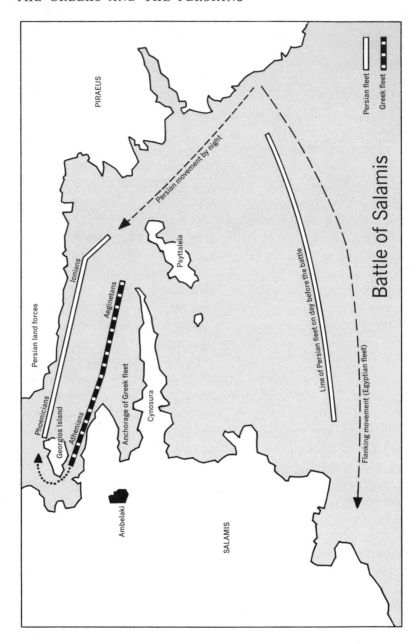

Battle of Salamis

PIRAEUS

Persian movement by night

Psyttaleia

Ionians

Persian land forces

Aeginetans

Phoenicians

Georgios Island

Athenians

Anchorage of Greek fleet

Cynosura

Line of Persian fleet on day before the battle

Flanking movement (Egyptian fleet)

Ambelaki

SALAMIS

Persian fleet

Greek fleet

Both sides fought with great valor. On the Persian side the Carian Princess, Artemisia of Halicarnassus, especially distinguished herself by sinking an allied ship from Calydna so as to escape pursuit by an Attic trireme. Her exploit won the admiration of Xerxes, who was watching the great drama from the heights of Aegaleus, where a throne had been erected for him.

Ironically, the numerical superiority of the Persians quickly proved to be a drawback. Their ships hindered each other's movements, especially after an Athenian flank attack had crowded them even more closely together. As a result the Persian losses were considerable, but they can hardly have amounted to 500 ships, as a later source (Ctesias) reports. Meanwhile a detachment of Greek hoplites, under the command of the Athenian Aristides, had landed on the island of Psyttaleia and had overwhelmed the Persian garrison. The entire naval battle lasted twelve hours, from morning till dark. Finally, at the command of Xerxes, the remainder of the Persian fleet withdrew from the roadstead of Phalerum back to the Hellespont. Xerxes himself returned with the land army to Thessaly, where he turned over the command to Mardonius and after a march of forty-five days finally reached the Hellespont. Despite the great losses suffered by his fleet, the King had by no means abandoned his plan to conquer Greece.

The causes of the Persian defeat at Salamis are not far to seek. The Greeks were better tacticians and in addition were fighting for their very existence as a nation; if the sea battle had been lost, deportation and slavery would have been their certain fate. Added to this, there were grave errors in naval tactics on the Persian side, above all in their plan of battle. Nobody among the Persians seems to have realized that in such narrow waters, not numbers but the quality of the ships and of their crews would alone be decisive. Finally, the Persian leaders were too unfamiliar with navigational conditions in the Greek waters. All these things certainly weighed in the scales—but it must be repeated again that it was the psychological attitude of the Greeks that proved absolutely decisive.

The later measures of the Greek naval leaders were not as

consistent as their first moves. The retreating Persian armada was indeed followed as far as Andros, but Themistocles' counsel—to finish the job with an attack on the Hellespont, the nerve center of the Persian line of communications—was not followed. In Herodotus we read of a second secret message that Themistocles allegedly sent to the Persian King, telling him that the attack on the Hellespont had been abandoned on his own advice. This story is inherently implausible. After all, the Persians could hardly have forgotten Themistocles' earlier false message, which had induced them to give battle at Salamis.

On their return to Salamis, the Greeks offered due sacrifice to their gods. To the god at Delphi they consecrated a colossal statue of Apollo holding in his hand the bow of a trireme. Although the Delphic Apollo had in this war been little inclined toward the Greeks, they did not hold it against him.

The Greeks were by no means out of danger. The Persian land army remained intact; as long as it stood on Greek soil the outcome was in doubt. From his headquarters Mardonius generated constant diplomatic activity, aiming above all at destroying the Hellenic League. Commissioned by him, King Alexander I of Macedon journeyed to Athens to present offers of far-reaching import. When the Athenians remained firm, the Persians once again invaded Attica. It was this second occupation that produced the grievous acts of destruction in the city and countryside that so inflamed the Athenians against the Persians. The inhabitants of Athens had already been brought to safety in Salamis. But it was no wonder that Athens in particular pressed hard to have the Greek allied army committed to battle. At Marathon the Attic hoplites had shown themselves superior to the Persians; there was no reason not to assume that the combined strength of Athens and Sparta could defeat the Asiatic hordes.

In Athens, during the winter of 480/479, a political upheaval took place. In the elections for the offices of *strategoi,* Themistocles had been defeated. In his place appeared the names of Aristides and Xanthippus, the latter connected by marriage with the family of the Alcmaeonids. The reason for it is not known, but this abrupt shift in the leadership of Athens is remarkable.

In preparing for the decisive conflict with the Greeks, Mardonius showed himself a very circumspect commander. In order to bring his far superior cavalry into effective action against the Greeks, he evacuated Attica and withdrew to Boeotia. There, in the plain of the Asopus, not far from Plataea and opposite the heights of Cithaeron, he found ideal terrain for his cavalry which, by certain modifications, e.g., the felling of trees, he was at pains to make still more suited to his purposes. Moreover, he controlled the road to Thebes, which was his main line of communication. The Thebans were the most reliable of his Greek allies. The Phocians, however, caused him greater difficulties. But this small contingent of 1,000 men hardly mattered, and besides, Mardonius had made it clear to them on their arrival that he was not a man to be trifled with.

On the Greek side, the supreme command was held by the Spartan Pausanias. He was the nephew of Leonidas and regent for the young king Pleistarchus. The bulk of the army was composed of Lacedaemonians and the contingents of the Peloponnesian League, but there were also Athenians and Plataeans; the Greeks may have numbered altogether about 30,000 fighting men. In numbers the Persians were certainly superior, though definitely not to the degree alleged by Herodotus. Herodotus' figure of 300,000 men is quite mythical; Mardonius can hardly have had more than 40,000 to 50,000 men under his banners. From Herodotus' account it appears that the Greeks were hard-pressed by Mardonius' superior cavalry; at the same time it is clear that the Persian commander was fully aware of the superiority of the enemy hoplites, especially those of the Spartans.

The Persian cavalry succeeded in rendering the Gargaphia spring in the rear of the Greek position unusable; Pausanias was then forced to make the difficult decision to withdraw his army if he was not to get into serious difficulties with his water supply. The retreat proved to be an extremely dangerous undertaking. In his own ranks Pausanias had to contend not only

61

with opposition but even with open disobedience. The Greeks were not accustomed to having someone else tell them what to do and not to do. Since each city-state was traditionally autonomous, the Greeks found it difficult to subordinate themselves in wartime to the will of another. The Athenians, it appears, refused to take part in the withdrawal ordered by Pausanias, which was carried out largely by the Spartans and the Tegeans. Nevertheless they not only beat off all Persian attacks but in the end destroyed a large part of the Persian army. Mardonius himself was killed. Even the Persian camp, which is said to have been fortified by a wall made of Persian shields, was captured by the Greeks, who gave no quarter.

"It is difficult," writes the Austrian Lieutenant-Colonel Georg Veith, "to imagine a commander in a more difficult and thankless situation than that of Pausanias in the year 479. The decision to make the campaign was positively forced upon him by the Athenians, and he—a Spartan and accustomed to leading the Spartan elite corps—found himself at the head of a hastily assembled militia." Nevertheless there is no question that the Hellenes owed their victory solely to the leadership of Pausanias, who with his Spartans kept his head in the general melee, and thus reversed a tactically impossible situation; Pausanias won the initiative from a numerically superior enemy, and not only overthrew but completely destroyed him. It would not be correct to maintain that the victory of Plataea was a victory of Greek unity. The exact opposite is true: Plataea was won by Pausanias and his Spartans, and here they made history. No one begrudges the Greeks in general, on the other hand, for celebrating the victory as their own. Special honors were accorded the Plataeans, and in Plataea itself a quadrennial victory celebration was established. These memorial games were still being celebrated in the age of Imperial Rome, the victor being honored with the title, "Best of the Hellenes." The alleged decision of the Greeks after the battle, to establish a common force of 10,000 hoplites, 1,000 cavalry, and 100 warships, is, however, not historic fact. This legend is rather an anticipation of conditions that came into existence with the founding of the Corinthian League in 338 B.C.

The Thebans who had fought on the Persian side—they were stationed opposite the Athenians in the battle—were now given short shrift. Thebes itself withstood a siege of twenty days, but in the end its inhabitants handed over to the Greeks those leaders of the "Medizing" party who had not already been able to escape to safety. On Pausanias' order they were put to death.

The military actions of the year 479 concluded with the battle of Mycale, which was not far from Priene in Ionia. A considerable part of the Persian fleet had already been dismissed and sent home when the Greeks disembarked under the command of the Spartan King Leotychides. The shore camp where the Persian ships were beached was taken by storm. Here again the high figures given by Herodotus for the size of the Persian army are hardly credible. The statement that the battle of Mycale took place on the same day as the battle of Plataea, moreover, is mere legend—another of those "fables of simultaneity" of which there are so many examples in ancient and modern times. After all, the Greeks would hardly have dared to undertake an overseas expedition as long as Mardonius' army stood intact in Greece.

The date of the battle of Mycale can probably be fixed in the late autumn of 479. In the months that followed, operations in the Aegean were pushed forward. Mycale was the signal for the defection of many Ionian cities from the Persians, and thereafter the Ionians took part in the annihilation of the Persian troops.

Victory over the Persians brought new problems for the Greeks. What should they do about the pleas of the Ionians, who were seeking protection against the Persians? Did they have sufficient power to undertake such campaigns on the other side of the Aegean? It is no wonder that the Spartans in all earnestness advised the Ionians to resettle in Greece, and there occupy the cities of those Hellenes that had made common cause with the Persians. Would this counsel have been at all practicable? The large islands off the coast of Asia Minor were more fortunate; on Athens' endorsement, Samos, Chios, and Lesbos were received into the Hellenic League. These islands all had significant fleets, which brought a very desirable strengthening of the Greek naval forces. Since the Spartans refused to give the Greeks on the mainland of Asia Minor any guarantees against the Persians, a number of cities in Ionia and on the Hellespont concluded treaties with Athens.

Meanwhile operations continued in the northern Aegean. Under the command of Xanthippus, the Athenians and their new allies undertook to besiege the city of Sestos, key to the Hellespont, which fell in the spring of 478. With this event, Herodotus' history closes; whether or not his ending at this point was intentional is a perennial subject of scholarly dispute, for the siege of Sestos certainly did not mark the end of the Persian Wars. Persian occupation forces were to be found in Thrace more than a decade later, and the state of war was only concluded by treaty, we believe, with the Peace of Callias in 449–448 B.C.

Another incident of this period concerned the Delphic Amphictyony, the religious federation of all the Greek states of the mainland. Sparta demanded the expulsion from this body of all those states that had joined the Persians. Had this been done, only a very few members would have been left, and these few would have been under the absolute leadership of Sparta. It was to Themistocles' credit that he resisted this proposal, thereby in the final analysis saving the Delphic Amphictyony. This episode occurred at the end of 479 or, at the latest, 478.

In this controversy can already be seen the opening moves of the impending war between the two most important Greek states, Sparta and Athens. The building of the Athenian wall was another portent. As early as the winter of 479–478 the Athenians had begun to build a city wall. That they worked in great haste is evident from the fact that in the construction they used any kind of stone that they could lay their hands on, even gravestones. The Spartans, displeased with this activity, decided to send emissaries to intervene, but Themistocles, who was in Sparta at the time, was able to delay the departure of the emissaries until the wall was completed and the immediate danger to Athens removed. K. J. Beloch and others have dismissed this as a legend, but quite unjustly. Twice Athens had been abandoned to the enemy, and the city still bore many marks of the destruction committed during the Persian occupations of 480 and 479. It was understandable that the Athenians should try to protect themselves against a similar turn of events. The army of Athens' ally, Sparta, could be considered protection enough, but had it not required the greatest effort to get the Spartan leaders to join battle on land with the hosts of Mardonius? Besides, the interests of Sparta were no longer completely identical with those of Athens. To be sure, the conquest of the city of Byzantium and part of Cyprus by the Spartan Pausanias had certainly been welcomed by the Athenians. But the way Pausanias had conducted himself, in the manner of a Persian satrap, had raised such a scandal that the Spartan leaders had finally been forced to recall him. Pausanias, the victor of Plataea, appears in this episode as an outright individualist, boldly disregarding the obligations that up to now had been binding for all Spartans. Nevertheless he obeyed the order recalling him from Byzantium, which only makes his conduct the more enigmatic. A few years later Pausanias returned once more to Byzantium and settled there, this time, however, for only a short period (477–476). A naval expedition under the Athenian Cimon soon put an end to his glory. We shall subsequently return to his career later in this book (see p. 76).

In the meantime a significant change had taken place in the Aegean. In 478–477, when Timosthenes was archon in Attica, the first Athenian Maritime League was established, a development which added an entirely new element, under the leadership of Athens, to the Greek alliance. This new league, which was able to guarantee protection against the Persians to Greeks on both sides of the Aegean, became the real standard-bearer of the struggle against the Persian Empire.

In the Sicilian Greek world, too, the year 480, which saw the defeat of the Carthaginians, was a turning point in history.

It was not the city-state system, however—as in Greece proper —but the power of the great tyrants that delivered the Siceliots from the threat of foreign domination. As Persia's allies, the Carthaginians put powerful resources into their campaign, but with the battle of Himera it ended in failure. The great leaders of the Sicilian Greeks were the tyrants of Syracuse and Acragas, Gelon and Theron, but it was Gelon who may justly be called the real victor. Despite their defeat at Himera the Carthaginians continued to maintain bases in the western part of the island, above all at the important city of Panormus (Palermo), as well as at Motya and Soloeis. Thus the danger of a new Carthaginian attack continued to hang like a sword of Damocles over the Sicilian Greek world.

At first, the rapid rise of Syracuse under Gelon and his successor, Hieron, prevented further Carthaginian encroachments. Then in 474, in a battle fought off Cyme (Cumae) in Campania, Hieron was victorious over the combined fleets of the Carthaginians and the Etruscans—a great victory not only for Syracuse but for the entire Western Greek world. To be sure, their liberty had been dearly bought, for the Sicilian Greeks still lived under the rule of tyrants who were able to direct the life of the city-state as they pleased.

Hieron had not only the interest but the wealth necessary to turn his court at Syracuse into a seat of the Muses. A whole series of brilliant poets made their home for a shorter or longer time in Syracuse: Simonides and his nephew Bacchylides, Epicharmus, and possibly Xenophanes. Above all, Pindar and Aeschylus honored Syracuse with their presence and proclaimed the renown of Hieron and his house to all the world.

For the Greeks of Greece proper, Salamis and Plataea marked the beginning of a new era. The onslaught of the powerful Persian army and great armada had been turned back. On water and on land, Sparta and Athens had proven their superiority. The days of the placid life of the small city-states had passed; new perspectives were opening up in the politics of the ancient world, and there were great individuals, far in advance of their time, who understood how to use these new possibilities, above all Themistocles and Pausanias. But they faced a phalanx of those who forever lived in the past, who (as always in history) had learned nothing and forgotten nothing. Nevertheless Hellas was again free of the enemy, and on the far side of the Aegean, too, the Ionians' sense of freedom was stirring.

> The world-historical perspectives of the Greek victory over the Persians are almost incalculable. By overcoming the onslaught from the East, the Hellenes gave a goal and direction to the political and cultural development of the West for a full century to come. It was only through the Greeks' victorious struggle for freedom that Europe, as idea and reality, was born. The objectives for which the Greeks risked their lives are still today the highest values in the life of western man. That Greek culture, enjoying full freedom in domestic and foreign affairs, was able to rise to those heights of achievement in sculpture, drama and historiography that are today revered throughout the western world as models beyond compare—that all this came to pass we owe to the fighters of Salamis and Plataea, Themistocles no less than Pausanias (Bengtson, *Griechische Geschichte,* 2nd ed., pp. 174–175).

We should not belittle the significance of the Greek victories of 480 and 479, but should try to understand, calmly and soberly, what the domination of the Persians might have meant. A victory of the Orient (said Eduard Meyer many years ago) would have meant above all a strengthening of priestly authority, a more or less far-reaching hieratic rule. As the history of the Jews demonstrates (so Meyer's thesis continues), the Persians would have employed the national religion of the Greeks and the rule of their priests in order to keep the people in subjection. Greek thought would have been smothered under the weight of an organized church and a developed theology, and every tendency to freedom would have been suppressed, so that the new Greek culture would have emerged with as strong a theological stamp as the Oriental already possessed. These speculations obviously exceed the limits of our knowledge, though they may well contain a grain of truth. The real meaning of the Greek victory over the Persians, we believe, lies rather in this: that the Greeks, because of their native political forms, were able to hold their own brilliantly against an enemy many times as strong as they were. The victories on land and sea were the victories of the Greek city-state, for which outstanding leaders had arisen at precisely the right time. And with the triumph of the city-state system, the Western concept of the free constitutional state won out over the absolutist system of the Orient. The Greeks were fighting not only for their homeland and their gods, but also for the ideal of intellectual freedom and for a higher civilization in a free Western world.

It is hard to understand how a historian of the stature of Arnold J. Toynbee could even consider the question of whether it would not perhaps have been better for the Greeks if unity and peace had been imposed upon them by the Persians in the fifth century B.C. Such a result (says Toynbee) would have spared the Greeks the four and a half centuries of misfortune they brought upon themselves, between the time of King Darius and that of Caesar Augustus. To make such a judgment is to forget that Western culture today, or essential parts thereof, is based directly upon what the Greeks achieved after they had turned back the Persian invasion in the fifth century.

A scholar like Alexander Rüstow is completely justified in stating, in opposition to Toynbee, that

> . . . the victory of the Greeks in the Persian Wars was one of the great miracles of world history. That they dared, in a situation that was hopeless by any human calculation, to risk everything in waging this fight for freedom, and that—amazingly—they won, is an enormous achievement, a mighty example of how the ideal of freedom can shine not only in beautiful and lofty words, but also in deeds. It is an example in which thousands and tens of thousands of men sacrificed their lives for the ideal of freedom, and thereby proved its validity in the most concrete and convincing way. In human affairs this is indeed the only way in which man can prove his loyalty to an ideal.

5

The Founding of the Delian-Attic Maritime League: The Rise of Athenian-Spartan Rivalry

The year of Timosthenes' term as archon, 478–477 B.C., was an epochal one in the history of Greece, marking as it did the founding of the Delian-Attic Maritime League. It was this confederacy, during the years before the Peace of Callias (449–448), that really carried the burden of the Greeks' war against the Persians. And it was the first instance of an organized union of Greek states—in this case under Athens' leadership—to arise outside of the territory of Sparta's Peloponnesian League. In contrast to the essentially defensive attitude of the latter, its aim was to take the offensive against Persia. Thus alongside the Hellenic League of 481 there now stood a special confederacy under the leadership of Athens, whose large fleet had contributed so decisively to the defeat of Xerxes. With the founding of the Maritime League the old Hellenic League had by no means ceased to exist; the war against the Persians went on, but the real initiative in the struggle now lay with Athens and its allies, while the other members of the old alliance—even Sparta, whose services in the liberation of Greece were unquestioned—now moved back into the second rank. Modern political science classifies the Delian-Attic League as a "plural symmachy"; it was a league between Athens on one side and a multitude of allies on the other. The precise number of allies is not known, since the earliest tribute lists preserved date only from about twenty-five years after the founding of the League. But one will not go far wrong in thinking of a number between 100 and 200; at the time of the Archidamian War, for instance, there were more than 400 members. The alliance, it appears, was to be valid for all time. This is indicated not only by the formula that is mentioned in Aristotle's *Constitution of Athens* (Ch. 23, par. 5), which states that the allies are to have friends and enemies in common. It is also shown above all by the fact that red-hot pieces of metal were dropped into the sea in confirmation of the mutual oath taken; just as these fragments vanished for all time, so also was the symmachy to last forever.

Of the organization of the League in its earliest years little is known. Historical sources report that Aristides was especially active in its affairs during this period. He fixed the levels of payments to the common war treasury for the individual allies, a difficult task which he solved to the satisfaction of all, gaining himself thereby the surname of "the Just." But Themistocles, too, took part in the organization of the League; this we would have to assume even if it were not attested by the verses of Timocreon of Ialysus, on the island of Rhodes, an author who had little love for Themistocles.

The headquarters of the Maritime League were on the little Aegean island of Delos. Here the delegates (*synhedroi*) from the member states assembled, and here too the treasury of the League was housed in the Temple of Apollo. While the large islands, such as Chios, Lesbos, Samos, Naxos, and Thasos, provided ships, which Athens welcomed as a valuable accretion to its own navy, the smaller cities were hardly in a position to do this and were perhaps not even willing to do so.

Instead, the latter were assessed a *phoros* (tribute), payment in lieu of military service, which went into the League's treasury. The total sum was fixed by Aristides at 460 talents, and the burden was distributed among the member cities in accordance with their importance and economic capability. So precise and practical was the initial organization of the League that this total amount for the tribute was adhered to without change for more than fifty years. Only after the victories of Pylos and Sphacteria in the Archidamian War did Cleon not only double but more than treble the tribute, to 1,460 talents.

The sharing of the financial burdens of the League by its members had not only an economic but also an ideological purpose. The allies could hardly expect Athens, the leading state of the League, together with the other large maritime states, to shoulder the entire burden of the defense against the Persian peril while the smaller cities simply stood by and watched. By contributing the *phoros* the latter did their share —and in general this should not have been difficult for them. By assessing tribute upon the allies, on the other hand, Athens had placed the union on a firm financial basis. In this respect it was far in advance of Sparta, which never created a federal treasury for the Peloponnesian League or anything of the kind. Even in the Peloponnesian War the Spartans were still more or less dependent on voluntary contributions from their allies.

In searching for earlier models that may have influenced the financial organization of the Delian League, one must turn inevitably toward the East. The Achaemenid Empire possessed a sound system of taxation, of which Herodotus has given a very thorough description. Naturally one cannot speak in any literal sense of an adoption of the Persian system. Nevertheless, taxation as such was characteristic of the empires of the Orient, whereas parallels in the Greek world are lacking. It must also be pointed out that most of Athens' new allies had up to now paid tribute to the Persians.

The military operations of the Delian League reveal from the very beginning a skillful, purposeful leadership. As early as 476–475, Eion on the lower Strymon was wrested from the Persians and its inhabitants sold into slavery. The same treatment was given to the Dolopes, the inhabitants of the island of Skyros. The reputed bones of Athens' legendary founder, Theseus, were found on this island and returned to his city— an early example of the cult of relics in ancient times. The date of the action against Skyros must probably be fixed before

470, as well as the subjugation of Carystus on Euboea. No precise date, on the other hand, can be given to the revolt of the island of Naxos. The events on Euboea and Naxos, however, are both very revealing. The territory of Carystus comprised the whole southern part of the island of Euboea. Its entry into the Delian League marks the forced inclusion of a city-state into that organization for no other reason than that it served Athens' purpose, which was a rounding off of the confederacy's boundaries. Athens was unwilling to tolerate an independent Carystus as an alien element in her immediate vicinity. However, the inhabitants of Carystus, the Dryopes, were treated very mildly.

The reason for Naxos' defection from the Maritime League is as little known, as are the terms that the city received after its capitulation. The case of Naxos, however, shows that member states were not at liberty to leave the league of their own volition. Since the League had been established for all time, Athens, the hegemonial power, was determined to block all attempts to escape its obligations. It is clear that what was involved here was hardly a legal question but one of sheer power.

A decisive event in the history of the Delian League was the battle fought on the Eurymedon in Pamphylia, probably in the years immediately following 470, possibly in 469. Eurymedon was the victory of the Athenian *strategos* Cimon, and beyond that of Athens and its allies. The Persians suffered heavy losses on water and on land; and once again the Phoenicians learned that the Greeks were their superiors in aggressiveness and daring when properly led and committed to battle purposefully. Before the battle Cimon had used the maritime city of Phaselis as his base, and after it a good many Hellenic cities on the southern coast of Asia Minor joined the maritime confederacy. As a result the sphere of influence of the Persian Empire was pushed back from the coast far toward the East. The Aegean had become a Greek sea, and for many decades afterward no Persian warship ventured to cross its waters. Thus the battle on the Eurymedon formed the capstone to the Greek victories of Salamis, Plataea, and Mycale.

Themistocles had no part in the victory on the Eurymedon. Since 471 the man to whom Athens and all Greece owed its freedom had suffered political eclipse. His followers, who in time of need had willingly stood at his side, now quailed at the onslaught of his enemies. They proved too weak to prevent Themistocles' ostracism in 471. Today we still have several hundred ostracism ballots marked with Themistocles' name. It must be assumed that a supply of them, so to speak, were produced and that they were then put into the hands of the Athenian citizens when Themistocles' enemies judged that the time was ripe for his political destruction.

It is not enough to see in this episode merely the shouldering aside of the older generation by the new. The conflict between Themistocles and his opponents went much deeper. Themistocles had realized, with clear foresight, that Athens could never rise to power if she continued to support the interests of her Lacedaemonian brothers-in-arms. Athens had to free herself from these burdensome fetters if she was ever to occupy that leading position in Hellas which she deserved because of the achievements of her fleet in the struggle for liberation. This view, however, not only ran strongly counter to the opinions of many citizens, but also threatened to disrupt the many personal ties between Athens and Lacedaemon that had grown up in the time of trouble with the Persians and had come to be cherished. But in politics gratitude, as Themistocles knew, is no foundation upon which to build a state's future. He who wants to move forward must not look back.

Themistocles' fall can more easily be understood if it is viewed in conjunction with the fate of Pausanias, the Spartan regent and victor of Plataea. Pausanias had been able to maintain himself securely in Byzantium until 476, when Cimon drove him out. He had then gone to Persian territory, to the Troad, and there he resided in the little town of Colonae. Why he let himself be persuaded thereafter (469?) to heed the ephors' renewed summons and return to Sparta remains a mystery. Sparta at this time was in a dangerous position. An anti-Spartan movement had arisen in the Peloponnese, and once again its leader was Argos, which, in alliance with Tegea

73

and the Arcadians, was so strong that it was able to prove itself almost the equal of Sparta in the field (battles of Tegea and Dipaea, both probably before 470). Moreover, a democratic movement had come to power in Elis about 470, so that here too Spartan influence was melting away. Were the Spartan leaders expecting new miracles from Pausanias' proven generalship? It does not appear so, for the first thing they did was to accuse Pausanias of collaborating with the Persians. This was the charge of Medism, which in those days not only meant disgrace but could also lead to the death of the accused. No quarter was given anyone who had dealt with the national enemy, whether in Sparta or in Athens. But in the case of Pausanias, no proof could be produced of collaboration with the Persians, so the indictment had to be dropped.

Then Pausanias made a move that was to lead straight to his ruin. He attempted to form an alliance with the helots, which would have undermined the foundations of the Spartan state. To forestall his threatened arrest by the ephors, Pausanias fled into the temple of Athena Chalcioecus in Sparta. The ephors had the temple walled up, and only brought Pausanias out of the sanctuary when he was on the point of death from starvation and lay in his last agony.

Thus died miserably the greatest general in Sparta's entire history, a death that he brought upon himself. For to conspire with the helots was a sin that could never be forgiven in Sparta, from which it is evident how little Pausanias felt himself bound by the Spartan political order, the *Kosmos*. It is quite likely that the revolt of the Messenian helots, which broke out only a few years later, was foreshadowed by the conspiracy of Pausanias. But this hardly justifies a view of Pausanias as a far-sighted politician. Sparta's power—to put it brutally—was based upon the subjection of the Messenians. Anyone who disregarded this fact was a political dilettante, who placed his own hunger for power above the safety of the state.

It is not a proven fact, nor in the nature of things can it be proved, that Themistocles was in league with Pausanias. The Athenian leader, after his banishment, had stayed at first in

Argos, and from there had journeyed about the Peloponnese. When it became known to him that both Athens and Sparta intended to take him prisoner, he fled to Corcyra and thence to Epirus, to the court of Admetus, King of the Molossians. But since he did not feel secure even in Epirus, he went to Macedonia, and from there took ship to Asia Minor, to Ephesus. During the crossing Themistocles is said to have come within a hair's breadth of falling into the hands of an Athenian naval fleet off Naxos. (Another manuscript of Plutarch's, *Life of Themistocles*, 25, 2—the Seitenstettensis ms.—gives the location of the incident as Thasos.)

In the Persian Empire Artaxerxes I, son of Xerxes, had been Great King since 465–464. He received the fugitive Themistocles with all honor and gave him in fief the city of Magnesia on the Maeander, as well as the towns of Lampsacus and the Ionian Myus. In Magnesia, as a vassal of the Persian King, Themistocles lived a few years longer, dying probably before the year 450.

The life of Themistocles is full of riddles which scholars will probably never succeed in elucidating. When one contemplates the face of this man—his bust was restored to us a few decades ago through a lucky find in Ostia—one understands why he was so completely different from his contemporaries. Themistocles was the first Greek statesman to possess what may be called the politician's sixth sense. He possessed in a high degree—if anyone ever did—the art of political foresight, for which the historian Thucydides (I, 138, 3) gives him full credit.

But political foresight in Themistocles was combined with (one might say) a completely amoral utilization of all political means that served to forward a course of action, once that course had been correctly perceived. Themistocles knew no compunction of any kind. His statesmanship resembled a game of chess, with each move producing a countermove, and Themistocles, of course, always one move ahead of his opponent. We need only recall the history of the building of the Athenian wall. It is not surprising that Themistocles' opponents within and outside Athens had little understanding of his kind of politics. They raised against him the charge of perfidy, and from their standpoint they were right.

And yet the uncanny Themistocles saw deeper than all the others. He probably lived long enough to realize that Athens would have to fight not only against Persia but also against its old ally Sparta, and in a war that, in magnitude and expenditure of resources, would tax the Athenians' powers to the utmost. There is no doubt about it: Themistocles would have taken another course and, if the situation required it, would not have hesitated to come to terms with the Persians against whom he had once fought, at Artemisium and Salamis, for the freedom of Athens and of all Greece. The clear, cold atmosphere of political calculation—this was the world of the man whom even the Persian adversary could not but respect.

With the ostracism of Themistocles in 471 the era of Cimon, the son of Miltiades, begins in Athens. It lasted almost exactly a decade and ended with Cimon's banishment in 461. In several respects this period is of great significance, not only for the internal development of the Delian League, but also for Spartan-Athenian relations and for Greek policy toward the great power in the East, the Persian Empire. Before we turn to the political events, we must say a few words about the man who placed upon this epoch the stamp of his own personality.

Cimon was born about 510 B.C. of the distinguished aristocratic family of the Philaids. His mother, Hegesipyle, was of Thracian princely stock. He was uncommonly wealthy, and made use of this wealth in a lavish fashion, his liberality being attested to above all by the buildings he constructed in Athens. As early as 476–475, after the capture of Eion, he received permission to consecrate hermae in the new Hall of the Hermae and provide them with inscriptions. Opposite this Hall of the Hermae Cimon's brother-in-law, Peisianax, erected the Stoa Poikilé, while Cimon himself built the Theseum, in which were housed the reputed bones of Theseus. Cimon also erected the great supporting walls of the Acropolis, which made it possible to enlarge greatly the area of the citadel. The gardens of the Academy, too, were the result of his initiative.

Like the great tyrants he also gathered around himself a number of poets, who proclaimed his renown. It is not by chance that Cimon's sister Elpinice holds a much more prominent place in historical tradition than other women of Attica. Though much that is reported of her may not be based on very reliable historical evidence, it can scarcely be disputed that her position resembled that of a princess more than that of a citizen. When we read how, in the battle of Tanagra (457), the members of Cimon's deme, the Lakiadae, rallied around his armor as around an emblem, we realize once again the unusual reverence that Cimon evoked in Athens even after his banishment. Cimon's attitude toward the Athenian state, it is true, was that of a great independent lord; nevertheless his political activity fitted to perfection the overall direction of Attic policy. It is not surprising, for instance, that this very decade from 471 to 461 was a period of Athenian success, which to a large extent can be attributed to the policies of Cimon.

The events in the Persian Empire during this period exercised almost no influence on Greece. The death of Xerxes in 465–464 and the accession of Artaxerxes I meant little outside the Persian Empire. Nevertheless the succession took place in an extremely bloody manner. Xerxes was murdered in his bedchamber, and his eldest son—named Darius, after his grandfather—was killed by the younger brother Artaxerxes. Another son of Xerxes, Hystaspes, revolted in Bactria, but Artaxerxes was able to eliminate him. In the events at court an important role was played by a number of Persian notables, led by Artabanus and Megabyzus. For us today it is hard to understand what actually took place, for over the events lies a thick web of intrigue, fostered by the suffocating atmosphere of the court.

For years now the real opponents of the Persian Empire had been Athens and the Delian League. How did matters stand in the alliance in the year 465, twelve years after its founding? That was a fateful year for the League. The rich island of Thasos defected from Athens. The causes are unknown, but that Persian intrigue played a part is as good as

77

excluded as a possibility. It is more reasonable to think of influences coming from Macedonia, but even this is hard to prove. About this time Athens had undertaken a large-scale colonization on the lower Strymon; no less than 10,000 colonists had been settled in the plain at the "Nine Ways" (*Enneahodoi*). The Thasians must have watched with concern while Athens secured a foothold in the Thracian interior. After all, the wealthy island of Thasos held extensive territory on the nearby Thracian coast, from which it received large revenues, especially from the gold mines. However, the Athenian advance was soon brought to an end when the settlers were defeated by the native Thracians at Drabescus, a disaster that cost Athens heavily. Nevertheless Thasos turned to Sparta. The latter is said to have promised the Thasians an invasion of Attica in order to give them a breathing spell. The promise, however—if indeed it was ever made—was never fulfilled, for in the year 464 a mighty earthquake devastated Sparta and wiped out part of its manpower of military age. Following this the helots rose in Messenia, in the so-called Third Messenian War, so that Sparta was for the time being incapable of action.

The Athenians commissioned Cimon, the victor of the battle on the Eurymedon, to suppress the Thasian revolt. The city was invested and finally, in the third year of the siege (463), forced to capitulate. Its inhabitants were forced to tear down their walls, surrender their fleet, defray the expenses of the war, and finally pledge themselves to pay an annual tribute to the treasury of the Delian League (up to now Thasos had only been required to provide ships). In addition the Thasians lost their valuable possessions on the mainland. Once again, as in the case of Naxos, Athens had punished a member of the Delian Confederacy that had dared to make an attempt to throw off the Attic harness—a warning example to any city that, like Thasos, nursed hopes for emancipation.

If the much-discussed inscription containing an Attic decree on the status of Erythrae (see Bengtson, *Staatsvertraege,* No. 134) could be dated exactly, we would have a valuable document illuminating the relations of Athens with another member of the League at about the time of the Thasian revolt. Unfortunately, all that can be said is that this inscription—the original of which has long been lost—seems to date from some time after 465. The possibility of setting a later date, perhaps as late as the middle of the fifth century, is of course by no means excluded. Be that as it may, the document shows very clearly the ever more overriding influence of Athens upon the internal affairs of a member city of her confederacy.

Erythrae was an Ionian city lying opposite the island of Chios, on a tongue of land extending far toward the west. Not only were there Athenian supervisory officers in the city, the *episkopoi* and the *Phrourarchos* (garrison commander), but these officers even had the right to review appointments to the city's council or *boule*. Moreover the councilmen of the city expressly pledged themselves not to defect from the Athenians nor from the other allies. The document draws an unbreakable line between the League and Persia, with which it was in a state of war. Thus it is expressly forbidden to receive within the walls of the city anyone who had fled to the "Medes." Furthermore care is taken to see that in Erythrae tyranny shall never come to power: whoever betrays Erythrae to a tyrant shall die. The document shows that Athens, as the hegemonial power of the League, exercised a strict domination over its ally. Though the city maintained local autonomy, in the conduct of foreign policy it was bound by the wishes of Athens.

After Cimon's return from Thasos to Athens, charges were brought against him. He was accused of having neglected to turn his forces against King Alexander I of Macedonia. It is not difficult to suppose that behind this accusation were the followers of Ephialtes and Pericles, since Pericles in this trial was the prosecutor appointed by the people. This was the first public appearance—with the exception of his choregy * in 473–472—of this man who was later to become so famous. As for the charge against Cimon, H. Swoboda has called it absurd; so indeed it was, but it is nonetheless very revealing. It shows that in Athens the upper hand had been gained by a movement that seems to have lost all sense of proportion in

* A citizen's provision of a dramatic chorus at his own expense.

foreign policy. First Thasos, then Macedonia—what would come next? Just as Cimon had taken the place of Themistocles, so new men—in the persons of Ephialtes and Pericles—were now pressing forward, men who were using every opportunity to discredit Cimon. The trial ended in an acquittal; the story that Cimon's sister Elpinice interceded with Pericles for her brother is certainly false.

Not long afterward the Spartans, unable to subdue the Messenians, whom they had surrounded on Mount Ithome, sent Athens an official request for help. The feeling in Athens toward the Spartan request was by no means unanimous. Ephialtes was violently opposed to it, but Cimon finally succeeded in having an auxiliary force of 4,000 hoplites sent into the Peloponnese (462).

During Cimon's absence on the Messenian battlefield, a fundamental change in the Constitution had been enacted in Athens. Its author was Ephialtes, and so radical was this reform that from now on it is possible to speak of the beginnings of total democracy in Athens (462–461). Ephialtes' reform, of which more will be said in another connection (see p. 82), as well as the action of the Spartans in sending back the Attic contingent, shook Cimon's position. His adherents in Athens were no longer able to control the newly rising forces under Ephialtes, and the internal struggle for power—during which Cimon tried in vain to have the reforms annulled—ended with the ostracism of Cimon in 461. For the time being the career of the victor of the Eurymedon was ended.

From this date Athenian policy took an entirely different course. The action of the Lacedaemonians in sending home the Athenian auxiliary corps revealed the latent conflict between the two leading powers in Hellas. Sparta, to be sure, had long since left the conduct of the Persian War to Athens and the Maritime League. Perhaps this renunciation was not even deliberate, for the Lacedaemonians had run into a great deal of trouble in the Peloponnese, most recently with the revolt of the Messenians. Nevertheless, the mounting antagonism between Athens and Sparta was to be very dangerous from the standpoint of Greece as a whole. The great national idea, which during the wars with the Persians had inspired the Greek will to defense, was now driven more and more into the background. The fortunes of individual states again became the dominant motive in politics, and it seemed to the other Greeks more and more a matter of course that Athens, with her fleet, should see to it that no Persian ship crossed the waters of the Aegean. Did anyone in Greece reflect on the fact that Persian inaction was merely the result of a slackening of the reins in the hands of a weak government? One must clearly realize, too, what Athenian dominion in the Aegean meant. Wherever the banner of Athens waved, security and peace prevailed, undisturbed even by pirates.

But between the Maritime League and the Persian Empire a barrier had now been erected, and this condition was to last for about thirty years. For an entire generation of Hellenes, the Persians were known only as the "barbarians," the archenemy, with whom a state of war had existed as far back as anyone could remember, and the charge of "Medism," of being Persian in one's sympathies, had become a deadly weapon in the internal political struggles among the Greeks as well as in their external wars. The gulf between the Greek and Persian peoples grew ever wider. Remote were the times when a rich cultural and material interchange had flowed freely between Greeks and Persians.

6

Pericles and Athenian Democracy

In the person of Pericles, a man ascends the stage of Athenian politics whose name will remain forever linked with the zenith of Athenian history. The period of his leadership, beginning with the death of Ephialtes in 461 and ending in the year 429, we call the Periclean Age, which has had countless admirers in both ancient and modern times. Indeed in the generation between 461 and the beginning of the Peloponnesian War (431) the Athenian people were brought—above all by Pericles—to a height never attained by Greeks before or since. Athens was without dispute the leading state in Greece, not only in the maturity of its political institutions, but even more so in its cultural achievements, which are to be laid in large part to the initiative of Pericles himself.

A number of reforms are connected with the name of this great statesman which, taken together, represent a decisive step on the road to complete democracy in Athens. The contributions of Pericles can only be understood, however, when viewed within the framework of the reforms that had already been inaugurated by Ephialtes. Aristotle tells us, in his *Constitution of Athens* (Ch. 25), that the Areopagus, with its lifetime members, was in control of Athens until Ephialtes, the son of Sophonides, turned against it. Ephialtes' first move, according to Aristotle, was to eliminate many members of the Areopagus by involving them in prosecutions for the misuse of their office; then he fought the Areopagus itself as an institution and eventually took from it all its powers. For this, down to Aristotle's day, he was called "guardian of the Constitution." Ephialtes transferred the powers of the Areopagus partly to the Council of Five Hundred and partly to the people and to the courts, a work in which, according to Aristotle, Ephialtes collaborated with Themistocles. But this allegation has long since been proved a capital error on Aristotle's part, for Themistocles was then living in Persian territory, and the assumption that he had returned from Asia Minor to the Athens that had outlawed him is so improbable that it needs no refutation. Besides, Aristotle's account is elsewhere adorned with so many questionable anecdotes that it seems advisable to treat it with reserve.

However, the fact that Ephialtes' reforms (462–461) were directed primarily against the Areopagus is indisputable. K. J. Beloch has expressed the opinion that the overthrow of the Areopagus was completely justified, that in the long run no institution could be tolerated whose members held power in the state on a lifetime basis, who were, in other words, in a completely impregnable position. Of Beloch's view, this much is correct: the character of the Areopagus was certainly altered after the archons ceased to be elected and were chosen, instead, by lot (487–486). Beloch, however, is exaggerating when he speaks about the many dubious characters who served on the Areopagus from that time on. Whether or not the Areopagus was substantially changed in its composition, there is no doubt that Ephialtes had deprived it of its basic administrative and judicial powers (with the exception of its jurisdiction in certain homicide cases), and had transferred these powers to the people—to their constitutionally elected organs and their courts.

These changes were the underpinning for everything that now followed. In 457–456 the *zeugitai*—the majority of the people of Attica, both urban and rural—were also made eligible for the archonate. Hitherto this highest office of the state had been confined to the two upper tax classes, the *Pentakosiomedimnoi* (see p. 33) and the knights. In 453–

452 the institution of the judges of the demes was again re-established, an institution about which we unfortunately know very little. It can be assumed, perhaps, that this move was connected in some way with the democratization of the courts.

It is difficult to envisage the last two reforms without the collaboration, indeed the initiative, of Pericles, who had become the real successor of Ephialtes. For Ephialtes had been murdered in 461, probably a sacrifice to the bitterness the internal political struggle in Athens had engendered.

The pages of Plutarch's biography of Pericles reveal a great deal about the life and deeds of that great man, but the reliability of Plutarch's portrait is another question. His details are often taken from late and biased sources; moreover Plutarch attempts to glorify his hero, in his own fashion, by associating him with events for which he is not responsible. Thus, for example, the constitutional reform of 461 is attributed to Pericles instead of to Ephialtes.

What do we actually know about Pericles? His father was Xanthippus, the victor of Mycale and opponent of Cimon; his mother was Agariste, daughter of Hippocrates, the brother of Cleisthenes. On his mother's side Pericles was thus descended from the House of the Alcmaeonids. He was the second son of this marriage, born probably about 495, so that he was old enough to have actually experienced the campaign of Xerxes and the evacuation of Athens.

What he looked like is revealed to us in portraits surviving from ancient times; they are probably all replicas of the famous bust by Cresilas. The peculiar, allegedly onionlike shape of his head became a repeated butt for the humor of the comic poets—Cratinus, Telecleides, Eupolis. That as a member of a distinguished family he must have received a good education is something that we may assume, even though it is not explicitly stated in historical tradition. His teachers, besides Damon and Pythocleides, who are unknown to us, included above all Zeno of Elea and Anaxagoras, the latter being bound to him by ties of deep friendship. Although it is certain that Anaxagoras did not come to Athens until Pericles had grown

84

to adulthood, the influence of the Ionian natural philosopher upon Pericles was nevertheless extraordinarily great.

Apart from these details, little is known about his youth. All the ancient sources agree, however, that Pericles was an orator of outstanding ability. Great rhetorical skill and an uncanny power of persuasion—these were the qualities for which he was repeatedly praised, and there is no doubt that this talent served him well in politics.

His internal political measures, to which we now turn, are readily understood when viewed in the light of the democratic reforms introduced by Ephialtes. Pericles continued on the path taken by his predecessor; he consolidated the power of the sovereign *demos* of Athens, thereby creating a real "democracy" for the first time in the history of the Western world. Periclean democracy, of course, cannot be equated with democracy as we know it today; the differences, both internal and external, are too great. Modern democracy is an indirect democracy. Power, to be sure, proceeds from the people, whose will is manifested by means of the ballot; but the governing process is carried on, as in England for instance, by a Cabinet of Ministers under the control of a Parliament elected by the people. In Athens, as in so many other Greek city-states, popular sovereignty was vested in the *Ekklesia,* the "People's Assembly." The Greek word *ekklesia* comes from *ekkalein,* which means "call out" or "call upon (someone) to do." All men had a right to participate in the debates of the Assembly, as long as they were in possession of civic rights and were of age. The degree of public participation, however, does not appear to have been very great; many citizens preferred to pursue their own affairs, or appeared only when the subject debated was one in which they were personally interested. This was the case not only in Athens but also in the other Greek cities. In these Assemblies the critical decisions as to war and peace, alliances with foreign powers, embassies, and other matters were made, and the citizens present were summoned by a herald to take part in the debate concerning the items on the agenda. As a rule, of course, the speakers were those men

85

who had made politics their life's work, the "demagogues," as they were disparagingly called. For them the People's Assembly was the arena in which they unleashed their eloquence.

Just as important as the *Ekklesia*, however, and in many respects even more important, was the *Boule*, the "Council," which had been established by Solon, and which since Cleisthenes' day had numbered 500 instead of the original 400 members, fifty from each *phyle* (tribe). Any Athenian citizen of more than thirty years of age could become a Councillor. In Pericles' time the candidates were chosen by lot, but no one could become a Councillor more than twice. This activity exempted one from military service, and in addition the members of the Boule had a place of honor in the theater. The work of a Councillor, on the other hand, was certainly strenuous and time-consuming, and it is no wonder that on occasion it was difficult to find the necessary candidates. The Council met daily, with the exception of festival days. These sessions were in principle open to the public, but sometimes the audience was excluded when secrecy would be in the public interest. The resolutions of this body either were *Probuleumata* ("preliminary resolutions"), which were then submitted to the Assembly as the decision-making body, or were independent executive resolutions on many different matters of administration and adjudication. If only because of its size, a body of 500 members (even if it is assumed that the Boule never assembled in full strength) is not in a position to act as quickly and flexibly as the moment may require. The Council was therefore divided, according to phylae, into ten divisions of fifty members each, which alternately took turns dispatching current business. The phyle holding the executive function was called the prytany, and its members prytanes. They assembled in a building that was circular in shape, called the Tholos. From their number they elected a president, the *Epistates*, who for one day held the chair in the Boule and also in the Assembly—and could thus boast of having been for twenty-four hours the leader of the Attic state. One third of the prytanes, together with their president, were required to remain constantly in the magistrate's office for the transaction

86

of current business. It can easily be imagined that in times of unrest these prytanes and their *epistatai* had plenty of work to do: officials, citizens, and foreign emissaries would turn to them, and they then had to decide which matters should and which should not be laid before the full Council.

Next to the officials, the Council, and the People's Assembly, the most important organ in Athens was the popular court. This institution, the *Heliaia,* was also originated by Solon, who had set it up to compete with the Areopagus. During the course of the fifth century the Heliaia was divided into a number of independent courts and for these courts not less than 6,000 citizens were chosen annually by lot to serve as jurors. This very large number is explained by the fact that there were seven courts and that some jurors were appointed as supernumeraries. Generally, 501 jurors sat in the courts, the number being occasionally increased to 1,001 or 1,501 according to the importance of the trial. In private cases, however, it was usual to call upon a very much smaller number of jurors.

Boule, Ekklesia, Heliaia, and the officials, of which the ten strategoi were the most important—these, then, were the organs of government that dominated the political life of Athens at the time of Pericles. Only Athenian citizens, however (with the exception of women, who were, of course, excluded), had access to these bodies. Neither the metics (the "co-residents" —citizens of other Greek city-states who were living in Athens) nor the slaves were represented in them. Attic democracy was, then, the rule of a minority over a majority which held no political rights. In his *Constitution of Athens* (Ch. 24) Aristotle states that in the fifth century B.C. more than 20,000 citizens of Athens were supported by public taxes and the *phoroi* of Athens' allies. He specifically lists 6,000 jurors, 1,600 archers, 1,200 horsemen, 500 councillors, 500 guards for the shipyards, 50 city guards, about 700 men to fill the city's administrative offices, and (probably) an equal number overseas, though the last figure may well be corrupted. Be that as it may, this is a remarkably large number of people to be maintained at state cost. Aristotle says that the salaries were established by Aristides. This is certainly an error; not Aristides but Pericles was responsible, as is unquestionably clear from other sources, according to which Pericles introduced *per diem* remuneration (*diaitai*) for jurors, and later also for councillors and for all officials appointed by lot. What the level of this remuneration was is to some extent a matter of dispute. The jurors of the Heliaia probably received two obols per day of session, which would approximate the minimum subsistence figure; the councillors, on the other hand, received one drachma (six obols). Whether Pericles (as Plutarch reports in his *Life of Pericles,* Ch. 9) also introduced the so-called theater funds (*theorika*), which were paid to the citizens for attendance at the dramatic performances, has not been fully ascertained. In this connection it must be understood that the performances fell within the sphere of religious worship, more specifically of state religious worship; they cannot be thought of as cultural events in today's sense. Payments to the citizens taking part in the Assembly, on the other hand, do not seem to have been instituted until much later, probably not before the beginning of the fourth century B.C.

K. J. Beloch has expressed the view that the *diaitai* payments were necessary in Athens because otherwise it would hardly have been possible to muster the necessary number of jurors, councillors, and officials. There is undoubtedly some truth in this. In all periods of history the popular interest in public affairs has not generally been great, so that a certain incentive has always been necessary. The citizen serving in the Heliaia or on the Council or as an administrative official was thereby often prevented from pursuing his own private profession, and for this he had to be compensated. In the early days of Athens it was usually only those citizens who were economically independent who offered themselves for public service. After the introduction of the practice of choosing archons by lot (487–486), however, and above all after Ephialtes' overthrow of the Areopagus and his other reforms, conditions were altered. Now the mass of the Athenian citizens were also to be given the opportunity to take active part in the politics of the state, whether as officials, councilmen, or jurors.

Pericles' introduction of the *diaitai* was in some respects, however, a benefit of a dubious, even questionable nature. Inevitably some Athenians would come to count upon being fed and supported by the state. Although the state paid them only enough for a minumum subsistence, there were nevertheless a great number of recipients of these state funds, and thus the spirit in which these sums were accepted, as well as the actual amount of the sums, became a factor in the political situation.

Certainly many citizens, it must be noted, were already well enough off so that the *diaitai* made little difference to them. Thus it was primarily the poorest class that was interested in the financial awards for public service. Nevertheless the measure introduced by Pericles marked the beginning of a downward path that was to be followed much further by Cleon and other demagogues. Already the phantom of the welfare state was visible in the background, a danger which hitherto had been completely unknown, not only in Athens but in all of Greece. Then there was the additional fact that the major part of the moneys thus dispensed in Athens was contributed by the member states of the Maritime League—contributions that not only made it possible to build the great edifices in Athens, but also provided many an Athenian with a very welcome addition to his personal income.

How self-serving the Attic *demos* could be is shown by the Law on Athenian citizenship introduced by Pericles (451–450). According to this law, only those persons could be citizens of Attica who were of Athenian ancestry on both their father's and their mother's side. If a man had a foreign mother, in short, he was not regarded as a citizen. The law was not retroactive, however. Those affected by it were not so much the lower classes of the population as the aristocracy, which had family connections in all of Greece and far beyond. This Periclean law reveals a positively tragic blindness that is all the more surprising in that Pericles' own family—as far as his sons by Aspasia were concerned—would not have met the requirements of the new law.

What idea lay behind this law? Was the intention really, as H. E. Stier has asserted, to form an Attic nation on the basis of bloodlines? We may assume that such a thought, then as always, could never have swayed the minds of the Athenians. The new law was actually intended to achieve a restriction in the number of persons living at the expense of the Attic state. Those who did not meet the requirements of the citizenship law would in the future receive no more daily allowances, and would also have no share in the distribution of grain. (It is reported that in 445–444 the Egyptian ruler Psammetichus sent the Athenians a large cargo of grain.) Here is evidence for a rather appalling group-egotism, which Pericles, far from discouraging, actually promoted.

It would be an error to assume that the damage resulting from the overstraining of the democratic principle had already come to light in the time of Pericles. Actually in his day Athens proved substantially equal to all its tasks, in particular to the burdens of foreign campaigns, which in the Periclean period often reached the limit of Athens' power to support.

When Pericles took up the political inheritance of Ephialtes, the Persian Wars of many years' duration were still continuing. It is most likely, however, that after the battle on the Eurymedon (469?) no further major collisions took place between Athens and Persia, although nothing can be stated as fact; the historical information is so inadequate that it scarcely permits an exact judgment. In any case it was necessary for Athens to be always on her guard, for the Persian fleet might at any moment appear in the Aegean and could put the existence of the Delian League to a severe test.

To the latent Persian peril was added the growing breach with Sparta and with the Peloponnesian League of which it was the leader. It is not surprising to find the Athenians searching for allies to cover their rear against the Peloponnesians. The most available were the Argives, Sparta's mortal enemies; thus Athens concluded a treaty of alliance with Argos and with the Thessalians, and a little later with the city of Megara on the Isthmus.

The importance of winning Megara as an ally—the city had left the Peloponnesian camp to go over to the side of Athens—could hardly be overestimated, since in the Megaran port of Pagae the Athenians now possessed a base on the Corinthian Gulf. This advantage was to be paid for, however, with the bitter enmity of Corinth itself. In the decades that followed and down to the outbreak of the Peloponnesian War the powerful trading city on the Isthmus was repeatedly to be found among the enemies of Athens; and in the later struggle of the Peloponnesians against Athens the interests of Corinth were not infrequently decisive.

Though Athens did not officially take part in the war between Sparta and Argos, it sent the Argives an auxiliary corps which in the encounter at Oenoe (about 460) gained a victory over the Lacedaemonians. This battle—which must not be confused with the battle of Oenophyta—made such a profound impression in Athens that it was immortalized in a painting in the Stoa Poikilé. Of Athens' adversaries at that time, besides Corinth and Epidaurus, the most important was the wealthy island of Aegina which, as a Dorian base in the Saronic Gulf, had always been a thorn in Athens' side. Even before Xerxes' campaign against Greece, relations between Athens and Aegina had reached the point of open conflict, which had to be arbitrated by Sparta. Meanwhile the balance of power had shifted very much in Athens' favor. Even with the help of Corinth, which suffered a defeat on land at the hands of Athenian forces, the Athenian investment and blockade of Aegina could not be prevented.

That Athens in all this fighting was able to maintain the upper hand, despite its Egyptian expedition (see p. 93), is explained by the fact that Sparta and the Peloponnesian League still had not entered into open hostilities against Athens. In the spring of 457, however, this situation changed. A large Spartan levy moved over the Isthmus northward with the ostensible purpose of bringing aid to their fellow Dorians of

91

Oetaea against the Phocians. In reality, however, this Spartan incursion into central Greece was actuated by frankly political aims, of which the size of the levy alone is sufficient proof. The objective was Spartan supremacy in Boeotia; but a Spartan hold on this region would mean a grave threat to Attica. Thus for the first time Lacedaemonians and Athenians met on the open field of battle at Tanagra, not far from Thebes, and the Lacedaemonians emerged victorious (457). Since a strategic pursuit of a beaten hoplite army was unusual (and probably also impossible), the Athenians were able to withdraw their army in good order back across the border into Attica. Among the Athenian strategoi, by the way, was Pericles.

Two months later the Athenians under Myronides won a decisive victory at Oenophyta over the Boeotian levies. With this, Attic supremacy was restored over all of Boeotia, with the exception of Thebes. How greatly the region was under Athenian influence is evident from the fact that in a number of Boeotian cities democratic movements came to power. Aegina had already surrendered unconditionally in the winter of 457–456 (Bengtson, *Staatsvertraege,* No. 141). The terms dictated to Aegina were essentially the same as those imposed on Thasos, no distinction being made in this respect between member states of the Maritime League and nonmembers. Like Thasos, Aegina too had to pay no less than thirty talents' annual tribute into the Treasury of the Delian confederacy. How strong Athens' position had become in central Greece is to be seen by the alliance concluded (probably at this time) with the Delphic Amphictyony (Bengtson, *Staatsvertraege,* No. 142).

The successes of Myronides in Boeotia and in Eastern (Opuntian) Locris were overshadowed by the naval expedition of Tolmides, undertaken with Athenian volunteers, most probably in the year 455. With fifty triremes and 4,000 hoplites on board, Tolmides sailed first to Methone on the western coast of Messenia and took the town. Then as the Lacedaemonians approached he weighed anchor and headed for Gytheum. Here too he succeeded in taking the city and burning the ships' wharves. Next the island of Zacynthus was subjugated and the towns of Cephallenia forced to join Athens.

Finally Tolmides sailed into the Corinthian Gulf, to Naupactus, where he settled refugee Messenian helots. An alliance was concluded with Achaea, so that Athens actually now had footholds on both sides of the strait of Rhium, the bottleneck of the Gulf. This posed a mortal threat to Corinth, whose lines of communication to the west were to all intents and purposes under Athenian control.

The importance of Tolmides' campaign can hardly be overestimated. Athens had shown how far its naval power could be extended, and it is even possible that the Athenians at the time were trying to dominate the communication routes westward to Sicily, which had previously been controlled primarily by Corinth. We are in possession, for instance, of fragments of a treaty between Athens and the Sicilian city of Segesta; unfortunately, it can be dated only tentatively to the archon-year of Habron, 458–457, since the name of the Attic archon on the inscription can be read only in part (Bengtson, *Staatsvertraege*, No. 139).

In 460 Athens had plunged into an enterprise whose importance hardly anyone in the city could have evaluated correctly at the time. This was the famous Egyptian expedition (460–454). Egypt, since 525, had been a part of the Persian Empire, but at various times rebellions had broken out, clearly indicating that the Egyptians were by no means reconciled to Persian rule. Therefore when the Libyan dynast Inaros established his rule in Lower Egypt, in the Delta region, he could be sure of the support of at least a part of the Egyptian population. A Persian army under the satrap Achaemenes, the brother of Xerxes, met him at Papremis, but Achaemenes was defeated and killed (460); the remnants of the Persian army were besieged in the citadel of Memphis. Meanwhile Inaros had established contact with the Athenians, apparently making them promises extensive enough to make them readily accept his offer. It is possible that colonization plans played a role in the Athenian decision. Undoubtedly Pericles was in part responsible for the acceptance of the offer of alliance. The Athenian fleet, rerouted from Cyprus to Egypt, took part in the siege of the Persian garrison in the "White Castle" of

Memphis, and at first seems to have been in unquestioned control of the situation. The fleet even appeared off the coast of Phoenicia to measure its strength against the Persians.

The Achaemenid Empire required, as usual, a long time to complete its military preparations. It was not until 456 that a relief army under Megabyzus was sent to Egypt. Megabyzus not only was successful in breaking the siege of Memphis but also invested the besiegers, Greeks and Egyptians together, on the Nile island of Prosopitis. Taking advantage of the lowest level of the Nile, he was able to take possession of the island by digging a canal that diverted and dried up one arm of the river. Part of the garrison on Prosopitis were massacred by the Persians, and the remainder were taken into captivity. Of the Athenians, only a few were able to escape and make their way back to Greece, reportedly by way of Doric Cyrene.

The Athenian losses are in general greatly exaggerated in various sources. In this case Ctesias, who around 400 B.C. lived for some time at the Persian court, may be given credence, though he is otherwise not noted for his reliability. He speaks of Athenian losses of 50 ships and 6,000 men. To this misfortune was added another. An Athenian relief fleet, unaware of what had happened, was surprised by the Persians at the Mendesian Cape and destroyed (454). Thus after six years Athens' Egyptian adventure was a complete failure; the Persian Empire had proved its superiority in Egypt and had made good the defeat on the Eurymedon.

In the same year as the Athenian catastrophe on the Nile, 454, the treasury of the Delian League was brought from Delos to Athens and placed in the Temple of Athena. It is clear that the two events cannot be divorced from each other, since when the Samians made the motion in the League assembly to transfer the treasury to Athens, they, like the other allies, must certainly have been under the influence of the dismal news from Egypt, even though the full extent of the defeat was perhaps not yet known. This year 454–453 marks the beginning of the so-called tribute lists of the League; they were actually lists of tribute quotas, in which were marked one sixtieth of the tribute (phoros) paid by the allies, i.e., one mina for every talent. The records extend, with many gaps, almost to the end of the Peloponnesian War, and are a valuable source of information not only on Athenian financial history but also on the composition of the League, its organization in districts, and the wealth and military capacity of its individual members.

In Greece too, in the year 454, there was no peace. The Athenians had little success with their campaigns in Thessaly and Acarnania, the latter under Pericles. The sources tell of a five-year armistice between Athens and Sparta, negotiated, allegedly, with the mediation of Cimon. If this is true the armistice could not have taken effect before 451, when Cimon returned from his ten-year exile. There is much doubt, however, as to whether Plutarch (*Life of Cimon,* 18, 1) should be given credence. In many other places Plutarch has attributed to his heroes events with which they had nothing to do (see p. 35). Diodorus (XI, 86, 1), on the other hand, gives us the date 453. Though in general Diodorus' chronology must be treated with reserve, he may well have hit the mark this time. For instance, the year 453 accords well with the fact that Sparta a little later (451) reached an agreement with Argos that was to last thirty years.

Cimon's participation in the Athenian naval expedition against Cyprus in 450, on the other hand, is definitely established. It was a considerable force, two hundred ships, of which sixty were diverted to Egypt to aid the rebel Amyrtaeus. The rest of the fleet set about laying siege to the city of Citium, but before a decisive victory could be achieved Cimon was carried off by an illness (450), and thus did not live to see the victory, by sea and by land, at Cyprian Salamis. The Athenians were not successful in incorporating Cyprus into the maritime confederacy, if indeed this was ever their intention.

The Cyprus expedition and the death of Cimon bring to a close an epoch marked by a continuing and sharp antipathy between Athens and Persia. Both sides, however, had been denied decisive victories, and it is no wonder that a search now began for possible ways of bringing to a close the war that had already been going on for several decades. In fact the sources report that an agreement was concluded between the belligerents, probably in the Attic year 449–448. This was the Peace of Callias. (The term "Cimonian Peace," which appears in a few ancient sources and even in some modern historical works, obviously makes little sense.) For this peace treaty, of course, we have no contemporary sources. Thucydides does not mention it, and it is first noted in the *Panegyric* of Isocrates (117 ff.), which dates from the year 380 B.C., almost seventy years later. Still one is inclined to regard the treaty as historic fact, even though it is contradicted by the two historians, Theopompus and Callisthenes. These, however, cannot be considered authoritative on this point (Bengtson, *Staatsvertraege*, No. 152).

What provisions were contained in the treaty? Probably the most important were those stipulating that the Greek cities of Asia Minor were to be autonomous. The Persians, furthermore, pledged that their land forces would not come within three days' march (or a one-day, nonstop horseback ride) of the Ionian coast. For Persian warships, too, limits were fixed—in the south the Chelidonian Islands, in the north the Cyaneic Cliffs at the entrance to the Thracian Bosporus. The Athenians, on their part, pledged themselves not to attack the territory of the Great King. The Peace of Callias was probably not a formal treaty but rather a binding commitment that was agreed upon and sworn to by both sides, including Artaxerxes himself.

The Peace of Callias was above all a victory for the Persian Empire. Athens had given up the conduct of the war against the Persians after coming to the realization that it was no longer possible to achieve a decisive victory. The Peace of Callias, therefore, marks an important turning point in Pericles' foreign policy. Probably not all Athenians and their allies welcomed the agreement with joyful hearts. What it brought, in reality, was a state of suspended action that could at any time break out again into open war. And though for the time being the Greek cities of Asia Minor were free of Persian pressure, this unstable condition could be altered in a day, whenever the Great King felt like breaking the agreements.

The greatest danger, however, was an ideological one. Up to now the idea of a war of defense against the Persians had held the Delian League together. With the relaxation of this pressure after the Peace of Callias, Athens' claim to leadership of the League was, in effect, also nullified. Would not the Greek cities of Ionia and the islands of the Aegean henceforth believe that they no longer needed Athens' help? It is to Pericles' credit that he now began to propagate a new idea, the idea of peace, a peace that would embrace all Greeks in the same way as the old defensive alliance. This idea, however, could only be translated into reality if Athens' great opponent, Sparta, did not exclude itself from the plan.

Now it so happened that in this very same year (448) the conflicting interests of Athens and Sparta had once more brought them into collision. This sequence of events in central Greece is usually summed up in the term the "Second Sacred War." Delphi, the common shrine of Greece, had come under the dominance of the Phocians; Sparta sent a force there to expel them then withdrew. But the Athenians sent troops to Delphi and undid everything again. Soon afterward the Athenian hegemony in Boeotia collapsed. The anti-Athenian movement originated in the cities of Orchomenus and Chaeronea, where oligarchic governments had come to power in 447, or 446 at the latest. Although Tolmides—again at the head of a volunteer Athenian army—succeeded in retaking Chaeronea, he was defeated and killed on the return march on the battlefield of Coronea, and a large part of his army was taken into Boeotian captivity. A treaty was signed in which Athens was forced to agree to evacuate all of Boeotia in order to secure the release of the prisoners. Phocis and Locris, too, defected from Athens, so that at a stroke the entire Athenian hegemony in central Greece was lost.

In 446 there was a rebellion against Attic rule on the island of Euboea. Almost at the same time the Doric city of Megara revolted, and here the Athenian garrison was able to hold only the two important ports of Nisaea and Pagae. To all this was

97

added the invasion of Attica by a Peloponnesian League army under the Spartan King Pleistoanax. At that time the Long Walls connecting Athens with its harbor of Piraeus had been finished, but the flat country around lay open to the Peloponnesians. Nevertheless, to everyone's surprise, the Peloponnesians withdrew. The assertion that Pleistoanax and his adviser Cleandridas were bribed by Pericles naturally cannot be proven. Pericles at all events was freed from danger on this front and was able to devote his entire strength to the suppression of the Euboean revolt. Left to fend for themselves, the cities of the island offered no further resistance.

Two resolutions of the Athenian Assembly containing directives for the Euboean cities of Eretria and Chalcis are extant (Bengtson, *Staatsvertraege,* Nos. 154 and 155). The second document, relating to Chalcis, is especially revealing. Chalcis had already capitulated, and the terms imposed upon it had been particularly severe. Though they were now eased somewhat, they were still hard enough. The oath required of the Chalcidians contains a pledge not only never to defect from the Athenians, but also to apprise them of any defections by others. In addition there was the usual obligation to pay tribute and to render military service to the Athenians. Chalcis was left its judicial sovereignty, but with the restriction that the native courts were not permitted to pass sentences of death, banishment, or *atimia,** these Athens reserved to herself. When one adds that in Histiaea (Oreos) the Athenians settled a cleruchy (*klerouchia*)† on the land they had taken from the Euboean polis, it becomes clear that Pericles was taking very rigorous measures here in order to render any future defection by the important island impossible.

The subjugation of Euboea was the work of Pericles. But so too was the thirty-year peace treaty that was concluded in 446–445 between Sparta and Athens. The historical records, though more than usually full of gaps, nonetheless show that both parties made concessions. Athens formally renounced the two ports of Megara—Nisaea and Pagae—and Troezen and

* Loss of civic rights in various degrees.
† Colony of Athenians, as a resident garrison.

Achaea besides. These provisions are probably to be regarded as concessions to Corinth. Furthermore the Athenians recognized the autonomy of Aegina as an accommodation to Sparta, which could not abandon the Doric island. The neutral city-states were conceded the right to form alliances, and from this provision perhaps both parties to the treaty hoped to derive some benefit. Lastly, and most important, courts of arbitration were to be established from the settlement of disputes. This was a significant step forward, even though it is not known how often thereafter courts of arbitration were actually formed. Later the Megarans, in their conflict with Athens, cited the fact that the free flow of commerce had been stipulated by treaty, and presumably this too was contained in the document of the Thirty Years' Peace. All in all, it was a treaty that either eliminated or considerably eased existing differences. Corinth in particular obtained almost unrestricted dominion over the gulf that bears her name, even though Athens continued in possession of Naupactus.

With the signing of the Thirty Years' Peace ended an era marked by great deeds on the part of Athens. But these were not all successes, for the losses in manpower were considerable. We are in possession of an inscription containing the list of dead for the *phyle* of Erechtheis, which shows that in a single year (459 or 458) this single tribe lost no less than 187 men killed in action. If this figure is taken as an average, ten phylae would have suffered almost 1,900 dead in a single year. (Aristotle, *Ath. Pol.* 26, 1, sets the number of dead as high as 2,000 to 3,000, though the latter figure is probably exaggerated.)

Were these losses justified by the successes of Periclean policy? The question must be answered in the negative. Although in the fighting against Persia an equilibrium had been achieved, in the struggle against Sparta and her other opponents in Greece Athens had been defeated. Of all her conquests, only Aegina and Naupactus remained in Athenian hands. Pericles had had to renounce everything else, in particular the hegemony in central Greece. Must it then be said that Pericles' foreign policy had failed? This would probably be an exag-

99

geration; but in fact events had shown that the tasks Athens had set herself had far exceeded her strength.

It is probably correct to hold Pericles above all responsible for the sudden change in policy that resulted in the conclusion of the Peace of Callias with Persia and the Thirty Years' Peace with the Peloponnesian League.

In addition there was a new factor, the idea of a Panhellenic Peace Congress. Plutarch, in his *Life of Pericles* (Ch. 17), has given us its program. According to him Pericles fathered a decree in the Assembly which was addressed to all Greeks in Europe and Asia (i.e., Asia Minor). All these communities, large and small, were called upon to send deputies to Athens to take part in a Peace Congress, whose agenda would include the following items: restoration of shrines that had been destroyed by the Persians; sacrifices that the Greeks had owed to the gods when they were fighting the Persians; security of the seas; and, finally, general peace. Plutarch reports that the Athenians sent out twenty emissaries who traveled in four different groups throughout the Greek territories around the Aegean, disseminating the proposals of Pericles. The Lacedaemonians are said to have opposed the project. Of the existence of such a plan for a general congress there can be no doubt; the difficulty lies in determining its date, which must have been during the years immediately following the Peace of Callias, 449–448, or in the years immediately following the Thirty Years' Peace of 446–445. A more precise dating is not possible.

That Pericles' proposal was seriously meant cannot be doubted, and it seems that he may really have hoped to achieve an enduring peace in Hellas. Such a peace would have served his own plans very well. But was his move really "a diplomatic action to excite our admiration—from the standpoint of Panhellenic international law, a highly exemplary deed," as K. Dienelt calls it? This view is certainly exaggerated. What was lacking in Pericles' project was a wholesome dash of *Realpolitik*. It must have been assumed from the very start that Sparta would refuse to join in implementing such a plan, which would have placed Athens at the head of all Greece. To portray Pericles "as the discoverer of the European or— at that time—the Panhellenic League of Nations," as Gregor does, is a piece of wishful thinking on the part of modern historians that has little to do with reality.

And yet this proposed congress, as a forerunner of the many attempts to establish a universal peace in Hellas, is certainly not without interest. The fourth century B.C. especially saw a whole series of attempts, beginning soon after the Peloponnesian War and ending in the time of the Diadochi, to realize in Greece the idea of the *koine eirene,* a general peace.

These decisive events, above all the Peace of Callias, were to have their repercussions on the Delian League. The immediate effect of the Peace Treaty is revealed in the tribute lists, which for the year in which the Peace Treaty was concluded show that the tribute payments either were very small or were discontinued entirely. This is a clear sign that at least some of the allies already regarded the League as superfluous. It must be assumed that Pericles vigorously opposed this view; that his opinion won out is shown by the tribute lists for the following years. In general the period following the Peace of Callias was significant for the internal transformation of the Maritime League; but this is not to imply that the formation of an Athenian Empire (*arche*) was restricted to these years alone. Documentary sources, such as the Athenian decree concerning Miletus (Bengtson, *Staatsvertraege,* No. 151), prove the contrary.

Athenian preponderance developed above all in two areas, the courts and the mint. The jurisdiction of the various courts of the Athenian *Heliaia,* for instance, was extended to numerous cases originating in the sphere of the Maritime League. The aforementioned Athenian decree on Chalcis (see p. 98) is evidence for this practice. More and more frequently citizens of a confederate city were forced to await their turn in Athens for a hearing in the People's Courts. Moreover the effect of the Coinage Law, enacted about 450 B.C., was to force many cities of the maritime confederacy to discontinue their own coinages. Nor was this all. It is an established fact that the Athenians repeatedly tried to bring democratic movements to power in the dependent cities.

As an overall result of these moves, many cities of the League began to show a dangerous accumulation of hatred against Athens, whose rule was felt to be more and more oppressive, especially since there was no longer any need to fear the Persians. But there was also a positive side to the maritime domination by Athens. There was no longer any piracy to speak of; significantly, the power of the pirates revived only when the Athenian maritime empire had been destroyed.

In many cases Athens also concluded the usual commercial treaties (giving the citizens of one state legal protection in the courts of another) with member states of the League. In these treaties the parity of both parties was guaranteed—as, for example, in the Treaty with Lycian Phaselis about 450 B.C. (cf. Bengtson, *Staatsvertraege,* No. 149), or the Treaty with Chios. But particular dissatisfaction was aroused among the allies by the fact that Athens did not feel itself obligated to render an accounting of the use to which it put the tribute money. Plutarch (*Life of Pericles,* Ch. 12) says that the Athenians felt they did not owe their allies any reckoning of the moneys because they were their champions and protectors against the Persians, and had put the barbarians in their place. There is certainly an element of truth in this; on the other hand, this attitude on the part of Pericles was the reason why Thucydides, son of Melesias, made the cause of the confederate allies his own.

It would be incorrect, as we have seen, to assume that the transformation of the League into an instrument of Athenian power took place only after the Peace of Callias. The Athenian decree on Erythrae—whatever the date to be assigned to it— is sufficient to prove the contrary. The recasting of the League, on the other hand, undoubtedly led Athens to seek to stabilize its power not only through supervisory officers (*episkopoi*) and garrison commandants installed in the subject states, but also by other means. The establishment of cleruchies on the territory of confederate states was likewise a thorn in the flesh of many allies, although for Athens there was the advantage that they absorbed a number of Athenian citizens, especially those that could find no livelihood in Athens. There were Attic cleruchies in Naxos, Andros, the Thracian Chersonese (Gallipoli), Brea on the lower Strymon, and Oreos (Histiaea on the island of Euboea).

The system of Athenian cleruchies proved very valuable in time of war, above all, of course, in the Peloponnesian War. The cleruchies are also of special interest because they remained a part of the Athenian state, and their inhabitants, though living in foreign parts, were still Athenian citizens. For the native population, of course, the existence of an Attic cleruchy meant an infringement on their rights, especially a preemption of their landed property. But Athens was never petty in this respect, and it is clear from the tribute lists that in many cases she decreased the tribute rate for the member state concerned.

In order to gain a picture of the financial arrangements of the League and its member states one must study the tribute lists. The lists for the year 446–445, for instance, show that the following states paid the highest tribute: Thasos, Aegina (30 talents each), Paros (18 talents), Byzantium (15.7 talents), Mende and Abdera (15 talents each), Lampsacus (12 talents), and Lindos (10 talents). From this survey it is clear that the cities that were then regarded as the strongest financially were for the most part located on the Thracian coast and in the region of the Hellespont. Through this same area passed Athens' most important lines of communication, which connected Athens with the Black Sea and southern Russia, whence was imported the grain indispensable to the feeding of the Athenian population.

Originally the Delian League was a free federative union, with all its members having equal legal status. This relationship shifted slowly, though more and more distinctly, in Athens' favor. Nevertheless even today this union, led by Athens, deserves our fullest admiration. Founded as an alliance against the Persians, the League lasted for almost three quarters of a century, from 478–477 to 404, and during this period it proved to be an indispensable influence for order in Greek politics. The achievement of Athens is all the more admirable in that the military resources at its disposal were by no means unlimited. Each revolt threatened the very existence of the League and was put down only with the greatest effort. Especially troublesome was the lack of a trained bureaucracy, which could be found nowhere in Greece at that time. The Athenians had at their disposal only a few functionaries, and even these were used only in emergencies. The only permanent agents of government were the League Treasurers, the *Hellenotamiai.*

How we are to picture the division of the League into regions has not yet been fully clarified. There seem to have been five such regions: the Thracian, Hellespontine, Ionian, Carian, and Insular. Of these, the Carian Region was dissolved soon after 440 and the Carian cities added to the Ionian Region. This arrangement was not based upon any division into provinces, but rather upon the collection of the tribute, with the individual cities listed on the tribute register according to their region. Athens governed the confederacy, not through bureaucratic measures, but rather by the sheer weight of its prestige, which rested preeminently on the achievements of its great men, Cimon and Pericles.

The fifteen years of Athenian history between the conclusion of the Thirty Years' Peace (446–445) and the outbreak of the Peloponnesian War (431) bear the unmistakable mark of Pericles. It was this man who gave Athenian foreign policy a new direction. For the first time, with the founding of the Panhellenic colony of Thurii in southern Italy in 443, Athens entered into the politics of the Greek world of the West. It is possible that in so doing Pericles was in a sense retreating from Spartan pressure toward the West, in order to create there, on neutral ground, a new potential of expansion for Athens. After an Athenian attempt in 445 to reestablish the city of Sybaris (which had been destroyed in 511–510) had more or less failed, Pericles proposed the idea of a participation by all the Greek tribes in the founding of a Hellenic colony in southern Italy. This was the city of Thurii, the ground-plan of which had been drawn up by the architect-philosopher Hippodamus of Miletus. The citizens of the colony included the famous historian Herodotus of Halicarnassus and the great sophist Protagoras of Abdera. Empedocles of Acragas, the philosopher-poet, also lived in Thurii. Even when his opponents in Thurii gained the upper hand, Pericles held fast to his Panhellenic idea, and did not intervene when Thurii came into conflict with the more powerful Spartan colony of Taras. The question remains, however, whether he lacked the will or the power to do so. For Athens was by no means without supporters in the West. It was allied with Sicilian Segesta; it was also allied with Rhegium and Leontini, with whom it had, at some earlier date unknown to us, concluded treaties which were renewed on the eve of the Peloponnesian War (Bengtson, *Staatsvertraege,* Nos. 162 and 163). Especially important was the friendship with Rhegium, which enabled Athens to use the Straits of Messina undisturbed. For Athens' trade with central Italy, and especially with Etruria, this was of the greatest importance.

But this was by no means the sole connection between Athens and central Italy. The great archaeological discoveries in the Etruscan necropolis of Spina (near Comacchio in the Po Delta) show how important a role Athens played there. From Spina, overland trade reached the whole of northern Italy and perhaps even the region beyond the Alps that had formerly been within the exclusive trading area of Massilia. Athens was thus pushing forward into a sphere which until then had been reserved for Corinth, the great Greek trading city on the Isthmus—another reason for the bitter enmity between Athens and Corinth which contributed to the outbreak of the Peloponnesian War. But Corinth was not Athens' only competitor in the West. Syracuse, which since its founding had enjoyed close relations with Corinth, was hardly enthusiastic about the expansion of Attic trade, all the more so because Athens had allied itself with her rivals, the Chalcidian colonies of Rhegium and Leontini.

The rising on Samos in the winter of 441 was a severe crisis for the maritime confederacy. The great island, which had considerable territory in Asia Minor, was, like Chios and Lesbos, one of those members of the League that had been accorded the privilege of providing ships instead of money. In a dispute between Samos and Miletus over the question of the possession of Priene, Miletus was supported by the Athenians, who were of kindred stock. The conflict was intensified by domestic party struggles on Samos. After Pericles had brought a democratic party to power on the island, it was again overthrown by the oligarchs, an action in which the Persian satrap Pissuthnes made common cause with the latter. Although the Athenians had the upper hand at sea, they were in constant fear of intervention by the Persian Empire, for the Samians had not scrupled to appeal to the Persians for help. But their appeal was ignored, and their city was invested and besieged. In the fighting at sea against the Athenians the philosopher Melissus distinguished himself, while on the Athenian side the siege machines of Artemon of Clazomenae helped materially to bring about the fall of the city. After a long siege Samos was forced to capitulate—probably in the spring of 439 —and like all other rebellious allies, it was punished severely. It may have lost the island of Amorgos, and in addition had to pay the costs of the war (Bengtson, *Staatsvertraege,* No. 159). In its defection Samos had been joined by Byzantium, but the latter was soon subdued. The conflict between Samos and Athens showed that the weaker states would not hesitate to turn to the Persians, just as Sicilian cities did when they appealed to Carthage for help.

In 443 B.C. Thucydides, son of Melesias, the son-in-law of Cimon and Pericles' most important adversary, was ostracized and expelled from Athens. Even though he was no match for Pericles, as spokesman for the opposition he had wielded great influence, and in particular had repeatedly espoused the cause of the confederate allies. Thus he had, for instance, used the large and splendid edifices built in Athens by Pericles as an occasion for turning against the latter's financial policy. In another respect, too, the banishment of this man was an important milestone in Pericles' life; after it he became the real ruler of the Attic state, being elected strategos year after year from that time on.

In ancient times Pericles' character was regarded as having been formed largely by his education in the school of natural philosophy, the philosophy of Anaxagoras above all being credited with placing a permanent stamp upon his mind. In actual fact Pericles had a shrewd understanding of the difficult art of leadership, which he displayed brilliantly in his speeches. In power of conviction these surpassed the oratory of all of his contemporaries. To play a political role in Athens it was particularly important to be able to sway the Popular Assembly to one's will, employing the most subtle psychological insight in order to win the minds of the listeners to one's purposes. Many witnesses testify to the high level of forensic art exhibited by Pericles. Eupolis, the poet of the Old Comedy, who had himself heard Pericles, was inspired by it. No less enthusiastic was the great historian Thucydides.

More recent historians have charged that Pericles, like Bismarck, lacked the ability to surround himself with able collaborators. K. J. Beloch even goes so far as to say that the people around Pericles were, to a man, intellectual ciphers. Although there may be some truth in this charge, we are unable to say whether it is correct or not because the materials upon which to base a judgment are lacking, in particular the contemporary source materials. However, we may deduce from ancient tradition that Pericles did after all have a few able collaborators, of whom Phormio was the most important. This man distinguished himself particularly in military and naval affairs, achieving great successes in the first years of the Peloponnesian War. Another associate of Pericles' was the poet Sophocles—although the two men were hardly of one mind in their basic outlook. Sophocles was *Hellenotamias* in 443–442; two years later he was *strategos* in the Samian War, in which he was able to discharge without difficulty the task assigned him. Still another member of Pericles' circle was Callias, son of Calliades. It was he who, in 434, made the motion—naturally under the direction of Pericles—for the famous financial decree that bears his name. Beside this, Callias was the

107

author of the decree concerning the renewal of the alliances with Rhegium and Leontini.

The person of Pericles was the target of numerous attacks, especially by the comic poets. The invective was mostly very personal in nature, Pericles' onion-shaped head being a favorite subject. It would be a mistake to take too seriously the attacks of the comic poets—Cratinus, Hermippus, Telecleides, and others—especially since after Pericles' death (429) his positive qualities were highly praised in comedy. In the comedy of his own day Pericles and his contemporaries, including Socrates, are portrayed as the people of Athens saw them or at least as they wished to see them. The citizen was delighted to hear from the mouth of the player that the great Olympian, too, had human weaknesses. Significantly, Pericles' connection with Aspasia was a repeated target of ridicule. Nor could people in Athens understand it when this freedom of speech in comedy was temporarily restricted by decree, as actually happened once, in 440–439, under the archon Morychides.

Worse than the strictures of comedy, from whose barbs nobody in Athenian public life was exempt, was a series of prosecutions in court. Not only was Aspasia brought to trial, but also some of Pericles' personal friends, Anaxagoras the philosopher and Phidias the architect and sculptor, to whom Athens owed the creation of the statue of Athena Parthenos. The trial of Anaxagoras, who was accused of impiety, probably can be dated as early as around 450. That of Phidias must have taken place either in 438–437 or in 432–431 B.C. (the latter date is the more probable). At any rate Phidias in the first years of the Peloponnesian War was still active in Olympia, and cannot therefore have died in an Athenian prison as tradition reports; it is much more likely that he died shortly before 420 B.C., a date based on the findings of recent research, in which the rediscovery of Phidias' workshop in Olympia was of decisive importance. As for Aspasia, she too appears to have been accused of *asebeia* (impiety), but was acquitted, most probably shortly before the beginning of the Great War.

Are we to believe that these trials shooks the authority of Pericles? It would be an exaggeration to assume it. Moreover it is doubtful that the trial of Phidias was a political one. The artist had been accused of embezzling gold, entrusted to him for the decoration of the goddess' image, a charge the justice of which can today be neither proved nor disproved. There is also no proof to support the hypothesis that behind these charges stood Thucydides, the son of Melesias, who had returned to Athens after the end of his ten-year exile.

Much more destructive than the attacks of his enemies was Pericles' own financial policy. Although we do not know much about it, since the surviving historical sources say little about these matters, this much is clear: Pericles laid out enormous sums of money for the splendid edifices he built in Athens, and the money he used was not Athenian but was primarily tribute money from the member states of the League. Some scholars make the point that the sums involved were really those that were in the Treasury of Athena Polias, but this makes hardly any difference. Certainly Athens itself had many other revenues at its disposal, but there is no reason to assume that the charges brought against Pericles—that he squandered allied funds—were unfounded. Since the beginning of the Egyptian expedition (460) the burden on Athenian finances had been growing ever greater. The outfitting of the fleets for Egypt and Cyprus must have consumed immense sums of money. In addition, there was the Samian rebellion. No wonder the financial reserves were dwindling.

It must not be forgotten in this connection that the Greeks had no knowledge of modern finance. They would continue to draw upon the various financial depositaries for the running of the state until these were empty. Not until 434 did it occur to the Athenians to establish a permanent financial reserve. The author of this motion, as we have seen, was Callias, son of Calliades, the well-known partisan of Pericles. His proposal, which called for 3,000 talents to be conveyed into the Treasury of Athena as a reserve, can only be understood in the light of the fact that by 434 the political situation was growing ever darker. The reserve, in other words, was intended to make provision for the event of war, which by then already seemed quite possible. When the Peloponnesian War began, there were 6,000 talents in the Treasury of Athena; 9,700 talents was the highest level the reserves ever reached. But Pericles and his friends cannot be spared the reproach that they paid too little attention to what the times required in the field of finance, which after all was supposed to be the backbone of any healthy state. Thus Athens entered the war with insufficient financial preparations, a war in which not only the continuance of the Maritime League but Athens' own existence were at stake.

7

Cultural and Intellectual Life in the Age of Pericles

From ancient times the name of Pericles has been inseparably linked with the image of a Periclean Age and Periclean culture. Indeed the cultural brilliance of Athens in the fifth century is unthinkable without the influence of the great Attic statesman. Through his political measures he created the external prerequisites for Athens' cultural achievement. Not only this, but he also took an active part himself in cultural life. He was the personal friend of numerous artists and scholars, and thanks to his initiative Athens was adorned with buildings and works of art that are among the most beautiful creations of the human spirit.

Athens owed its leading role in Greece in great part to its hegemony of the Delian League. But Athens' rapid rise would not have been possible had not a significant shift in the economic center of gravity in Greece begun soon after the victories over the Persians. In the sixth century the city-states of Ionia, especially the city of Miletus, dominated the economic, trade, and intellectual life of Greece. But the flowering of Ionia was blighted by the unhappy outcome of the great revolt; Miletus was completely destroyed in 494, and only in the Hellenistic period was it to recover a certain importance. Athens, above all, and cities like Corinth and Aegina were to become the heirs of Ionia's splendor. While Aegina had been a serious competitor of Athens in the Saronic Gulf, it was of course humbled in its struggle with Athens, and its capitulation in 457 pretty much spelled the end of its golden age. Corinth, on the other hand, with its strong navy and with the help of its colonies, was able to dominate the sea routes westward to southern Italy and to Sicily. By the middle of the fifth century the greatest and most populous cities in the Greek world were Athens, Syracuse, Gela, Acragas, and Corinth and, among the islands, Thasos, Paros, and Corcyra.

Since detailed statistics are lacking, population figures can only be given approximately. The population of Athens in the Age of Pericles has been estimated at about 105,000 to 120,000, of whom only about 35,000 were citizens. The overall population of Attica is estimated to have been 210,000 to 235,000 (De Sanctis). Attica thus appears to have been much more populous than Boeotia, which, being a predominantly agrarian region, may have numbered 110,000 to 125,000 inhabitants. For Sparta, scholars have arrived at a figure of more than 200,000, of which, however, only 4,000 to 5,000 were full citizens. According to recent calculations this tiny elite dominated some 40,000 Perioeci (subject peoples) and no less than 150,000 Helots (serfs). Again, however, these figures can only be considered approximations.

Even in ancient times Greece was already dependent upon imports from abroad to feed its people. While Solon had already prohibited the export of Attic grain, he permitted and even encouraged the export of oil. Grain was brought by ship from the Pontus, from Sicily, and from Egypt. The latter, above all, was a very rich granary; in the second millennium B.C., for example, it was already shipping grain to the Hittites. Athenian import figures were very high. In the middle of the fourth century 800,000 *medimni* (1,200,000 bushels) of grain were unloaded at the Piraeus annually, imports that were all the more necessary because Greek agriculture continued to adhere to long outmoded methods. In Attica the crops that flourished were chiefly the grape vine and the olive tree, which were cultivated with meticulous care. Greek wine and oil had won widespread markets abroad as early as the sixth century, and were the most important items in the Greek export trade. Yet despite this flourishing trade a barter economy continued to prevail in part in many areas of the Greek world, especially in the outlying districts.

Alongside this there was, of course, a developed money economy, as evidenced by the numerous coinages of the Greek city-states. The Greek coins of the fifth century, however, are something more than just an important source of information on Greek trade. Many are stamped with splendid images, especially those of Syracuse. Silver for these coins was available in sufficient quantity. The Athenians had their mines on Mount Laurium, which were rented to individual entrepreneurs. They were worked mainly with the help of slaves, often under very primitive labor conditions. Besides these mines (whose yields were evidently growing smaller in the latter part of the fifth century), there were also the mines of Thracian Pangaeum, which later came under the dominion of the Macedonian kings.

In the course of time immense riches accumulated at the great Panhellenic shrines, especially at Delphi and Olympia, where not only rich votive offerings were received but also cash deposits that private persons or Greek cities had entrusted to the temples for safekeeping. Since, as we know, the possession of precious metal was forbidden in Sparta, the medium of exchange was the clumsy iron money. Nevertheless many Spartans, who had managed to obtain gold and silver, sent it to safety beyond the Spartan borders.

In addition the great sanctuaries often functioned as banks, frequently lending money—of course at the prevailing rates of interest. The Temple at Delos, for instance, charged ten percent interest. At the time this was a customary rate and was generally exceeded rather than the contrary. The increased circulation of money had the effect (as it always does) of driving prices slowly upward. A bushel of barley in the time of Solon, for instance, cost only a drachma; two hundred years later it cost twice as much. Over the same period, on the other hand, the price of a sheep increased ten- to twenty-fold. A person seeking an especially profitable investment would often place his money in a maritime loan, which drew

113

enormously high interest, partly because of the risks involved. Seafaring, by the way, was still largely restricted to coastal voyages. In order to travel from Greece to Sicily, one had to take a Corinthian ship, which would call at Corcyra and Taras on the way. There were few maritime maps, lighthouses, or beacons—a situation which would hardly be improved until the time of the Roman Empire.

Wages in the fifth century were very low. An oarsman received three obols a day and really had to work for them. Intellectual pursuits were generally no better paid than physical labor. Thus the overseer of the construction of the Erechtheum in Athens received only a drachma daily, the same as a stonecutter. Physicians and Sophists, on the other hand, were well paid, and many of these amassed considerable fortunes.

To the Greeks' credit it must be said that their daily life was very modest. Their private homes were wooden, mud-walled, or frame houses; there was no luxury of any kind. In dress, the long Ionian chiton of linen gradually went out of fashion and was replaced by the Peloponnesian chiton made of wool, linen clothing being reserved for women only. "Purple" (i.e., dark scarlet) chitons were the official dress of the Attic strategoi, as well as the uniform of the Spartan hoplites.

Meals were very simple, consisting principally of grain in the form of gruel or cakes, as well as greens and other vegetables. As side dishes there were olives, figs, cheese, and salt fish. Meat and game were to be had only on feast days. The per capita daily quota of barley meal was reckoned at one choenix (about 1½ pints dry measure) which cost ¼ obol. When one considers that a worker's total daily wage amounted to no more than about three obols, it can be seen that large families often had to manage with very slim rations.

One of the obligations the wealthy citizen was bound to perform was the support of special public services. These public works (*leitourgiai,* "liturgies") consisted mostly of the outfitting of warships (trierarchy) and the assembling of choruses for the performances of tragedies and comedies in Athens (*choregia*). The trierarchy in particular, a very costly affair, was enough to ruin even the wealthiest citizen. The equipping of a single warship during the Peloponnesian War, for instance, cost nearly a talent (about $1,200 in gold values; as much as fifteen times that in purchasing power). On occasion the cost of a trierarchy was borne by two citizens jointly. Nevertheless, the Greek tradition of public service worked on the whole in exemplary fashion. Many hundreds of citizens unquestionably gave to the state much more than they ever received from it. Even as late as the age of the Roman Empire the obligation to serve the general public was a marked characteristic of the Greek way of life.

The expenditures of the Attic state itself were not small. Large sums had to be raised to pay both citizens and officials. The prytanes were fed in the Prytaneum at the cost of the state; the 500 councillors received the *diaitai* (*per diem* allowances), as did the jurymen, though of course the jurors' pay was substantially covered by the court costs. The expenses of public worship and festivals were also large. Thus in the year 410, in the midst of the war, no less than six talents were spent on the Greater Panathenaea festival. If to this one adds the costs of building the public edifices (under Pericles no less than 2,000 talents were spent in construction on the Acropolis alone) and the enormous, annually recurring costs of war, it will be seen how great was the burden on Athenian finances.

Where did the money come from? There were no direct taxes, except a property tax, the *eisphora,* which was levied only in emergencies. Direct taxation could not be imposed on the Athenians, who would have considered it a sign of tyranny. Instead there were numerous indirect taxes, such as the port duty (*ellimenion*) levied on imported and exported goods, mostly at a rate of two to five percent *ad valorem,* though in the Piraeus it was only one percent. There was no occasion for smuggling, for there were no customs barriers, and even at the state boundaries no customs duties were levied. On the other hand, the ancient records occasionally mention transit tolls; for example, for passage through the Bosporus a *dekate,* or ten percent toll, was imposed. Fees also had to be paid for use of the marketplaces. But there was no trade tax on capital and earnings; only conjurors, fortune-tellers, and members of what were considered other more or less dishonorable occupations were subject to a tax.

Athens, on the other hand, realized considerable revenue through a tax on metics, citizens of foreign communities who had settled in the city and in the Piraeus, and who were obliged to pay a protection fee. In addition there were the revenues derived from the confiscation of the property of condemned persons. Inscriptions still exist today which list inventories of the contents of the house of Alcibiades, who was condemned and outlawed for profanation of the hermae. The Attic state, in other words, possessed numerous sources of revenue quite apart from the tributes; but even at that time it was difficult to obtain an overall picture of such sources of revenue, particularly since the Greeks were always rather backward in the art of establishing a state budget.

The Age of Pericles was distinguished by its architectural activity, and the influence of Athens in this regard led to vigorous competition throughout all of Greece. Sicily in particular was not far behind Athens in its architecture, owing to the initiative of the tyrants of Syracuse and Himera, which led, after the victory over Carthage in 480, to an outburst of major public construction on the island.

The erection of the Long Walls between the city of Athens and the harbor of Piraeus was an exclusively military undertaking. A plan for the walls had been formed immediately after the break with Sparta in 461, but its execution dragged on for some time. The walls were only completed after Athens and Sparta had, at Tanagra in 457, for the first time faced each other with hostile intent. About fifteen years later a third wall was added to the two walls, evidently to serve as a second line of defense. With this the city of Athens and its harbor, the Piraeus, had become a single great fortress, which from the land side was practically impregnable. In the event of a foreign invasion, according to Pericles' intention, the population of Attica was to be given protection in the space between the two long walls. In other words from the beginning Athens planned to conduct a purely defensive warfare on land, and a major factor in the scheme was the redevelopment of the Piraeus. The ground plan for this project was the work of the architect Hippodamus of Miletus, who later drew up the city plan for Thurii in Magna Graecia. In his plan for Piraeus, by the way, Hippodamus for the first time created a grid plan, with streets intersecting at right angles, a type of city plan that had not hitherto been known in Greece. Naturally the Long Walls and the installations in the Piraeus cost a lot of money, and this had to be raised in part through the tribute payments of the allies.

A rebuilding of the temples of Athens had already begun under Cimon, but the epoch of Pericles marks a radical new departure. The most famous of the Periclean temples is, of course, the Parthenon, or the Temple of Athena Parthenos, the building of which had begun immediately after the Peace of Callias. The architect was Ictinus, and in all it took fifteen years to complete the task. Built of shining Pentelic marble, the Parthenon was designed with exquisite proportions, which were never again to be achieved in later times. With its Doric columns and gold-and-ivory statue of the maiden Athena, the work of Phidias, the temple became an emblem of Athens, the city which under Pericles had become the center of the Greek world. As a processional entrance and gate to the Acropolis, the monumental Propylaea was erected. (It was finished in haste at the beginning of the Peloponnesian War, and not quite according to the original plan.) At the same time the so-called Theseum was built at the foot of the Acropolis, which actually was a temple of the god Hephaestus. The Parthenon survives in our own day only as a shattered wreck. (It was struck in 1687 by the cannon-shot of a German gunner in the service of the Venetians, when the Turks were using the temple as a powder magazine.) The "Theseum," on the other hand, is the only one of all the sanctuaries of ancient Athens that has remained essentially undamaged. With the Odeon, situated on the citadel's eastern slope, and many

117

other edifices no longer in existence today, Athens had acquired a completely new appearance. It was admired throughout the world and was visited by many foreigners. In the rest of Attica, too, there was much activity. In Eleusis, famed for its mystery rites, Ictinus built a new temple; on Cape Sunium rose the Temple of Poseidon. Looking far out over the sea, it was a welcome landmark for ships returning home.

Without doubt the greatest of the Greek sculptors was Phidias, who worked not only in Athens but also in Olympia, where the great Temple of Zeus was under construction between 470 and 455. Phidias' contribution was the statue of Zeus, though he probably did not make it until the decade after 430. The statue made a profound impression on the people of that age. As late as A.D. 100 Dio Chrysostom wrote of it: "When one entered the Temple of Olympia, one believed that one was looking at God the Father himself, as Homer has described him: calm, mild and sublimely grand. The beholder felt himself transported to a higher sphere, and at that sight might forget all the cares and troubles of life." Today coins of Elis still give us some idea, however sketchy, of the magnificence of this statue.

For painting, too, a new age began in the fifth century. Before this time painting had been cultivated primarily in Ionia. Thus Mandrocles of Samos, who built the bridge over the Bosporus for King Darius, immortalized his work in a painting which he dedicated in the Temple of Hera in his native city, and which showed the passage of the Persian army over his bridge. But the great master of the fifth century was Polygnotus of Thasos, who worked not only in Athens but also in Boeotia and Delphi. Pliny said of him that he was the first to free the human countenance from its old rigidity (Pliny, *Natural History,* XXXV, 58), by which he probably meant that Polygnotus had moved beyond what we now call the archaic style. In addition Polygnotus boldly designed gigantic murals, said to have been about a hundred square yards in area. For instance, he decorated the Painted Portico (Stoa Poikilé) in Athens with paintings of scenes from the battle of Marathon, and in Delphi painted the fall of Troy and Odysseus' journey to Hades. The Athenians, in recognition of his achievements, conferred citizenship on him, which was a very rare distinction in those times. Polygnotus is also said to have been the first painter to employ some measure of perspective in his work.

The plastic arts were richly cultivated in Greece. Temples were adorned with sculptured figures which were often arranged in mythological scenes. On the east pediment of the Parthenon, for instance, the birth of Athena is portrayed, and on the west pediment the famous contest betwen Poseidon and Athena, while the metopes on the north and south fronts show the Greeks in battle with the Trojans, as well as the struggle between men and centaurs. Around the cella, the temple's Holy of Holies, runs a frieze which portrays the procession of the Athenians at the Great Panathenaic festival, with several hundred figures and more than two hundred horses—all this, too, a masterwork of Phidias.

Among bronze-founders, Polycleitus of Argos holds a preeminent position. The statues cast by him are distinguished by the beauty of the proportions of the human body, to a degree never previously achieved and clearly visible even in our late copies of his works. (The originals, without exception, have been lost.) A famous example is his *doryphoros,* or spear-bearer. Another much-praised statue is the Nike of Paeonius (of Mende on the peninsula of Chalcidice), representing the goddess of victory hovering over the earth. This work of art, a votive offering in Olympia from the Messenians of Naupactus, is the first known attempt in the plastic arts of antiquity to capture the movement of flying. Equally esteemed was the famous discus-thrower of Myron (of Eleutherae in Attica); here the artist has perfectly succeeded in capturing not only the idea of athletic competition, but even that fraction of a second in which the young athlete stands motionless before throwing the discus.

It was inevitable that the great art of the bronze-founders and sculptors should have had its effect upon vase painting, although by the middle of the fifth century the latter art had already passed its peak; nevertheless many splendid works were then still being created. The famous cup by Brygus (now in the Martin von Wagner Museum in Wuerzburg) is, to be sure, of earlier date (between 490 and 480), but here a very realistic representation has been ennobled in the most charming way by the brush of the artist. Pictured on many other vases are scenes from the world of the Greek heroic epics. Gradually, however, themes from the drama also begin to appear, which shows how interested the people of Attica were in the tragic drama and the myths it portrayed. A newer art was the creation of so-called *lekythoi,* slender ointment vessels with long necks, fired in white clay. Placed in the grave with the deceased, they have been found in great quantities, almost all of them in Attica.

In Pericles' speech in honor of the fallen, Thucydides has him say: "For the relaxation of the spirit from labor we have made many provisions, in part the festival games and sacrifices which we celebrate the whole year through, in part tasteful private establishments, in which we can delight ourselves day by day and thus dispel melancholy." Indeed the people of ancient Greece thoroughly enjoyed their festivals, which were dedicated to the gods and formed an inseparable part of political life. Politics and worship belonged together. Many of these festivals were the occasion for gymnastic competitions; at others there were contests in song and music; and at still others, dramatic contests, in both tragedy and comedy. In Athens the year began in midsummer with the month called Hekatombaeon, at the end of which the Panathenaea (the great national festival of Athens) was celebrated. The Panathenaea took place annually, but with particular pomp every four years. Its high point was always the procession from the Kerameikos, or potter's quarter, through Athens to the Acropolis, where the goddess Athena was presented with a new garment, which was placed upon her statue in the temple. In March occurred the Greater Dionysia. At this festival tragedies and comedies were performed in honor of the god, Dionysus being the deity of the dithyramb and of the theater. Attending the performances were numerous guests from the entire

Greek world, in particular many delegations from the confederate states, who on this occasion delivered their tributes in Athens. Performances also took place at the Lenaea, which fell in the month Gamelion (about January); this festival was celebrated by the Attic people among themselves.

Almost every Greek city had a theater, the theater in Athens being situated on the south slope of the Acropolis. (The Theater of Dionysus in Athens, in its present form, dates from the time of the Roman Empire.) In a few Attic demes, too, theaters were built. The outstanding acoustics achieved in Greek theaters can still be admired today in Epidaurus.

There are probably no nobler testimonials to the intellectual life of Athens in the fifth century than Attic tragedy and comedy. Here was an unimaginable prodigality of intellectual talent. Year after year, for the Greater Dionysia, three poets each composed a trilogy of dramas and, in addition, a satyr play. Moreover, five comedies were played at this festival (during the Peloponnesian War only three). And added to all of these were the performances at the Lenaean festivals. But of this intellectual richness only fragments have come down to us. Aeschylus, eldest of the triad of classical Attic tragedians, wrote ninety tragedies in all, but only seven have survived. The performance of the plays was always part of a dramatic contest (*agon*), and ten judges were selected by the people to decide which poet, which choregus and which protagonist (leading actor) should be awarded the prize.

The people of Athens must be given credit for being a most enthusiastic theater public. For three full days thousands of people, usually for seven to eight hours a day, would watch the sequence of dramas, each day a trilogy and a satyr play. At the Greater Dionysiac festivals no less than seventeen different pieces were performed (if we add the five comedies for which a separate day was reserved), among them probably a good many for whose loss we need not mourn. Each performance was preceded by detailed preparations, in particular the drilling of the choruses and the so-called preliminary

121

competition (*proagon*), a kind of dress rehearsal which was held, not in the Theater of Dionysus, but in the Odeon before the Attic authorities.

When we consider that not even wars—not even the great Peloponnesian War—were allowed to interfere to any extent with the performances, and that the Athenian state continued even in wartime to stage tragedies and comedies that were hardly in agreement with official policy, we cannot but be overcome with admiration for the Athenian *demos,* which gave its finest minds a free public forum unequaled in the history of the world.

The great triad of Attic tragedians—Aeschylus, Sophocles, and Euripides—dominated the Athenian stage for approximately seventy years, or two full generations. The *Persians* of Aeschylus was produced in 472, at a time when most of the veterans of Salamis were still living. Themistocles, too, was certainly present at the performance. The zenith of Attic tragedy was reached in the Pentecontaetia, the fifty years between the Persian and the Peloponnesian wars, with Aeschylus holding the dominant position until his death in 456. With the name of Aeschylus is linked a significant improvement in dramatic technique. To the first player, the protagonist, he added a second actor, giving the performance of tragedy far more vitality. Incidentally, we note with amazement that the epitaph of Aeschylus says nothing about his magnificent works but only mentions his participation in the battle of Marathon, a particularly striking example of the Greek sense of public service.

In Aeschylus' *Persians* he gave Themistocles, the great Athenian statesman, a monument more durable than iron. Although his name is never mentioned in the tragedy, Themistocles is obviously the off-stage adversary of the Persian King Xerxes. In the *Eumenides,* the third play of the trilogy *Oresteia,* we find not only allusions to the reduction of the power of the Areopagus,* but also a reference to the city of Sigeum on the Hellespont. In the time of Peisistratus, Sigeum had belonged

* The play was produced in 458, only three years after the reforms of Ephialtes.

to Athens; at the time of the tragedy, around the middle of the fifth century, it appears to have joined the maritime confederacy.

Sophocles (496–406), from the deme of Colonus, was Aeschylus' rival and some twenty years his junior. In 468, while still comparatively young, he had won his first victory over the older poet in the Greater Dionysia. The judge was Cimon. For almost sixty years thereafter the plays of Sophocles dominated the Athenian stage. The chronicle shows eighty victories in the Dionysia and six more in the Lenaea. Many of Aeschylus' characters are exalted to a superhuman level; Sophocles portrayed people as they really were in his time, although his characters still lack individuality. For all that they are capable of arousing an intense emotional response. The contrast between human and divine justice, as embodied in the figures of Creon and Antigone, was never more impressively depicted in antiquity than by Sophocles. The choral lyric, "There are many amazing things, [but] none more amazing than man," may be taken as a summing-up of the inner meaning of Sophocles' work. Sophocles, an innovator no less than Aeschylus, added a third player to the two already employed in Greek drama.

The youngest of the trio was Euripides (born about 480, died 407–406). In comparing him to Sophocles, the difference between the generations is crucial. The older man was still greatly influenced by the experience of the Persian Wars. Euripides must be thought of in connection with the new teaching of the Sophists. The very fact that he held aloof from politics all his life makes him a new kind of Athenian. Political allusions are not wholly lacking in his dramas, but they have no great significance in his work or in his thought. If historical tradition is correct, he wrote no less than twenty-two tetralogies, i.e., twenty-two dramatic trilogies and an equal number of satyr plays. He brought his first play to the stage in the year 455. He was not exactly pampered by the public; in his long life he gained only four victories.

Euripides' surpassing skill is shown in his *Alcestis,* which was performed in 438 and is his earliest surviving drama.

Here a purely human, nontheological problem is transferred to the stage with great subtlety. Alcestis is the wife of King Admetus, who is fated to die; since all his friends refuse to do so, she decides herself to make the journey to Hades in place of her beloved husband. Her sacrifice is not in vain, for Heracles rescues her from death and returns her living to her husband the King. This masterful drama shows us the whole breadth of Euripides, and it is no wonder that his tragedies have had a worldwide influence. Yet in the life and work of this poet there are many riddles; the most puzzling of all is that presented by the *Bacchae,* his last drama, which he wrote in Macedonia in extreme old age, and which reflects his turning toward mysticism.

By the early part of the fourth century the tragedies of Euripides were already regarded as classics, and it is therefore not surprising to find that a great number of papyri containing works of Euripides have been found in Egypt. Goethe (in his diary, November 22, 1831) justly said of Euripides:

> What astonishes me is that the philological aristocrats do not grasp his superiority; with their usual refinement they rank him below his predecessors, on the authority of that clown Aristophanes. After all Euripides made an enormous impression on his age, from which it follows that he was eminently a man of his time; everything that matters depends on that. And has any nation since then produced a dramatist worthy even to hand him his slippers?

Euripides' effect on his times can be seen reflected in the strictures heaped on him by the comic poets, especially Aristophanes. Aristophanes of Cydathenae lived from about 445 to 388, and reached the zenith of his career in the latter part of the Peloponnesian War. He is the most important representative of the Old Comedy, eclipsing his predecessor Cratinus as the best of comic poets. Attic comedy was a part of public life; its verses reflected the hopes, fears, humor, and sheer bravado of the broad masses of the people. When Aristophanes presented his first play on the Athenian stage in 427 (it was the *Daitales,* or *Banqueters*), he was still part and parcel of a tradition that mixed crude peasant customs and sophisticated dramatic techniques. It was the task of comedy to entertain, to make the audience laugh; in this Cratinus as well as Aristophanes was repeatedly successful, and many of their characters have lived on in literature. The comic poets' favorite targets were the leading politicians, particularly Pericles and later Cleon; even if many of their attacks seem extremely crude to us, their verses are never lacking in the grace of real poetry.

The numbers of Atttic peasants, citizens, metics, and slaves appearing in the comedies give a colorful picture of the whole range of the Athenian population and their occupations; their work, their interests are portrayed with a wealth of detail which can scarcely be matched anywhere else in literature. To be sure, the characters are often simply caricatures. Who does not remember Aristophanes' ludicrous picture of Socrates, the seeker after truth, drawn in the *Clouds:* "I wander through the air and with my mind investigate the sky!" In the Old Comedy the personal and the political go hand-in-hand: the *Poleis* (*Cities*) and the *Demoi* (*Townships*) of Eupolis reveal the poet's political interest in their very titles (their subjects are the allied states of the Delian Confederacy, and the mainland communities of Attica). The last-named play was produced in 412, when Athens was already on the road to catastrophe after the failure of the Sicilian Expedition.

Years earlier, in the *Babylonians* (426), Aristophanes had leveled a sharp attack on Cleon. In *The Wasps* (422) he scourged the Athenians' unbridled passion for jury service. And in his *Peace,* performed at the Dionysiac festival of 421, he foreshadowed the Peace of Nicias. A very famous comedy is *Lysistrata* (411), in which the women on both sides put an end to the bitter war between Athens and Sparta (at least on the stage), by going on strike in a manner which has amused posterity. Jakob Burckhardt held that the production of this play could not have been more inopportune; for at the time, in the year 411, the Spartan enemy was at Decelea, in the heart of Attic territory, and was allied with Persia; obviously, then, the Spartans did not have the slightest reason to long

125

for peace, as the Spartan envoys did in the comedy. What impresses us today in *Lysistrata,* from the political standpoint, is that the poet was permitted to give expression to a mood that was undoubtedly felt by the Athenian people as a whole. Whether it was politically wise, at this time, to allow a pacifist drama to appear on the stage is another question entirely.

In the Greek world, in the time of Pericles, there began an intellectual movement which we call Sophism. The Sophists were men who offered themselves as teachers of wisdom, taking fees from those who studied under them. Today it is difficult for us to imagine how profound and far-reaching was the influence of these men and their doctrines. The Sophists brought about a basic transformation in the public and private life of the Greeks, and their teachings are reflected in almost all the literary works of the second half of the fifth century. Plato, in the fourth century, was a bitter opponent of Sophism, taking issue with it by setting up the ideal figure of Socrates in opposition to its teachings.

In a general way Sophism may be compared with the eighteenth-century concept of the Enlightenment, although we must constantly remember that the two terms are by no means identical. The most that can be said is that the two showed parallels in their effects on the world at large. Oddly enough, not a single Athenian is to be found among the more famous Sophists. All of them were born elsewhere; however, almost without exception, they lived for a time, sometimes for a considerable period, in Athens and disseminated their teachings from that city. Thus Protagoras (ca. 485–410), born in Abdera on the Thracian coast, was at home in the entire Greek world. In Athens he became the friend of Pericles, who set him to drafting the laws for the Panhellenic colony of Thurii. Since Protagoras also had enemies in Athens, he was threatened with an indictment for impiety (*asebeia*), and his books were publicly burned. Other major Sophists were Prodicus of Ceos, Hippias of Elis, and Gorgias of Leontini.

What was the essence of this movement and of the doctrine

126

that these men propagated? The Sophists offered to teach practical accomplishments and provide a general education, in which rhetoric occupied a central position. Knowledge of rhetoric was to make their pupils capable of taking part in public life, and in such a way as to excel all others. Rhetoric was also supposed to help form an intellectual elite. No question but that the Sophists were highly successful in their efforts; in particular, they contributed substantially to the spread of formal education in the Greek world. They were the founders of the liberal education, and at the same time may be called the first professors. Just as the Sophists announced their programs of instruction in advance, so professors do today, in course catalogues and on university bulletin boards. Of the work of the Sophists—apart from some fragments and a couple of speeches—practically nothing has survived. The degree to which they were masters of rhythmic prose is shown today in Gorgias' surviving set speech, the *Helen*.

The Sophists and their teaching made an unimaginably powerful impression. Until then the great athletic contests had been the ideal of Greek youth, and its most cherished achievement was to win a victory in the great Panhellenic Games. The adolescent male, the ephebe, had formerly spent the greater part of his time on the athletic ground, in the *gymnasion*. But after the Sophists appeared, the young men of Greece were to be found sitting at the feet of these teachers, and inevitably intellectual problems now appeared to the young to be the decisive ones. Of course in the past, too, the rough uneducated athlete had been an object of mockery. Preserved in Euripides, for instance, is a fragment from the work of Xenophanes of Colophon in which the Ionian thinker deals with the subject of athletes in no friendly fashion: "The polis has small joy of it if someone wins a victory on Pisa's shores [i.e., at Olympia]; for that does not fill the coffers of the state." To the Sophists these words spoke directly, for they thought of themselves as far above the competitive activity then engaged in by most Greeks. In offering their doctrine to mankind the Sophists were convinced that, through their instruction, they could make a decisive contribution to education. And so appeared the problem of education, which from that time on was central to Greek history.

From Protagoras comes the famous dictum *homo mensura:* "Man is the measure of all things: of those which are, that they are; of those which are not, that they are not." No matter how one interprets this famous sentence, to measure all things, to view all things, from the standpoint of man was an entirely new concept. The images of the gods, which had been bound up with the life of the state, the family, and the individual, began to lose their luster. Thus Protagoras declared: "Concerning the gods, I can say nothing—neither that they are nor that they are not, nor of what kind they are. For much limits our knowledge, the obscurity of the subject itself and the shortness of human life." Certainly this statement is still a long way from a denial that the gods exist; but mere agnosticism was no less dangerous than atheism, and the fact that people were more and more concerned with the question of the existence of the gods is attested by Euripides' treatment of the gods on the stage. We are therefore not surprised to see the appearance, toward the end of the fifth century, of an outright atheist in the person of Diagoras of Melos, known to history by the surname of the godless (*atheos*). Nor was he alone in his stand: Critias, Plato's uncle, declared religion to be an invention of shrewd men for the purpose of keeping the masses in check, and of forcing people to adopt an ethical conduct.

Among the Sophists there were men with a clear bent for academic research. Hippias of Elis was the first to draw up a list of the victors in the Olympic Games, a record that proved of value for Greek chronology. But the Sophists also busied themselves with the problems of language such as synonymy (Prodicus), ethnic nomenclature (Hippias), and of course basic philosophic questions. Are we therefore to consider them the founders of modern scholarship? This has been occasionally asserted in the past, but without much foundation. What is certain is that the Sophists transmitted knowledge, both formal and practical knowledge, and that they laid the foundations of the liberal education. Of special importance for political theory was the fact that the Sophists opposed to customary law (*nomos*) a universal natural law. Since, as we know, the right of the stronger usually prevails in nature, it is no wonder that even at that time there were many who preached that justice is the right of the stronger. However, really gross abuses of the Sophists' teachings did not appear until later decades (for instance, Alcibiades, or the Athenian expedition against Melos in 416); a philosopher like Hippias of Elis could point out that all men are by nature brothers, and Protagoras himself could speak of the need to consider the rights of others, since we do not live in a primeval state like wild animals, but in human society.

To understand the enormous influence of the Sophists we must realize that public education did not exist in Athens, nor in most of the other Greek states. If a man wanted to have his children educated, he sent them to a teacher in a private elementary school. In Athens this was done with no compulsion whatsoever on the part of the state, in direct contrast to the education of the Spartans. The Seven Sages, with their proverbial wisdom that could be memorized with ease, were familiar to every Greek from his youth. To these earliest impressions were added, as soon as a boy came of age, the performances in the theater, which of course exerted a profound influence. The dramas were played before audiences of 20,000 to 30,000, a number seldom reached again even in modern times.

It would be difficult to underestimate the effect of these performances. When, for example, Aristophanes, in the *Clouds,* discusses at great length how the weaker case can be made the stronger with the aid of rhetorical devices, he was treating a particular Sophistic problem that was familiar to every Athenian. Here, in the theater, its point was driven home with the full force of wit. It was, of course, an outrageous slip on the part of Aristophanes to have represented Socrates, of all people, as a typical Sophist. Socrates, after all, was anything *but* a Sophist; he merely made use of the Sophists' formal methods.

It is astonishing to find that Plato, one of the towering intellects of Greece, refused to believe that performances in the theater had any ethical effect. Quite the contrary, he went so far as to condemn the tragic drama as immoral. True, the conduct of the public in the theater was hardly exemplary. On occasion they shouted and howled and, in token of their displeasure, threw all sorts of things at the stage and at the actors.

The fifth century saw an imperishable achievement in still another field, when Hippocrates of Cos and his school laid the foundations for the science of medicine. Of Hippocrates himself (born about 460) very little was known even in ancient times. Descended from the noble line of the Asclepiads of Cos, he is said to have been born there on the twenty-seventh day of the month Agrianos under the eponym Habriadas. But since we know nothing about the calendar of Cos, neither the month nor the year of his birth can be stated with certainty. We possess a great sheaf of Hippocratic writings from ancient times, no less than fifty-two in number, comprising seventy-two books. They are written in the Ionian dialect—an interesting fact, since Doric was the dialect of the island of Cos. Even ancient writers, from Aristotle onward, strongly questioned the authenticity of many of these Hippocratic writings. The Greek physician Galen (second century A.D.) thought that only fourteen, or at the most fifteen, of them were genuine. Today criticism has reached the point where it seems hardly possible to prove the genuineness of even a single Hippocratic document. In recent scholarship, however, the point has quite rightly been made that an important, and perhaps decisive, criterion for the genuineness of the individual writings is the presence of the theme of illness as a function of the whole man. Also considered "Hippocratic" is the doctrine of the four humors—the so-called humoral pathology—and in general all attempts to see man in close connection with nature. This was finely and cogently expressed in a book on the effects of the environment on man, called, in Greek, *On Airs, Waters, and Places,* which probably belongs to the last decades of the fifth century. It certainly had its origin in the school of Hip-

130

pocrates. The spirit of these Hippocratic doctors is best expressed in the famous Hippocratic Oath, which runs:

> I swear by Apollo the physician, by Æscalapius, Hygeia, and Panacea, and I take to witness all the gods, all the goddesses, to keep according to my ability and my judgment the following Oath:
>
> To consider dear to me as my parents him who taught me this art; to live in common with him and if necessary to share my goods with him; to look upon his children as my own brothers, to teach them this art if they so desire without fee or written promise; to impart to my sons and the sons of the master who taught me and the disciples who have enrolled themselves and have agreed to the rules of the profession, but to these alone, the precepts and the instruction. I will prescribe regimen for the good of my patients according to my ability and my judgment and never do harm to anyone. To please no one will I prescribe a deadly drug, nor give advice which may cause his death. Nor will I give a woman a pessary to procure abortion. But I will preserve the purity of my life and my art. I will not cut for stone, even for patients in whom the disease is manifest; I will leave this operation to be performed by practitioners (specialists in this art). In every house where I come I will enter only for the good of my patients, keeping myself far from all intentional ill-doing and all seduction, and especially from the pleasures of love with women or with men, be they free or slaves. All that may come to my knowledge in the exercise of my profession or outside of my profession or in daily commerce with men, which ought not to be spread abroad, I will keep secret and will never reveal. If I keep this oath faithfully, may I enjoy my life and practice my art, respected by all men and in all times; but if I swerve from it or violate it, may the reverse be my lot.

Two of the greatest of the thinkers of the Periclean circle were Hippodamus of Miletus and Anaxagoras of Clazomenae. Hippodamus was the first to attempt an abstract approach to an understanding of the Greek polis. The same schematic thinking that he employed as city planner of the Piraeus and Thurii, he brought to bear on the field of political thought,

131

and thereby became the father of political utopias. His most famous successor was Plato in his *Republic* and his *Laws;* from Plato the line of descent passes through Augustine to the Middle Ages and, in early modern times, to the English Chancellor Thomas More's *Utopia*. Hippodamus divided the inhabitants of the polis into three classes—soldiers, farmers, and artisans—and drew a distinction between sacred, public, and private property. In his speculations the triad obviously played an important role.

In the field of the natural sciences, Anaxagoras of Clazomenae (ca. 500–428), approximately contemporary with Pericles, put forward revolutionary physical theories. He is said to have given away his large fortune in order to be able to devote himself entirely to research. He was a firm believer in the indestructibility of matter, and was the first to make a distinction between force and substance, spirit and matter. In doing so, he also replaced the concept of becoming and passing away with the concept of motion, to which the world-soul (*nous*) had given the first impulse. Anaxagoras also declared that the sun was a fiery metal ball, larger than the Peloponnese, and that the moon was another earth inhabited by humans. This doctrine, far in advance of its times, was of course in complete contradiction to the convictions of the many. No wonder, then, that its author was persecuted for impiety.

The diversity of Greek life can be seen in the methods used by various Greek states for computing time. Each individual polis had its own calendar, which was used to regulate both public and private life. A significant step forward in this field was made at Athens in the time of Pericles, when a man named Meton calculated the length of the year at $365\frac{5}{19}$ days. On this basis he drew up a nineteen-year calendar-cycle which he then had set up on the Pnyx, probably in the year 432 B.C. What is surprising is that the Athenians made no use of this discovery in their daily life. Such an exact calculation simply does not seem to have been needed. And so this scientific triumph, remarkable for its time (Meton's year was only a half hour too long), remained an abstract achievement without practical effect. We may note, by the way, that there is evidence that the same nineteen-year cycle was also known in Babylonia after 381 B.C. Whether the two are connected has thus far not been determined.

The importance of science must be measured, at least in part, by the ability not only to acquire new knowledge but also to disseminate it in the wider world. Only when it is freely communicated can science contribute to the welfare of the human race. The Age of Pericles, especially the years following the Peace of Callias (449–448), was an epoch in which the world once again lay open to the Greeks. Even the Persian Empire, which had been isolated from the outside world, was again accessible to Greek merchants. How great were the possibilities that existed for a Greek is shown by the travels of Herodotus, whom we honor as the creator of the first historical work really deserving of the name.

Born in Halicarnassus, Herodotus not only gained a detailed knowledge of the coast of Asia Minor from the Troad to Lycia, but also investigated almost every place of any importance at all in Greece itself. Thus he visited Salamis, Plataea, Thermopylae, Cape Artemisium, and even the Vale of Tempe in Thessaly. Other journeys took him almost to the limits of the then known world; he was probably in southern Russia (i.e., Scythia), at Tyras (Akerman), and at Olbia, at the mouth of the Bug and the Dnieper. On the latter river he traveled for forty days upstream. Especially famous is his visit to Egypt, though it lasted only three or at the most four months. However, he went up the Nile as far as the island of Elephantine. He even traveled in Babylonia. It is doubtful, on the other hand, that he visited Susa. He also knew the Greek world of the West, taking part in the founding of Thurii, and from there it is certain that he set foot on Sicilian soil.

The great physician Hippocrates, it must be assumed, also traveled extensively. He visited not only Scythia but also remote Colchis on the Black Sea. He may even have traveled to Cyrene in North Africa—that is, if his remarks about the Libyans are the result of his own observation.

Journeys between Sicily and the Greek mother country were quite common. Many embassies traveled back and forth; also many poets and Sophists (the famous Gorgias of Leontini was an example) crossed the Ionian Sea several times in both directions. Naturally, as a rule one traveled by sea only in the sailing season, i.e., in summer when the winds were predictable and relatively mild.

Travel was facilitated for the Greeks by the fact that they used a language whose different dialects—especially the most important, the Ionic and the related Attic—had many features in common. For those who spoke these dialects it was not easy to understand a Lacedaemonian, as is shown by the documents in the Laconian dialect that are to be found in the *History* of Thucydides. However the rise of Ionic as the language of literature, philosophy, and medicine—and somewhat later of Attic, especially in the area of the maritime confederacy—had a unifying and, in the final analysis, a salutary effect. It was Attic that finally became, in the form of the *koiné* or "common" dialect, the universal language of Greeks, Macedonians, and educated men of many other nations in the centuries after Alexander the Great.

The possibility of bridging great distances by water and by land undoubtedly contributed heavily to the growth of a Greek feeling of community. Greeks began to feel themselves something special *vis-a-vis* the alien world of the "barbarians," the nations to the east and to the west, and the Greek national idea found its most powerful expression in the Panhellenic Games in Olympia. Here, every four years, all Greece met to witness the athletic competitions. On the lists of victors appear not only the names of Greeks from the mother country but also, over and over again, those from many different colonies: from Cyrene, for example, or the Sicilian cities of Messana (today Messina) and Camarina, and from Locri Epizephyrii and other localities in southern Italy. Herodotus is said to have recited his *History* in Olympia, while other great writers, Pindar and Bacchylides, for example, glorified the victors of the Olympian Games in their poems. Euripides, too, composed an *epinikion* (victory poem)—of which a few lines have been preserved—in honor of Alcibiades' victory in the chariot races in 416.

A victory at Olympia was regarded as the crowning point of a man's entire life. Here we must realize what a central role the idea of the *agon*, the contest, played in the life of the Greeks who, from their youth onward, took pleasure in pitting themselves in competition against their contemporaries. The education of the young was moreover to a substantial degree oriented toward gymnastics. The *gymnasion* was primarily a place for physical competition; academic instruction took second place. There was probably a *gymnasion* in most Greek cities, and it usually owed its existence to private endowment. In the *gymnasion* the young Greeks carried out a variety of physical exercises; their elders, too, met here to watch the youths at their games and to discuss the issues of the day. Thus Socrates as a rule passed his time in the public square and in the *gymnasion*, drawing all those present into endless discussions. Besides gymnastics there was also training in music, both vocal and instrumental, and finally literary instruction, which will be discussed further on.

The *gymnasion* was preceded by the elementary school, which was probably attended, as a rule, until the beginning of adolescence. There was no compulsory education. Elementary schools, like *gymnasia*, probably existed in all Greek cities. If they are seldom mentioned in the ancient sources, this may be because their existence was taken as a matter of course. Only in special cases are they mentioned at all: thus we learn that in Chios in 494 B.C. the roof of a school collapsed, and almost all the children lost their lives. In addition the Duris Vase, which probably dates from the Age of Pericles, depicts some of the activity of the schools. It shows instruction in music (flute and cithara) and in writing and reading. The teacher holds in his hand a papyrus roll, on which a verse of Homer is written (not quite correctly).

The elementary school was probably attended only by boys; not until the Hellenistic Age was there any concern with the education of girls. The teacher's fee was paid by the parents. When the Athenians evacuated their city before the onslaught of the Persians and moved their women and children to safety in friendly Troezen, the people of the latter city decided that the refugees would be provided for, and the teachers of their children paid, at the city's expense. In other words, in Troezen too there were only private and no public schools. However, most Greeks of the educated classes were probably able to read and write, though here, as always, the exceptions prove the rule. That there were illiterates is shown by a well-known anecdote. During an ostracism a worthy Athenian citizen, encountering Aristides without knowing him, asked him to write the name of Aristides on his *ostrakon*. Asked what he had against him, the citizen replied: "Oh, it annoys me to hear everybody calling him 'the Just.'"

What was read in the children's schools? Homer, and then —more Homer. The works of this great poet held a dominant position in the schools, and maintained it throughout the whole of ancient history; the many Homeric papyri from the Egyptian Desert are the best testimonials to this. Besides Homer, preference was given to Hesiod and, among the lyric poets, to Solon in particular. In short, the schools emphasized didactic reading matter, and there is no doubt that for the Greek boy the sentences became a part of his very bones. The instruction actually began with reading. The original meaning of the Greek word for "read" (*anagignoskein*) is "to recognize again." Now it must be understood that the process of reading in ancient times was by no means so simple as it is in our own day. The words were written in capital letters alone, and without any gaps between them. The reader himself was forced to break down the uninterrupted flow of letters into syllables, words, and sentences. In addition, it was the practice in ancient times to read aloud; only when we realize this do many allusions in the ancient authors become intelligible. The art of printing had not yet been invented; books were written by hand, and a book could be distributed only by making copies of it; this was a tedious business, very time-consuming and very expensive. There were probably few people, for instance, who possessed the whole of Homer on papyrus. In compensation for this, however, the faculty of memory—not only that of students but of people in general—was much better developed than it is in our day, when hardly anything is learned by heart any more, even in the schools. In ancient Greece there were always men who could recite the whole of Homer by heart.

The method of learning to read in ancient Greece was the direct opposite of ours. Whereas today we try to teach children to grasp not only the whole word but the whole sentence, the Greeks began with learning the names of the individual letters. From the letters they moved to the syllables, at first syllables with only two letters, then with three or more. Then short words with a few letters were formed (often obscure and seldom-used words): *aix, bous, gryps, drys* (goat, ox, griffon, oak). Finally the pupil set about writing whole sentences. It is clear that with such a method only the slowest progress could be made. As a rule the boys required years of training before they could read and write to any extent.

The elementary school was followed by training in the *gymnasion,* which, with its physical exercises, was actually a pre-school for military service. The exercises were held in the arena of the school (*palaestra*), and the boys performed them entirely naked (*gymnos,* hence the word *gymnasion*). The most important items for gymnastics were oil and sand. The oil was rubbed over the body and the sand strewn over the skin before the exercises. After the contest, the sand, which had become mixed with oil and sweat, was sloughed off the body with a scraper. The gymnastic exercises usually took place to the music of the "double flute" (actually an oboe).

In Athens the exercises of the pentathlon were practiced by preference: wrestling, running, broad jump, discus throwing, and javelin throwing. In wrestling the pairs were chosen by lot. If there was an uneven number of contestants, the extra man was paired with one of the victors of the previous contests. In the footraces there were various distances; the shortest was a *stadion* (about 200 yards in length); others were twice or four times as long. Besides these there was the long-distance race—a distance of up to twenty-four *stadia*. The races were not run on a circular track, but forward and back again over a straight distance of exactly one *stadion*. At the end of the stretch stood columns which the runners had to round, the number of times depending on the length of the race. It can easily be imagined that this kind of running required a special technique, especially at the turning point (*terma*).

The Greeks' technique in the broad jump, too, was quite different from ours. In each hand they held a jumping weight in the form of a dumbbell weighing up to eleven pounds. Apparently the Greeks believed that these weights strengthened the spring and made balancing easier, a view that has long since been proved erroneous. Ancient sources speak of broad jumps of up to fifty-two feet (Phayllus of Croton), but this is an obvious exaggeration.

The discus throw was made from a standing-still position. The turning motion, which alone can give the throw the proper swing, had not yet been discovered. In the javelin throw, a distinction was made between precision-throwing and distance-throwing. At the balance point of the spear, there was a leather loop for the thrower's index finger (or the index and middle fingers), probably to give more force to his cast.

In addition to the sports of the pentathlon there were boxing and all-in wrestling (*pankration*). (The latter had the reputation of being especially fierce and rough, which it fully deserved.) For boxing, the fists were wound round with leather straps, which often led to severe injuries. Much worse were the dangers of the *pankration,* for this was a mixture of boxing and wrestling, in which every kind of blow was allowed. This form of fighting was forbidden in Sparta, which speaks well for the Spartans' good taste.

These exercises, to which the young Greeks devoted themselves so passionately, helped create and maintain a genuine competitive spirit in Hellas. But excesses were inevitable, and the Sophists raised their voices against the overvaluation of physical exercise—for the most part no doubt in vain. The agonistic inscriptions reveal a wealth of material on social history, only a small part of which has thus far been exploited.

Many of the athletes also played a role in politics, for example, Phayllus of Croton, the only leader from the Western

138

Greek world to help in the defense of the Greek mother country against the Persians. On the Acropolis of Athens can be seen the votive dedication of a man named Callias (the name occurs frequently in the Athens of that day), who was a pancratiast and a political adversary of Pericles. He had won victories at all the great Greek festivals; he was what was called in later times a *periodonikes,* the title given to those who had won victories at all four of the great Greek national games. Politically this Callias seems to have been a partisan of Thucydides, son of Melesias. About the middle of the fifth century he was ostracized and was forced to leave Athens.

Some athletes were actually elevated to the rank of heroes, i.e., of demigods, after death. (For the ancients, we must remember, the distance between gods and men was much smaller than it would be from our point of view.) For instance, there is a dedicatory inscription from Olympia, dated around 470 B.C., which concerns a famous boxer from Locri Epizephyrii, one Euthymus, for whom a hero-cult was instituted at Temesa in Lucania. The reason for this cult is very revealing, as we read in Erwin Rohde (*Psyche,* 1, 9 and 10 [1925), pp. 192–193):

> What such hero-tales must have been like (many of them were probably once current but have now been lost) can be learned from a single example that has been preserved for us by chance. Once upon a time, the tales runs, the inhabitants of Temesa in Lucania were being terrorized by a hero who strangled any of them he could seize. In their extremity, the people of Temesa, who were already thinking of emigrating from Italy, turned to the Delphic oracle, which told them that the hero-spectre was the ghost of a foreigner who had once been slain by the inhabitants of the country for raping a virgin, and that therefore they must dedicate a sacred precinct to him, build a temple, and sacrifice to him every year the fairest of Temesa's maidens. When this had been done the hero left Temesa in peace—except for the horrible sacrifice that was made to him each year. Then in the year of the 77th Olympiad a famous boxer of Locri, returning to Italy from Olympia crowned with victor's laurels, heard of the impending sacrifice at Temesa and forced his way into the

139

temple. There he found the doomed virgin waiting for the hero. Seized with compassion, he fell in love with her, and when the hero-spectre approached, the victor of so many past contests grappled with him and finally drove him into the sea, thus freeing Temesa from its monster. The story is close to that well-known German fairy tale of the boy who went out to learn what horror is really like. In the end, of course, the brave Greek boxer was wedded to the liberated beauty in a splendid ceremony, lived to an extremely advanced age, and then, instead of dying, was carried away alive, and is now himself a hero.

There were no standing armies in ancient Greece. In principle, all citizens were obliged to perform military service and served, each according to his means (i.e., his capacity to supply his own horse or arms), in the cavalry, in the phalanx of the heavy-armed infantry (hoplites), or in the light-armed infantry. The Lacedaemonians held an unquestioned military superiority on land, since the Spartan's entire life, from his earliest youth, was oriented toward war and training for war. Little time was left for private life. The strict military discipline of the Spartan army (the great mass of which, incidentally, consisted of perioeci—literally, "those who dwell around") made it an instrument of war that was feared throughout the known world. No other state in Greece could stand up to it in pitched battle. The Helots were employed as camp servants and, in cases of emergency, as light-armed infantry and skirmishers. To be sure, Sparta too had its problems. The earthquake of 464 had caused great loss of life among the young, a loss which could not quickly be made good, and the dissension between kings and ephors led to repeated clashes. In earlier times the cavalry had played an important role in Greece, but the development of the hoplite phalanx radically changed the situation as early as the seventh century. Only in Thessaly and Boeotia, and, outside Greece, in Macedonia, was there a cavalry worthy of the name.

There was in Athens a muster-roll, on which the names of all those obliged to perform military service were entered. The muster-roll contained not less than forty-two age-groups, from eighteen to sixty. Naturally, the lower age-groups, say, from twenty to fifty years of age, were used on campaigns, while the older age-groups were usually drawn upon only for garrison duties. Only the members of the three highest tax-classes served in the hoplite regiments; the *thetes* (laborers) were excluded. Only in the later years of the Peloponnesian War were the latter called upon, when losses had begun to thin the Athenian ranks. The Athenian hoplite army was divided into regiments according to phylae; occasionally, for special military tasks, only the levies of certain individual phylae would be called up. Thus in 446–445 Pericles marched to Euboea with seven phylae, while three others were directed against Megara. The levies of the phylae were also known as *taxeis,* and were headed by a *taxiarch.* The subdivisions were *lochoi* (companies), led by *lochagoi* (company commanders). The citizen was required to provide his own equipment, and to bring with him provisions for the first three days. Athens had a cavalry totaling 1,000 men, but it had no great role to play on the field, being no match for the Thessalian and Boeotian horse. Use of the stirrup was unknown, as was that of a proper saddle, so that no rider could count on a firm seat; in fact we find many cases of riders falling off their horses in the shock of battle.

With the exception of the Spartans, the Greeks regarded military service as burdensome; the longer the Peloponnesian War lasted, the more men attempted to evade service under arms. The Spartan troops, on the other hand, had an entirely different outlook. For them, military service and warfare were a matter of honor; draft dodgers and cowards were rare exceptions. The Spartan levies consisted almost entirely of heavily armed infantry, being divided into seven regiments, each numbering about 600 men. An eighth regiment, the *Skirita,* was employed as light-armed infantry. Each regiment had a subdivision called the *pentekostys,* numbering 128 men. The smallest unit (32 men) was the *enomotia.* The chain of command was precisely regulated, every order passing from the

141

king down through each of the lower levels of command to the last hoplite. Since this was unique in Greece, it was especially emphasized by Thucydides (V, 66).

In Sparta the men were liable to the draft for forty years, almost their entire lifetime; the small number of full citizens, or Spartiates, made a long period of active service inevitable. In the last resort they could fall back on the Helots—but, of course, only such as had been set free. These appear as *neodamodai* (newly enfranchised), especially in the Lacedaemonian armies of the fourth century. Sparta did not possess any naval force to speak of; in the Peloponnesian War only Persian gold made construction of a fleet possible. Warships for Sparta's naval ventures were provided for the most part by the maritime cities of the Peloponnesian League, primarily Corinth, also Megara and Sicyon. Except for the Corinthians, these forces were inferior to the Athenians in naval battles.

In Athens the naval construction program under Themistocles had created entirely new conditions. From that time on, for instance, a great number of *thetes,* whose military potential had been little utilized in the past, served as oarsmen on Athenian warships. Naval squadrons were also occasionally manned for training purposes. There are said to have been 300 warships available at the outbreak of the Peloponnesian War, of which 100 were assigned to the defense of Athens. The equipping of the warships was done by means of the trierarchy; Athens' needs in wartime required no less than 400 citizens who would assume this obligation. The first syntrierarchy is not recorded before 405–404, at the end of the Great War. By that time it had become necessary to distribute the financial burden of equipping a ship among several citizens at once, since private wealth had greatly dwindled. Nevertheless Athens' navy, together with the ships of the great allied states of the maritime confederacy (Chios and Lesbos), had become a formidable instrument of sea power unmatched in all of ancient history; only the navies of the Carthaginians were remotely equal to it.

The real problem of the citizen army, in Greece as in every other country where the institution was established, was a

142

psychological one. In the army and navy alike the men had to be welded into battle-fit tactical units, and naturally this could be achieved only through hard training. But this was precisely what the adult citizens most disliked. It was necessary therefore to begin with those who were not yet old enough to bear arms. These were the ephebes, the young men of eighteen to twenty years of age, from whom one could expect not only endurance of hardship but also submission to a strict discipline. Under the supervision of older trainers (*paidotribai, kosmetai, sophronistai*) these young men busied themselves, as we have seen, with physical exercises that were actually preparation for service under arms. From an Attic document of the fourth century B.C., we know the text of the ephebic oath:

> The arms that I bear I shall not cover with shame. I shall fight for the holy places and for the state, and I shall transmit to future generations a fatherland that is not smaller but larger and mightier, according to my powers and with the help of all. I shall obey my superiors, the laws now in force, and those laws which may lawfully be passed in future. If however anyone plots to overthrow the laws, I shall not allow this, so far as it lies in my power to prevent it, and [this too] with the help of all. I shall hold in honor the public worship inherited from my fathers. Witnesses of my oath are the gods Aglauros, Hestia, Enyo, Enyalios, Ares and Athena Areia, Zeus, Thallo, Auxo, Hegemone and Heracles; and further, the boundary stones of the fatherland, the fields of wheat and barley, the grape vines, the olive trees and the fig trees.

In a recent study Louis Robert has rightly pointed out that this oath contains a number of older elements that lead us to assign it to an early date, perhaps to the Age of Solon. In any case, this ephebic oath is an interesting relic of the early history of Attic civilization. For the history of Athenian religion, too, it is not without significance, for among the gods named are some who had been largely forgotten by the classical period, gods like Aglauros, Thallo, and Auxo, who were connected with the growth of crops. The view has been widely advanced by classical scholars, notably by Ulrich von Wilamowitz, that the Attic ephebic training dates only from the last third of the fourth century B.C. This supposition, although it has found much support, is nevertheless untenable. In itself the oath given above is sufficient to refute it. We need not hesitate to assume the existence of ephebic military training as early as the fifth century. Such training was of inestimable value, for it implanted in the young a love of their country and awakened in them a readiness to engage themselves for it with all their strength. No state can exist without courage and self-sacrifice on the part of its citizens. That the words of the ephebic oath were not empty ones is proved by Athens' achievements in the Pentecontaetia, and no less in the dark days of the Peloponnesian War.

With the exception of Lacedaemon, there were no basically military states in Greece. Athens, to be sure, had the largest navy by far, but the foundations of its prosperity were commerce, industry, and agriculture, and the last continued to be the backbone not only of the Athenian economy but also of the Greek economy as a whole. In Athens the reforms of Solon had led to the creation of an efficient farmer class, based mainly on medium and small-sized holdings. In other parts of Greece such as Thessaly, on the other hand, many large estates still existed in the fifth century. Agricultural methods continued to be primitive; the iron plowshare was still unknown, and there was still no change in the practice of letting fields lie fallow every other year. Moreover, the increasing aridity of the land, due in part to progressive deforestation, raised extremely difficult problems. It has been conjectured that in all Attica only about one fifth of the land was actually cultivated, and of this fifth, half lay fallow. The principal crops were wheat and, more frequently, barley. But the yields were not nearly sufficient to feed the population, so that the difference had to be made up through imports. In Thessaly and Boeotia the situation was substantially better.

Agriculture was regarded as a highly honorable occupation, but it was quite the contrary with hand crafts and retail trade. The man who engaged in these ran the risk of being ridiculed as a *banausos,* a person without intellectual interests. Socrates alone was a laudable exception to the rule. He spoke out for the necessity of physical labor, provided of course that it left some opportunity for leisure.

Industrial enterprise continued to be limited. One Cephalus, toward the end of the fifth century in Athens, employed 120 slaves in his shield factory, but this was a rare exception, as was the use of many hundreds of slaves in the mines of Mount Laurium. Most businesses were very small. Only two or three workers other than the owner were employed—free men or slaves. The difficulties that grew out of the intense industrialization of the nineteenth century were unknown in ancient Greece. Nor was there any of the intensive specialization that would have dulled minds of the workers. As a rule, a genuinely patriarchal relationship existed between the owner and the workers, since each was dependent upon the other. Many articles were manufactured on a cottage-industry basis.

During the fifth century Greek commerce underwent a decisive change. Athens took the place of Miletus and the other cities of Ionia, as well as of Chalcis and Eretria on the island of Euboea. Athens, however, had an important rival in Corinth. Aegina's prosperity was blighted by the city's subjugation in 457, and at the beginning of the Peloponnesian War the Aeginetan population was replaced by Attic cleruchs. This brought to a temporary end the history of a city that, up to the time of the Persian Wars, had played an outstanding role in Greek commercial life. Megara was for a long time under the control of Athens; only with the Thirty Years' Peace, signed in 446–445, did it again recover its independence. The trade blockade imposed on Megara by Pericles was one of the immediate causes of the Peloponnesian War.

The expansion of Greek long-distance commerce was spurred by the building of larger and larger ships, of ever increasing speed. Some interesting evidence, dating from the first years of the Peloponnesian War, reveals the wide scope of Attic overseas trade. It appears in a comedy of Hermippus, the *Phormophoroi* (*The Basket-Carriers*), which dates from sometime between the beginning of the Peloponnesian War and year 425. The text is made more interesting, but more difficult, for us by some pointed contemporary allusions. According to a passage in the play, the following goods were being shipped to Athens by sea:

> From Cyrene silphium stalks and ox-hides; from the Hellespont, mackerel and salted fish; from Italy, spelt and ribs of beef; from Sitalces the Thracian King, slag for the Lacedaemonians; from Perdiccas the Macedonian, whole ship-loads of lies; from Syracuse, swine and cheese; from Egypt, sails and papyrus; from Syria, incense. Crete delivers cypresses for the gods, Rhodes delivers raisins and dried figs that cause sweet dreams. From Euboea come pears and plump sheep, from Phyrigia slaves, from Arcadia mercenaries. Pagasae sends slaves and branded thieves, the Paphlagonians send chestnuts and oily almonds, Phoenicia sends dates and fine wheat-meal, and Carthage sends carpets and many-colored pillows.

This interesting passage has been quoted often, and rightly so; more than any other source it throws light on Athens' connections with all the known world. It is corroborated by a pseudo-Xenophontic work dating from about the same time, the *Constitution of Athens,* in which we read (sections 11–13):

> The wealth of the entire Hellenic and barbarian world the Athenians alone possess. For if any state is rich in wood for shipbuilding, where shall it sell its wood, if it does not win the consent of the state that rules the sea? Or if a state is rich in iron, copper, hemp, or wax, where shall it sell these unless it win the consent of the state that rules the sea? For from these very materials ships are made. From the one state is taken wood; from another, iron; from another, copper; from another, hemp; from another, wax. It will not be borne that these things be exported to our rivals; rather than that, the sea will be blockaded against them. Thus, without doing anything, I receive from all quarters all these things by way of the sea, whereas no other state has two things at the same time. Instead, where there is much flax the land is flat and sparsely wooded, and likewise iron and copper are not found in the territory of the same city. Nor of the other products does one state have two or three together, but rather this state has this one, the other has that.

It would be a fatal error to form too primitive a picture of Greek commerce in the fifth century B.C. Though it cannot, of course, be compared with modern international trade, still it was quite considerable in scope, and to underestimate its size, as has been done by Hasebroek and his school, is a mistake.

In Greek society of the fifth century B.C. an important role was played not only by citizens but also by metics and slaves. The numerical proportion of the three groups is not known; but an interesting document of 409–408 B.C., on the composition of the team of workers engaged in the construction of the Erechtheum in Athens, throws some light on the problem. Seventy-one names are mentioned in all, of which twenty are citizens, thirty-five metics, and sixteen slaves. Are we justified in drawing conclusions, on the basis of a document that was preserved by chance, on the composition of the population as a whole? This would be very dangerous. For instance, the relatively small number of citizens involved can easily be explained by the exigencies of war; many were under arms or were needed for other tasks. The state of war also explains the high number of metics, whose work was especially important in Athens at the time. Though the metics had no political or civil rights, they were drawn upon for military service on land and sea. Many of them were wealthy men, who felt themselves closely linked to the life and the fate of their host-country. Not only were they prominent in commerce and manufactures, they also played an important role in the artistic and intellectual life of the city. A vivid picture of the status and the life of a metic in Athens is given in the trial speeches of Lysias. His family originally came from Syracuse, whence his father Cephalus emigrated to Athens about the year 460. Cephalus was a friend of Pericles, who is said to have invited him to come to Athens. Lysias, born probably about 444 in Athens, went to Thurii at the age of fifteen, where citizenship was conferred on him. Expelled from Thurii, he returned to Athens in 412–411. Here he acquired a considerable fortune by the large-scale production of shields in wartime. Under the rule of the "Thirty" (404–403) he was forced to flee from Athens to Megara. Although he returned to Athens after the democracy was restored, he took as little part in the struggle against the "Thirty" as he had previously taken in the Peloponnesian War. In his activity as a logographer (legal speech writer), Lysias reveals himself as the sort of hair-splitting advocate for whom no means is too base to insure victory for his side. This judgment of K. J. Beloch's will be confirmed by anyone who has gone through Lysias' orations. But not everything for which Lysias has been reproached was his own fault. The Greek world of his time was split up into countless city-states, all of them zealously independent. There was no such thing as a single Greek nation. Between citizens and noncitizens—and the metics, of course, belonged to the latter class—there yawned a deep and unbridgeable gulf. The consequence of this was a class of the population that flowed from one city to another, whose motto was *ubi bene ibi patria* ("My country is wherever things go well for me").

Presumably not all metics had Lysias' earning power. Moreover, in the Peloponnesian War many metics risked their lives for the Greek state whose guests they happened to be, and in the expulsion of the "Thirty" from Athens in 403 many metics lent what assistance they could. The Athenians were exceedingly chary of granting foreigners their citizenship; it is therefore not surprising that so many metics plunged with particular single-mindedness into business, since the field of political activity was closed to them.

Slavery in the Greek world had many different aspects. There were whole population groups that had been reduced to the status of serfs, mostly in connection with the conquest of a country. Typical of these were the Helots in Lacedaemon. The Penestae in Thessaly, the Cyllyri in Syracuse, and others had also been reduced to a similar and similarly unenviable status. The fear of Helot revolts reappears, like a specter through Sparta's entire history. This is understandable when we consider the great superiority in numbers of the oppressed over their oppressors. There was no change in this situation in the classical period, until Epaminondas created a free Messenia (see p. 235).

Entirely different was the nature of the slave problem in Athens and in most of the other Greek city-states. Here slaves were employed in the workshops of the city, and above all as domestics. They were acquired on the slave market, if they had not already been born to bondage in their master's house. There must have been regular associations of slave dealers, whose connections and business relations spanned more or less the entire Mediterranean world. How else can it be explained that in a single household, that of Cephisodorus in Athens, there were slaves from Thrace, Caria, Illyria, Colchis, Scythia, Lydia, and Malta? The number of slaves was considerable. Thus Nicias is said to have had no less than 1,000 slaves; he rented them out, primarily for mining work, and realized huge profits from their labor. Even as early as the fifth century it appears to have been possible for a slave to acquire money of his own and to purchase his own freedom. But the first evidence we have of large-scale manumissions of slaves is documents dating from the fourth century, especially from Delphi.

In recent years a question often discussed is to what extent were the slaves in ancient Greece considered by their masters as fellow human beings (J. Vogt)? If we consult ancient sources, the answer must be, hardly at all. For the Greeks, slavery was so firmly established as an institution that no one seriously dared attack it. The slaves were needed; for Greek civilization they were a vital necessity. That people were concerned about their slaves and about their bodily well-being goes without saying. From the Hippocratic writings it is clear that medical care was given to slaves. But all this is rather marginal, and we shall understand the Greeks better when we realize that even men of enormous breadth of spirit such as Plato and Aristotle regarded slavery as the natural state of things. This picture is little altered by the fact that many male slaves, as tutors (*paidogogoi*), and still more female slaves as nurses, felt the closest kind of ties to the children who were entrusted to them.

Women held similarly subordinate status in the Greek world. They lived quite shut off from the outside world in the women's chamber (*gynaikeion*), and when Pericles says that the best

149

women are those of whom the least is heard, whether in praise or blame (Thucydides II, 45, 2), he is certainly expressing the prevailing opinion among Athenians and among the Greeks as a whole. (Consider the contrast with, for instance, conditions at the time of the Renaissance.) It goes without saying that women did not participate in the political life of the classical period. In addition, they were under legal guardianship their entire lives. A woman's guardian (*kyrios*) was either her father or a male relative or, if married, her husband. She was not consulted before being married; her opinion in the matter did not have the slightest weight. Her activity was exclusively in the household; in the man's professional life she had no share. If her husband decided to do away with a newborn baby by means of exposure, he did not even have to ask her opinion. The status of the Greek woman was little different from that traditionally held by women in the Orient, and her role as a wife was further undermined by the existence of the hetaerae, who had the masculine world at their feet, as well as by the presence of domestic female slaves. These facts resulted in many conflicts within the family. Added to this was the practice of pederasty, which was widespread not only in Sparta but in all of Greece.

For practical purposes it meant very little that there were, in the contemporary literature and among contemporary intellectuals, occasional voices raised in behalf of equal rights for women. Euripides in his dramas, Socrates in his dialogues, put forward these revolutionary notions. The position of Aspasia in Athens was, however, quite exceptional. It has been thought that her image influenced Euripides in his portrayal of women, and in particular in his tragedy *Medea* (431), but this is not at all certain. Antisthenes, the founder of the Cynic philosophy, wrote a dialogue that had her name as its title, and so did Aeschines of Sphettus (about 386). Although individual poets and thinkers might maintain that man and woman possessed equal ability, the obvious conclusions were never drawn from this.

The life and the history of the Greek people cannot be understood without taking their religion into account. The

Greeks believed that their entire life, public and private, was directed by the gods. Their imagination peopled nature with many divine forms, which were also active in the life of the individual. In the Persian Wars the gods had visibly helped the Greeks, and they were given due thanks by the construction of shrines and the organization of feasts and sacrifices in which the entire city took part. There was no professional priesthood; the priests were simply civic magistrates from the individual communities and were either elected or appointed. The masses enjoyed the feasts and the sacrifices, and it would never have occurred to them to doubt, for instance, the existence of Pallas Athena, the great protective goddess of Athens. This gives us the explanation of the trials for atheism that were so often brought against philosophers. Religion and state belonged inseparably together: whoever turned against religion also attacked the foundations of the state.

Nilsson has correctly pointed out that the religion of the Greeks contained a healthy element of self-interest. When the Greeks presented to the gods the sacrifices they owed them, they expected prosperity in return; the farmer especially hoped that his fields and cattle would prosper. Nevertheless it must be understood that in Greece, too, there were genuinely pious men. The great masses of the people, of course, believed in the simple externals; they were convinced that *hybris* provoked *nemesis,* the envy and the vengeance of the gods, and that it was therefore better not to climb to too great heights, so as not to have too great a fall. The story of Polycrates and Amasis, related by Herodotus (III, 40 ff.), is a well-known example.

How vivid was the Greek belief in the supernatural is shown by the influence of the oracles, above all of the great Delphic Oracle. After their victories over the Persians, the Hellenes showered the Delphic Oracle with votive gifts, even though in the struggle for freedom Delphi's priesthood had adopted a suspiciously neutral attitude. The conduct of the devout man is seen in the life of Nicias, who bore a large share of the responsibility for the failure of Athens' Sicilian expedition. Nicias made expensive gifts to the shrines on the Acropolis, as well as to those at Delos and Delphi, and there was no doubt about the sincerity of his piety. It is reported on good authority that he sacrificed daily to the gods. In his house he kept a seer constantly with him, with whom he used to discuss every possible subject, even matters of business. His trust in seers is known to have plunged him and his country into misfortune: when the moon went into eclipse, they counseled him to postpone the departure of the Athenian forces from Syracuse by three times nine days, i.e., one full moon. Nicias followed this advice into defeat.

The level of superstition among the mass of Greeks is revealed by the Hippocratic book on the Sacred Disease (epilepsy). The first chapter gives us an entire catalogue of dark superstitions. We are told of men who refused certain foods, and men who considered it harmful to wear black clothing; others believed that it brought misfortune to sleep upon or to wear a goatskin; that a man must not put one foot before the other, nor lay one hand upon the other—and all this to heal the so-called Sacred Disease. There were people, says the author, who claimed that they could bring down the moon from the sky, darken the stars, and create storms and good weather. In general the author criticizes the popular view that the human body is contaminated or infected by the gods—as, for example, when popular belief associated certain symptoms of illness with particular deities. All of which makes it perfectly clear that we simply cannot assume the fifth century to have been a period of general enlightenment, entirely without superstition. The opposite is obviously true; parallel to higher notions of the nature of the gods, revealed to us in the works of the poets and sculptors, there existed also, as in every age, an unbridled superstition. We see this, for instance, in the tablets of magical curses, which were to be found all over the Greek world.

For deeply religious spirits the civic religion, with its world of gods inherited from the past, was no longer satisfactory. This is why the mystery rites found so large a following, especially the Mysteries of Eleusis in Attica. "The Eleusinian religion," says Nilsson, "spoke to the heart of man; for that the great gods had become too aristocratic." The strong appeal of the mysteries was based upon the deep secrecy of their practices, and the high spirituality of their doctrines. In all ages of history man has longed for that pure happiness which cannot be realized here on earth but only in the hereafter. The Eleusinian Mysteries were built upon the doctrine, not of individual immortality, but of the immortality of the race, the species, one's kindred, as manifested in nature—for example, in the seed grain. The initiates expected to continue the celebration of the mysteries in the hereafter, and this was a thought that cheered them on their way, giving them joy and confidence for life on earth, and hope for a life in the future.

For the broad masses, however, the mysteries held little appeal. Their attitude toward the mysteries was probably about midway between the *deisidaimonia* (superstitious piety) of Nicias and the cool skepticism of Pericles. The little that we know of the religion of Pericles leads us to suppose that he was neither an especially devout man nor an atheist. Religion for him was inseparably bound up with the state, and this connection was something that Pericles—like every Greek public man of his time—had constantly to keep in mind. The religion of Pericles was conventional; in thanks for the rescue of a worker, for instance, he dedicated a statue to Athena Hygieia. On the other hand when he fell sick of the plague—as Theophrastus tells us—he is said to have shown one of his friends an amulet that the women had tied around his neck. The story is not at all incredible; indeed it aptly illustrates the ambivalence of his religious attitude.

8

The Peloponnesian War
(431–404 B.C.)

The Greek victories over the Persians at Salamis and Plataea were followed by the so-called Pentacontaetia, a period of about fifty years (479–431 B.C.). In this epoch the Greeks rose to the position of the leading nation in the Mediterranean world. The Persian Empire was not in a position to prevent this. With the Peace of Callias, a truce was reached in the long confrontation which enabled both the Persians and the Athenians to turn to their own domestic problems. During the Pentacontaetia, or "fifty-years"—the term is Thucydides'—the conflict between the two leading Greek states, Sparta and Athens, grew increasingly tense, finally exploding in the crisis of the First Peloponnesian War (457 to 446–445). The war brought no real decision. The Thirty Years' Peace signed in 446–445, though it eased the tensions between Athens and the Peloponnesians, did not wholly eliminate them.

The Second Peloponnesian War is the theme of the famous *History* written by the Athenian Thucydides. Who was this man? Of his life very little is known, but still enough for us to be able to understand something of the origin of his history and the attitude of its author. Thucydides, of the deme of Halimus in Attica, was the son of Olorus, whose name—if it has come down to us in correct form—indicates a Thracian origin; and it is in fact likely that his mother's

154

family was of Thracian princely stock. Thucydides was born about 460, perhaps somewhat later. In 424 he was one of the Athenian *strategoi* in Thrace whose task was the defense of Amphipolis on the lower Strymon. Unfortunately he was unable to hold that important city against the Spartans under Brasidas, retaining only the harbor, Eion. Knowing the consequences that faced him in Athens, Thucydides voluntarily went into exile. Where he lived for the next twenty years is not known—perhaps in Skaptehyle in Thrace, where he had family property. Toward the end of the war a decree introduced by Oenobius recalled him to Athens. There he is supposed to have died a few years later, though the exact date of his death is not known.

His literary intentions and his ability to realize them is attested by his *History,* which has made his name immortal. He left his work unfinished; it breaks off in the midst of his account of the Ionian War (441), confirming the ancient tradition that the historian died suddenly. In the form in which we possess it, the work has been edited posthumously. What part in it was played by the "editor"—faced repeatedly with difficult philological problems—is an insoluble question. A prime indication of the work's incompleteness is the fact that the eighth and last book contains none of the quoted speeches that are so characteristic of the earlier books.

Thucydides begins with an account of Greek prehistory (*archaiologia*), in which he attempts, by a method that seems rather modern, to arrive at some definite conclusions about the early ages of Greece. After depicting the underlying as well as the immediate causes of the Peloponnesian War, he then discusses the Pentacontaetia. With the Second Book begins a detailed description of the war, commencing with an account of the night surprise attack of the Thebans on Plataea in the spring of 431 B.C.

Thucydides' *History* is above all the history of a war; military and political affairs are always in the foreground, while diplomatic proceedings, for instance, are mentioned only insofar as they are absolutely necessary to his narration. This is the reason for the drastic one-sidedness of his work: but it is also the reason for its strength, so greatly admired by ancients and moderns alike. It is a tremendous drama that Thucydides unfolds before the reader's eyes. Unlike Herodotus, who regarded the intervention of the gods as a matter of course, Thucydides refrains from any supernatural explanations, and for this reason has been called, not unjustly, the "natural scientist" among historians. He was not untouched by the intellectual currents of his time. The ideas of the Sophists, for instance, are to be found in the famous Melian dialogue in the Fifth Book, and in a number of other speeches inserted throughout the entire work.

That these speeches—in the form in which we now read them—were not actually delivered by the speakers, has long been a matter of common knowledge to historians. They serve rather to throw light on the situation at a given time, from the point of view of various sides and various attitudes of mind. Thucydides even goes so far as to compose speeches for occasions when in fact no speech was given at all. We must, then, reconcile ourselves to the fact that, in the form in which they are related by Thucydides, the speeches are not authentic. It is another matter with the documents that he has incorporated into his work. Although it cannot be expected, considering the prevailing practice of ancient writers, that Thucydides has given a literal rendering of these documents, nevertheless they are of great historical value. For example, Thucydides alone has given us the texts of the treaties concluded between Persia and Sparta in 412–411, which are of priceless value to every historian. (Bengtson, *Staatsvertraege,* Nos. 200–202).

What Thucydides' original intention was as regards the design of his work, and to what degree he did or did not change it as he went along, is a problem endlessly discussed. First raised in 1845–1846 by Franz Wolfgang Ullrich, Professor at the Johanneum in Hamburg, it has cast its shadow over every subsequent work on Thucydides. According to Ullrich, Thucydides originally intended to depict only the Archidamian War (431–421), i.e., the first part of the Second Peloponnesian War. In Book One, Chapter One, Thucydides (so Ullrich maintained) was referring to the Archidamian War alone. Only as the war progressed did Thucydides become conscious of the interrelationship between the Peloponnesian War's individual parts i.e., the Archidamian War, the Sicilian Expedition, and the Decelean and Ionian Wars. This new awareness resulted in an entirely new conception, which was reflected in his work as it progressed. Ullrich and his partisans, including above all the great classical philologist, Eduard Schwartz, believed that they had found conclusive support for their thesis in the so-called Second Preface of Thucydides (V, 26), which in their view, for the first time in the *History*, presupposes a knowledge of the entire war. There are two schools of thought—the school of Ullrich, which stresses the original separateness of the war's component parts in Thucydides' mind, and the unitary school of Eduard Meyer, H. Patzer, and others, who hold that Thucydides saw the war from the start as a single struggle. The pendulum still swings back and forth between them. Though the hypothesis of Ullrich is, in the nature of things, not fully verifiable, it has proved an extremely rich mine of suggestions for scholars. However, it is not likely that this question will ever be answered with entire certainty.

Thucydides says, at the beginning of his work, that he is writing his account of the Peloponnesian War in the expectation that the struggle would turn out to be the greatest and most important of all events in Greek history up to that time. In this he was entirely correct. In itself the extension of the war was remarkable. It reached from Asia Minor across the Aegean to Greece and thence to Sicily and to southern Italy. Even the Persian Empire intervened and in the end, by its subsidies, decided the struggle in favor of Sparta. The resources brought to the war by both sides were enormous. Athens fought on until it had completely exhausted its material resources. Moreover, tens of thousands, Pericles among them, were carried off by the great plague of 430–429. If in addition it is borne in mind that the war lasted an entire generation, in the course of which external and internal changes of the very greatest magnitude took place in Greece, and that at the

157

war's end there were evident not only great destruction but also unexampled symptoms of intellectual decline—then the Peloponnesian War will be seen to be the great revolutionary event, the *peripeteia* of Greek history in classical times. The war was an example on a grand scale of the effect of destructive, indeed ruinous, psychological fixations in the life of nations. Not only individuals like Cleon, Alcibiades, and others were caught up in this, but also the mass of Athenians; the longer the war lasted the more they became obsessed with the exercise and increase of their power, until they had thereby dug their own graves. After the death of Pericles in 429, it is impossible to find a single statesman who might have brought forward new and constructive ideas, capable of putting an end to the chaos in political life.

The military scene, to be sure, forms a sharp contrast to this dismal picture of Greek politics. On sea and on land the war saw a number of brilliant achievements, of which Brasidas' expedition across Greece and Macedonia to the Chalcidice is but one example. Thanks to Thucydides' precise data, we are able to find in his book outstanding material for the study of military history, and in addition much evidence that, even today, has not lost its value for the study of psychological warfare.

Thucydides was the first historian to try to distinguish between the deeper causes that underlie a war and the more immediate external events that precipitate it. Without doubt, one of the underlying causes of the Peloponnesian War was the inherent conflict between Sparta and Athens. The contrast between them is to be seen even in the way in which each power exercised its hegemony. Athens held the maritime confederacy in a state of strict dependence; Sparta granted a large measure of internal freedom to the members of the Peloponnesian League. But the Peloponnesians felt threatened by democratic ideas which, with their source in Athens, were showing an increasing power of attraction for the Peloponnesian states. A more fundamental factor, however, was the irreconcilable clash between Athens and Corinth, the Queen of the Isthmus; the interests of the two cities collided sharply in two areas: in the Adriatic and in Potidaea on the

Chalcidice. Corinth watched with great concern the expansion of Athenian trade with the West, and when the Athenian colony of Thurii severed the ties that bound it to Athens, and allied itself with the Spartan colony of Taras, Corinth must have welcomed the event with a sigh of relief.

The war was precipitated by difficulties that had arisen between Corinth and its colonies on the Adriatic. From the time of the tyrants Corinth had created an extensive colonial empire. Most Greek colonies were autonomous city-states, but in the cities settled by Corinth the will of the mother city continued to prevail, and indeed the mother city often intervened in the internal affairs of the colonies. The island of Corcyra, in the Adriatic, was one such colony; it in turn settled the coastal town of Epidamnus (Durazzo) jointly with Corinth. When internal dissensions developed in Epidamnus, the democratic party called on Corinth for help, whereupon Corinth secured Epidamnus by means of a garrison (435). The oligarchic party of Epidamnus, however, did not give up; they secured the support of Corcyra, whose fleet proceeded to besiege Epidamnus. When Corinth, with a number of allied states, met the Corcyraeans at sea, the encounter ended in a Corinthian defeat off Corcyra's Cape Leucimne. On the same day Epidamnus signed terms of surrender to the Corcyraeans (Bengtson, *Staatsvertraege,* No. 160).

Corcyra's success could not disguise the fact that the island's situation, in view of Corinth's superior forces, was very difficult. The Corcyraeans therefore established contact with the Athenians, and a defensive alliance (*epimachia*) was concluded (Bengtson, *Staatsvertraege,* No. 161), in which Athens pledged itself to render partial assistance (433). If Athens intended to adhere to the terms of the Thirty Years' Peace of 446–445, it would not conclude a full defensive and offensive alliance with Corcyra. But according to Greek conceptions of international law, Athenian aid in defense of Corcyra need not violate Athens' treaty with the aggressors, nor involve her in war with them. The Athenians therefore proceeded cautiously, to avoid arousing the anger of the Peloponnesians.

At first Athens dispatched only a small squadron of ten

ships to Corcyra, a force that was scarcely decisive, but which showed that Athens intended to adhere to her treaty with Corcyra. The fleets of the Corinthians and the Corcyraeans met off the Sybota Islands. With 150 ships to the Corcyraeans' 110, the Corinthians held the advantage. As they were on the point of gaining the day, the Athenians—meanwhile reinforced to a strength of 30 ships—attacked, depriving the Corinthian squadron of the victory that had been within its grasp (433).

Athens, in the following winter of 433–432, renewed the earlier treaties with Rhegium and Leontini. Were the Athenians already planning war? But these treaties were as important for Athens' relations with the West as they were for insurance against a possible war with Corinth.

As in the Adriatic, so also in the northern Aegean there was a collision of Athenian and Corinthian interests. The city of Potidaea, which had been founded by the Corinthian tyrant Periander, was a member of the Delian-Attic Maritime League. However, it had always maintained ties with its mother city; Corinth continued to send to Potidaea its supreme magistrate, the *epidamiurgos*. Athens now became mistrustful, and made the unreasonable demand that Potidaea tear down its city wall where it faced the sea and refuse to receive the Corinthian *epidamiurgos* in future. Thus threatened, Potidaea found support from the Macedonian King Perdiccas II and, having assured itself of the assistance of Sparta, took a decisive step. Together with a number of Thracian and Chalcidian cities, Potidaea announced its withdrawal from the Delian League (432). The Corinthians dispatched an auxiliary corps to Potidaea, while the Athenians began the investment of the city by land and sea.

The responsibility for Athenian policy rested with Pericles. Was it mere coincidence that, immediately before the outbreak of the war, a series of trials took place involving charges against his followers, and even against Aspasia? Are we justified in seeing, in these trials, the expression of opposition to the leading Attic statesman and, in the war that followed, the means that he adopted to quell it? Apart from the fact that the dating of some of these trials—such as the trial of Anaxag-

oras and that of Phidias—is not certain,* the acquittal of
Aspasia, who was accused of being an atheist and a procuress,
shows that Pericles' position was still unshaken. These events
therefore had no repercussions on foreign policy.

The Megarian *psephisma,* on the other hand, was something
else again. This decree, passed on a motion by Pericles in
432, laid on the city of Megara a strict embargo that completely cut off the Isthmian city's access to its markets in
Athens and in the territories of the Delian League. A few
border incidents—naturally exaggerated by Pericles—served
as justification. Behind this aggressive act against Megara lay
Athens' old grudge against its neighbor, which in 446–445
had broken away from the sphere of influence of Athens, and
since then had again become a zealous member of the Peloponnesian League.

It was Corinth that from now on accelerated the drift toward
war. On a motion by the Corinthians and the Megarians, the
Apella, the Spartan assembly of full citizens, declared that
Athens had broken the treaties (by which was meant the
Thirty Years' Peace). The congress of the members of the
Peloponnesian League also, and by a great majority, decided
upon war, although here the feeling was not unanimous
(autumn of 432). Moreover, Delphi too placed itself on the
side of the Peloponnesians, not only encouraging the Spartans
to go to war, but even holding out a sure prospect of victory
and the assistance of the Delphic god. There is no question
that after the meeting of the congress of the Peloponnesian
League, war with Athens was inevitable. The war did not
break out, however, until the following spring (431). On
both sides, but especially on that of the Spartans, the interim
was filled with negotiations designed to place the enemy in
the wrong. These negotiations, by the way, are a striking
proof that at the time international public opinion was already
a factor of the greatest importance in Greece.

Sparta's first demand was for the expulsion of the descendants of those who had had a part in the sacrilegious murder of
Cylon. This was aimed primarily at Pericles, who was de-

* The trial of Anaxagoras certainly belongs to an earlier time (see p. 132)

scended on his mother's side from the Alcmaeonids, who, by violating the right of asylum, had originally brought the curse upon themselves. Athens made counterdemands; it demanded that the Spartans exorcise the curse that lay upon them for the killing of Helots in the sanctuary of Poseidon in Taenaron, and for the death of Pausanias in the Temple of Athena Chalcioecus. These religious demands were soon followed by political ones. The Lacedaemonians demanded that Athens discontinue the operations against Potidaea, give Aegina back its freedom, annul the Megarian *psephisma* and guarantee the Greeks' autonomy. According to Thucydides (II, 140), Pericles thereupon branded the Lacedaemonians as aggressors and violators of the peace, declaring that they had not adhered to the terms of the Peace Treaty of 446–445, which had provided for appeal to a court of arbitration in the event of differences arising between the two states.

Could Athens have avoided war by fulfilling the demands of the Lacedaemonians, on a few points at least? The answer can only be no. The view that Pericles consciously worked toward war in order to evade internal political difficulties— a charge brought against him by Aristophanes and, in recent times, by K. J. Beloch—proves to be entirely unfounded. It is refuted not least by Pericles' essentially defensive strategy. Pericles did not want war, but he also did not go out of his way to avoid it when it became clear that peace could be maintained only at the cost of humiliation for Athens. The question of guilt can be answered unequivocally: It was Corinth above all that carried the reluctant Lacedaemonians along with her, and thereby ignited a war that marked the beginning—in terms of power politics—of the fall of the Greek world.

What was at stake in this war? For Athens it was her predominant position in the Aegean, her hegemony over the maritime confederacy, and the continued development of her economy and of her trade, which had no equal in the entire Mediterranean world. Sparta and the Peloponnesians, on the other hand, maintained that they were drawing the sword in behalf of freedom of the seas and the autonomy of the Greek

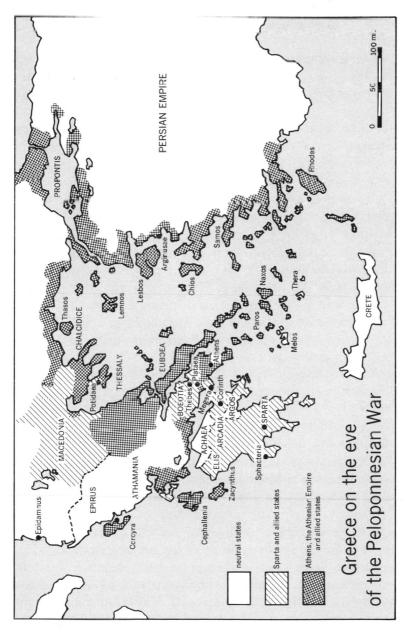

Greece on the eve
of the Peloponnesian War

neutral states

Sparta and allied states

Athens, the Athenian Empire
and allied states

states, both of which were being threatened by the power of Athens.

The distribution of forces on both sides is revealing. Sparta was the strongest land power in Greece. Together with the other members of the Peloponnesian League, she was capable of putting a considerable hoplite army, totaling close to 40,000 men, into the field. In addition there were the central Greek levies of the Boeotian League, the Phocians and the Locrians. In the Peloponnese, only Argos and Achaea remained neutral; Argos was bound by treaty not to war on Sparta (see p. 178). The navy of the Peloponnesians, on the other hand, was far inferior to that of the Athenians: the maritime cities of Corinth, Megara, and Sicyon made the most substantial contributions to the fleet, but it consisted of less than a hundred triremes. As to the overall strategic situation, Athens' enemies had a great advantage: with the bulk of their forces they could operate from a main base in the Peloponnese, and by employing their allies in central Greece as well, they could catch the Athenians from both south and north in a deadly pincer movement.

Against the mass levies of the Peloponnesian League, the Athenians were unquestionably inferior on land. Athens could raise only 15,000 hoplites for its field army; the older age-groups, said to total 16,000 men, could be used only for occupation or defense purposes. But the Athenian navy with its 300 triremes was an imposing instrument of war. In addition there were the naval contingents from Chios and Lesbos, and the ships of the new allies in the Ionian Sea, Corcyra, Cephallenia (see p. 167), and Zacynthus. The navy had little trouble in keeping open the sea routes to Athens, thereby assuring her the importation of vitally necessary goods.

Pericles' design was to remain on the defensive on land while seizing the initiative at sea, unsettling the Peloponnesians by surprise landings on their coasts. This plan naturally put great demands on the Athenians' discipline and dedication. Since an invasion by the superior Peloponnesian army had to be reckoned with, plans were made for the evacuation of

Attica. The entire rural population was to be quartered in the area between the Long Walls, while the open country, with the exception of a few forts, was to be left to the Peloponnesians. Athens, the Long Walls, and the harbor of Piraeus formed a single gigantic fortress, the defense of which was assigned to the hoplites of the older age-groups, leaving the field army free for operations against the Peloponnesians. The field army could also be transported by the fleet to overseas areas, if the war situation required. No one in Athens dared think in terms of crushing the enemy; only a strategy of exhaustion could achieve Athens' goal.

The Peloponnesian War was a fratricidal war among Greeks, a fact that was not altered by the intervention of foreign powers, Macedonia, for instance, and later the Persian Empire. We note with amazement that during this conflict, which lasted almost three decades, the idea of a common national identity of all Greeks was never once taken up by either side. The jealously guarded autonomy of the Greek city-states, the narrow patriotism of their inhabitants, ruled this out entirely: it was the sharp antagonisms among the Greeks that were in the end decisive; the commercial jealousy of Corinth, the oppression of Megara, and in general the Peloponnesians' fear of further expansion by Athens.

Like the globe-girdling British Empire, Athens had secured important bases everywhere: in Thessaly, in Thrace, on the Hellespont and the Bosporus, on the western coast of Asia Minor, on the islands of the Aegean, in the Ionian Sea, and even on the Straits of Messina and in Sicily. As far as the sea extended, there the fleet of Athens sailed unchallenged; her power was respected and feared throughout the world. The Peloponnesians, not least the Lacedaemonians, could not fail to realize that the day would come when nothing could be done in the Greek world without the assent or express approval of Athens. In Sparta, as elsewhere, perceptive statesmen felt it was their duty to take measures against Athens before it was too late. From the standpoint of Sparta and the other Peloponnesians, it was to be a preventive war: Athens' power was

165

to be reduced to a level tolerable to the Peloponnesians. But it is hardly likely that the Peloponnesians originally counted on a complete victory over Athens.

The first phase, the Archidamian War, lasting from 431 to 421, takes its name from the Spartan King Archidamus, who led the Peloponnesian levies to Attica, although he himself was not enthusiastic about the war. Hostilities began with a Theban night surprise attack on Plataea in March, 431. For some time tensions had existed between Thebes and Plataea. Thebes, striving to extend and straighten the frontiers of its Boeotian League, was unwilling to abandon its designs on Athens' ally Plataea. Peloponnesian chances were favored by the existence in Plataea of a group friendly to them. The surprise attack failed, however; the 180 Thebans who had forced their way into the city were taken prisoner and, in violation of an express promise, executed. The Athenians, in response to the Plataeans' request for help, placed a garrison in the city, women and children were evacuated, and the city was prepared for a siege. These events constituted an open breach of the Thirty Years' Peace.

Two months later, in May, 431, the Peloponnesian army appeared on Attic soil. The Lacedaemonian King Archidamus made one more attempt to induce Athens to make concessions, but Pericles remained firm; in fact the Assembly of Athens had passed a decree that prohibited negotiating under pressure of enemy arms. The Athenians moved their families and their most valuable possessions to safety in the area between the Long Walls, where the entire Attic population, crowded into the narrowest space, was housed in emergency quarters. It must have been a hard test of their resolution to watch, from the battlements, the grain fields of Attica going up in flames, and the vineyards and olive orchards being destroyed by the Peloponnesians. When the Peloponnesians' food supplies gave out they drew closer to Boeotia, and finally began to withdraw toward home, dismissing the contingents of the various states. The campaign had lasted only one month.

The Athenians' revenge was to dispatch a fleet of 100 triremes to the coast of Peloponnese. Aboard the ships were

1,000 hoplites and 400 archers. An attack on Methone failed, since here the Spartans had an outstanding leader in Brasidas. A landing on the coast of Elis was more successful. Much more dangerous than these needling tactics was the fleet's invasion of the Ionian Sea, where the island of Cephallenia soon joined the Athenian side. Meanwhile, in the Saronic Gulf, the inhabitants of Aegina were expelled by Pericles, but were permitted, with the assent of the Spartans, to resettle in the Thyreatis region, a rare example of humanity amidst the horrors of the Peloponnesian War. Later, when Nicias landed at Thyrea in 424, the Athenians were to go back on this by taking the Aeginetans prisoner and bringing them back to Athens, where they were executed.

The Athenian operations on land were insignificant. Pericles destroyed some places in the region of Megara. In the northern Aegean fighting continued before the city of Potidaea, which the Athenians had invested, and whose fall was now only a question of time. Potidaea was supported by the Macedonian King Perdiccas II, while the Athenians gained a valuable ally in Sitalces, King of the Odrysian Thracians. Thrace, with its wealth in raw materials and slaves, was invaluable for the Athenian economy. But the extravagant hopes the Athenians placed in their new ally were not fulfilled.

In the early summer of 430 the Peloponnesian army invaded Attica for the second time. A few days later appeared another, equally uninvited guest, the plague. Brought to Athens from overseas, it caused the most frightful losses, finding in the dangerously overcrowded city all too rich a prey. Thucydides has described the epidemic in detail (II, 48–54), remarking that he himself had the disease and saw others suffering from it. If we are to believe him, the plague appeared first in Ethiopia, then in Egypt and Libya, and later in Asia Minor, whence it was brought by ship to the Piraeus. Thanks to Thucydides' description we know the course of the sickness in detail. It began with a high fever and an inflammation of the eyes, soon followed by nausea, violent spasms, and ineffectual retching. The body was covered with boils, and the sick suffered from terrible fever, restlessness, and insomnia. In most cases the crisis was reached on the seventh or ninth day. If this was survived, the disease moved to the abdomen and the victim was tortured with violent ulcerations and diarrhea, so that many died of weakness. Those who survived this stage were attacked in their extremities; some lost the use of their limbs, others went blind or lost their memories. There do not appear to have been successive attacks of the disease on the same person. All medical aid against the epidemic proved to be in vain. Even today medical science has not been able to define the nature of the disease. Bubonic plague and typhus appear to be out of the question, and it can only be said with certainty that it must have been a severe infectious illness.

The pestilence raged in Athens for two years, and also spread to other areas. In faraway Rome an epidemic is recorded for the year 436 which is without doubt identical with the plague in Athens. Incidentally, it follows from this that the traditional chronology of Livy (IV, 21) is six years too early at this point. In Athens, during the four years of 430, 429, 426, and 425, the plague carried off a third of the population. Just as severe as the loss in human life was the effect of the plague on Athenian morals. Indifference and ruthlessness spread with the disease or, in their absence, frivolity and a lunatic thirst for pleasure.

On hearing of the outbreak of the epidemic the Peloponnesians at once evacuated Attica. With minor exceptions (Phigalia) the plague did not appear in the Peloponnese, where very drastic preventive measures were taken: every Athenian and every member of the Delian League taken prisoner was killed on the spot. In Athens the people's anger was directed against Pericles, whose strategy, by concentrating the Attic population within the Long Walls, had offered the pestilence an easy prey. At first an attempt was made to come to terms with Sparta. When this broke down over the intransigent demands of the Lacedaemonians, the opposition in Athens, supported by the hostility of the populace, began a major attack on Pericles. A decree of the Assembly deposed him as strategos; in addition he was accused of embezzling public funds and condemned to pay a fine. This charge was in all likelihood quite without foundation, for if any Greek refrained from enriching himself at the expense of the community, it was Pericles.

With the capitulation, after a two-year siege, of Potidaea in the spring of 429, Athens gained a significant success in the northern Aegean. The terms granted Potidaea were very mild: each individual was permitted to leave the city with his family, the men being allowed to take one garment and their wives two, as well as subsistence money for the journey. They were free to choose their new homes. A few months later, this Athenian victory was offset by the defeat of her hoplite army in battle against the Chalcidians at Spartolus. This was the first encounter in which cavalry and peltasts (light-armed infantry) showed their superiority over hoplites.

In the elections for the strategoi in the spring of 429, Pericles was returned to power; but it was too late. Marked by the plague, having lost his two legitimate sons, he was already a broken man. He died in the summer of 429, after only three months in office, and the entire epoch on which he had set the stamp of his genius was buried with him. He had left behind him no political heirs in the real sense of the word. Politicians of the type of Eucrates, Lysicles, and Cleon took his place—all of whom, as businessmen, felt the pressure of the war far less than the farmers whose fields were repeatedly burned by the Peloponnesians. Eucrates ran a mill and a hemp business; Lysicles, who later married Aspasia, was a cattle dealer; Cleon, the most important of the three, owned a tannery and a leather business. Later there appeared on the political scene Nicias, son of Niceratus, who distinguished himself on several occasions during the Archidamian War. But Nicias, too, was no Pericles; he was incapable of exerting enough influence on the Assembly to bring the war to a conclusion favorable for Athens.

Phormio's operations in the Gulf of Corinth (429) were among the most brilliant in the naval history of Attica. In spite of the enemy's numerical superiority, he was able to establish and maintain a blockade in the Strait of Rhium which bottled up the greater part of the Peloponnesian navy in the Corinthian Gulf, thus effectively eliminating it from the war. After a side campaign in Acarnania, where Athenian partisans were helped to power in various communities such as Stratos, Phormio returned, by way of Naupactus (Lepanto), to Athens; but there, despite his indisputable successes, he was soon brought to trial and condemned to pay a fine. Unable to raise the money, he fell into *atimia* (loss of political rights) and never again held a command.

A very dangerous crisis for Athens occurred in the year 428. The rich island of Lesbos (with the exception of the city of Methymna) defected from the Athenian side. For half a century Lesbos had been one of Athens' most loyal allies. Its defection was very awkward, for it might draw others in its wake, endangering Athenian domination of the coast of Asia Minor and of the Hellespont. Lesbos allied itself with Sparta, and was even received into the Peloponnesian League with due formality. But effective Peloponnesian aid was very much lacking, while the Athenians dispatched the strategos Paches to Lesbos, with a thousand hoplites on board his ships. (There were evidently no available oarsmen, since the hoplites had to pull the oars themselves.) Paches invested the city of Mytilene by building a wall around it. This expedition was ruinously expensive; for the first time in the war, Athens was forced to levy a direct income tax (*eisphora*), which realized 200 talents. The tributes also were collected from the allies with particular strictness. Cleon, who had actively collaborated in putting the decree on the income tax through the Assembly, was elected *hellenotamias* the following spring. Nicias, Eurymedon, and Demosthenes were also placed in important positions, all three being elected as strategoi.

Meanwhile the citizens of Mytilene were waiting in vain for Peloponnesian help. The commander of the Spartan fleet, Alcidas, lacked courage; his intelligence system failed completely; not until the Peloponnesians were near Erythrae on the Asia Minor coast did they receive reliable word that Mytilene had already capitulated a week before (July, 427). The treaty concluded between the Athenian strategos Paches

and the Mytilencans (Dengtson, *Staatsvertraege*, No. 170)
was relatively mild, on the face of it. The Mytileneans, to be
sure, had to surrender unconditionally, but Paches gave a
pledge that none of them would be put to death, jailed, or
sold into slavery until the embassy of the Mytileneans had
returned from Athens. In Athens, however, other emotions
prevailed. In a dramatic Assembly meeting it was resolved,
on the motion of Cleon, to execute all adult Mytilenean males
and sell the women and children into slavery. The following
day the monstrous decree was revised: only the Mytilencans
that Paches had sent to Athens were to die, 1,000 in all.
The high figure that we find in the text of Thucydides (III, 50,
1) has always been a stumbling block; it has been thought to
be an error in transcription, so that instead of "A" (1,000)
the text should read "Λ" (30). The question will have to
remain open, unless documentary evidence someday provides
the answer. With the exception of Methymna, which had remained loyal to the Athenians, the cities of Lesbos lost their
independence; their territory was taken from them and assigned to Attic cleruchs.

Shortly afterward, in midsummer of 427, the siege of
Plataea came to an end. Ever since the summer of 429 the
unhappy city had been besieged by Peloponnesians and Boeotians, and Athens had been in no position to help its ally. After
half of the garrison, 212 men, made a successful sortie and
fought their way to Athens (winter 428–427), only a small
band of soldiers continued to hold the city. The Spartans
would have had little trouble in taking it by storm, but they
had hesitated to do so, for they realized that after the conclusion of a peace treaty they would have to return to their former
owners all the places they had taken by force. The Spartans
had previously pledged themselves to set up a court and to
punish only the criminals among the Plataeans. But when the
city surrendered, a proper trial never took place; instead the
Spartan judges put an insidious question to each prisoner: Had
he aided the Peloponnesians during the war? Since none could
answer this question in the affirmative, all the prisoners—200
Plataeans and 25 Athenians—were executed.

The behavior of the Spartans is a horrifying example of

war psychosis. That the treatment of the Plataeans was a mockery of all principles of international law is obvious. Of course the Plateans, too, had been guilty of a flagrant violation of international law when, contrary to their pledge, they killed the Thebans who had forced their way into the city (p. 155). But now Plataea came into Theban possession, and was entirely destroyed; the name Plataea disappears from the roll of Greek states.

The year 427 was marked by the outbreak of an oligarchic revolution on Corcyra. The island had allied itself with Athens, but the return from Corinthian custody of the Corcyraeans who had been taken prisoner in the battle of the Sybota Islands sparked a revolution. The internal struggle on Corcyra, which was fought out on both sides with the greatest bitterness, is a proof of the enormous mutual hatred that had accumulated between oligarchs and the democrats in Greece. Even the intervention of Athenian forces under the strategos Nicostratus did not lead to a resolution of the conflict. Corcyra did conclude a treaty of full alliance with Athens (Bengtson, *Staatsvertraege,* No. 172), which replaced the former epimachy (see p. 159), but party warfare once again broke out. With the tacit acquiescence of the Athenian Eurymedon, the democrats' thirst for blood raged unchecked in Corcyra, and many who held opposing views became its victims.

Scarcely had Athenian influence in Corcyra been restored than the Athenians sent a squadron of twenty warships on a voyage to Sicily. This was the First Sicilian Expedition, which in the autumn of 427 left the Piraeus under the command of Laches. It was preceded by the famous embassy in Athens of the Sophist Gorgias of Leontini, at that time at war with mighty Syracuse. On Leontini's side were the Chalcidian cities of Sicily, the Doric colony of Camarina, and Rhegium. The Syracusans were supported by a number of Doric cities (Gela, Selinus, Messana, Himera) and, in southern Italy, by Locri Epizephyrii.

The Athenians dropped anchor in the harbor of allied Rhegium, but were able to achieve very little, if only because of the small number of available triremes. Among other things a raid was undertaken against the Lipari Islands, which were allied with Syracuse. In the following year (426) Messana went over to the Athenian coalition, and as a result Athens and its allies now controlled the straits between Italy and Sicily. Halicyae in western Sicily concluded a treaty of alliance with Athens of which a few letters have been preserved (Bengtson, *Staatsvertraege* No. 174). Also, the treaty with Segesta was renewed by Laches.

What did the Athenians hope to accomplish in the West? There is no doubt that they wanted above all to strike at the lines of communication between Corinth and Syracuse. Moreover, they had to reckon with the fact that the Syracusans were capable of sending warships to the Peloponnesians, which would have meant a substantial strengthening of the enemy fleet. It was Laches' task to pin down the Syracusans on the island of Sicily and to minimize the influence that the Peloponnesians, especially the Corinthians, had in the West. In 426, the Spartans also established a base in central Greece, not far from Thermopylae. This was the colony of Heraclea near Mount Oeta. Their hopes, however, were only partially fulfilled, for the Thessalians made bitter war upon the colony.

In general this year was marked by the expansion of the war to new theaters. Under Demosthenes and Procles, the Athenians advanced into Aetolia, but the results were at first so meager that Demosthenes, after the expiration of his term of office, did not dare return home. But then, in league with the Acarnanians and Amphilochians, he succeeded in defeating the Ambraciotes and the Peloponnesians in a pitched battle. But at this point the Greeks of the West, who had up to then been mutual enemies, concluded a Hundred Years' Treaty among themselves, the purpose of which was to prevent Athenian dominance (Bengtson, *Staatsvertraege*, No. 175).

The year 425 marked a turning point in the war. In the spring an Athenian fleet of forty ships put to sea, with the mission of bringing reinforcements to Sicily. Among those on board was Demosthenes, but without a command. This strategically gifted soldier recognized an opportunity to damage the Spartans by a landing on the coast of Messenia. When a storm forced the fleet to seek shelter in the Bay of Pylos (Navarino), Demosthenes convinced the two commanding strategoi, Eurymedon and Sophocles son of Sostratides, that the peninsula of Coryphasium should be occupied, in order to establish contact from there with the Messenians. While the bulk of the fleet continued to Corcyra, Demosthenes remained behind with five warships and a few hoplites. In their countermoves the Spartans showed little skill. Though they were able to occupy the rocky island of Sphacteria on the western side of the Bay of Pylos, the Athenian fleet, recalled from Zacynthus, blocked the two entrances to the bay, leaving 420 Lacedaemonian hoplites, among them 200 Spartans, stranded on the island. In view of the threatened loss of these completely irreplaceable soldiers, Sparta concluded an armistice for the area of Pylos, and was prepared to negotiate with Athens for peace.

Had there been a real statesman in Athens, he would have seized this momentary advantage to arrive at a tolerable peace with Sparta and the Peloponnesians. Unfortunately, the political leadership in Athens lay in the hands of the radicals, more specifically Cleon. When attempts to capture the Lacedaemonians stranded on Sphacteria did not succeed, the Athenian Assembly finally empowered Cleon, who had been boasting of how *he* would handle the situation, to attend to the matter. The Athenians landed a force on the island several times the size of the enemy's, and the remnants of the Peloponnesians—292 hoplites, 170 of them Spartans—were compelled to surrender. Credit for this success belongs especially to Demosthenes, who had given Cleon excellent counsel.

But the fruits of the victory were harvested by Cleon. Honors were heaped upon him, and he saw and seized an opportunity to convert further resources into ready cash for the conduct of the war. Cleon trebled the tributes of the allies so that the total now came to 1,460 talents. The per diem allowance for Athenian jurors, however, was raised from two to three obols.

The Athenians also showed their mettle in several other engagements with the Peloponnesians. In the same year, 425, they occupied the Methana peninsula near Troezen. The following year Nicias conquered the island of Cythera, and from it great damage was inflicted on Peloponnesian commerce. Finally, the port of Nisaea near Megara fell into Athenian hands. But these successes were clouded by a sharp Athenian defeat at Delium, in 424. Here, in Boeotia, the first pitched battle of the war between major armies took place, and the Boeotians routed the Attic hoplites. The outcome of this battle is striking proof of the soundness of Pericles' war plans, proposing a strictly defensive strategy on land.

In Sicily, too, Athenian influence was on the decline. In view of the Athenian reinforcements the Siceliotes had decided on peace (424), at the urging of the Syracusan Hermocrates. A general peace was concluded at a congress at Gela, and when the Siceliotes invited the Athenians to become a party to the treaty, they agreed. Consequently the Athenian fleet left Sicily. An enterprise that had been begun with great hopes had ended without result. Naturally, however, internal strife among the Sicilian Greeks broke out again soon afterward.

The Spartan Brasidas gave the war a new direction. This officer had already distinguished himself on several occasions by his great boldness and decision, and had been severely wounded in the fighting around Pylos. Thanks to him the Peloponnesians were able to hold Megara despite the loss of Nisaea. Brasidas now brought forward a new strategy for Sparta. Till then the Peloponnesians, almost year after year, had laid Attica waste, but had otherwise, of necessity, confined themselves to the defensive, with no major offensives being undertaken. It was obvious, however, that Athens had an Achilles' heel in Thrace and on the peninsula of Chalcidice. If the Peloponnesians, together with the Macedonians, could make a major effort here, a major success might be achieved.

With 1,700 hoplites Brasidas marched in the spring of 424 from the Isthmus through central Greece to the Spartan base at Heraclea, and from there through Thessaly and Macedonia to the Chalcidice peninsula. The first cities to range themselves on his side were Acanthus and Stagira, but the most significant success was the conquest of Amphipolis. Toward the former members of the Delian League Brasidas was extraordinarily lenient. The treaties of capitulation are refreshing in their generosity (Bengtson, *Staatsvertraege,* Nos. 181–182). The loss of Amphipolis decided, among other things, the personal fate of the historian Thucydides; the necessary materials for pronouncing a judgment on his responsibility for its fall are lacking. By the loss of other places to the Peloponnesians, especially Torone on the Sithonia peninsula, Athens' position in Thrace was severely shaken. Many cities, exasperated by the increase in the tribute, were only waiting for the opportunity to defect.

In Athens as well as in Sparta the longing for peace grew stronger by the day. And this feeling was expressed politically, in Athens by Nicias and others, in Sparta by King Pleistoanax. The Spartans, for instance, were obsessed by the plight of the prisoners taken at the battle of Pylos; the Athenians, who regarded them as hostages, had threatened to execute them if the Peloponnesian army dared to invade Attica again. The result was the conclusion of an armistice in 423 between Athens and Sparta, which included the allies on both sides (Bengtson, *Staatsvertraege,* No. 185). The document, which has been preserved in Thucydides (IV, 118), gives us an interesting insight into the diplomatic practices of the Greeks. In the treaty various local demarcation lines between the forces were fixed; in general the existing territorial holdings of the two belligerents were confirmed. Disputes during the truce were to be submitted to arbitration.

But hopes for an early conclusion of a formal peace treaty were dashed. Two days after the signing of the armistice, the city of Scione on the Pallene arm of the peninsula of Chalcidice defected to the Spartans. It was supposed to be returned to the Athenians, but Brasidas refused to do so. So the war continued. Through an alliance with the unstable King Perdiccas II of Macedonia and with Arrabaeus, Prince of nearby Lyncestis, the Athenians increased their power in the north (Bengtson, *Staatsvertraege,* No. 186). Cleon now appeared with a strong force in the northern theater of war, and the reconquest of Torone was followed by other successes. Unluckily, however,

Cleon let himself be enticed into an attack on Amphipolis, was surprised by Brasidas and utterly defeated. Cleon and 600 of his Attic hoplites lay dead upon the field. The enemy is said to have lost only seven men; but one of these seven men was Brasidas. It was the autumn of 422.

In Sparta, as well as in Athens, the war party had lost its leader. In both states the desire for peace was gaining ground. Sparta was having difficulties in the Peloponnese, and besides was concerned for the fate of its prisoners in Athenian custody. Nicias above all, despite the opposition of radical elements, was responsible for bringing the Athenians to favor the conclusion of a treaty, which became effective at the beginning of April, 421, and was to be valid for a period of fifty years. Its provisions are known from the document preserved in Thucydides (V, 18; see also Bengtson, *Staatsvertraege,* No. 188). Essentially the peace treaty provided for a restoration of the *status quo ante bellum.* Amphipolis was to revert to Athens; the inhabitants of cities that were to be returned to Athens were given the right to seek new homes. A number of cities of Chalcidice were declared autonomous, on condition that they pay Athens the old tribute that had been fixed by Aristides (not the amounts set by Cleon). Athens was to give up the places it had occupied on the Peloponnesian coast. Delphi and its shrine were expressly proclaimed autonomous.

The Peace of Nicias ended ten years of struggle in which the tide of battle had swayed to and fro without a clear decision. Both opponents had generally held their ground, but no one could fail to see that Athens had emerged from the war far weaker. It still had not recovered from the losses suffered from the plague, and the death of Pericles had left a gap that could not be filled. These disasters were not fully offset by the position that Athens had built up in the Ionian Sea as a result of its alliances with Corcyra, Cephallenia, and Zacynthus. To be sure, these islands were the stepping-stones of a route linking Greece to Italy, but everyone must have foreseen that Corinth would do its best to destroy the Athenian command of the Ionian Sea.

In fact, it was not only Corinth that disliked the peace that had been contrived by Sparta. Megara, Elis, and Boeotia also refused to become parties to the treaty. Sparta felt isolated by the behavior of its allies, and therefore concluded a fifty-year defensive alliance with Athens. Each of the two parties pledged itself to come to the other's aid if attacked by a third party. Athens also promised the Spartans its aid in the eventuality of a Helot revolt (Bengtson, *Staatsvertraege,* No. 189). There may well have been men on both sides who were hoping for a joint rule by both states over the whole of Greece.

The disillusionment of the former Spartan allies took form in a comprehensive Peloponnesian alliance that excluded the Lacedaemonians. Its members, besides Argos (which up to now had kept out of all quarrels) were Corinth, Elis, Mantinea, and the Chalcidians. The effect of this alliance (Bengtson, *Staatsvertraege,* No. 190) was positively explosive. It tore the Peloponnesian peninsula into two separate parts, for neither Megara nor Tegea wanted to break with Sparta. Moreover, the Boeotians had little trust in Argos.

For the Athenians, too, the trend of events was disappointing. The Spartans, even had they wished to, were simply not in a position to fulfill the terms of the Peace of Nicias. Most of all, Sparta could not take it upon itself, by force of arms and before the entire world, to compel its refractory allies—especially Corinth and the Chalcidians—to accept the conditions of the peace. To this was added the fact that a political movement that was anything but moderate was rapidly gaining ground in Athens. In the spring of 420 Alcibiades, son of Cleinias, had been elected strategos. Alcibiades, who grew up in the house of Pericles, was an absolute egotist. Both in his personal life and in politics, every means was right for Alcibiades if it achieved his ends. Formed by the spirit of the Sophists, endowed with rich intellectual gifts, affable and winning in his personal relations, Alcibiades radiated a charm that was able to captivate even his most sober-minded contemporaries. His goal was the complete ruin of Sparta, whose power of resistance he underestimated to a fatal degree. The means to his goal was to be the political cooperation of Athens with Argos and the other disaffected Peloponnesian states.

The shifting political moves and countermoves led first to an alliance between Sparta and Boeotia in 420 (Bengtson, *Staatsvertraege,* No. 192); this was capped by Alcibiades with a hundred-year treaty of alliance between Athens, Argos, Mantinea, and Elis (Bengtson, *Staatsvertraege,* No. 193). The only significant thing about these treaties was their temporary character, for the political constellation was changing almost month by month.

The tension finally exploded in the battle of Mantinea (August, 418); under the command of King Agis the Spartan army was victorious over the forces of the dissident federation, and Lacedaemonian ascendancy in the Peloponnese was once more fixed. The sudden change finds expression in two treaties of alliance that Sparta now concluded, one with Argos, Perdiccas II of Macedonia, and the Chalcidians, the other with Mantinea (Bengtson, *Staatsvertraege,* No. 194). Both treaties can probably be dated as early as 418. The resurgence of Sparta was, of course, a heavy blow to Alcibiades' war policy; there is no doubt that it was this policy that had driven the Peloponnesians back into the Spartan camp.

In Athens the antagonism between Alcibiades and Nicias seemed irreconcilable. The issue was posed: war or peace? It was decided to use the machinery of ostracism to force a political decision on the question. The outcome ought never to have been in doubt, for the farmers, who feared for their fields in the event of war, would surely have turned the scales against Alcibiades. That they did not was the fault of Nicias alone. Deceived by the promises of Alcibiades, he allied himself with the latter, so that the votes of the supporters of both men were directed, not against each other, but against a third figure, Hyperbolus, who was condemned to exile.

This ostracism of the year 417 was a sign of a grave internal crisis in the Attic state and among the Attic citizenry. Eduard Meyer correctly said:

> The decision was fateful, not only for the future course of political events, but for the whole character of the Attic state. The safety-valve that had preserved it in all previous crises had now become unserviceable. Personality had tri-

umphed over the power of state as a whole. In showing itself no longer capable of wise decision, Attic democracy had pronounced judgment upon itself.

The policy of Athens now lay in the hands of Alcibiades and Nicias, both of whom had been elected strategoi for the year 417–416. It was Athens' naked drive for domination that brought the island of Melos to ruin in 416. Until then Melos had been neutral. Although it is listed in a register of tributes for the year 425, this must be regarded as a fictitious claim on Athens' part, and the evidence cannot outweigh Thucydides' express statement to the contrary. What had Melos done to deserve to be treated by Athens in so shameful a manner? For its men were killed, its women and children sold into slavery. In the famous Melian dialogue Thucydides (V, 85 ff.) wrote that, in this case, might for the Athenians came before right and that the Melians in vain implored the gods for help. Nor would Sparta lift a finger in defense of the unhappy island. Historians rightly see in the Melian expedition a brutal embodiment of the Athenian will to power. Alcibiades, or whoever it was that counseled this move, did not serve his city well; on the contrary he covered it with shame and disgraced the weapons that Pericles had forged for its defense.

If the Melian expedition was soon forgotten, this was because it was shortly overshadowed by another and more memorable event. This was the Athenians' great Sicilian Expedition (415–413). How did this fateful undertaking come about? In Sicily, Syracuse had had little trouble in reestablishing its former hegemony; Leontini had been conquered, and victory gained in a war with Segesta. A call for help from Leontini and Segesta, however, found willing ears in Athens, for in earlier years certain Athenian politicians—Cleon and Hyperbolus—had cherished far-reaching plans of conquest: the two demagogues had seriously considered a war of conquest against Carthage. The prospect of acquiring great riches in Sicily now aroused the most extravagant hopes among the Athenian masses. We read in Plutarch's *Life of Nicias* (Ch. 12) how in Athens young and old plunged into discussion of Sicilian intervention. In the palaestrae, the workshops, and the public square, groups stood around arguing the problems involved. Sketches of the island of Sicily were drafted, and plans of its harbors and other places. In the background lay the hope of bringing not only Carthage but the entire Western Mediterranean area under the power of Athens. That these plans far exceeded Athens' capacities seems to have occurred to no one.

Was it really possible to achieve a decisive victory so far from Athens, when the Athenians had not even been successful in establishing order in the northern Aegean? There was still so much for Athens to do in the Chalcidice, and Amphipolis still had not returned to the Delian League. In all earnestness Nicias appealed to the good sense of his countrymen. Nevertheless an embassy was sent to Segesta, which returned with great hopes and still greater promises. Alcibiades' cause had won; the Assembly resolved to grant Segesta the aid it had requested against Selinus. Command of the expedition was given to Alcibiades, Nicias, and Lamachus; all three strategoi had special plenary powers for the enterprise. In Athens there was complete certainty of victory; only a few incorrigible pessimists were worried, and among them, we are told, was Socrates. From Athens to Rhegium was a sea journey of ten days, barring bad weather. In winter, however, there would usually be a several months' interruption of navigation.

Immediately before the fleet's departure for Sicily the hermae (pillar-busts of the god Hermes) standing in the public squares and streets of Athens were mutilated under cover of darkness. We may be sure no political motive was involved; most probably a band of youths, arrogant with wine, had laid violent hands on the sacred statues. Under normal circumstances this boys' prank would have been a case for the regular courts. But in the highly charged political atmosphere of Athens, it was immediately suspected that the offense signaled a real *coup d'état*. The council established an extraordinary investigative commission composed of ten men, which learned nothing as to the identity of the offenders. Alcibiades, however, was denounced for having profaned the sacred Mysteries of Eleusis in his house. It seems doubtful that this accusation was at all justified; but that Alcibiades was believed capable of the deed is significant. Although he urgently requested an immediate clearing-up of the affair, this was postponed until the return of the fleet from Sicily. So Alcibiades was allowed to retain his command.

It was an imposing force that embarked on the long voyage to Sicily. In all there were 134 triremes, with a complement of about 20,000 men. In addition there were 5,100 hoplites and 1,300 light-armed troops on board. The land force was, of course, too small for a large-scale war, but the fleet was far superior to the potential enemy in Sicily, the Syracusans, and in armament the Athenians had the advantage.

The Athenians were received very coolly in the West. The south Italian cities of Taras and Locri adopted a hostile attitude, and even in Rhegium the Athenians were not exactly welcome; the Greek cities of Sicily hesitated to declare themselves on their side. Only when Catana opened it gates to them were the Athenians able to shift their fleet from Rhegium to Sicily. The first engagements with the Syracusans now began. A fateful act was the recall of Alcibiades, who had been the soul of the enterprise. Thessalus, the son of Cimon, had denounced Alcibiades for desecrating the Eleusinian Mysteries, and the Athenians sent the dispatch-boat *Salaminia* to Sicily to bring him home. But they had reckoned without Alcibiades, who, following the *Salaminia* in his own trireme as far as Thurii, simply put himself ashore there and, by way of Elis, reached Argos. When the Spartans let him know that he had nothing to fear from them, he went to Lacedaemon.

In Sicily the Athenians landed in the large bay south of Syracuse, but had to give up the position: in an unlucky encounter with the Syracusans their lack of cavalry showed to ill effect. In Syracuse the citizens armed themselves with frantic determination. Messengers went to Sparta, calling upon the Spartans to resume the war against Athens without delay. But Syracuse's trials were far from ended. Nicias, after a victory over the Syracusans, began to lay siege to the city, cutting it off from the rest of the peninsula by a system of field fortifications. The Syracusans threw up counterworks, but were unable to free themselves from the investment.

Athens' simultaneous intervention in Caria, however, was to prove fatal. In supporting the rising of the dynast Amorges against the Persian Great King, the Athenians had committed an open infraction of the Peace of Callias. But by now they seemed to have neither scruples nor sense.

In response to Syracuse's request for help in the winter of 415–414, the Spartans decided to renew the war with Athens. The decision was by no means an easy one for the Spartans; it was Alcibiades personally who persuaded them to do it. Actually, however, if Sparta had borne the events in Sicily in silence, if she had allowed the Athenians not only to overcome the Doric colony of Syracuse but also to win hegemony over the whole island, Sparta's prestige among its allies would have been at an end. Inaction would have meant Sparta's abdication as a great power, its reduction to the role of a petty agricultural state. Moreover, the Athenians were already guilty of inroads against Spartan coastal towns in 414, at a time when Sparta was at war with Argos.

The Spartans dispatched the commander Gylippus to Syracuse; this proved an effective aid to the besieged. Gylippus succeeded in passing through the straits of Messina before the Athenians, and landed at Himera. With his auxiliary troops he then forced his way through to Syracuse, and Nicias did not dare challenge him to battle. From this time on the fortunes of the Athenian besiegers of Syracuse went downhill. At the beginning of the winter of 414 a message from Nicias arrived in Athens, urgently asking that either the undertaking be broken off or sufficient help be sent to maintain the siege of Syracuse.

For the Athenians this was a hard blow, but for the time being they did not allow their hopes to be shaken. While the arsenals and the shipyards echoed with the noise of armaments being prepared for Sicily, the Peloponnesian army under the Spartan King Agis marched into Attica in the spring of 413, fortified the town of Decelea, and placed a garrison there. This was done on the counsel of Alcibiades, who had placed his personal desire for revenge above all other feelings. Athens was no longer master in its own house. Peloponnesian raids were disturbing the whole of Attica; only Eleusis and Salamis could be protected. To the devastation of Attic agriculture was added a marked decline in commercial life. No less than 20,000 slaves ran away, many of them from the mines of Mount Laurium. For its food Athens was now entirely dependent on imports.

What war had done to the humanity of men is shown by the fate of the little Boeotian town of Mycalessus, in the year 413. The Athenians had enlisted a troop of Thracian mercenaries totaling 1,300 men. They were originally intended to embark with Demosthenes for Sicily, but were sent back because their provisioning was too expensive and because there were already men enough for the expedition. After passing through the Euripus, the strait between Boeotia and Euboea, the Thracians devastated the countryside near Tanagra, and then, directed by the Athenian Dieitrephes, advanced on Mycalessus. They seized the town, whose walls were in poor condition and whose city gate, through criminal negligence, had been left unlocked. The Thracians literally massacred the entire population, sparing neither women nor children. Even the cattle were slain. We learn that they forced their way into a school and slew all the children they found there. Rushing to the site, the Thebans pursued the Thracians to the Euripus, where many of them, unable to swim, lost their lives in attempting to reach their ships. To read this account in Thucydides (VII, 29–30) is to sense something of the historian's indignation at this atrocity, which was no isolated instance in the endless Peloponnesian War.

Both sides meanwhile had sent reinforcements to Sicily. The Athenian force was imposing. Under his command Demosthenes now had 73 triremes, with 5,000 hoplites and many light-armed infantry aboard, a contingent totaling altogether about 20,000 men. Athens was betting everything it had on a single card; if this card did not take the game, not only the Sicilian Expedition but Athens itself was lost.

Meanwhile, in the spring of 413, the tide had turned before the walls of Syracuse. Gylippus had carried out a night assault on the Athenian fort at Plemmyrion, and now the Athenians found themselves forced onto the defensive. Demosthenes, on the other hand, had had no success with a night assault on the fortifications of Euryalus, for the Syracusans, panicking at first, took heart and drove the Athenians from the heights. At this point Demosthenes would have preferred to call off the whole enterprise, but since his co-commander Nicias was opposed to it, several weeks were wasted in total inaction. Just when Nicias had finally agreed to leave, a lunar eclipse occurred on August 27, 413 B.C., whereupon the superstitious Nicias postponed the return for a whole month.

In an attempted breakthrough nearly half of the Athenian fleet was lost. Perhaps another such attempt might have succeeded, but the Athenians were by now so discouraged that they had no heart for another naval battle. This left only the land route, and though the difficulties here too were considerable, still a large part of the army could have been saved if its leaders had proceeded to put their plan into execution without delay. But precious hours slipped by, and meanwhile the Syracusans had succeeded in blocking the roads into the interior of the island. It was still a quite imposing force—Thucydides numbers it at 40,000 men—that now took the road westward up the Anapus. But because of Syracusan resistance the direction of march had to be altered, and in the night before the sixth day, the army headed south. An attempt to reach the sea ended in utter failure.

First Demosthenes and the greater part of the now dissolving army were overtaken; two days later, on the Assinarus River, the remainder of the Athenians under Nicias were taken prisoner (autumn, 413 B.C.). The prisoners were put in the stone quarries of Syracuse, where most of them died of the rigors of the climate. Nicias and Demosthenes were executed. That was the end of the great Sicilian Expedition, which the Athenians, on the advice of Alcibiades, had begun with such extravagant hopes.

The outcome of the campaign is an example of the consequences of inadequate political and military leadership. Certainly Nicias was not alone at fault, but he was responsible for the fact that the expedition was not called off while there was still time. His conduct is excused to a certain degree by the fact that the whole expedition had been undertaken, so to speak, blindfolded. Athenian policy had not been governed by hard factual knowledge; rather the Assembly's decision had been based upon vague dreams, hopes, and speculations. It is tragic to watch Nicias insisting, in the hope of discouraging the entire project, that the expedition would take many more ships and men than its supporters had allowed for, only to see the Assembly blithely vote a larger expeditionary force, and fatally compound its original error. Athens, with its restive maritime confederacy and with its deteriorating relations with the Persian Empire, had every reason to proceed with the greatest caution. An undertaking that ended with the loss of the lives or liberty of almost 50,000 men seems even less justified, when from the very beginning it was lacking in any clarity of aim. Unlucky accidents, to be sure, also hurt the Athenians, but fundamentally the fault lay with the demos of Athens and its demagogues for having, in inconceivable delusion, consented to dig their city's grave.

It was fortunate for Athens that the catastrophe in Sicily happened at the end of the campaigning season. During the following winter of 413–412 Athens was thus able to arm itself anew. The great fleet was irreplaceable, but by mobilizing its last sources of funds Athens was able to lay down the keels of new ships. Thus an *ad valorem* tax of five percent was laid on all imports and exports of the entire area of the Delian League, a measure that the subject cities naturally felt to be especially oppressive.

In the meantime, changes had been taking place in the Persian Empire that marked a new turn in Persian policy toward Greece. The Great King Artaxerxes I had died in the winter of 425–424. His forty-year reign had not been very glorious, but still he had been able to repel the Athenians' invasion of Egypt and retain the island of Cyprus for the Empire. His son and successor, Xerxes II, had reigned only one and a half months when he was murdered by his brother, Sogdianus. But Sogdianus, too, was unable to keep the throne. His stepbrother Ochus, satrap of Hyrcania, had him killed and himself took possession of the throne in 424 under the name of Darius II. Little is known of the internal history of the Persian Empire at this time; the sources as a rule indicate only the usual harem intrigues, typical of the Persian court. For the Greeks a much more important figure than the Great King in remote Susa was his representative in nearby Asia Minor, the satrap of Sardis.

In 412 the satrap of Sardis was Tissaphernes, who is well known from Xenophon's *Anabasis* as the adversary of the younger Cyrus. Tissaphernes had been of great service to the Persian Empire. Before his appointment as satrap he had distinguished himself in battle against his predecessor, Pissuthnes. He had also fought against Amorges, a relation of Pissuthnes, who had revolted in Caria against the Great King. In this contest the Athenians had been incautious enough to support Amorges (see p. 183). When the full extent of the Athenian defeat in Sicily became known, the Persian King demanded of the Greek cities of Asia Minor the arrears in their tribute to him; he began, that is, once more to treat them as subjects of the Empire. This new policy of the Persian King fell in with the ambitions of the Lacedaemonians, who, after the Sicilian catastrophe, now began to find favor everywhere. Euboea, Lesbos, Chios, Erythrae, and other cities of Ionia began to negotiate with Sparta, negotiations in which the Persian satraps Tissaphernes of Sardis and Pharnabazus of Dascyleum also joined, for the Persian King could be a very important ally. Even though his forces could exert no power outside of Asia Minor, Persian gold was always valuable, and for the Spartans, by now, every means toward victory was permissible.

When Miletus fell into the hands of the Spartans, the latter signed a treaty with the Persian King in the spring of 412. The text of the document is given verbatim by Thucydides; it is the first of the three treaties concluded between Sparta and Persia (Bengtson, *Staatsvertraege,* Nos. 200–202). For Sparta the terms were anything but gratifying. The Lacedaemonians were forced to renounce all cities and territories that had formerly been in the possession of the

Great King or his predecessors, and they pledged themselves to cooperate with the Persians in preventing any incursion of the Athenians into Asia Minor. The war against Athens was to be continued by both parties, and a separate peace by either party was prohibited.

The mention of Tissaphernes' name in the text of the treaty —it appears after the name of the Great King—shows us who was responsible for the conclusion of this treaty. Tissaphernes was in fact the real gainer; the Peloponnesians helped him to defeat the dynast Amorges in Iasus (Caria). Soon, however, the first differences appeared between the new allies, the issue being the level of Persian payments for the mercenaries. It was necessary therefore to formulate the terms more precisely. This was done in the second treaty (Thucydides, VIII, 37), but this treaty also did not endure for long. Alcibiades, formerly the moving spirit of the Spartan-Persian rapprochement, was resorting to new tactics. He had convinced Tissaphernes that it was by no means in the Persian interest to give Sparta unreserved support, but that, on the contrary, a certain equilibrium between Athens and Sparta would be more to the Great King's profit.

The events that took place after 412 were shaped by Alcibiades and the Persian satrap Tissaphernes, not by the combatants. The absence in Athens of any clearly conceived policy became increasingly evident, as well as the lack of a leader able to unite the forces of the city in the service of any plan. A heavy blow for Athens was the loss of the greater part of Ionia in 412. Cnidus and Rhodes as well went over to the enemy, so that only a few islands, including Lesbos and Samos, and a few coastal points, Halicarnassus and Clazomenae being the most important, remained in Athenian hands.

By the beginning of the year 411 Athens was so far gone that one final effort by the Peloponnesians, the Syracusans, and the Persians would have sufficed to destroy her once and for all. The responsibility for this unending chain of misfortunes obviously lay with the Athenian democracy. Small wonder that in Athens the opponents of democracy— led by Antiphon of Rhamnus, a celebrated orator—began to raise their heads. Probably at the end of 413 or the beginning of 412, an executive authority of ten probouloi ("precouncillors") had been established in Athens, which took over part of the former functions of the council. These oligarchic efforts in Athens were not distasteful to Alcibiades, who was hoping to effect through them a return to his native city. So he undertook to mediate an alliance between Athens and Persia, on condition that the democratic government in Athens be dissolved. It appears, however, that Alcibiades had overestimated his influence with Tissaphernes, for just at this juncture came the signing of the third Spartan-Persian treaty. Persian subsidies appear in this treaty for the first time, as well as a promise by the Persians to commit their fleet in the Aegean—an action that, as we know, was for whatever reasons never carried out.

A revolution nevertheless took place in Athens, although it is hardly likely that it took such an orderly form as the documents reproduced in Aristotle would lead us to suppose. Democracy was buried; from now on political rights were to be held by only 5,000 citizens, and the Council of Five Hundred was dissolved (May, 411). The most important governing body was the new Council of the Four Hundred; from its members were elected the strategoi and the other officials. It was the real director of the Attic state. Salaries for public office were abolished, substantially easing the burden on the Treasury. The fall of the democracy marks a deep caesura in Athenian constitutional life. The Cleisthenean political order was set aside; Athens had become an oligarchy. Whether or not it was politically wise to change the constitution at this critical point in time was a question that only the future could answer. There were serious difficulties on Samos, where an oligarchic revolution had also broken out. It was not supported by the mass of the Athenian naval crews present there, and was suppressed by them with no great difficulty.

The instability of conditions on Samos is shown by Alcibiades' election as strategos by the naval forces there. The man's dazzling personality, the deteriorating military situation, the uneasy political conditions at home in Athens—all these probably help to explain why the sailors threw themselves into Alcibiades' arms. To Alcibiades, the form of government at Athens was basically not very important; the new Council of the Four Hundred, however, was a thorn in his flesh. He demanded its elimination and the restoration of the old Cleisthenean Council of the Five Hundred. As a consequence the ground under the Athenian oligarchs' feet began to tremble. One of their leaders, Phrynichus, was slain. Eventually the oligarchs and democrats arrived at a compromise: the rule of the 5,000 was to be preserved, and from their number a new council was to be elected. Further failures in the various theaters of war, particularly the loss of the cities on the Hellespont, as well as of the rich island of Thasos, and finally Euboea, which was completely indispensable for the feeding of Athens—all these events contributed decisively to the downfall of the oligarchs in Athens.

From now on all decisions lay with the 5,000 citizens who alone were allowed to equip themselves with weapons. They elected a council of four hundred members, divided into four sections, whose task it was to dispatch current business. All the top officials of the state came from the membership of this council. Furthermore a commission was formed to record the current laws of Athens, a task, however, which it fulfilled only inadequately and with great waste of time. The new constitution gave decisive power to the Council of Four Hundred, which must be regarded as the actual ruler of Athens at this time. Thanks to the moderation of Theramenes, the ideological leader of the oligarchs, the change of the constitution took place without any violence.

The energy with which Athens, sorely beset, roused itself once more to resume the war at whatever cost deserves our admiration even today. Alcibiades' help was, of course, again available, and he dealt the Peloponnesians two bitter naval defeats, at Abydos in the autumn of 411 and at Cyzicus in May, 410. The losses at Cyzicus in particular caused the Spartans rather unexpectedly to ask for peace (summer, 410). Sparta went so far as to offer the Athenians peace on the basis of each side's retaining territorial control of what it held at that time. It was prepared to evacuate Decelea in return for Pylos and Cythera. To be sure, it would have been hard for Athens to renounce control over all the cities that had defected since the resumption of the war, but better terms could not reasonably be expected; and Athens would still have emerged from a war she had so arbitrarily unleashed with a very considerable sphere of influence: Samos and Lesbos, the Cyclades and the Thracian Chersonese, and a number of lesser possessions.

As a result of the victories on the Hellespont, however, the democratic party in Athens had returned to power. Its leader was Cleophon, a lyre-manufacturer. The rule of the 5,000 was at an end, and democracy was introduced once more. Theramenes, who had won a great deal of credit in connection with the settlement between the democrats and the oligarchs, had previously sailed off to Ionia at the head of a naval squadron. With that the oligarchic interlude was over. From July, 410, sessions of the Council of Five Hundred were resumed, and the juries of the popular courts also took up their activities as though nothing of importance had happened either in domestic affairs or in the theaters of war. The citizens pledged themselves to the democratic constitution by a special, and compulsory, oath, laid down by a decree introduced by Demophantus. As for salaries—no democracy without salaries! Cleophon reintroduced them for members of the Council and the courts. In addition, there was a payment of two obols to each citizen not otherwise entitled to the *diaitai,* the expense allowances. It can be imagined how these measures further worsened the already strained financial situation of the Attic state.

The great day of the newly resurrected Athenian democracy came at the June Festival of the Plynteriai for the year 408. On this day Alcibiades returned to his native city, which had prepared for him a triumphal reception. Everything that he had done to his Attic homeland was forgotten; no one spoke any longer of his treason; the curses that had been pronounced against him were retracted; the stones on which the verdict against him had been inscribed were smashed; he was compensated for his confiscated property by the state. The Athenian people entrusted to him the supreme command of the land and naval forces. He became, in other words, a kind of generalissimo (*hegemon autokrator:* Xenophon, *Hellenica,* I, 4, 20). But the hopes that his return had aroused were based on wishful thinking; they stood in sharp contradiction to Athens' real situation.

On the Spartan side, Alcibiades now faced an opponent who was not only his match but in many respects his superior. Lysander had devoted his energies all his life to the service of his country. Born in humble circumstances, he possessed, like Alcibiades, the ability to draw men to himself and make them serviceable to his designs. Moreover he was completely incorruptible, a quality that in a Greek deserves special mention. A further misfortune for Athens was a change that now took place in Persian policy. Darius II decided to end the seesaw policy between Athens and Sparta; its author, the satrap Tissaphernes, was removed from Sardis and compensated with the satrapy of Caria. His place in western Asia Minor was taken by the Great King's second son, the younger Cyrus, who from now on, as supreme commander (*karanos*) of all Persian forces in Asia Minor, and as satrap of Sardis, intervened tirelessly in Greek affairs. The collaboration of Cyrus with Lysander soon brought Athens to the edge of the abyss. The Spartans, with the aid of the Persian subsidies, were now in a position to pay their ships' crews a salary of four obols to the Athenians' three. When Lysander won a victory at Notium in the spring of 407 over one of Alcibiades' subordinate officers, Alcibiades was finished. He had been unable to work the miracle that the Athenians expected of him; he was relieved of his command. He betook himself to his private possessions in the Thracian Chersonese, there to lead the life of a great independent lord. Still exiled by the Athenians at the war's end, and having nothing more to hope for from Sparta, he fled to the court of Pharnabazus, satrap of Dascyleum, who, at the instigation of Lysander, had him put to death in the autumn of 404.

In 406 Athens once again assembled a great fleet. To make this possible even the votive offerings in the Parthenon were not spared. In August, 406, the Athenians were actually victorious at Arginusae, an island group in the sound between Lesbos and Asia Minor. However this was Athens' last great naval victory. The Spartan Admiral Callicratidas fell, and seventy of his ships were taken by the Athenians, but because a storm suddenly arose from the north, the Athenians were not able to rescue their own shipwrecked sailors. For this the six Athenian strategoi in command were brought to trial, not in the regular courts but in the Assembly, and, in a proceeding that was a mockery of all justice, were condemned to death and executed. One of the six was Pericles, son of Pericles and Aspasia. Even if the strategoi and their lieutenants did not do everything possible to rescue the sailors who were drifting on the wreckage, the verdict was still unjust; with it, the Athenian democracy had passed sentence on itself. The delusion of the Athenian leaders, especially Cleophon, is also shown by the fact that a renewed offer of peace from Sparta was summarily rejected.

The final blow came with the Athenian defeat at Aegospotami ("the goat rivers") on the Thracian Chersonese (Gallipoli) in the summer of 405. At this place Lysander surprised and destroyed the beached Athenian ships and their crews. The 3,000 Athenian prisoners were brought to Lampsacus and executed, a horribly bloody deed for which Lysander bears full responsibility. His justification was that this was in retribution for Athenian atrocities.

When the news of the defeat arrived, Athens was placed on a defense footing. Lysander appeared with his fleet before the harbor of Piraeus, and in Attica the Peloponnesian army under King Pausanias joined forces with the garrison of the fort of Decelea. The blockade was total; provisions in Athens were soon running short, and negotiators were sent to the Peloponnesians. But only after the Athenians had got rid of Cleophon, and Theramenes had joined the negotiators in his place, were they able to come to terms with the Peloponnesians.

To Sparta's credit it must be said that it resolutely resisted

193

the demands of its vengeful allies, especially the Corinthians, for the complete destruction of Athens. The Spartans' terms were, however, anything but lenient. The Long Walls and the walls of the Piraeus were to be torn down; in short the fortifications of Athens were to be completely destroyed. All warships, with the exception of twelve, had to be surrendered. Exiles were to be permitted to return. All overseas possessions, even the long-standing cleruchies of Lemnos, Imbros, and Skyros, were to be evacuated. With the acceptance of this peace treaty, in April, 404, Athens abdicated as a great power. It had not only lost its rule over the maritime confederacy, but had also been forced to renounce the cleruchies, the Attic citizen colonies overseas, and moreover was obliged to join the Peloponnesian League and render the Spartans military service. We read in Xenophon (*Hellenica,* II, 2, 23): "After the acceptance of the peace terms by the Athenians, Lysander entered the Piraeus with the fleet, the exiles returned, and the walls were joyfully torn down to the music of girl flute players, for people believed that with this day freedom for Greece had begun."

9

The Greeks of the West in the Fifth Century B.C.

As Athens' day was drawing to a close, a new danger appeared in Sicily. This was Carthage which, after its defeat at Himera in 480, had for seventy years refrained from any intervention in Sicilian affairs, though it still held some bases in the western part of the island. It was the Elymians of Segesta, involved in a struggle with the city of Selinus, who called on the aid of the Carthaginians in 409. With this Carthaginian intervention a new age began for the island; the struggle of the Siceliotes with the Carthaginians was to last more than a lifetime. The great adversary of the Carthaginians was the tyrant Dionysius I of Syracuse, whose reign was the high point in the history of the Western Greek world.

Between the fall, in 466, of the ruling dynasty of Syracuse, the Deinomenids, and the beginning of Athens' Sicilian Expedition in 415 lies a half-century of political history that saw changes of the first importance in the West. In many of the major Sicilian cities, the era of the tyrants was followed by a period of internal dissension. Severe conflicts broke out in various Greek cities with the mercenaries who had previously been the military mainstay of tyranny. In Syracuse, the rule of the tyrants was followed by a democracy (the view that the tyranny was replaced by the rule of the *Camoroi,* or landed nobility, is not correct), and in imitation of Attic ostracism, the institution of *petalismos* was established. The word is derived from *petalon* (leaf), the name of the person to be banished being written on an olive leaf. Democracies were also established in Messana and Rhegium, while in Acragas Empedocles exercised a powerful influence on his fellow citizens, not only as a philosopher but also as a statesman. Hand in hand with the strengthening of democratic movements went the development of formal oratory (Gorgias of Leontini).

But the fifty years between the fall of the old tyrannies and the appearance of the Athenians in Sicily also saw an enormous liberation of artistic energy. Many cities were adorned with splendid temples, in particular the city of Acragas where the construction of the shrines at the south wall was still in progress when the Carthaginians began their attack on the city. It was the same in Selinus. On the whole, the cultural efforts of the tyrants were continued successfully in this period, the necessary funds coming mostly from the intensive trade of the cities with Carthage as well as with Italy and Greece proper.

An event of great historical interest was the revolt of Ducetius. Here for the first time, the indigenous Sicels reacted against the Greeks. Until now, the native population had been silently reconciled to Greek rule. That it ceased to be so is to be attributed to dissension among the Greek cities between 460 and 440. Ducetius, the leader of the Sicels, caused a great deal of trouble for the Greeks. His headquarters was at Palici, where there was a famous temple of the Palikoi, revered as the protective gods of the Sicels. It appears that the full extent of the danger was only gradually recognized by the Greek cities; otherwise it would be difficult to understand why Syracuse and Acragas did not unite against Ducetius until almost 450. He was eventually defeated in the field and, no longer feeling safe among his own disappointed countrymen, turned to the Syracusans, who sent him out of the country to Corinth. But Ducetius returned once more and attempted to establish a settlement at Caleacte on the northern coast of Sicily. The result was tension between Acragas and Syracuse, for it is possible that the Syracusans not only approved his

196

plans for the colony but may even have fostered them. But in 440/439 Ducetius died.

His attempt to unite the indigenous Sicels was paralleled in Italy. Here, too, in the course of the fifth century there was a gradual awakening of the native peoples. In 473 the Tarentines suffered a severe defeat at the hands of the Iapygians and the Messapians, in a battle that Herodotus describes as the greatest blood-bath ever inflicted on Greeks. Moreover, in 421 the rich Greek city of Cyme (Cumae) in Campania fell to the Italic Samnites; part of the Greek population found refuge in Neapolis (Naples). We know very little about these events in Italy, since the sources report them only occasionally. These developments, however, are significant, for they show that the Greek element in these regions was on the defensive.

After the defeat of the Athenians' Sicilian Expedition, Syracuse sent a strong naval contingent to aid the Peloponnesians. In command was the Syracusan Hermocrates. But there were no great successes; on the contrary, many of the ships were destroyed in the battle of Cyzicus. Even after the year 413 fighting continued in Sicily, particularly at Catana, to which a small part of the Athenian army had fought its way, and where they continued to offer the Syracusans resistance.

The vanguard of the Carthaginians, which had begun to press the Greeks on Sicilian soil in 409, was followed in 408 by a large army composed of Carthaginians, Libyans, and mercenaries from all over the world. Within a short time Selinus was subdued, and Himera suffered the same fate. In both cities the Carthaginians were guilty of severe excesses, the Greek prisoners of Himera being put to death by the Carthaginian commander Hannibal as a sacrifice for his dead grandfather. Finally in the winter of 406–405 Acragas, too, had to be evacuated by the Greeks. In the fighting over this city the Syracusan commander Daphnaeus had shown little skill, so that together with his colleagues in office he was formally deposed.

In Syracuse a party came to power which was led by Hipparinus and Philistus (later a historian). These men were

197

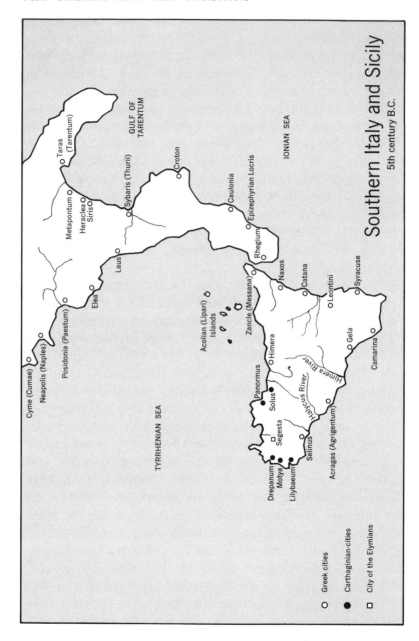

Southern Italy and Sicily
5th century B.C.

Greek cities ○
Carthaginian-cities ●
City of the Elymians ☐

responsible for the rise of the young Dionysius, who, using the position of strategos with plenary powers as a springboard, succeeded in taking full control of the state (405). Surrounding himself with a bodyguard, he took possession of the city and deliberately resumed the policy of Hermocrates (who had died in 407), marrying his daughter. Dionysius is one of the outstanding figures not only of Sicilian but of all Greek history. The historian Timaeus has portrayed him as a large and powerful man with reddish-blond hair and a freckled face. Dionysius' success was due not only to his boldness and decisiveness but also to the difficult situation of his native city, a situation that called for more than normal measures.

But quite unexpectedly—thanks to an epidemic that broke out in their army—the Carthaginians were ready for peace. The peace was signed in 405 on the basis of each side retaining what it held at this time. This meant that Carthage not only had secured a foothold in Sicily but now held practically half of the island. In addition to its old domain, which included the cities of Motya, Panormus (Palermo), and Solus, the Elymian and Sicanian peoples had now come under a Carthaginian protectorate. Inhabitants of the Greek cities that had been conquered by the Carthaginians—Selinus, Himera, Acragas, Gela, and Camarina—were allowed to return on condition that they pay tribute to their Carthaginian masters. In the eastern part of the island Leontini and Messana were to be autonomous. Dionysius was recognized as lord of Syracuse. The Peace of 405 is of special significance not only because it established Carthaginian rule over half the island, but also because it recognized the independence of all Sicels. This was a heavy blow to the Greeks, especially to the Syracusans.

In 406 the Athenians had attempted to establish ties with the Carthaginians in Sicily, efforts which are probably related to the appearance of a Carthaginian mission in Athens at the beginning of that year. A fragmentary inscription indicates that the Athenians sought a formal alliance with Carthage (Bengtson, *Staatsvertraege,* No. 208). Nothing, however, came of the attempt.

Both in the Eastern and the Western Greek world, the course of history was determined at this time by the power of one great personality. In the East it was the Spartan Lysander who subdued Athens and forced her to sue for peace. The heights to which Lysander had risen is shown by the monument that he had erected in Delphi after his victory at Aegospotami. This was called the Hall of Lysander, with no less than thirty-seven statues immortalizing the Dioscuri, Zeus, Apollo, Artemis, Poseidon, Lysander himself, and thirty of his helpers who had had a decisive share in the victory. Lysander was paid semidivine honors by the Samians.

In Syracuse things had not yet gone so far; but the young Dionysius, not yet thirty years of age, had, with unparalleled energy, improved his position in the city. Ortygia, also known as Nasos (the "island"), was tranformed into a fortress and shut off from the rest of the city by a high wall. The residence of Dionysius, the Acropolis, was built on the isthmus that linked Nasos with the city. An important revision of the citizenship laws was decreed, and partial redistribution of land. A great many slaves were set free, and these, together with Dionysius' friends and the mercenaries, were the strongest pillars of his rule. This unprecedented social realignment is the background to the whole later political history of Syracuse, and of Sicily as a whole. Naturally these changes were not carried out without resistance on the part of the citizens of Syracuse. A mutiny of the hoplites attacking the Sicel city of Herbessus developed into a general revolt of the Syracusans, which brought Dionysius, besieged in Ortygia, to the verge of ruin. Not until Campanian mercenaries came to his aid was he able to subdue the rebellion. The Spartans also played a role; the surrender of Athens left them free to intervene in Syracuse, and Sparta intervened on the side of Dionysius; in so doing, she not only reversed her traditional policy of enmity toward tyrants, but paid homage to the greatness of the man. In return, Dionysius became the Spartans' loyal ally from then on (spring of 403).

10

Sparta's Hegemony and
the Corinthian War (404–386 B.C.)

The capitulation of Athens in April, 404, marked the end of the Peloponnesian War. Samos continued to resist the Peloponnesians for a short time, until she, too, opened her gates to Lysander in the summer of 404. The victory of the Peloponnesians was complete; Lysander was the most important man in all Greece. To be sure, victory had been gained only with the aid of the Persians; Persian gold had played a decisive part in the downfall of Athens and its maritime confederacy. The Spartans now replaced Athens as overlord of the cities of the former maritime league. Everywhere the partisans of Athens were expelled and oligarchic constitutions were installed. For the individual cities Lysander appointed commissions of ten men (decarchies) which, together with the Spartan military commanders (harmosts), exercised full power over the lives of the inhabitants.

After a short time this Spartan system of rule provoked an enormous hatred of the Lacedaemonians, and many cities that had willingly changed over to the Spartan camp now longed for the former rule of the Athenians. There could be no illusion of real autonomy for the individual states; what Lysander prescribed was law. In many places the grim Spartans added outrage to unpopularity. On the island of Thasos, for example, the Spartans' opponents were lured out of their asylums in the temples and, in violation of the promises given them, were put to death. In the former area of the maritime confederacy, at any rate, the state of affairs was far removed from freedom. Lysander had, in reality, established a military dictatorship. A few thousand Spartans ruled over a million or more subjects. Sparta, exactly like Athens, imposed a tribute, reportedly in the amount of 1,000 talents a year.

It is true that our knowledge of Spartan rule after 404 is based mainly on the Attic rhetorician Isocrates, whose anti-Spartan bias is perfectly clear. But even taking this into account, the individual facts still speak against the Spartans and, above all, against Lysander. With the elimination of Athens, Greece had lost its most important trade center. This had crippling effects on the exchange of goods and on the provisioning of the cities. Piracy reappeared on the seas, a nuisance that Athens had previously rooted out almost completely. The result was uncertainty on the seas and higher cargo rates, consequently higher prices in Greek markets.

Athens, too, was affected by the general reaction against Spartan rule. The peace treaty stipulated that in Athens "the constitution of the fathers" (*patrios politeia*) was to be restored. With Lysander's support, the oligarchs in Athens tried to interpret this concept in their own way. Under the protection of the Spartan garrison on the Acropolis, the oligarchs, led by Critias, Plato's uncle, established a ruthless reign of terror in Athens. We read of full-fledged proscriptions, to which a large number of citizens—reportedly 500, as well as many metics—fell victim. Even Theramenes, who had mediated again between the democrats and the oligarchs, was put to death by Critias. All power in Athens lay in the hands of thirty men, who were popularly known as the "Thirty Tyrants." But in one of the most glorious actions of Athenian history, many citizens living abroad in exile now risked their lives to bring the Thirty's reign of terror to an end. At the head of this courageous band stood Thrasybulus. He first laid siege to the fortress of Phyle on the heights of Mount Parnes, and from there advanced toward Athens, not even hesitating to engage the Spartan garrison in battle. The Piraeus and the fort of Munychia fell to him. Critias was killed in the street fighting. (The excavations in the Athenian cemetery at the *kerameikos* have uncovered the graves of the Spartans who fell in this fighting; there were thirteen in all, some of them slain by arrows.) The Thirty were now replaced by an Assembly of 3,000 citizens, who set up a committee of ten men chosen from among themselves to draw up a constitution. But not all citizens approved the new course of events. The confirmed oligarchs left Athens and founded a separate community in Eleusis hostile to the resurrected Attic democracy.

Athens, on the verge of civil war, was saved by the Spartan King Pausanias, who brought about a reconciliation between the two parties in September, 403. This was in the term of the eponymous archon Eucleides (403–402), which also saw the introduction of the Ionic alphabet for the inscription of public documents. Henceforth, Ionic replaced the archaic Attic alphabet on public and soon on private inscriptions. Under Eucleides, an amnesty was decreed also for all but the most gravely incriminated oligarchs, members of the administration of the Thirty Tyrants. Full unity was, however, not achieved until 401–400, when the separate oligarchic state of Eleusis was reunited with Athens.

Pausanias' conduct toward the Athenians was hardly compatible with Lysander's policy of force. We may be almost certain that in Sparta a party had now gained power that strongly disapproved of the policy of Lysander. Sparta, in fact, could not afford to continue to ignore the outcries against Lysander that came to her from every quarter. Lysander fell from power, and with him the decarchies that he had established in the dependent cities. Sparta had now abandoned his policy—too late, for it had already aroused almost the whole of Greece against Spartan leadership. Public opinion was no longer on the side of the Spartans. With Lysander's fall, Sparta's policy of rule by force collapsed, and there was a return to the traditional Peloponnesian policy. A special problem, of course, was the status of the Greek cities of Asia Minor. In return for Persian financial aid, the Lacedaemonians had surrendered them to the Persian King, which did not particularly add to Sparta's prestige. From this time on, the fourth-century Greeks were repeatedly challenged by the problem of the freedom of the Greek cities of Asia Minor.

The Persians wisely refrained for the time from availing themselves of their rights in the Greek cities of Asia Minor. The result was a state of suspended activity that lasted several years. The reason for the Persian's behavior is obvious. The empire had to contend, as so often before, with internal difficulties and tensions. These become visible in the Anabasis (expedition into the interior) of the younger Cyrus (401–400 B.C.).

Darius II had died in the spring of 404. He was succeeded by his eldest son, Arsaces, who, under the name of Artaxerxes II, reigned for more than forty years (404 to 359–358). The new king, to whom the Greeks gave the surname Mnemon, took over a difficult inheritance. In 405, a rebellion had broken out in northern Egypt. Its leader, Amyrtaeus, ruled Egypt for six years, but even after his death Egypt remained independent, and could not be subdued again until 343–342. The loss of this rich grainland was extremely serious for the Persians, and it is not surprising that repeated attempts were made to suppress the Egyptian rebellion (see p. 347).

If the Greek sources are to be credited, Artaxerxes II had come to the throne over the opposition of his mother, who favored her younger son Cyrus. The two sons were very dissimilar and had been enemies from their youth. Cyrus is said to have made an unsuccessful attempt on the life of his elder brother; Artaxerxes, however, permitted him to return to his previous position as satrap of Sardis. The Persian Empire was by this time anything but a unified state. Some of the satraps were declared enemies, and waged regular wars among themselves. For example, Cyrus warred against Tissaphernes, the issue in this case being possession of the wealthy Greek city of Miletus. Only when the existence of the Empire was put in question did the Great King bother to interfere in these conflicts. In the fighting among the satraps the Greek mercenaries played an important role; unemployed after the end of the Peloponnesian War, they were easily hired for good wages everywhere.

The Anabasis of Cyrus the Younger, his expedition to Babylonia in an attempt to replace his brother by force of arms, is essentially an event of Persian history. But because many Greek mercenaries took part, particularly those from the Peloponnese, and because a firsthand account of the campaign was written by the Athenian Xenophon, the event also belongs to Greek history. The Spartans sent Cyrus an auxiliary corps under Cheirisophus, although they later tried to deny this. The fighting ability of the Greek hoplites cowed the enemy troops; the Anabasis would undoubtedly have achieved its goal had not Cyrus the Younger been killed in the decisive battle of Cunaxa in Babylonia in the autumn of 401. With that, the campaign had lost its purpose. The Greeks' return march from Babylonia, through the inhospitable mountains of Armenia to the Black Sea, which they reached at Trapezus in March, 400, is justly regarded as one of the most brilliant feats of Greek military history. The courage of the Greeks was more than equal to the difficult terrain and the rigors of the climate. Xenophon's *Anabasis* offers, especially in the final books, a mine of materials for the history of civilization, as well as for the history of warfare. It informs us of the customs and usages of the peoples of Armenia and Anatolia, and describes the condition of the remote Greek cities on the Black Sea, all with a vividness that does honor to Xenophon as a writer. It is no wonder that his narrative of the march of the 10,000 Greeks (actually there were over 13,000, of whom 8,600 returned) overshadowed other accounts, such as that of Sophainetus of Stymphalus.

The Spartans had now decided to give up the policy of Lysander, but the decisive reasons for this were not necessarily considerations of prestige. More important was the realization by Sparta's political leaders that there were not enough Spartan troops to maintain a system that had aroused opposition over all Greece. If we consider that the total number of Spartiate citizens was only 2,000 in 402, and that all others were either Helots, Perioeci, Hypomeiones (citizens with lesser rights), or Neodamodai (Helots who had been raised to a higher status), we can see why, in 398, Cinadon tried to have the citizen roll enlarged by admitting Perioeci and Helots. But the attempt failed, and Cinadon, whose proposal would have destroyed the existing order of the state, was executed.

The Greeks of Asia Minor then approached Sparta with a request for aid against the Persians. With the return of Tissaphernes to Asia Minor—where he took over the position of Cyrus the Younger—the Ionian question entered on a new stage. Tissaphernes attempted to make the Greek cities subject, in fact as well as in theory; he was, without question, entitled to do so on the basis of the Spartan-Persian treaties of 412–411. But could Sparta, the leading power in Greece, the victor over Athens, allow the Greeks in Asia Minor to be surrendered to barbarians? If Sparta failed to answer the Ionians' call, she would be abdicating her position as a hegemonial power; she would have shown to all the world that she was unable and unwilling to take over Athens' role as protectress of the Anatolian Greeks.

Sparta undertook the liberation of Asia Minor with very small forces: a thousand Neodamodai, 4,000 Peloponnesians, and 300 Athenian cavalry were all that she sent out to Ionia. This Spartan-Persian War in Asia Minor (397–394) was waged with very small forces on both sides. However, the superiority of the Spartans—who had drawn to themselves the remainder of Cyrus' 10,000—soon became clear. The Persian satraps Tissaphernes and Pharnabazus avoided major battles, so that the Spartan commanders, first Thibron and later Dercylidas, had an easy time of it. A turning point in the war came when the Persians, acting on the advice of the Athenian Conon, resolved to seek a decision not in a land battle but by sea. Conon, after the battle of Aegospotami, had not returned to Athens; instead he had found refuge at the court of the Greek Prince Evagoras of Salamis on Cyprus. So it was on Cyprus, in secrecy, that the keels were laid for a great Persian fleet. For a long time the Spartans were ignorant of what lay in store for them, until by chance they got wind of the Persians' naval preparations from a Syracusan merchant who had been trading in Phoenicia.

Meanwhile, in 396, the Spartan King Agesilaus (who had reached the throne with Lysander's help) crossed over with an army from Euboea to Ephesus. In 395 he won a major victory over the Persian cavalry at Sardis. The Persians tried to delay Agesilaus' progress by diplomatic negotiations, especially after Tissaphernes was replaced as satrap by Tithraustes. For the Persians, the war was one of no great importance; it was a frontier war, the conduct of which the Great King left to his satraps in Asia Minor.

Little is known about operations in the naval war after 396. Xenophon, in his *Greek History*, passes over the naval war completely, perhaps in order to improve the luster of his hero Agesilaus' actions in the land war in Asia Minor. In reality, however, the decisive battle was fought not on land but at sea, at Cnidus, in the beginning of August, 394. Cyprian, Rhodian, and Phoenician ships, under the command of the Athenian Conon and the Persian Pharnabazus, won a decisive victory over the Spartan nauarch Peisander. At Cnidus the Spartan maritime empire, after a life of almost exactly ten years, ceased to exist. All the islands off the western coast of Asia Minor were lost, from Cos in the south to Lesbos in the north. The Greek cities of Asia Minor also deserted Sparta in large numbers, many of them opening their gates to the Persians without further ado. So great was the Persians' strength at sea that their fleet was able to raid the coasts of Greece, where it had not been seen since Xerxes' invasion of 480.

On setting out for Asia, Agesilaus had intended to present a sacrifice in Aulis, but was turned away by the Boeotarchs, the leading magistrates of Boeotia (396). This was the first sign of Boeotian hostility toward Sparta. The behavior of the Boeotarchs is an indication of the prevalent mood in the states of central Greece. They were anything but content with Sparta and her policy; the Spartan victory over Athens had brought them little or no benefit. Their disaffection was stirred up further by the Persians, whose emissaries traveled through Greece, paying hard currencies to incite the Hellenes of mainland Greece against Sparta. One of these Persian agents was Timocrates of Rhodes. He operated on behalf of the satrap Pharnabazus of Dascyleum in Thebes, Corinth, Argos, and Athens, and was unsparing in his use of Persian gold.

In 395, war had again broken out in Greece. It stemmed from a quarrel between the Phocians and the Locrians (whether the Ozolian or the Opuntian Locrians is not clear). The Locrians, in any case, were the aggressors, and had the support of Thebes, while the Phocians turned to Sparta for aid. Athens intended to risk nothing vital in this conflict, but in the beginning it sided with Thebes. The text of the defensive alliance (which was to last in perpetuity) has been partly preserved (Bengtson, *Staatsvertraege,* No. 233). It is hardly to be doubted that here, too, Persian gold played its part.

Sparta had little luck with its Boeotian campaign. The appointment of Lysander and King Pausanias as joint commanders proved to be a mistake, for the two men were unable to cooperate with one another. After a Boeotian victory in the battle of Haliartus (autumn of 395)—in which Lysander was killed—Pausanias evacuated Boeotian territory. Sparta was enraged at the King, who had withdrawn to safety in Tegea. Now only Agesilaus could help; with heavy hearts, the Spartans recalled him from Asia Minor. "Thirty thousand Persian archers," * Agesilaus is supposed to have said, "drove me out of Asia Minor." The Persian navy controlled the seas; Agesilaus had to return to Greece by the arduous land route through Thrace. He therefore arrived too late for the battle of the Nemean brook near Corinth in July, 394; but he took part in the battle of Coronea in the following month, and contributed to the Spartan victory there. The victory was not decisive, however, as the enemy coalition remained in being. Thus, the war in Greece continued, though without major pitched battles.

For Athens, too, brighter days were approaching. In the spring (or summer) of 393, Conon, the victor of the battle of Cnidus, returned to his country. His native city honored him in a striking manner; Athens erected a bronze statue to him

---

* On the Persian coins the Great King was represented as an archer in a kneeling position.

"because he had brought freedom to the Athenians' allies." It was the first time since the tyrannicides that a statue had been erected in honor of a mortal man at Athens. Furthermore, Conon received the *ateleia* (privilege of freedom from taxes), for he had brought back to the Athenians something more than glory; he had brought back Persian funds sufficient to allow the rebuilding of the Long Walls and the walls ringing the Piraeus.

It was during this time that the old Attic cleruchies of Lemnos, Imbros, and Skyros were recovered; these were vital for supplying the surplus Attic population with land. Under the protection of Conon's fleet, Athens prepared to reestablish her ties with a number of the Aegean islands. Alliances were concluded with some that had formerly been members of the Delian League, such as Eteocarpathus, Cos, Cnidus, Rhodes, and also Mytilene on Lesbos and Chios. It is even possible that Athens, at this time, again allied herself with the Greek cities of Asia Minor (Xenophon, *Hellenica,* IV, 8, 12). Naturally, this is in no way a formal restoration of the old Attic maritime empire.

All these alliances were possible only with the Persians' assent, or at least with their tacit toleration. Conon, moreover, was anything but a first-rate statesman; he was long on imagination, short on sense. One of his ideas, for example, was to bring about an alliance between Evagoras of Cyprus and Dionysius I of Syracuse, a fantastic plan which was hopeless from the start, and which foundered under the Carthaginian attacks on Sicily.

The Greeks of the homeland were nevertheless beginning to realize that unity was the prerequisite of power. This is shown by the political union of Corinth and Argos in 392, an event unique in Greek history. Here, for the first time so far as we know, the boundaries of the city-state were swept away. Even the stone markers on the border between the two states were torn out of the ground. But this dual state was not long-lived; six years later it was dissolved by the terms of the King's Peace. In the same year that this union was founded (392), Athens for the first time began to put out peace feelers. A delegation went to Sparta, and among its members was the rhetorician Andocides, armed with special plenipotentiary powers. In his "Peace Oration"—which was the report he delivered on his return—Andocides, for the first time, publicly expounded the idea of the *koine eirene,* that is, the idea of a general Greek peace which was to play a significant role in Greek history in the rest of the fourth century.

Indeed, every intelligent man must by now have realized that the Greeks' incessant wars among themselves could not go on indefinitely. Hellas was divided into two camps. On one side were Sparta and its allies—those few who had remained loyal to Sparta. On the other side were Sparta's opponents: Thebes, Athens, Corinth, Argos, and the rest. Trade in general was at a standstill; the recovery of the economy after the great Peloponnesian War had now bogged down, the seas were unsafe, and even communications with Sicily were disturbed by the new Carthaginian War. It was fateful that Sparta, in order to save its hegemony, now fell back on an idea that it had put forward during the Peloponnesian War and that, in later years, decisively contributed to the downfall of the Greek political order. Sparta demanded that all Greek poleis be free and autonomous. To secure the aid of the Persians in this, the Spartans did not even shrink from formally surrendering the Greeks of Asia Minor to the Great King. But the Athenians protested against the betrayal of their Ionian brothers; the peace congress that convened in Sardis in 392, under the presidency of the Persian satrap Tiribazus, therefore achieved nothing. Tiribazus, the satrap of Lydia, had favored the Spartans, and thereby lost the Great King's trust and was relieved of his post; his place was taken by Autophradates. The Ionian cities were detached from the Lydian satrapy and constituted as a new satrapy under the satrap Struthas; Caria was given to the dynast Hecatomnus of Mylasa. Clearly the Great King was determined to eliminate, once and for all, the commanding position of the satrap of Sardis.

The years 391 and 390 were years of misfortune for Sparta. In 391 a new Spartan expedition came to grief in Asia Minor;

the Spartan Thibron fell into an ambush laid by the satrap Struthas and was destroyed together with 8,000 men. The following year Athenian light-armed infantry (peltasts), in cooperation with hoplites, under the command of the Athenian mercenary general Iphicrates, surprised a Spartan regiment (*mora*) at Lechaeum in the vicinity of Corinth. This was a heavy blow to Sparta, which lost no less than 250 Spartiates, an irrecoverable diminution of her waning citizen population.

Athens, on the other hand, gained surprising successes at sea. They were won by Thrasybulus, the leader who had restored the Athenian democracy. Athens once more sought to reestablish her rule over the Hellespont and the Bosporus. Byzantium was won and the Athenians resumed their alliance with Chalcedon, but they were unable to expel the Spartans from their strongpoints in Sestos and Abydos on the Hellespont. The successes of Thrasybulus were nevertheless considerable. Besides Thasos and Samothrace, he had in the spring of 389 won Lesbos, Halicarnassus, and Clazomenae. In addition, he imposed a ten percent toll on all goods shipped through the Bosporus. Again, one cannot speak of a restoration of the Delian League. The successes of Thrasybulus were of too transitory a nature; they were made possible only by the weakness of Spartan naval power broken by her defeat at Cnidus.

Thrasybulus' exit from the scene is a sign of the usual weakness of the Athenian demos, inconstancy. Summoned back to Athens to answer for his actions, Thrasybulus refused to obey and continued to act on his own in the Aegean. On a money-raising expedition in remote Pamphylia, on the southern coast of Asia Minor, he met his death at the hands of the people of the city of Aspendus (388), outraged by the violence of his troops. His death was a severe loss to Athens. As a convinced democrat he had twice performed the greatest services for his native city; in 411, in Samos, he had stood out resolutely for Attic democracy; in 404–403, he had liberated Athens from her oligarchic oppressors. To be sure, he was quite human. He was anything but altruistic in money matters; complaints against his extortions were only too justified. His name, nevertheless, is forever linked with the resurgence of Athens after the disasters of the Peloponnesian War.

Meanwhile, in Sparta, it was becoming obvious that a clear decision could not be reached in the struggle against her main Greek opponents—Argos, Boeotia, and Athens. The time was ripe for peace negotiations. Significantly, these negotiations were initiated not in Greece but by the Persians. In Sardis, the satrap Struthas had been recalled and again replaced by Tiribazus. Tiribazus was a friend of the Spartans; the latter sent Antialcidas to Sardis to negotiate. Tiribazus and Antialcidas set out together on the long journey to Susa in order to learn the Great King's conditions for the conclusion of a peace treaty. These conditions were crushing for the opponents of Sparta; it was no wonder that they refused to accept them.

In Susa, peace was concluded between Sparta and the Persian Empire. To compel the rest of the Greeks to accept the Persian peace terms, the Spartans, with the help of a Syracusan naval contingent, stopped Athenian imports of grain from the Black Sea by a blockade of the Hellespont. Once food ran short in Athens, the Athenian demos too was ready for peace. In 387, a great peace congress assembled in Sardis, and emissaries from all the states that had taken part in the war were present. An imperial edict was read out, listing the conditions that Artaxerxes II had declared to Antialcidas at the beginning of 387. It read as follows:

> Artaxarxes the Great King deems it just that the cities of Asia Minor belong to him, and, of the islands, Clazomenae and Cyprus; that other Greek cities, large and small, be autonomous with the exception of Lemnos, Imbros, and Skyros, which, as of old, should belong to the Athenians. Whoever does not accept this peace, I shall make war upon him, together with those who agree [i.e. those agreeing to the peace], with ships and with money.

This document, which is preserved in Xenophon's *Hellenica*, V, 1, 31 (Bengtson, *Staatsvertraege*, No. 242), is fascinating evidence of the Persian King's political attitude and of Persian diplomacy. The man who gave the Greeks orders in this peremptory manner must have had a strong sense of his commanding position. Technically, the document is an extract from the Instrument of Peace that was agreed upon by Antialcidas and the Great King in Susa in 387. This extract had been reworked into the form of an edict of the Persian King, with the addition of a sanction formula in which all those who might refuse to accept the Peace were threatened with war. The King's Peace, or the Peace of Antialcidas (as it is called in Greek tradition), was accepted by the Greeks at the peace congress in Sparta that followed. This was solemnized by a "general peace," a *koine eirene,* to be seen as a side effect of the Peace of Antialcidas.

Among the losers were, without doubt, Thebes and Argos. On these states the principle of autonomy, as established by the King's Peace, had worse effects than on any of the others involved. Thebes lost her hegemony over the Boeotian League. Argos had to renounce her union with Corinth. Athens, on the other hand, got off relatively lightly. She was certainly better off than in 404, because she had her cleruchies back again. On the whole, however, the Peace was a sign of the ascendancy of the Persian Empire, which now achieved the height of its influence over Greece. No one in Hellas dared oppose the decree of the Great King, and Sparta had voluntarily sunk to the status of warder for the Persians. She pledged herself to see that the peace terms were carried out in Greece. The following decades of Greek history are an unrelieved display of Persian domination. With the acceptance of the King's Peace in 386, the Greeks including the Spartans, subjected themselves to the Persian King's command. The Colossus of the East had extended its sphere of influence to the Ionian Sea. In Greece it was the Persian party, supported by Persian gold, that gave the orders. A direct line leads from Conon to Antialcidas to the Theban Pelopidas. All three not only accepted Persian gold but also acted as agents of Persia's interests in Greece.

To be sure, the achievement of a general peace was some

213

progress. Though in the following years and decades there were still repeated wars in Hellas, the idea of a peace embracing all Greek wars was constantly taken up anew. It was the star of hope for a people who, more than almost any other in history, had had to suffer under the scourge of unending war.

11

The Decline of Greek Independence and the Idea of the General Peace (386–362 B.C.)

The quarter-century between the King's Peace (386) and the battle of Mantinea (362) sealed the fate of the city-state system in the Greek homeland. That system depended, for its survival, on the Greeks' capacity to turn themselves from a congeries of warring independent units into a nation, when threatened from without. In other words it depended on the Greek states' capacity to accept the leadership of one of their number in time of trouble. In Sicily, this was still possible. In Hellas, it was not. The clear need for national unity, as the only antidote to Persian interference in Greek affairs, produced no genuinely national hegemony in Greece. Leading states there were, but they did not lead the Greeks against the Persians; they led them against Greeks, with Persian encouragement. Sparta, for example, continued to exercise an ascendancy of sorts beyond the borders of the Peloponnese until 371, but this was possible only because the Persians permitted it, regarding the Spartans as their pawns. Much the same is true of the brief hegemony of the Boeotians from 371 to 362 B.C. Athens did succeed in again building up a maritime confederacy (378–377), but it was only a shadow of the Delian League; it, too, could not have been established without Persia's imperial assent.

The autonomy of the city-state, as proclaimed in the King's Peace, was decisive in perpetuating the instability of Greece. A parallel has occasionally been drawn to the "freedom" of the states of the Holy Roman Empire, as established by the Peace of Westphalia in the seventeenth century; the parallel is exact. But even more critical was the absence of genuinely commanding personalities from the Greek political scene. Agesilaus, despite his glorification by Xenophon, was only a mediocre figure; the Boeotian Epaminondas, however admirable his character, failed as a statesman because Boeotia, even with Persian support, was as unsuited to the role of a hegemonial power as any state possibly could be. In the Thessalian tyrant Jason of Pherae Greece did produce a man capable of national leadership, but Jason fell to a gang of assassins before he could carry out his plan for a war against Persia.

No wonder, then, that the idea of a general peace in Hellas now made more and more headway. The land was visited by incessant wars, most of which, as a result of the complex system of alliances, involved a large number of states. These wars brought misfortune and insecurity, paralyzed trade, and involved the individual states in enormous expenses, particularly for recruiting mercenaries, who more and more took the lead in the military affairs of Greece. A general peace was only possible, however, if the Persian King exerted sufficient pressure on the Greeks to adopt it, first through the Lacedaemonians, later through the Boeotians. But a peace by the grace of Persia was only a half-peace, and rightly voices were repeatedly raised against it in Greece. Isocrates, for example, pointed to Athens' glorious past, and saw in it a special obligation for leadership resting on his native city. But in a world that was increasingly open to the influence of money, national enthusiasm was a minor motif. There were too many politicians who were in contact with Persia, who did not object to accepting the "archers" of the Great King. Greece seemed to have sold her soul; no Greek seemed to know how to win it back again. It became more and more clear that the Greek polis did not possess the strength it needed to restore itself. A deliverer would have to come from outside, if ever there was to be a new age for the Greeks.

The first few years following the King's Peace were Sparta's, to do with as she wished. First of all, the Lacedaemonians made a clean sweep of opposition in the Peloponnese, doubtless on the advice of Agesilaus; the other King, Agesipolis, was still too young to exert any influence. To begin with, Mantinea was forced back into the Spartan alliance. In 418–417 Sparta and Mantinea had concluded a thirty-year peace treaty which had now expired. Sparta did not long delay an attack on Mantinea; this came in 385 or 384. The Spartans diverted the waters of the River Ophis against the walls of the city, softening the sun-dried bricks and eroding the foundations, so that the town had to capitulate. Mantinea was divided into five separate villages, each of which had to send its contingent to the army of the Peloponnesian League. No different was the treatment the Spartans gave the city of Phlius. For twenty months the inhabitants withstood a siege by Agesilaus before they were starved into surrender. The oligarchic party in Phlius, with Sparta's support, again took power in the city (379).

The last demonstration of fourth-century Spartan power was the Lacedaemonian intervention on the Chalcidice peninsula. Here, during the Archidamian War, many of the cities had formed a league with Olynthus as its capital. We are justified, perhaps, in viewing this as a true federal state; common federal institutions are known from the inscriptions. There was no doubt of the effect of this Chalcidian League on the balance of power; all the neighboring states, especially Macedonia, had to reckon with it. On an inscription now in Vienna (Bengtson, *Staatsvertraege,* No. 231) we find an alliance and a trade treaty between the Chalcidian League and Macedonia. The treaty was probably signed in 393, for a period of fifty years. The signatories promised mutual support in the event of an attack on either party; unfortunately, the remaining terms of the treaty have been lost. The Chalcidians were granted free access to pitch and wood from Macedonia for ship construction, but importation of the valuable white pinewood was permitted only for the League government's use. Each party pledged itself to conclude no alliances with a number of specified states without the consent of the other: Amphipolis, the Bottiaeans, Acanthus, and Mende (which shows us that none of these states were at that time members of the Chalcidian League). For the time being the Macedonians and the Chalcidians were on the best of terms. We know that in 393 a present of land was made to the Chalcidians by King Amyntas III. In other respects, too, the Macedonian-Chalcidian Treaty is instructive. It shows, among other things, that the King of Macedonia could sign a treaty on behalf of his country; in other words, modern theories that king and state in Macedonia were separate institutions are quite erroneous. The Chalcidian League's commanding position was shown when Amyntas III had to ask assistance against the Illyrians, who were overrunning large areas of Macedonia. Troops of the Chalcidian League occupied parts of Macedonia, especially lower Macedonia, and the League showed a definite reluctance to evacuate them once the war was over.

But northern cities, outside the League, among them Acanthus and Apollonia, called on Sparta to intervene in defense of their autonomy, threatened by the Chalcidians. True to its principle of the autonomy of individual states, Sparta intervened. A large force of the Peloponnesian League, no less than 10,000 men, was sent by the land route to northern Greece, and the Macedonian king lent the Lacedaemonians aid. The fighting, which took place mainly before Olynthus, the Chalcidian capital, lasted quite some time. The city was finally surrounded and forced to capitulate (379). The Chalcidian League was dissolved, and its individual cities forced to join the Peloponnesian League. Despite painful losses— Teleutias, the brother of Agesilaus, had fallen before Olynthus, and King Agesipolis had died of an illness—Sparta had shown her power. She had upheld the principle of autonomy, and broken an experiment in unity that might have developed great importance in the northern Aegean. Sparta, victorious over the Chalcidians, stood at the zenith of political and military prestige. But in the name of what cause? The principle of autonomy simply furthered the policy and power of the Great

King, and sapped the strength of the city-state system in Hellas.

In 382 Sparta had been guilty of an aggression that aroused the indignation of all Greece. When the Spartan force, on its march northward, reached Thebes, Leontiades, the leader of the Theban oligarchic party, approached the Spartan Phoebidas and offered to help put the Cadmea—the Acropolis of Thebes—into Spartan hands. The Spartan gladly agreed, occupied the citadel, and took the leader of the democratic party, Ismenias, into custody. There is an explanation for his behavior: Thebes had expressly refused military aid to the Spartans on their march to the Chalcidice, although she was obligated by the terms of her alliance to provide it. Even in Sparta opinion regarding this coup was divided; the ephors and the Spartan assembly, the Apella, were not at all delighted by Phoebidas' actions; Agesilaus considered them perfectly proper. He was wrong. Though Sparta had secured an important base, the moral damage caused by this outrage against autonomy, Sparta's own slogan, was irreparable. Sparta had acted against her word, and the several hundred Theban democrats who fled to Athens did not tire of pointing out the injustice that had been inflicted on their state.

Spartan rule in the year 379, then, extended from the southernmost tip of the Peloponnese to the Chalcidice. With Macedonia, Thessaly, and the Molossians in Epirus, Sparta was on as friendly terms as she was with the great tyrant Dionysius I of Syracuse. Sparta's alliance system spanned the whole of Greece; almost all of the Hellenic states were obligated to give the Spartans military service. Yet the foundations of Spartan supremacy were fragile. The number of full citizens continued to decline, and pro-Spartan sympathies had, for the most part, been replaced by the exact opposite. There were still, to be sure, Greeks who admired the old Spartan discipline and training. Evidence of this is to be found in the works of Xenophon, especially his *Constitution of the Lacedaemonians* (*Lakedaimonion politeia*), written toward the end of his life, probably about 360. But Xenophon could not return to Athens, because he had been exiled, probably for taking part in the battle of Coronea on the side of Sparta. He therefore lived at

Scillus, a small estate in Elis that Sparta had granted him, and wrote in praise of his benefactors.

Late in the year 379 the Greek world was stirred by a remarkable feat of daring. Seven Theban democrats, disguised as women, managed to slip into their native city and assassinate the leaders of Leontiades' oligarchic government. A second group of Thebans, supported by an Attic contingent under two strategoi, invaded the city in force. The commander of the Spartan garrison on the Cadmea lost his nerve and concluded a treaty with the democrats, agreeing to evacuate the Cadmea in return for the right of free withdrawal. Thebes was free— but the Spartans were not willing to be forced out of this important position at so low a price. The officers in command on the Cadmea were either executed or severely punished. The Spartan King Cleombrotus (who succeeded Agesipolis, fallen before the gates of Olynthus) marched to Boeotia with the army of the Peloponnesian League. But he was not equipped for a siege of Thebes, and therefore had to withdraw, leaving part of his army behind under the command of Sphodrias. Athens had obviously lent the Theban democrats not only moral but also military support. Sparta was well aware of this, and Sphodrias' attempt to take the Piraeus by surprise (378–377) is fully understandable. Athenian policy in 379 and 378 was not calculated to inspire Spartan confidence; Athens was not in a position to offer resistance to the united strength of the Peloponnesians, and did not want an open conflict with Sparta, but she hardly concealed her sympathies for the Thebans. A formal treaty between Athens and Thebes in the year 379–378 is not likely. But the Sphodrias affair ended Athens' hesitancy once and for all. In 378–377 (probably in the first months of 377), Athens concluded a formal alliance with Thebes and openly sided against Sparta. An inscription of this treaty has been preserved (Bengtson, *Staatsvertraege,* No. 255), but the left side of the document is missing, so that there are difficulties in interpretation. But the formal initiative had clearly come from the Thebans; Stephanus made the motion in the Athenian Assembly for the conclusion of a treaty of alliance. Evidently an Athenian embassy had pre-

viously gone to Thebes, and one of its members was Thrasybulus, son of Thrason, from Collytus (not to be confused with
the famous Thrasybulus of Steiria). Thrasybulus of Collytus
had especially good connections in Thebes, where—if Aeschines (III, 138) may be believed—he stood in high regard.
In general, many personal ties would seem to have been established between the two cities as a result of the presence in
Athens of Theban democrats, which makes the alliance all
the more understandable.

While the treaty was being ratified in Athens and in Thebes,
a great change was already in the making in the Aegean. This
was the founding of the Second Attic Maritime League in
378–377, one hundred years after the establishment of the
(First) Delian-Attic League.

The Second Attic Maritime League was not established on
any one particular day. It was built partly on the basis of contacts established in the time of Thrasybulus, which—as in the
case of Chios in 384 and Byzantium in 378—had led to treaties
of alliance with Athens. In addition, Athens had the good
fortune of having a great rhetorician and publicist, Isocrates,
who, in his formal orations, proclaimed the glory of his native
city to the entire Greek world. The *Panegyricus,* for example,
which appeared in 380, is a eulogy of the Athenian past.
Isocrates invokes historical examples to emphasize the greatness of the Athens of the past and the obligations on the present generation of Athenians that result from it. A particular
object of Isocrates' hatred was the King's Peace of 386, and
the *rhetor* tirelessly pointed to the great deeds of Athens under
Pericles, when the Peace of Callias (449–448) set bounds to
the pride of the Persians. Classicists (e.g., E. Buchner) have
now rightly turned from the views of U. von Wilamowitz and
others, who saw the *Panegyricus* as propaganda for the establishment of the Second Attic Maritime League. But the speech
did a splendid job of preparing the ground for Athens' purposes and, to that extent, ushered in a new epoch of Attic history. In Athens it was clearly understood that a new alliance
would have to rise on a different basis from that of the old
Delian League; in particular, the allies must not be allowed to

221

feel that Athens was exploiting the union for selfish or imperialist ends. By February-March, 377, the preparations had progressed so far that Athens was able to issue a manifesto calling on Greeks and barbarians on the mainland and on the islands to join the new confederacy.

This document—formally a decree of the Athenian Assembly on the motion of one Aristotle—is preserved on a tablet of Pentelic marble that has been pieced together from twenty fragments, and is one of the most important documents for the history of Greece in the fourth century B.C. (Bengtson, *Staatsvertraege,* No. 257). To those, Greek or barbarian, who wished to join the confederacy, freedom and autonomy were assured, and in addition freedom from occupation and tribute. Moreover, the Athenians pledged themselves not to acquire any territory in the areas belonging to their new allies. Finally, aid was assured to the members of the confederacy in the event of aggression. At the beginning of the document, of course, a polite (or ironical) bow was made to Spartan supremacy: the Lacedaemonians were asked to allow the Greeks freedom, autonomy, and peace as well as the undisturbed possession of their territory; in this connection a reference was made to the *koine eirene* (these words are restored in the document) invoked by the Persian King and the Spartans. The inscription lists the names of the Athenian allies; fifty-three, at most, appear here, but the total number (according to Diodorus, XV, 30, 2) was, in fact, seventy. Naturally, these were far fewer than the numbers of the First Maritime League. It is especially interesting to find, among the allies, the name of the great Thessalian tyrant Jason of Pherae (column B, line 15 of the inscription). The name has been restored: [*Iaso*]*n,* but the reading seems as good as certain. What happened was that the name was chiseled out later on, when Jason grew hostile to Athens.

The bases of the confederacy were the provisions of the King's Peace regarding autonomy. Athens occupied the position of the hegemonial power, and was directly recognized as such in the treaties of alliance with the individual states. Otherwise the confederacy's constitution stressed the equal rights of members. The allies were pledged to render assistance not only to Athens but also to each other. In contrast to the First Maritime League, a permanent League organ was created, the *synhedrion,* which held regular meetings. In this body one vote was held by each member state irrespective of size or population. Athens, however, was not represented in the synhedrion; she stood outside the confederacy, as its ally. Agreement between Athens and the confederacy was necessary before a decision could be carried out. Athens—or, more precisely, the Athenian Assembly—had, in other words, a general veto power.

But the confederacy, like its forerunner, could not manage without contributions. These were called *syntaxeis,* no longer *phoroi;* the latter had unpleasant associations from the days of the Delian League. Only those members who were not in a position to provide ships or soldiers were obliged to pay *syntaxeis:* Thebes, for example, never made any financial payments. Although in the founding of the confederacy equality of powers had been painstakingly observed, in the course of time Athens assumed a greater share of influence. Thus, it gradually developed that it was not the synhedrion of the allies but the Athenian Assembly that made decisions, not only on the reception of new members, but also on the allotment of the confederacy's funds, just as in the First Maritime League. Executive power lay entirely in the hands of Athens. It was Athens that held the supreme command, ordered the mobilization of ships and soldiers, and conducted the necessary diplomatic negotiations.

The Second Attic Maritime League, in its best days, comprised not only most of the islands of the Aegean but also a number of cities on the Thracian coast, the large islands of the Ionian Sea, and even Acarnania and parts of Epirus. The union was, however, anything but a federal state. It offered no federal citizenship, nor was there any federal government. It was, rather, a military alliance, formed to rebuff Sparta. It is significant that a Spartanophile like Xenophon, in his *Hellenica,* does not say one word about the founding of the Maritime League.

223

Athens at this time had the good fortune to have a number of able men on hand who served her as political and military leaders. The principal statesman of the day was Callistratus of Aphidnae, who was best known as a financial expert. Chabrias, the friend of Plato, distinguished himself repeatedly as strategos. A typical soldier of fortune was Iphicrates, who managed to gain both great honor and great wealth in the service of his city and as a mercenary leader abroad. With his name is linked a revolutionary innovation in the Greek art of war: in place of the cumbersone hoplite phalanx, Iphicrates relied on light-armed infantry (peltasts), with which he gained significant successes in the Corinthian War.

Parallel with the rise of the Second Attic Maritime League was the rise of Thebes. The two developments are connected: Athens was allied with Thebes, and Thebes was a member of the Maritime League. For Athens, the Theban alliance was of the greatest importance, as it forced the Lacedaemonians to concentrate their attention on Thebes and central Greece, and therefore prevented them from turning their full force against Athens. The Athenians did not fail to lend the Thebans support. When, in the summer of 377, Agesilaus appeared in Boeotia with the Peloponnesian army, he was met not only by the Thebans but also by the Athenians under Chares, who did not, however, venture a pitched battle against the experienced old Spartan commander. The incursion of Cleombrotus in 376 did not bring the Spartans the success they had hoped for, and at sea they were decisively defeated that year in the strait between Naxos and Paros. How strong Athens now believed herself is shown by the dispatch of Timotheus, the son of Conon, to the Ionian Sea. Here, he persuaded the islands of Corcyra and Cephallenia, Acarnania, and Alcetas the King of the Molossians to join the allies of Athens (Bengtson, *Staatsvertraege,* Nos. 262 and 263). Macedonia also joined the Maritime League, in either 375 or 373. This land, the source of wood for shipbuilding, was considered a very important partner in the alliance (Bengtson, *Staatsvertraege,* No. 264).

The conduct of the war, especially the Athenians' naval armaments, cost enormous sums. A declaration of movable and immovable assets in Athens was ordered to give a new basis for assessments. It showed a total of 5,750 talents in individual holdings. The citizenry was divided into 100 tax districts, called *symmoriai,* each of which was capable of producing about sixty talents in taxes. This new division superseded the Solonian tax-class system, to which the Athenians had adhered for over 200 years, and which had long since become unworkable.

For Thebes, the largest city of Boeotia, the regulation of its relations with the rest of the Boeotian cities was a question of survival. This problem, in the decade of the 70s, was quite successfully solved. The King's Peace had meant the end of alliances in Greece, including the Boeotian League; now, after the liberation of Thebes in 379, the Boeotian League was resurrected. The most important magistrates were the Boeotarchs, now seven in number. Besides these, there was an Assembly of all Boeotians, in which the affairs of the League were publicly discussed. In view of the political fragmentation of Greece, this was a great step forward. A united Boeotian state never existed, however, for the Boeotian cities were too strong individually to give up their independence. But they did subordinate themselves to Theban leadership, and, on this basis, the Boeotian League was able to carry out ambitious plans.

At about the same time a new power emerged in the north of Greece, in Thessaly. Its rise is inseparably linked with the name of the tyrant Jason of Pherae. In Thessaly the rivalries within the all-powerful aristocracy had long prevented the political consolidation of the country. Not until Jason, the son (or son-in-law) of Lycophron of Pherae, bludgeoned the warring parts of the country into unity did Thessaly assume its rightful place in Greek history. Like Dionysius of Syracuse, Jason was a man of great education and wide intellectual interests. He was a pupil of the Sophist Gorgias of Leontini. Naturally, the rise of Thessaly was watched with envious eyes by its neighbors, but especially by the Lacedaemonians. But the latter were too occupied with their own concerns to interfere with Jason's rise. The conquest of Pharsalus was the pinnacle of

Jason's achievement; he was now the sole master of Thessaly, and held the title of *Tagos* (commander). Thessaly was capable of mustering 8,000 cavalry and 20,000 foot soldiers. Even the Peloponnesian League, at that time, could assemble forces of that size only with the greatest effort. In Thessaly, the principle of individual autonomy was successfully disregarded, a tribute to the commanding personality of Jason.

It was probably fear of the increasing power of Thebes that brought the Athenians to sue for peace in 375–374. Through the mediation of the Persian King and Dionysius I, with Thebes also participating, a peace was concluded at Sparta in July, 374. This peace is significant in that it was a *koine eirene;* that is, it was supposed to include all Greeks. Under the peace terms, Athens gained no inconsiderable advantages. Above all, she had confirmation of her leadership of the Second Attic Maritime League, which now had official recognition as a counterpoise to the Peloponnesian League. Sparta had to pull back considerably; she had in particular to recall her garrisons from the Boeotian cities, a provision that was naturally to the advantage of Thebes. Though one source (Diodorus, XV, 38) reports the exclusion of the Thebans from this Peace of 375–374, this is an error based on a confusion of this treaty with the Peace of 371.

In Athens, an altar was erected to the goddess of peace (*Eirene*), and for this occasion the sculptor Cephisodotus cast a famous statue of Eirene with the boy Plutus on her arm. Peace supporting prosperity: a symbol of the hopes of all Greeks. It is possible, perhaps even probable, that the Athenians were promised the possession of Amphipolis in this peace, and perhaps even the Thracian Chersonese. The power dominating this peninsula could control the strait of the Hellespont.

The peace was of short duration. Xenophon blamed Timotheus, son of Conon, for the renewed outbreak of war. Timotheus had interfered in the internal affairs of Zacynthus, and put ashore there certain members of the democratic party. Athens, occupied with the extension of its Maritime League, had, of course, little to gain by another war. A sea power, after all, is affected much more severely by the hardships of war than is a land power, so long as the latter is strong enough to protect its frontiers. The Athenian citizens therefore brought Timotheus to trial in the hope of staving off reprisal (373). But Timotheus, without awaiting the result, entered the service of the Persian King as a mercenary commander. The fact that the oarsmen of the Athenian warships at Corcyra had to hire themselves out as farm laborers in order to earn their keep shows how far Athens had come from the great days of the First Maritime League. She could ill afford large-scale warfare.

But tensions also arose with Thebes. The Thebans made a surprise attack on Plataea and leveled the city to the ground (374–373 or 373–372); they proceeded to annex Thespiae, and even laid claim to Oropus. The destruction of Plataea, a heavy blow to Athens, is reflected in contemporary political oratory. Isocrates made propaganda against the Thebans in his *Plataikos*. The date of the oration is a matter of dispute among scholars, Werner Jaeger fixing it at 373, Mathieu at 371.

These events, however, were not sufficiently important to make the difference between peace and war. The Spartans, who were no match for the Athenians at sea, had meanwhile, through their intermediary Antialcidas, again invoked the intervention of the Persian King. On Persian initiative a Peace Congress assembled in Sparta in 371. In addition to the Greeks of the mother country, emissaries from Dionysius I of Syracuse and the King of Macedonia were present. Again the principle of autonomy enshrined in the King's Peace was recognized as the foundation of the treaty. The Persians, in other words, were still hovering over the affairs of the Greeks; Sparta took pains to do as the Great King wished.

The autonomy clause made it impossible for the Thebans to accept the peace terms. They tried to induce the congress to accord legal recognition to the Boeotian League, but their representative Epaminondas met the determined opposition of the Spartans, and Athens, understandably, was not inclined to side with Thebes. The Spartans commanded the Thebans

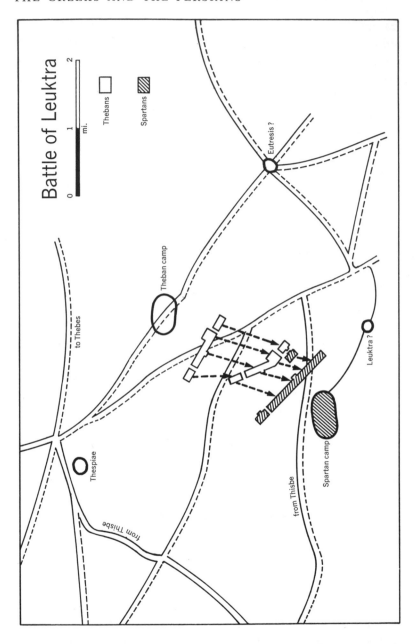

Battle of Leuktra

to release the other Boeotian cities from the League and restore their autonomy. An order went out to the Lacedaemonian King Cleombrotus to give point to this by advancing from Phocis into Boeotia. Despite the Lacedaemonian army's superiority in numbers, Epaminondas persuaded his countrymen to face the invader on the field. Battle was joined at Leuctra, six miles from Thebes, in July, 371. There the Lacedaemonians did something they had never done before in a pitched battle on an open field. They lost.

They lost to no ordinary commander. At Leuctra, Epaminondas introduced a revolution in military tactics, which won the day and changed the art of war. Before the battle he had strengthened his left wing until it stood no less than fifty men deep. In its first ranks stood the members of the "Sacred Band," the Theban elite troops, led by Pelopidas. The Spartan right was unable to withstand the impact of Epaminondas' charge, when the full weight of his left wing bore down on them. The traditional courage of the Spartans was in vain; their line broke; of the 700 Spartans, no fewer than 400 lay dead on the field. The Lacedaemonian wing could not even join battle; it too had to withdraw to the fortified camp on the heights, which the Thebans did not attack. But by their request for permission to recover their dead, the Spartans conceded defeat. Interestingly enough, the Spartanophile Xenophon's account of the battle of Leuctra is entirely inadequate. He does not mention Epaminondas once, and he gives no reason for the Lacedaemonian defeat (*Hellenica*, VI, 4, 1–14).

Who was this Epaminondas, who before the gates of his native city had defeated the undefeatable? Epaminondas, son of Polymnis, came of an ordinary Theban family that had little to offer their son in the way of wealth but in compensation gave him a very careful education. Like other boys of his age, he was trained in the arts and in gymnastics. In addition, he had the benefit of the instruction and friendship of Lysis the Pythagorean, who had had to flee from southern Italy. The ancient sources rightly stress not only that Epaminondas was entirely incorruptible but that, to preserve his complete independence, he lived in voluntary poverty. He never married, but he was a close friend of many Thebans besides Pelopidas. Even in ancient times men marveled that Epaminondas did not take part in the party struggles in Thebes. He played, at most, a very modest part in the liberation of his native city. But he must have been all the more active during the years from 377 to 371; in this period, the army of the Thebans and Boeotians was transformed into a first-rate tactical instrument of war, in which we must suspect the decisive influence of Epaminondas. Clearly, the new tactic of the reinforced left wing was not introduced overnight; on the contrary, it presupposes incessant drill and the strictest discipline, such as up to now had been found in Greece only among the Lacedaemonians. Certain models for his innovation might be found in Greek military history; thus the battle of Delium (424) had been decided by the thrust of the Boeotian right wing. Is it also possible that Epaminondas took over Pythagorean geometrical notions, applying them to the realm of tactics? We do not know. In any case, Epaminondas had now dealt the Spartan military state its death blow. He had also set an example for future ages. Leuctra was the model for the battle of Leuthen (1757), in which Frederick the Great, with an army far inferior in numbers, administered a crushing defeat to Austrian arms.

There was no longer a Spartan hegemony after Leuctra. A year later (370), Jason of Pherae was murdered. He had planned to appear with the Thessalian army in Delphi to seize the presidency of the Pythian Games. With the death of this man, who had seriously weighed plans for a war against Persia, Thessaly again fell prey to internal disorders, and for Thebes the road to hegemony was now entirely clear.

Meanwhile, in Athens, delegates from many of the Greek states had again assembled for a peace congress. Sparta was probably among them, but not Elis. The peace treaty put forward little that was new; once again, the rule of autonomy of the King's Peace was invoked by the Greeks. This measure was directed specifically against Thebes. Once again a *koine eirene* was concluded, which can be dated before the end of 371, after the battle of Leuctra (Bengtson, *Staatsvertraege,*

No. 270). It never occurred to any of the signers of this treaty to rebel against the terms of the King's Peace. On the contrary, the treaties of the Persian Great King were taken expressly as the basis for this Hellenic *koine eirene*.

But hopeful signs of a more national course now began to appear. The years following Leuctra saw the founding of several Greek confederations. The Arcadian League was founded in 370, and in 367–366 the *koinon* of the Aetolians appears on an Athenian inscription for the first time. There is no doubt that these federations introduced a new note into Greek history. While preserving the autonomy of individual states, whole tribes now merged together. The individual *poleis* (city-states) and *ethne* (tribes) had realized that only if they were united would they be capable of playing a role in history.

Theban policy was quite another matter. Thebes, which had made itself the leading power of Boeotia, concluded alliances with a number of other states: Phocis, the Arcadian League, Macedonia, the tyrant Alexander of Pherae, and Achaea. This policy of alliances was in part a preparation for the final struggle with Sparta. In part, however, it was also a consequence of Theban encroachment on the Peloponnese and on Thessaly.

The Theban offensive against Sparta began in 370, with the first Boeotian campaign in the Pelponnese. Greece at that time was essentially divided into three alliance systems, led respectively by Thebes, Sparta, and Athens. But no one of these hegemonial symmachies was strong enough to create anything really new and lasting. Not only material resources but constructive ideas that might have brought order out of the Greek chaos were entirely lacking.

Epaminondas' first campaign in the Peloponnese was a dramatic one. This was its origin: The Arcadians, who were at war with Sparta, were casting about for allies. When Athens failed them, the Arcadians naturally looked to Thebes. A formal alliance was concluded between the two states (370). Two alliances, then, joined forces against the Lacedaemonians. Supporters flocked to the Boeotians in the Peloponnese. It was with superior forces that Thebes invaded Laconia. Epaminondas forded the Eurotas at Amyclae, and the Boeotian cavalry penetrated to the environs of Sparta itself. But there no decision was reached; Agesilaus occupied the high ground of the city, and would not be provoked into a pitched battle. The credit for saving Sparta belongs, by right, to her tough old king.

In the city itself there was complete confusion. Perioeci and Helots had fled in large numbers. The Spartan women, until now renowned for their courage, filled the city with cries and commotion. Sparta's history could have been sealed then and there, had not Boeotians and their allies turned to plundering. Although Sparta was preserved from capture by a foreign enemy, the impression made in Greece and far beyond was enormous. The Boeotians became the first military power in Hellas. Together with their allies in central Greece and in the Peloponnese, they had power enough to transform the whole aspect of Greece, had they so willed.

The first result of this revolution in Greek affairs was the righting of an ancient wrong. The Messenian Helots were freed. Under the protection of Boeotian arms, they erected a new state of their own (369). And, under Epaminondas' direction, the newly founded state established a capital city, built on the slopes of Mount Ithome and given the name of Messene. The new Messenian state, founded at Sparta's expense, was a loyal ally of the Boeotians from the start, and resumed its ancient anti-Spartan tradition. It is at least probable that the legendary history of Messenia had its literary origin at this time.

Sparta had now lost the rich and important farm lands between the Taygetus range and the Ionian Sea, and with them, the greater part of its accustomed harvests. The whole Spartan military state had been based on the patient serfdom of the many thousands of Helots that Sparta had enslaved, kept under surveillance, and bled white for the benefit of their masters in arms. After the loss of Messenia, Sparta passed out of the ranks of the leading powers of Greece. From this time on, there is no such thing as a decisive Spartan influence in Greek politics. A development of several hundred years' duration had, in the end, proved to be one of history's blind alleys. But Sparta had done Greece good service in the Persian Wars. The Greeks owed their liberation from the Persian menace to the cold courage of Pausanias and his warriors at Plataea. Justice demands recognition for Sparta's merits, for the many proofs of Spartan discipline in the service of the state in both war and peace. While other Greek states sought strength in confederations, Sparta remained true to herself alone. One may regret Sparta's downfall, but even in that can be seen a spark of the old grandeur, the uncompromising quality of the Spartan ethos.

The founding of the city of Megalopolis, as a capital and rallying point for the Arcadian League, was also directed against Sparta. Its inhabitants were recruited from thirty-nine adjacent communities. This city, like Messene, appears to have been established under the protection of Boeotian arms. The site of Megalopolis was so chosen that the city, with its strong walls, blocked the entrance from the valley of the Eurotas to that of the Alpheus. With this, the main invasion route into Arcadia was closed.

There is little to report of the second expedition of Epaminondas (369). It evidently had a limited objective from the start. The Boeotians won the cities of Sicyon and Pellene, and the regions of Troezen and Epidaurus were laid waste.

Meanwhile, Athens and Sparta had concluded an alliance in which the supreme command was to alternate every five days, clearly a concession on the part of the Spartans (Bengtson, *Staatsvertraege,* No. 274). On the whole the Theban expedition had had little success, and upon its conclusion Epaminondas and Pelopidas were brought to trial and removed from office as Boeotarchs. With the Theban invasion of the north that followed into Thessaly and Macedonia, the Boeotians overtaxed their strength; one accomplishment, however, was an agreement with Ptolemy, the regent of Macedonia. As a pledge of fidelity to the treaty, the young Prince Philip (later King Philip II) came to Thebes in 368. There he had access to the homes of the most eminent families, and unobtrusively learned the military art from the greatest masters of the age. In Thessaly, however, a dangerous opponent to the Boeotians had arisen in the tyrant Alexander of Pherae. On an expedition to Thessaly, the Thebans Ismenias and Pelopidas fell into his hands, and they were liberated only by a treaty that Epaminondas succeeded in making with Alexander in 367 (Bengtson, *Staatsvertraege,* No. 281).

Nothing better displays the impotence of all Greece than the Peace Congress that assembled at Delphi in 368—on the initiative of foreign powers. The emissaries of Dionysius I of Syracuse dominated the preliminary negotiations; the Persian satrap Ariobarzanes of Phrygia had sent his agent Philiscus of Abydos to Hellas, and had been unsparing of outright bribes. Naturally Persia had the greatest interest in bringing about a peace which perpetuated the fragmentation of Greece. But since Sparta was unable to recognize an independent Messenia, the negotiations at Delphi came to nothing.

The following year (367), envoys from many Greek states journeyed to the Great King at Susa, among them the Theban Pelopidas; Sparta and Athens were also represented. In Susa, the old friendship between Persia and Thebes was renewed. Moreover, the Persian King issued a decree recognizing Messenia as independent and, in addition, decreeing the disarmament of the Athenian navy. With that Pelopidas had his will, but only in Persia, for the Greeks refused to accept the latest dictates of the Great King (Bengtson, *Staatsvertraege,* No. 282).

As early as 368, Athens had endeavored to establish relations with the tyrant Dionysius I. In the summer of that year the Athenians had honored the ruler and his two sons with a golden wreath and the right of citizenship. In March, 367, an alliance between Athens and Dionysius was concluded (Bengtson *Staatsvertraege,* No. 280). Each of the parties gave assurance of aid in the event of an attack on the other, and agreed to a nonaggression pact. This meant a triple alliance, since Sparta, too, was allied with Athens and with Dionysius. It never came into effect, however, because the Syracusan ruler (in the document he is called the "Archon of Sicily") was removed from the scene by the careless hand of death.

Epaminondas' third expedition into the Peloponnese, in 367, brought no substantial change in the political situation there. The Boeotians had difficulties with Arcadians, but were able to induce some Achaean towns to join the symmachy. Not for long: Thebes made the mistake of replacing oligarchic governments in these cities with democracies; as soon as the Boeotian armies left, the oligarchs, now irrevocably pro-Spartan, returned. This political instability was now the rule in the Peloponnese; in 370, hundreds of citizens had been massacred in the course of party struggles at Argos. Athens, too, was being drawn into the Peloponnesian maelstrom: she now concluded a defense alliance with the Arcadians. Since Athens was also allied with Sparta, this created an intriguing state of affairs: the Athenians were pledged to give aid to the Arcadians against Sparta and to the Spartans against the Arcadians, depending upon which state attacked which. A Peace Congress held in Thebes, in 366, showed some recognition of the leading role of the Boeotians in Greece: the liberation of Messenia was approved by treaty. For this very reason, Sparta found it impossible to become a party to the Peace (whether or not it was a *koine eirene* is a matter of debate), and the result was therefore more of an armed truce than a state of peace. Sparta's situation was in any case unenviable. Its coffers were empty, and the aged King Agesilaus had to hire himself out, for a time, to the Persian satrap Ariobarzanes as a mercenary commander, in order to earn revenue for his bankrupt country.

In Asia Minor, a rebellion of the Persian satraps had broken out, with Ariobarzanes of Phrygia and Datames of Cappadocia especially active. This revolt meant a considerable weakening of the Persian power in Anatolia; only after years of hard fighting (370–359) was it suppressed. All of which favored the Athenian expedition to Samos in 365. The Athenians, under Timotheus, snatched the valuable island from the Persian Empire and made their new possession more secure by the settlement of Athenian cleruchs. (The conquest of Samos, by the way, was a clear contravention of the Athenian promise —made in the original invitation to join the Second Maritime League—that she would make no conquests within the sphere of the confederacy.) The Athenians now obtained a foothold on the Thracian Chersonese and even in Byzantium. Still more remarkable were the Athenians' successes in Thrace. Although Amphipolis could not be taken, Timotheus won the cities of Pydna and Methone, of great importance for trade with the Macedonian hinterland. Torone and Potidaea also joined Athens; Athenian cleruchs were sent to Potidaea. The reappearance of cleruchies is easily explained: as usual, new lands for settlement were a vital necessity for Athens' steadily rising population.

But Athens found an unexpected competitor at large on the sea. The Thebans had proceeded to build a fleet, and for this purpose occupied the Locrian harbor of Larymna. They may have used the services of a Carthaginian for the building of their navy: we have a Boeotian decree honoring a certain Annobal [Hannibal?] son of Asrubal [Hasdrubal?] (Dittenberger, *Syll.* 13, No. 179 of the year 364).

On his fleet's first and only voyage, Epaminondas scored some surprising successes. Byzantium and the great islands of Chios and Rhodes defected from Athens; even the island of Ceos off the Attic coast shifted its alliance to Thebes. But the gains were surely temporary; Athens was soon able to win back the defectors. During Epaminondas' absence a group of citizens of Orchomenus, in Boeotia, in league with Theban exiles, had tried to overthrow the democratic constitution of Thebes by force. The attempt failed, and the Assembly of the Boeotian League imposed a frightful punishment. The 300 men who had taken part in the conspiracy were put to death, their wives and children enslaved, and Boeotian Orchomenus destroyed. This reflects the political antagonism between aristocrats and democrats; but it also shows the ruthlessness of the Boeotians toward their own countrymen.

Meanwhile a conflict over the district of Triphylia had broken out between Arcadia and Elis in the Peloponnese. Elis received help from Sparta, while the Arcadians were supported by a corps of cavalry from Athens. The Eleans temporarily lost their overlordship of Olympia. The place was occupied by troops of the Arcadian League, and the administration of the Olympic Games was placed in the hands of the people of nearby Pisa (July, 364). But the Eleans, supported by the Achaeans, did not let themselves be driven out without a struggle—a struggle that led to an actual pitched battle within the sacred precincts of Olympia. The Arcadians were the victors: they seized the temple treasures, which they needed to pay the Arcadian League's federal troops, the 5,000 *eparitoi*. The desecration of the property of the Temple at Olympia led to a split in the Arcadian League, in which two parties, led by Tegea and Mantinea, opposed each other from now on. The Mantineans expressly condemned the pillaging of the temple.

The divisions in the Arcadian League led Epaminondas to make his fourth and last expedition into the Peloponnese. Once again, the Thebans made a sudden attack on the city of Sparta; once again, it was inconclusive; Agesilaus succeeded in bringing his troops to the threatened city in the nick of time. Epaminondas was not successful in Mantinea either: the Athenian cavalry stopped the Boeotian horse, who were attempting to take the city by surprise. The two armies then assembled south of the city, the allies barring Epaminondas' way to Mantinea by disposing their lines across the plain between the hills. The two forces were probably about equal in numbers, with 20,000 men on each side. The idea that Epaminondas' army outnumbered the enemy by three to two originates with the historian Ephorus and deserves no credence. Once again, the tactical problem was brilliantly solved by the great Boeotian commander. Advancing with his strengthened left wing he went directly to the attack, while the right wing of his army held back. His objective was to gain control of the road to Mantinea in the rear of the enemy's position, and thus cut off his retreat. The thrust of the Boeotian left wing was masked by cavalry. Opposite stood the Mantineans, who obviously had not reckoned with an attack on this day. To break the enemy's line at the point of attack, Epaminondas had to prevent the shift of troops from one wing to the other; he therefore ordered a simultaneous attack on the enemy's left, held by the Athenians. The result was a clear-cut, clockwork success. The attack of the Boeotian left wing broke through as at Leuctra, the enemy—Mantineans and Spartans—were unable to sustain it. But Epaminondas, fighting in the front rank, fell mortally wounded. The battle dissolved into isolated engagements; neither side swept the field. Each side raised the trophy of victory, and each requested from the other permission to bury its dead, an acknowledgement of defeat.

The battle of Mantinea, fought on the twelfth of Skirophorion (July 12), 362, was followed by the conclusion of a peace treaty, once again a *koine eirene,* in which Sparta, alone of all the Greek states, had no share. The Peace confirmed the splitting of Arcadia into two separate Leagues, a southern one under Tegea and Megalopolis, and a northern one under Mantinea. The Spartans continued their efforts to recover Messenia, but their strength was inadequate to the task. This minor war continued for several years.

The history written by the Athenian Xenophon comes to a conclusion with the battle of Mantinea. It ends with the resigned observation that neither side possessed a grain more after the battle than it did before, but that the perplexity and confusion in Greece was even greater than it had been at the start. Xenophon's analysis is perfectly accurate. The world of the Greek poleis had not developed a new ideal that might have renewed the life of Hellas. The fighting among the various symmachies could have gone on for centuries, for all that Greek political intelligence could contribute toward its solution. Hellas had eliminated itself as an independent force; a renewal from within was no longer to be hoped for.

We may wonder, then, whether Epaminondas' work was not entirely in vain. There can be no doubt that Epaminondas was a Boeotian, not a Panhellenic, political figure. As a general, he succeeded in developing a completely original idea, but as a politician he was a traditionalist. He replaced the hegemony of Sparta with that of Boeotia, which was not really viable and succeeded only in overtaxing Boeotia's strength. He was ready to call the Persians into Greek affairs when it seemed to him to be advantageous. His political work was purely destructive in its long-term effect. The hegemony of Sparta was utterly destroyed. The ground was prepared for the later intervention of foreign powers, in particular Macedonia. The phase of Greek history that began with the King's Peace ends, with the battle of Mantinea, precisely where it began. Hegemonies had come and gone, the Western satraps had revolted at length (370–359), yet Greece was still fragmented into independent and antagonistic states, and the power of Persia to keep her so seemed undiminished.

12

The Greeks of the West in the Fourth Century B.C.

The history of the Western Greek world during the first third of the fourth century B.C. bears the stamp of the personality of the Syracusan tyrant, Dionysius I (d. 367). He gave the Sicilian Greek world security and freedom from the threat of Carthaginian conquest; he extended his sphere of influence to various parts of the Italic mainland, at a time when Rome did not yet play a significant role in the peninsula.

Two problems faced Dionysius after he came to power (see p. 199): the settlement of his relations with the Sicels, and the Carthaginian question. The latter, despite the peace treaty of 405, could in no sense be regarded as permanently solved.

To begin with, Dionysius forced the Greek cities of Aetna, Catana, and Naxos into subjection. Leontini was also conquered, and its inhabitants transported to Syracuse. At that time the first of a number of conflicts with Italic Rhegium broke out, which, however, was easily settled. This expansion increased not only Dionysius' self-confidence but also the prestige of Syracuse. The city was by far the most important power not only of Sicily but of the entire Western Greek world.

From 402–401 B.C. on, Dionysius strengthened the fortifications of Syracuse. In particular, the plateau of Epipolae in the northwestern part of the city was protected with extensive

240

walls, in the erection of which a huge number of laborers, reportedly 60,000, are said to have taken part. Of the citadel on the Euryalus impressive remnants are preserved today, especially the enormous main bastion, which towers over the Sicilian landscape. The end result of these preparations was that Syracuse was ringed by a gigantic wall no less than eighteen miles in circumference. These fortifications were, in fact, splendidly adapted to an offensive defense. Their layout, in other words, reflected the tyrant's strategic plans, which were certainly not confined to the mere defense of his city. In Syracuse, an army of engineers and technicians labored to produce a large quantity of war material. Here for the first time catapults were built, to be used in attacking enemy fortresses. The Syracusan navy was also considerably increased; with 300 ships, it was the largest at the disposal of any Greek state at this time.

Surrounded by new projects and new plans, Dionysius still found time to marry two women in a double wedding. His wives were Aristomache, the daughter of his friend Hipparinus of Syracuse, and Doris, the daughter of a respected citizen of Locri in southern Italy.

The war that Dionysius now began against the Carthaginians was an outright aggression; the latter had given him no grounds for attack. In Syracuse and the other Greek cities of the island the population turned on the Carthaginian merchants. In a terrible massacre, they were killed in large numbers and their property pillaged. Dionysius demanded that the Carthaginians set free the Greek cities that they then occupied; naturally this was refused. So, once again, the issue was decided on the field of battle (397). Dionysius had armaments superior in quantity and quality, and had engaged the services of a great many mercenaries. First, the Carthaginian base of Motya fell into his hands, then the Sicanians went over to him. Of the larger cities only Segesta continued to offer resistance. But a Carthaginian fleet landed at Panormus (Palermo), and Dionysius' luck deserted him by stages, until finally he was surrounded in his capital of Syracuse. But thanks to his connections with the Greeks of the homeland, especially the Spartans, his city did not fall. A dangerous epidemic broke out in the Carthaginian army, and Dionysius had won the campaign. He forced the Carthaginian general Himilco to capitulate. The Carthaginians were granted freedom to withdraw in return for payment of a large sum of money (300 talents).

This victory of Dionysius' can justly be set beside the other great Syracusan feats of arms, the victory of Gelon at Himera and the defeat of the Athenian expedition. The result was a revolt in Africa, during which Carthage came close to being captured. Dionysius made use of the opportunity to strengthen his control over the east and the north of the island. The founding of the city of Tyndaris dates from this time, a stronghold controlling the main road along the northern coast of the island from Messana to Panormus. In 392, a large Carthaginian army again appeared in Sicily, but there were no decisive victories on either side; peace was concluded that same year.

The Treaty placed the Sicels under the rule of Dionysius; Tauromenium also was conceded to him. Carthage continued to hold her suzerainty (*epikratia*) over western Sicily, but the indigenous peoples of the island and the Greek cities became part of the empire of Dionysius.

In southern Italy, the Greeks found themselves increasingly threatened by the Italic peoples, the Lucanians presenting the most pressing danger. Joining their forces, the Greek cities formed an Italiote League. Among its members were the cities of Croton, Sybaris on the Traeis, Caulonia, Thurii, Elea, and perhaps also Poseidonia (Paestum). Rhegium too, which was in the sharpest conflict with Dionysius, was received into the League. Dionysius' own most important strongpoint in southern Italy was the city of Locri. A battle was fought on the river Elleporus in which the Sicilian ruler was victorious over the troops of the Italiote League (388). The outcome for the Italiotes was disastrous. No less than 10,000 prisoners were taken by the tyrant. But Dionysius now showed himself to be a master of practical politics; he sent the prisoners home without demanding ransom, and concluded peace with the

1. Archer-bodyguard of Darius I:
relief from the palace at Susa

2. Horse and camel (left) and falcon and winged griffin (right):
Achaemenian cylinder seals

3. Bronze head
of ibex, Persian,
Achaemenian peri

4. Remains of the throne hall at Persepolis: Apadana (audience hall) and gate
of Xerxes in the background

5. Reliefs on stairway to council hall at Persepolis

6. Relief panels from stairway of the Apadana at Persepolis, showing Babylonians and Syrians bringing tribute, with Medean and Persian guards

7. Darius (seated) with Xerxes behind him: relief from the Hall of the Hundred Columns at Persepolis

8. Face of bull-man, from a pillar at Persepolis

9. Gold drinking horn, Persian, fifth century B.C.

10. Bust of Themistocles: Ostia, Italy

11. Amphorae from Rhodes (left) and Spain (right) dating from the
sixth century B.C. and found at Corinth (ruins of temple
of Apollo in background)

12. Speaker's platform at Athenian assembly on the Pnyx, a hill outside Athens

13. Bust of Euripides

14. Drinking vessel showing youth and teacher, Greek, c. 470 B.C.

15. Inside of chalice showing flute player, Greek, fifth century B.C.

16. Vase: Athens, showing battle of Greeks and Amazons, c. 460–450 B.C.

17. East frieze of inner temple, Parthenon, showing Poseidon, Apollo and Artemis watching the Panathenaean procession

18. Fragment of treaty between Athens and the Peloponnesian city of Hermione, 450 B.C.

19. Part of the west pediment: temple of Zeus, Olympia (central figure, Apollo)

20. The Acropolis

21. The Parthenon

22. Temple of Nike
on the Acropolis,
Athens, c. 440 B.C.

23. Remains of the theatre at Epidaurus, c. 325 B.C.

24. The Erechtheum on the Acropolis, Athens:
Porch of the Caryatids, c. 420 B.C.

25. Head of a maenad, late fifth century B.C.

26. Remains of temple of Apollo at Delphi

27. Temple of Poseidon, Paestum, fifth century B.C.

28. Temple of Concord, Acragas (Sicily), c. 430 B.C.

29. Bust of Plato

30. Stele of Ampharete, Athens, c. 405 B.C.

31. Alexander the Great

32. Mosaic from Pompeii, showing Alexander the Great attacking Darius III at the Battle of Issus, 333 B.C.

33. Naophorous statue of Henat, Egyptian, Twenty-sixth
or Twenty-seventh Dynasty

34. Naophorous statue of
Psamtik-sa-Neith, a minor
official, Egyptian, Twenty-
seventh Dynasty

35. Falcon: faïence hieroglyph from inscription on shrine,
Egyptian, Twenty-seventh Dynasty

36. Kneeling man: hieroglyph for *millions of years*, faïence inscription on shrine, Egyptian, Twenty-seventh Dynasty

37. Southern corridor, entrance hall, Temple of the Moon at
Marib (Temple 'Auwam), Arabia

League. Of course, the League had to cede the territory south of the isthmus of Catanzaro; with this, the cities of Caulonia and Rhegium were isolated and, in effect, delivered over to Dionysius. Caulonia was the first to fall, and its territory was added to that of Locri (389–388). Then Hipponium fell, and finally Rhegium, after eleven months of terrible suffering. The siege of Rhegium (according to Polybius, I, 6, 2) was simultaneous with the conquest of Rome by the Celts and with the Peace of Antialcidas (see pp. 212–13): its date, in other words, is 387–386 B.C.

Thus was ended the first phase of the expansion of Dionysius. He now held the extreme southern tip of Italy from the Gulf of Scylletium to the Straits of Messina. Even the Celts, who shortly before had conquered Rome, came within his orbit: after 386 his army included, besides Iberians and Campanians, Celtic mercenaries as well. Now the Syracusan fleet even ventured into the Adriatic Sea. Here, Dionysius colonized the island of Issa (the modern Lissa/Vis). The south Illyrian city of Lissus also came into his possession. A Syracusan settlement was founded in the Po Delta; it was the city of Adria, evidently first settled at this time. The name "Canal of Philistus" (*fossa Philistina*) reveals the presence in the area of the Po Delta of Philistus, friend and confidant of Dionysius. At the mouth of the Po stood the city of Spina, the necropolis of which has become famous as the result of recent excavations. A Syracusan colony also existed in Ancona. In the Adriatic as well as in the Tyrrhenian Sea, the principal threat to Dionysius' plans was the presence of Etruscan pirates. The Syracusan navy undertook repeated expeditions against them. In 384–383 the Temple of Leukothea in Pyrgi (the harbor of Caere in southern Etruria) was plundered. A Syracusan base was also set up in Corsica.

In the Third Carthaginian War (383–382 to 376 or 374) Dionysius also had to face enemies on Italic soil, where the Carthaginians had found allies. Again, no real decision was reached; on the contrary, the peace treaty confirmed anew the boundaries of the two spheres of influence. From now on the rivers Halycus and Himeras forced the dividing line between the territory of Dionysius and the Carthaginian *epikratia*. East of this line only the city of Heraclea Minoa belonged to the Carthaginians. This border continued in existence until the intervention of the Romans in Sicily. In southern Italy, Dionysius was able to take the city of Croton (379). In Taras, which had taken part in the war against him, the Sicilian ruler seems to have won a number of friends, among them the famous mathematician and statesman Archytas, the friend of Plato.

The empire of Dionysius had four divisions. Its nucleus was the territory of the city of Syracuse, which had grown considerably through the annexation of neighboring localities. The second category was the military colonies founded by the tyrant, where his discharged mercenaries found a new home. Among these were Catana, Leontini, Messana, Tauromenium, and Tyndaris. There were, besides, a number of allied cities such as Locri, which, by the will of Dionysius, assumed a leading position in southern Italy. The allied cities in Sicily included Acragas, Gela, and Camarina. But the tyrant's actual influence extended far beyond his empire and his naval bases. A great many cities and states were at pains to acquire his friendship. The Syracusan fleet fought in Greek waters in the Corinthian War and helped force Athens to accept the King's Peace (see p. 212). For long the relations between Athens and Dionysius were cold, but a change came shortly before his death, when both states concluded an alliance (see p. 234).

For all his successes as champion of the Western Greeks against Carthage, Dionysius, as long as he lived, remained a tyrant in Greek eyes. His rule, that is, was regarded as illegal and based on force, even though he had developed his position by the use of full military powers legally voted to him. Naturally, he had a considerable personal following in and outside Syracuse, and many friends and aides to help him build an empire. But basically he was, amid all his popularity and power, a solitary man. The strongest pillar of his rule was the army of mercenaries he had recruited from all parts of the world. The mercenaries cost a great deal of money, so that

Dionysius was forced to keep tapping new sources of funds. Personally moderate and unpretentious, he devoted his free time mainly to the arts. He was a writer of tragedies, one of which, entitled *The Ransom of Hector,* even won a prize in 367 at the Lenaean Festival in Athens. He took all conceivable measures for his personal protection. He surrounded himself with a bodyguard and maintained a secret police. We are told, for example, that he did not even trust the hair of his head to the barber's scissors, but let it grow or had his daughter singe it off with nutshells.

All this, however, cannot dim his great political achievement. He was greatly admired, and rightly, by Hannibal's opponent, the Roman Scipio Africanus Major. Under the scepter of Dionysius, the Sicilian Greek experienced a period of prosperity and of peace at home and abroad. All these blessings were, to be sure, purchased at a high price. Decisions in political matters no longer rested with the citizenry of Syracuse and the other Sicilian Greek cities; in these things the will of the tyrant was alone decisive, though he took pains to secure the formal assent of the Syracusan Assembly.

As a ruler and as a man, Dionysius I stands at a turning point in history. Himself a product of the polis, he set new goals in politics and statecraft and, over the opposition of his fellow citizens, achieved them for the most part. The figure of Dionysius points forward to the Hellenistic Age, in which the personality of the absolute ruler towers above all others: the will of the ruler is law, and his decrees are binding even on the city-states of the empire. When, in 367, Dionysius died a natural death after almost forty years of personal rule, he was once again in the midst of a war with Carthage. Under his son, Dionysius II, the war was brought to an end, probably in 366.

Dionysius was the eldest of six children, and did not always live in harmony with his brothers and sisters. But the old tyrant's officers, particularly the leaders of the mercenaries, refused to allow the supreme power to be divided, so Dionysius II came to the throne at the age of twenty-five. Tradition has given us, on the whole, quite an unfavorable picture of the young ruler. Politically he was a pawn in the hands of his brother-in-law, Dion. A decisive opponent of Dion was Philistus, just returned from exile. It was Dion who called Plato to Syracuse, and it was the influence of Philistus and his circle that later forced Plato to leave the city. But the younger Dionysius lacked the genius of his father. His rule, which began with various concessions to the people, soon deteriorated into despotism. He had some talent for literature; he made friends with philosophers and artists, the Pythagoreans being especially high in his favor. In 357, the exiled Dion forced his way back into the country, and Dionysius was besieged in the fortress of Syracuse. When he could no longer hope for aid from outside, he made his escape from the Acropolis, where his son, Apollocrates, continued to hold out. Dionysius II went to live in southern Italy, where the cities of Rhegium and Locri still remained in his possession. From Locri he returned once more to Syracuse (347).

The leading personality in Syracuse and in Sicily after 357 is unquestionably Dion, the son of Hipparinus. It was he who succeeded in liberating the city from Dionysius II. But Dion made major errors. He discredited much of his work by the murder of his rival Heracleides. In 354–353, Dion finally fell victim to assassination; his slayer was the Athenian Callippus, to whom he unsuspectingly entrusted himself.

Dion had close ties with the Platonic Academy in Athens; his murderer Callippus, for example, was a member of it. Plato himself, who was Dion's friend from 366 to 357, believed in all seriousness that through Dion he might realize his ideal political constitution in Syracuse. In this he was entirely wrong. An aristocratic form of government would simply not have worked in Syracuse; the city's upper classes were narrow-minded oligarchs, who had repeatedly demonstrated their refusal to make any concessions to the people, any sacrifices for the common good. Not only would such a constitution have been unworkable, it would have been fatal to Greek life on the island; and an end to tyrannical rule in Sicily would have spelled an end to effective resistance to Carthage. Says H. Berve: "The tragedy of the Hellenic world in Sicily was that, because of its exposed geographical position, reasons of foreign policy repeatedly forced the sacrifice of its cities' autonomy." The Platonic experiment could not be translated into reality on this soil. It stood in complete contradiction to the existing political realities.

Dion's failure was offset by another man's success. Timoleon, a Corinthian, had always been an ardent democrat and an enemy of tyrants. When the most respected citizens of Syracuse appealed to their mother city, Corinth, for aid against the returned tyrant Dionysius II, the Corinthians sent Timoleon to Syracuse as strategos. The choice was an excellent one; in the short space of fifty days, Timoleon succeeded in taking the Syracusan stronghold of Ortygia. Dionysius II had to capitulate in return for a safe-conduct. He was sent to Corinth (probably in 344), where he became an object of the citizens' curiosity, and reportedly lived down to the time of Alexander the Great.

Timoleon's second task was no less difficult: this was to expel the Carthaginians, who were again on the move in the Greek part of Sicily, this time in league with the tyrant Hicetas of Leontini, who had seized parts of Syracuse. Timoleon was able to recapture the citadel of Syracuse, which was then torn down, and the tyrants' houses and monuments destroyed. The Carthaginians suffered a complete defeat at the river Crimisus in 341. From then on they no longer ventured outside the bounds of their *epikratia*. The tyrants Hicetas of Leontini and Markos of Catana were also overcome by Timoleon. Finally, Messana too was taken. But as time went on, Timoleon was faced with impending blindness; he had to withdraw from politics, though he continued to serve the citizens with his counsels.

The Sicilian Greek world owed to Timoleon not only its liberation from the Carthaginians but also the internal settlement of the individual poleis, above all Syracuse. Timoleon expelled and executed the tyrants wherever they were to be found in Sicily; in this, he was inexorable. The single exception was Andromachus of Tauromenium (the father of the historian Timaeus), who had received and aided him on his

247

arrival in Sicily. In Syracuse Timoleon, with the aid of two other Corinthian lawgivers (*nomothetai*), established a mixed constitution, midway between oligarchy and democracy. The supreme office in the state was occupied by the priest of Olympian Zeus, a condition that, according to Diodorus (XVI, 70, 6), lasted more than three centuries. The inscription on his tomb honors him for restoring their laws to the Siceliotes— a reference to the revision of the old laws of Diocles. His services in the resettlement of the island were equally important; from Corinth large numbers of Greeks came to Sicily, among them many former exiles. The Greek element on the island was considerably increased, and the development of Greek culture strengthened there.

It was not Timoleon's fault that these measures could not prevent the rise of a new dictatorship after his death. The man who undid his work was Agathocles, the son of Carcinus, who was born in the Sicilian city of Thermae about 360 and took part as a young man in Timoleon's last war. Agathocles' rise to power began in 319–318, when he was appointed commander of the Syracusan fortresses in Sicily. He then followed the traditional road to a military command with full powers (316–315), and from there extended his influence until he had achieved the position of tyrant; all of which is reminiscent of the rise of the first Dionysius (see p. 199). The history of Syracuse in the fourth century leads us from tyranny to the constitutional government of Timoleon and back again to tyranny. The free Sicilian polis was unable to solve the great problems of domestic and foreign policy that beset it. Tyranny provided its own solutions; it was a prelude to Hellenistic kingship, which did the same for Greece proper: Agathocles, as we know, later assumed the title of King.

The Greeks of southern Italy had a different destiny. They welcomed with delight the end of the tyranny in Syracuse. But they thereby lost an important prop of their defense against the Italic peoples. They now turned for help to the Greek mother country: the Spartan King Archidamus III crossed over to southern Italy in 342. But he fell in battle against the combined forces of the Lucanians and the Messapians at Mandonium in 338.

The expedition of Alexander, King of the Molossians (334–333)—undertaken at about the same time as his nephew and brother-in-law Alexander the Great's departure for Asia—had an equally unhappy outcome. Summoned by the city of Taras, he fought against a series of southern Italic tribes. This Alexander is especially known for his treaty with Rome (ca. 333–331), probably occasioned by the need for a common front against the Samnites. It may be that Alexander, like Pyrrhus later on, intended to establish a kingdom of his own in southern Italy. In any event he came into conflict with the Greek cities, and lost his life at the hand of an assassin at Pandosia in 330. His brother-in-law, Alexander the Great, is said to have put his army into mourning on receiving the news of his death. Taras was at this time the most powerful of the Greek cities in southern Italy; in the last quarter of the fourth century, it enjoyed a period of relative peace, but it was an illusory one. The Samnites and Lucanians were involved in a life-and-death struggle with Rome which required all their energies (326–304); when it was over, the face of Italy was changed.

13

Greek Culture in the Fourth Century B.C.

The fourth century stands in the shadow of the death of Socrates (399 B.C.). The fact that a man went courageously to his death for his convictions, true to the laws of his native city, is by no means sufficient to explain the profound and far-reaching effect of his personality. In the death of Socrates there is much more: he gave his fellowmen a model that was never forgotten in all antiquity. When Seneca, on the discovery of the Pisonian conspiracy, went to his death by Nero's order, he consciously took heart from the death of Socrates, and used this as the model for his own. To some extent, of course, the fame of Socrates rests on his good fortune in having Plato for a disciple. The personality of this great philosopher and political thinker was profoundly influenced by that of his master. Though he saw Socrates in nearly super-human terms, nevertheless he understood him, and was able to transmit this understanding to his contemporaries, and to posterity, in an incomparable manner. The influence of this image of Socrates, as reflected by Plato, is so strong and lasting that, to this day, no one who has encountered it can escape it.

Who was Socrates? Only a few details are known of his life. He was born in 470–469. His father was the sculptor

Sophroniscus, his mother the midwife Phaenarete. In his youth he received the education customary in Athens. When he was nearly forty the Peloponnesian War broke out; he served in the war as an ordinary hoplite, and took part in the fighting at Potidaea (432–429), Delium (424), and Amphipolis (422). When the people, in an illegal proceeding, tried the strategoi who had been in command at Arginusae and condemned them to death, it was Socrates who dared to contradict his countrymen in the Assembly.

For the rest, he was little interested in external things, and just as the philosopher Kant seldom went outside Königsberg, so Socrates felt no urge to see the world that lay outside Athens. All the intelligence and charm of Socrates were devoted to, and developed by, one simple pursuit: conversation. One could constantly come across him in the *gymnasion* or in the marketplace, discussing, arguing, questioning, in the midst of a circle of astonished listeners. Socrates was not a Sophist, although he made use of Sophistic methods. He never received and never asked for monetary payment. To many people he may even have become a nuisance, exposing them with his penetrating questions, and repeatedly showing them how little they really knew of the fundamental questions of life and government and religion. It does not come as a complete surprise, therefore, that there were three otherwise quite honorable men who, in 399, were ready to accuse him in court of not believing in the gods of the Athenian state, but introducing other gods and corrupting the young. The charge was, in this form, naturally false. But as Socrates refused to arouse the sympathy of the jury, he was condemned by a narrow majority, and thirty days later was executed by a draught of hemlock.

The significance of this unique man lies not so much in his remarkable capacity for conversation—this was for him only a means to an end—but in his striving for the truth, which he sought out tirelessly, doggedly and brilliantly. But he was also motivated by the conviction that man, once he knows what is right, will be able to do what is right. Socrates' creed was therefore a kind of ethical optimism; he believed not only

251

in the value of truth but in the goodness of man. Nowadays we tend to disagree: a knowledge of the truth does not, as a matter of practical experience, necessarily lead men to live according to the truth. It is not knowledge alone that rules man; Socrates' equation of knowledge with ethics ignores the irrational. But, then, Socrates was a reasonable man.

Socrates was one of the first to realize the full extent of the problem of education. His idea of education extended to the training of a man's soul, so that it might take its proper place before all the external things of life. This conscious turning away from material goods was simply revolutionary for the Greeks of that day; it represented a complete break with the outlook on life that had prevailed up to that time. In the words of an anonymous drinking song:

> Health is the greatest good to mortals,
> The second, to be beautiful in stature,
> The third, possessions won without fraud,
> The fourth, to bloom in the radiance of youth among
>   one's friends.

Socrates' ethic could, of course, lead to extreme individualism. It could result in a turning away from the state. It could, but in his case it did not, for Socrates, by his life and his death, showed the world that the state for him, in particular his own city of Athens, was a sacred and inviolable union. To obey the laws of one's city even when they seemed unjust—this was an attitude in pointed contrast to that of the thousands who saw the state only as a common feeding trough.

The secret of Socrates lies in the inseparable tie between his personality and his doctrine. In his lifetime Socrates had a positively magical attraction for the best of the Athenian youth; after his death, he was revered by them as a saint. Without question the execution of Socrates, one of the best citizens Athens ever produced, was the worst condemnation of the resurrected Athenian democracy and, with it, of the entire political life of Athens. If, in a state claiming to be a constitutional democracy, such a monstrous miscarriage of justice was possible, then it was clear to all the world that the standards of right and wrong had gone astray in Athens. Equal injustice had been done in the trials of the Arginusae generals—but then Socrates had been alive to condemn it. With his death, and by his death, Athens lost her conscience.

Socrates worked only through oral conversation; he left behind no written record. It was his pupil Plato (427–347) who, in his *Dialogues,* cast the image of Socrates for all time. Xenophon's *Memorabilia,* written a full lifetime after the death of Socrates, is useful only for certain surface details. If anything is certain, it is that Xenophon did not understand the inner nature of his master. Aristotle, on the other hand, cannot be dispensed with entirely if we wish to reconstruct the image of Socrates; he is essential to a proper understanding of Socratic dialectic. But the most important source by far continues to be Plato, especially his so-called early dialogues, in particular the *Protagoras* and the *Laches.*

Of Plato's own life we know more than a little, thanks to his writing; the Platonic *Epistles* are an especially valuable source, and not only for his biography, as historians in recent times have come to recognize. The question of the degree of their authenticity cannot be discussed here in detail.

Plato was born in Athens in 427, of an old and noble Attic family. He was a typical Athenian child, it seems, devoted to athletics and the like; grown to young manhood, he found his way to Socrates, and from his twentieth to his twenty-eighth year (407 to 399) belonged to the circle of his pupils. These are the impressionable years in a man's life; the impressions Plato now received changed his world forever. Another important turning point came in 390, when he made his first Sicilian journey. On that journey he came into contact not only with the Pythagoreans in southern Italy but also with the great tyrant Dionysius I of Syracuse. Whether, after a quarrel, the latter had Plato sold on the slave market in Aegina may be left an open question; possibly this is one of the Platonic legends that began to form among his pupils soon after his death. Returned to Athens, Plato founded the Academy, so called from its location in the grove of the Hero Academus. There he created an intellectual center for his pupils, for

253

teaching and common inquiries. This Platonic Academy was the model for many other intellectual institutions. It was the oldest philosophical school of Athens, and existed as such for more than 900 years. When the Emperor Justinian I closed it in A.D. 529, he closed the chapter on almost a millennium of educational endeavor that was of incomparable importance for Western man. Plato made two more long journeys abroad, in 367–366 and 361–360. Again Sicily was his destination, where he vainly hoped to turn his political philosophy into reality.

But Plato's destiny did not favor him in politics. He has given a truly moving description of this in his *Seventh Epistle:*

> The older I grew, the more difficult it seemed to be effective as a statesman in Athens. It was impossible without faithful friends and comrades, and these were hardly available any longer; for our city was no longer governed according to the customs and institutions of our fathers, and to acquire new ones with any ease was not possible, for the letter of the laws, and our customs, were giving way to an ever greater corruption and disrespect. The result was that, whereas at first I had been filled with a strong desire for public service, now, when I considered these things, seeing everything being driven helter-skelter, my head was in a whirl; it was not that I gave up the hope that things might one day become better, but that I kept on waiting for the opportune moment to act, until at last I realized that all existing states without exception had irremediably bad constitutions. . . . So in praise of true philosophy I was obliged to say, that through it alone can we recognize what is right for states as well as individuals; and that the human race will never be delivered from its ills until either the race of right and true philosophers come into public office, or until, by divine dispensation, that of rulers of our cities become genuine philosophers.

Plato's disillusionment with the possibilities of politics was not unnatural; the management of his city's affairs was in the hands of men considerably less than ideal; his Sicilian experiment had foundered on his own misunderstanding of the nature of Western Greek tyranny. Plato therefore turned away from the affairs of this world, to the world of the imperishable and the eternal. This was a change that had already been adumbrated in Socrates; in Plato, it was fully developed, and produced one of the greatest intellectual revolutions ever seen in the world. To the world of appearances Plato opposed the world of ideas. The influence of the teaching of the Pythagoreans is plainly visible here. The nature of things reveals itself to Plato in things, not as they are, but as they ought to be—the ideas (*ideai, eide*). He is able to recognize them on the basis of recollection, *anamnesis*. "Over against the invisible world of what is truly real, the eternally unchanged essences accessible only to pure thought, there stands, midway between being and non-being, in a constant state of becoming, the visible world of appearance, of coming to be and passing away" (W. Capelle).

The Greek as we know him is devoted to the concrete and the palpable, to the here-and-now: to understand this is to grasp the astounding novelty of Platonic thought. Plato revealed to the men of his time a new world, a world that was bound to have a vast attraction for every thinking person. But this attraction was not without danger. It could lead to a denigration of life in this world, in particular to a neglect of political life. Yet Plato's real significance lies in the field of political thought. Although his more strictly political writings, the *Politeia* (*The Republic*) and the *Nomoi* (*The Laws*), hardly received the attention they deserved in his lifetime, they later exerted, through the philosophy of late antiquity and through the *interpretatio Christiana,* a towering influence on the political thought of Medieval and modern times.

Plato was not the first to concern himself with the plan of the ideal state. Many years earlier Hippodamus of Miletus, the friend of Pericles, drew up such a plan. It was influenced by the Spartan constitution, and envisaged a professional division of the citizens into soldiers, farmers, and artisans (Aristotle, *Politics* II, 1267, 13 ff.). About 400 B.C., a quarter-century before Plato, one Phaleas of Chalcedon wrote a similar work, in which the principles of equality of property and education and equal citizen rights for all free men were advanced. These ideas were in the air, so to speak, so it is not surprising that Plato concerned himself with these problems at this time.

The *Politeia* appeared in 374, at a time when Persia dominated the affairs of Greece. The fundamental idea of *The Republic* is this: a genuine statesman must be a man who has set the continual moral betterment of the citizens under his care as his only goal. This is the theme of *paideia,* of education, which plays a central role in all of Plato's thought. The population of Plato's ideal state is divided into three classes or castes, the producers (*demiurgoi*), the guardians (*phylakes*), and—selected from the latter class—the rulers. The highest task of the state is the education of the guardian class. Its members have no personal property, and they live and take their meals together. The Spartan model is unmistakable here. Since Plato held the revolutionary view that men and women were to a degree similarly gifted, women too were admitted to the ranks of the guardians. Equally revolutionary is his demand for the abolition of private property. Marriage also goes by the board; instead women and children are possessed in common. Through an extremely complicated system of eugenic mating festivals, the best men and the best women are to be brought together. The children of these unions are brought up by the state; the other children are left to die of exposure. From the guardian class the "rulers" are chosen. They receive an especially careful education, and after long years of proving themselves in the service of the state, they are, at the age of fifty, ready at last to rule. It is their obligation to see to it that the principles of the state are upheld. It is a state without wealth and without poverty, a state in which the number of citizens must remain substantially constant. It is also a state without progress and without development—to Plato, the best of all conceivable states.

There is no doubt that Plato, when he wrote this book, entirely expected to see this plan put into practice. He was then in the prime of life, having just passed fifty (Plato, we note, had prescribed that the "rulers" must have completed their fiftieth year); at this age one is, as a rule, not yet ready to retire. Plato had a contemporary model for the realization of such a plan in the Spartan state. To criticize the Platonic state is an easy assignment, for Plato's ideal state had a fatal structural flaw. Plato overlooked the fact that every viable state is based on power. If a state does not possess power, it will be crushed by stronger states. Its destruction is absolutely certain, unless it can join a larger system of alliances. Certainly every state must care for the education of its citizens; but of at least equal weight is its care for their defense and for the power of their community. This aspect of political life Plato neglected; the economic aspect he almost completely ignored. The compulsion of the individual in the Platonic state, which goes far beyond anything practiced even among the Spartans, makes of Plato's Utopia one enormous prison. Can Plato, for example, seriously expect his guardians to give up marriage and private property? As long as the state is a community of human beings, private property must continue to exist: pride of possession is inseparably bound up with human nature; the acquisitive impulse is a human instinct. The state cannot simply abrogate the nature of man; neither should political theory.

But let us not lose sight of Plato's purpose in writing *The Republic*. Plato's state was created in the service of an ideal. This was the ideal of justice, which he carried out, with unswerving consistency, to it furthest logical conclusions. The Platonic state is designed to last; everything must be subordinated to this, not least the happiness of the individual citizen. It will be perfectly obvious that the Platonic state stands in sharp contrast to liberalism as it has developed in Europe since the French Revolution. It should also be obvious that the virtues of Plato's state lie elsewhere; for unity, for self-sufficiency, no other political order ever imagined can touch it.

Plato's stay in Sicily and his association with Dion dashed his hopes for an early realization of the program of *The Republic*. In his last years Plato once more took pen in hand and wrote what became, so to speak, his political testament. It bears the title *Nomoi* (*The Laws*). The work was drafted by Plato himself, but was published only after his death by his pupil Philippus of Opus. While Plato was writing *The Laws,* a great change

257

was coming about in the Greek world: the rise of Macedonia under Philip II. This was observed with understandable anxiety by the Greeks, especially in Athens. In the *Nomoi* we find a different Plato than in his earlier works, and this profound change is one of the reasons why some critics have denied that Plato was the author of the *Nomoi* (see Gerhard Müller, *Studien zu den Platonischen Nomoi,* Munich, 1952). That the work is authentic should, however, be perfectly obvious to the student of Plato.

The state of *The Laws* is no longer the idealistic state; it is not the best imaginable, but the best that can be realized in this world and therefore the second-best state. And here, too, the problem of education is central. Plato even went so far as to demand compulsory education for all. In this, he was far in advance of his time. The ancient world never required compulsory schooling. King Frederick William I was the first major ruler to introduce it, in Prussia (a few small German states had preceded him in the seventeenth century). But compulsory education is simply one aspect of a state that is compulsory in every way in the *Nomoi*. Robert von Pöhlmann has termed this second-best state of Plato's a completely intolerable coercive state, in fact a police state of the most thoroughgoing kind. In *The Laws* everything is subjected to government control, even the raising of one's children. A central role in the *Nomoi* is played by religion; Plato was now, and increasingly, under the influence of Orphism. It is horrifying to see that this state which so honors the laws does not shrink from the heaviest punishments, not even from capital punishment, for those who, for example, dared reject the state religion.

How could Plato arrive at such a flat denial of his own principles? We read *The Laws* and find an ideal state in which the citizens' free will stands for virtually nothing, and compulsion stands for everything. Where is the heritage of his teacher Socrates, whose life was devoted to teaching men how to find the good in themselves, how to live a better life by their own free choice? It is nowhere to be found in *The Laws,* Plato's last word to the world.

The third great name among the philosophers is Aristotle,

whose master and guide was Plato himself. Concerning his life we are relatively well informed, with the exception of a few years after 340. Aristotle was born in 384 of a family of physicians in Stagira on the Chalcidice peninsula. His father, Nicomachus, was the personal physician of King Amyntas III of Macedonia, the father of Philip II. Medicine was the most empirical of the Greek sciences; Aristotle was therefore predisposed to a life of empirical research. This background also gave him a close relationship to the Macedonian King.

His life was a tapestry of changing fortunes. In 367, at the age of seventeen, he came under the influence of Plato, by then already a man of sixty. For twenty years, until the master's death, he sat at Plato's feet in the Academy before the gates of Athens and received the impressions that were decisive for his entire life. The bond between teacher and pupil was dissolved only by Plato's death in 347. In the same year Aristotle answered a summons from the tyrant Hermias of Atarneus, who had also been a pupil of Plato's, to come to Assos in the Troad. His three years in Assos (347–344) as Hermias' close associate must have given him extensive experience in practical politics. Hermias was able, for a time, to maintain the independence of his small state between the great powers Persia and Macedonia, but he was slain by the Persian mercenary Mentor of Rhodes in 342–341.

By this time, however, Aristotle had already arrived, after a stay in Mytilene (344–343), at the court of Philip II in Pella; Philip had summoned him there to become the tutor of his son Alexander, later Alexander the Great. In his later years Alexander repeatedly acknowledged the profound influence of Aristotle. That the great Macedonian King enthusiastically embraced Greek culture is at least partly the work of his teacher, Aristotle. From 340 to 335 we lose trace of Aristotle. Then he reappears in Athens. Here he established a school of his own in the *gymnasion* of the Lyceum, which soon took its place on an equal footing with the Platonic Academy.

In the Lyceum, or *Peripatos*—as the school was called, after its walks—Aristotle spent his most productive years. Here, surrounded by pupils from all parts of the world, he rose to become the acknowledged leader of Greek intellectual life. On the news of Alexander's death in 323, Aristotle fled from Athens to Chalcis on the island of Euboea, since he was known in Athens to be a friend of the Macedonians. He died in Chalcis in the following year. The Macedonian regent Antipater was named as executor of his will. His successor in the Lyceum was Theophrastus of Eresus.

Werner Jaeger, in his extraordinary book, *Aristotle: Fundamentals of the History of His Development,* has drawn a picture of the evolution of Aristotle's intellect that, in its basic outlines, is certainly correct. Three phases are to be distinguished in the life of Aristotle. During the first, which lasted till Plato's death, Aristotle is under the decisive influence of his teacher. After Plato's death the years of wandering begin, during which he slowly frees himself from Plato's influence. In the third and final period, from 335 on, Aristotle is the great master, the lord of the whole realm of knowledge. The broad lines have been drawn correctly by Jaeger, but one point is open to debate: whether Aristotle's great turning toward natural science and scholarship is entirely the product of the last period of his life. After all, as the son of a physician he was familiar with empirical research from his youth onward.

Whatever the cause, the results were remarkable. Aristotle left to posterity an astonishing wealth of writings. In philosophy proper he concerned himself with questions of logic and epistemology, with psychological and ethical problems; the whole range of the natural sciences—especially physics, zoology, and botany—was familiar ground to him; so also was the terrain of historical and literary research. For example, Aristotle prepared a complete list of the victors in the Pythian Games, which naturally meant a thorough study of the archives. His nephew Callisthenes worked at his side in this task. Aristotle examined the documents relating to the dramatic productions in Athens, laying the groundwork for the critical studies of the Alexandrian philologists; with Aristotle's *Didascaliae* (now lost) as a point of departure, the Alexandrian philological school was able to establish the basic chronology of ancient drama. Aristotle brought into his research work many of the pupils he had attracted to Athens from the entire Greek world. His methods of organizing research were unprecedented and had the most far-reaching influence. In his person he united the entire *universitas litterarum,* which fell apart after his death into a scattering of independent disciplines. This universal genius, therefore, stands at the end of an intellectual epoch, but also at the beginning of another, which takes its starting point from his all-embracing work. The rise of science and scholarship in the Hellenistic Age was squarely based on Aristotle; so was the whole intellectual culture of the Middle Ages, to which Aristotle's works were transmitted in part by the Arabs. Not until the Renaissance and the centuries that followed it did the world gradually free itself of the overwhelming influence of Aristotle. The immense effort and sacrifice that this cost are the measure of the power of his thought.

Like his teacher Plato, Aristotle was deeply concerned with political theory. Unlike Plato, however, he never attempted to intervene actively in political life. His was a predominantly theoretical nature; contemplation meant more to him than action. His greatest political legacy was the *Politics,* a book that has continually attracted historians and politicians, among them Wilhelm Oncken and Heinrich von Treitschke. Since Werner Jaeger's researches it may be taken as certain that the *Politics* was written over a very long period of time. The earliest parts date from the years at Assos; the book was completed and partly revised in the final period in Athens. In the older strata, the intellectual affinity with Plato is clear; later sections are already written with an eye to empirical knowledge. For Aristotle, man is a political being (*zoon politikon*); that is to say, man can fulfill his true function only as a member of the state. The state that Aristotle was thinking of, however, was the polis, which in his own day was being subjected to severe trial. In the book's later sections the practical foundations of the state are laid bare, much more clearly than they are with Plato. Aristotle not only thought about economic problems—unlike Plato he was a supporter of private property—he also paid attention to the protection of the state by armed

261

power. The forms of the constitution are very important to him; he distinguishes among monarchy, aristocracy, and middle-class rule (*politeia*); for all three forms there are corresponding deviational forms (*parekbaseis*), tyranny, oligarchy, and democracy, i.e., extreme democracy, which Aristotle rejects. To Aristotle the ideal constitution is the *politeia,* in which control lies in the hands of the middle class. Wealth and poverty are not to be banned from the Aristotelian state anymore than is slavery, to which Aristotle takes not the slightest exception.

The political theory of the *Politics,* in which the sum of long experience is digested, was supplemented by collection of Greek constitutions which Aristotle's pupils prepared at his direction. No less than 158 of these constitutions were recorded and described. One of them, and probably the most important, has been miraculously preserved on an Egyptian papyrus only discovered in 1889, which is now in London. This work was written shortly after 330 B.C., but perhaps not published until after the master's death. It gives a review of the development of the Athenian Constitution from the earliest times, and in a second, systematic section, a survey of the Athenian public officials and their tasks. Both parts are equally valuable, although to our disappointment the historical penetration of this study, especially the first part, leaves something to be desired. But our knowledge of earlier Athenian constitutional history has, by Aristotle's book, been placed upon a new foundation. That the author has let a few mistakes and oversights creep into his work may be forgiven him.

That the writings of Plato and Aristotle on political theory did not, in their own time and in their own city, receive the attention they deserved can be traced to various causes. The fact that the works appeared at a time when the polis had already passed its peak should not be overlooked. The rise of Macedonia, Alexander's later conquest of the Persian Empire, the formation of the kingdoms of the Diadochi, all put the Greek polis more and more into the background. Completely new problems arose, which could no longer be solved by traditional means. Plato only saw this new age approaching from afar; Aristotle, the teacher of Alexander, lived to see it come into existence. But in all his writings, there is not a single reference to the problem of universal monarchy, and this changed very little in the period following Aristotle's death. Theophrastus, for instance, his successor as head of the Peripatetic School, published a book under the title, *How the Poleis Can Be Best Administered* (the work has unfortunately not been preserved).

Finally, we must bear in mind that in the fourth century a large number of philosophers simply lost interest in the polis. Aristippus of Cyrene (ca. 435 355), who had sat at the feet of Socrates as a young man, is no longer prepared to assume any kind of function in the service of the city-state. He finds this activity a burdensome distraction; it is unsuited to his philosophical ideal of a life of hedonism. A low opinion of the Greek state was also held by his opponent Antisthenes, founder of the Cynic school of philosophy. Antisthenes was born about 450 and died sometime after 366; he was the son of a Thracian female slave, and therefore never became a full citizen of Athens. Significantly, it is in Antisthenes that we first find the complaint that expert knowledge is not sufficiently honored in the polis. Antisthenes is supposed to have said that one might as well appoint donkeys and horses to official posts as appoint people who understood nothing. From Antisthenes, it is no long leap to Diogenes of Sinope, his pupil, who declared that he was not a citizen of any single polis, but that his polis was the cosmos. Here lie the roots of the idea of world citizenship (cosmopolitanism) in antiquity, an idea that also contributed to the dissolution of the psychology of the city-state.

What was the polis like in the first half of the fourth century B.C.? We possess a treatise written by one Aeneas Tacticus, on the measures to be taken in the event of a siege. This book, which we can probably date sometime between 357 and 340, draws an interesting picture of a small city-state of the Greek homeland, a picture more realistic than any to be had from the other literary sources of the time. The author remains unknown to us; the attempt of earlier scholars (such as Casaubon and Hug) to identify Aeneas with the Arcadian strategos

Aeneas of Stymphalus, mentioned in Xenophon (*Hellenica,* VII, 3. 1), is not necessarily successful. Again and again in the early fourth century Greek cities came under siege; there was a siege of Phlius about 381–379 by the Spartans under Agesilaus, and Mantinea was besieged in 385. The precautions that Aeneas lists are therefore no theoretical exercise.

Aeneas gives a whole series of concrete recommendations. As soon as the danger of war appears, cattle, movable property, and slaves must be removed from the *chora,* or rural areas, and placed in the care of a neighboring city. (The deposit in neutral territory of property threatened by war was perfectly common at that time, as is shown by a treaty between the dynast Hermias of Atarneus and the city of Erythrae, in Asia Minor; we have this on an inscription dating from the period before 342–341.) (Bengtson, *Staatsvertraege,* No. 322.) If possible, the land (Aeneas continues) is to be completely evacuated, and the free population and the produce brought within the shelter of the walls. If anyone refused to comply, his property in the *chora* was to be left to be plundered with impunity. Particular care must be taken that no contact be made between the city and its exiles outside. For this reason censorship of mail is recommended. In fact, everything and everyone that enter and leave the city must be strictly supervised; foreigners are to be received within the walls only with the knowledge of the authorities, and it must be noted in whose house they intend to stay; this applies also to all those staying in the city as students. Those who import oil or grain into the city are to receive a public commendation and an award, the amount to be regulated according to the quantity of goods imported.

That the polis cannot manage its defense without mercenaries is taken for granted by Aeneas. He proposes that individual citizens recruit and provision mercenaries according to their means; the state can partially reimburse them later on. Those elements of the population who resist the prevailing social order must be won over to their city's cause; Aeneas suggests the reduction or cancellation of debts as a means.

It is clear that Aeneas is very much concerned with the

internal unity of the polis and its inhabitants; all his recommendations are designed, in the last analysis, to serve this end.
We know that precisely in the fourth century the internal
harmony of the Greek cities deteriorated sharply; again and
again we hear of attempted revolutions; exiles, of whom there
were a great number, were especially feared on this account.
Fear of internal discord is so ingrained in Aeneas that he ad-
vises against employing any aliens in the defense of the city.
When defense exercises were to be held, the aliens would
have to go to a special area assigned to them, or else remain
at home. Mistrust of the aliens, even of mercenaries, was only
too justified. Repeatedly they deliberately played into the
enemy's hand.

Against whom are all these preparations made? Aeneas is
thinking not only of neighboring cities but also of the great
mercenary leaders, who often acted on their own, leading
their troops to war in their own private interest. The exiles, as
we have seen, were forever a source of potential unrest; as-
tonishingly enough, Aeneas does not seek remedy for all this
in symmachies; on the contrary, he recommends that allied
troops be received into the city only in numbers that will not
outweigh its own forces. To these counsels of mistrust he adds
advice on a number of technical questions: he deals with the
correct way of shutting the city gates, with guard duty, signaling, and other matters.

To read this expert treatise is to sense something of the spirit
that animated the polis of the fourth century. The polis was
prepared to risk everything to secure its own existence; it
could do so as long as it had to reckon with enemies that were
also from the world of city-states. More powerful opponents
than these did not threaten it before 360 B.C. But waiting in
the wings were the siege engines of the Macedonian King.

Imagine the polis described by Aeneas seriously taking as
its basic problem the education of its citizens, as Plato demanded in his *Politeia* and *Nomoi,* and you have imagined
the impossible. Between Aeneas and Plato stands a deep abyss;
a state whose existence is continually endangered will pay far
more attention to military affairs than to education. The

internal instability of the polis, aggravated from outside by violent mercenaries and vindictive exiles, forms the background for whole chapters of Greek history in the fourth century. Plato describes the ideal state; Aeneas show us the historical polis.

Greeks as mercenaries can be traced back to the earliest relations between Greece and the empires of the ancient Near East. At the beginning of the sixth century B.C., Greeks served the Kings of Egypt and Babylon as hired troops. The names of Greek and Carian mercenaries are immortalized by graffiti on the colossus of Ramses II at Abu Simbel in Nubia. The Greek mercenaries were exceptionally valued because of their fighting qualities. In the fourth century they were to be found in all parts of the world, in the service of the Persian Great King or of his satraps, and in the West as well, with the Carthaginians. The soldier who acquired money and prestige abroad returned home to retire a wealthy man. Of the rest, who found ruin and death in foreign lands, history tells us nothing.

The Eldorado for recruiters of Greek mercenaries was the Peloponnese. The names of several mercenary captains appear in Xenophon's *Anabasis*. Among them were Clearchus from Lacedaemonia, an exile; Aristippus, a Thessalian who had been forced out of his country by his political enemies; Proxenus, a Boeotian; Sophainetus of Stymphalus; Socrates of Achaea; Xennias from Parrhasia; Pasion from Megara; Sosis from Syracuse, and others. At the same time, there were also Greek mercenaries on the Persian side—no fewer than 400 in the army of Abrocomas in Syria. Tissaphernes himself had a Greek instructor, Phalinus of Zacynthus, whom he held in high honor. When Athens and Persia were on good terms, between 375 and 373, Iphicrates and Timotheus, with their Greek mercenaries, served successively under the Great King Artaxerxes II in Egypt, though they were unable to give him decisive victories against the Egyptian rebels. In the reconquest of Egypt in the winter of 343–342, two Greek mercenary leaders distinguished themselves, the Theban Lacrates and the Rhodian Mentor, who was appointed supreme commander on the Asia Minor Littoral as a reward. His brother Memnon was

266

one of the dynasts in Asia Minor under the last Persian Kings and was the only Persian officer who could approach Macedonian Alexander as a strategist. The death of Memnon in 333 freed Alexander of a dangerous and worthy opponent, who had defeated his forces several times in the Aegean (see p. 309).

At home, in the armies of the Lacedaemonians and the Athenians, there were increasingly large numbers of mercenaries in the fourth century. Agesilaus owed his victory at Coronea (394) in large part to former Greek mercenaries of Cyrus under Herippidas; Xenophon was probably among them. Particularly sought after were certain special troops, such as archers from Crete, spearmen from Thessaly, Acarnania, and Locris, and slingers from Rhodes. There were several recruiting centers in Greece, of which the best known were Corinth and Cape Malea at the southern tip of Laconia.

The use of mercenaries had become necessary because citizens more and more regarded military service as a burden. Demosthenes' passionate laments on this falling-off from former standards are well known. The state compensated for this by forcing the citizens to pay an exemption tax, which found its way into the pockets of the mercenaries, many of whom amassed a considerable fortune. Men like Iphicrates, Timotheus, Charidemus, and Chares had a large body of followers, which made them almost independent of the Athenian state. The great mercenary captains have a commanding share in the history of Greece in the fourth century. The mercenary army's weakness lay in its lack of national purpose; the men risked their lives for anyone who could pay them.

Hand in hand with the practice of using mercenaries went the transformation in Greek military technique, most notably in the field of siege craft. It had been usual in the fifth century to subdue cities by starving them out, but around 400 B.C. this gave way to new methods. The Carthaginians brought new siege machines with them in their attack on the Greek cities of Sicily, including high movable towers on which were mounted not only battering rams but also catapults, here used for the first time. These were torsion catapults in which the tension required to fire a stone ball or heavy metal arrow was produced by twisting leather thongs. Even though hours might be required to make these machines ready for action, their mortal effect was enormous. The arrows shot from them pierced every armor at short and even middle distances, and the great stone balls swept the defenders from the walls. Dionysius I was the first Greek to build these instruments of war in imitation of the Carthaginians, improving in part on his models. Soon he possessed a great stock of siege engines and catapults. In Greece proper the new siege technique was introduced by Philip II of Macedon. The siege of Perinthus (340) ushered in a new age in warfare for continental Greece.

When Nicanor of Stagira, at the Olympic Festival in 324, read out Alexander's decree requiring that all Greek exiles be readmitted to their own cities, there were reportedly present at Olympia no less than 20,000 refugees from all parts of Greece. From the earliest times, exiles had been a danger to the political stability of the Greek states, for their whole will and energy was bent on returning to their native city and regaining their confiscated property. It was part of the normal process of Greek political life that the opponents of the ruling party in a city-state had to leave the field, losing not only their citizenship but also their property. A man thus exiled, unless he had a close friend outside his native city, was in a desperate situation; many had to become mercenaries or hired dependents. There were exiles in every city, and their numbers were seldom reduced, for when they returned to their native place —mostly in the wake of hostile armies, as the Athenian exiles came with Lysander in the spring of 404—their day of reckoning came, in which the banished exiled their banishers in turn. The number of exiles was further increased by the verdicts in the great political trials in Athens in the fourth century. The careers of many politicians, among them Timotheus, Callistratus, and Chabrias, were abruptly terminated. More and more as a matter of course, the Athenians shifted the blame for political failures on to the leading politicians of the day. But the death penalty was imposed in only a few cases, and many politicians had to interrupt their careers for only a short time.

But political life had now assumed forms that gave cause for concern. Freedom of speech, the palladium of democracy, had produced some very unwelcome side effects. Orators poured torrents of the most incredible abuse on each other, and we are shocked even today by the vocabulary in which Demosthenes described his rival, Aeschines: "scribbler" and "charlatan" are the mildest expressions. Aeschines' father is derided as a slave, his mother as a prostitute. Aeschines gave back as good as he got. He addressed Demosthenes as the scum of humanity, as a murderer, as the greatest villain in Hellas. Repeatedly the speeches incite the audience to outright violence against the political opponent of the moment. It was not unusual for the people to laugh the speaker off the rostrum, or even force him off. Attic fourth-century orators appealed to the worst instinct of the masses, promoting—consciously or unconsciously—the terrorization of political life. The people repeatedly placed themselves in the hand of the demagogues, where they served as tools for personal political ambition. Worse, they would not long remain loyal to any one demagogue. How could there be a stable policy when the mood of the demos, in its sovereign Assembly, was as changeable as a weather vane? The people have a short memory, and in all periods of history demagogues have been able to count on this. Thus in the speeches of Demosthenes there are lies, distortions, and disfigurements of fact, which often make his testimony completely worthless for the historian. Where, in Athens, was that internal harmony of the city's people that Aeneas Tacticus held up as the *sine qua non* of self-defense?

Extreme democracy gave its citizens political equality; this failed to satisfy many, who began to demand economic equality as well. The slogans here were "cancellation of debts" and "redistribution of land," and they aroused a ready response among the poorer part of the population. Repeatedly the state found itself forced to acquire new land for settlement, and the question of food supply became an issue by which the whole political life of the city could be manipulated. In the Assembly the naked self-interest of the demos governed the legislation and policy of the state, the self-interest of those who had become accustomed to "feed at the public trough" (Aristophanes, *Ecclesiazusae,* 873).

Bismarck once said that in general the Phaeacian way of life was more comfortable than the Spartan, since the Phaeacian style was to eat and drink and be protected in return for no sacrifices, or in any case as few sacrifices as possible. This describes a large percentage of fourth-century Athenians, especially the well-to-do. Interest in politics had been replaced by the striving for material wealth, economic questions dominated the debates in the Assembly, and every politician, whether he wanted to or not, had to cope with economic problems.

A contemporary document on economic thought is Xenophon's little book, *On Ways and Means (Poroi),* written shortly before 354. Xenophon makes it perfectly clear that the state's first obligation is to provide public assistance to its citizens; he regards the dole as a perfectly natural way of life. Athens' hope of flourishing and prospering depends primarily on the state of her finances; a city that has money is, he says, protected against all mischance, in particular against bad harvests, and even against war! The state is regarded as the great organizer of economic life, and he advances a series of proposals for improving state revenues accordingly. The work was probably written under the shadow of Athenian failure in the Social War (357–355), in which Athens again lost much of her empire. It is valuable testimony to the pacifist mood that resulted in Athens.

The art of drawing up a state budget had not yet been discovered in Greece. This, as can easily be imagined, made financial administration a practically insoluble task. The achievement of those men—Callistratus, Eubulus, Lycurgus— who brought order into the financial affairs of Athens must be rated all the more highly. Linked with the rise of economic thought in the fourth century was the development of a proper banking system. Many of these institutions began with quite modest resources, but some of them—the banking house of Pasion in Athens, for instance—accumulated sizable reserves. The origin of banking can probably be traced to the fact that, with the great number of coins of the most varied origin then current in Greece, extensive exchange operations were unavoidable. The principal source of a banker's earnings was naturally loans, which brought high rates of interest. The capital market was very sensitive to external crises, and the interest rates would shoot upward in wartime: it amounted to as much as 25 percent in the Corinthian War; it hovered around 12 percent per year in normal times. The man who was adept at banking could become the Greek equivalent of a millionaire. Thus Pasion, after thirty years in business, is said to have retired with a fortune of between forty and sixty talents. He had started with precisely nothing.

On the whole, a gradual rise in prices and a corresponding rise in wages are evident in the fourth century. Against the great numbers of the poor and destitute, there stood a handful of surpassingly wealthy citizens. At his death, Conon is said to have had a fortune of forty talents (one talent = 60 minae = 6,000 drachmas = 36,000 obols), of which seventeen talents were inherited by his son Timotheus: Conon, naturally, was regarded as one of the wealthiest men in Athens. In the year 378–377, an estimate was made of the private property in Athens, and the total was 5,750 talents, excluding state property and the possessions of the *thetes,* who were the lowest tax class. The wealth of the Athenian population as a whole in the fourth century was presumably very much higher. This property estimate was the basis for the apportionment of direct taxes, the level of which varies in accordance with current state needs.

But despite taxes and *leitourgiai* (an attempt was made to distribute the burdens of the latter more justly by the system of *symmoriai* after 357), in wartime great gaps in the state's finances still appeared. In order to fill these, the Greeks did not hesitate to collect compulsory loans from their temples and to apply temple funds to political purposes. If worse came to worst, they did not shrink from melting down the silver votive offerings. The Phocians' forced loans from the temple in Delphi became notorious, but even the Phocians, in the Third Sacred War (356–346), were only doing what others had done before them—the Athenians, for example, and the Arcadians, the latter in the national shrine of Olympia. Much bolder than the governments of the Greek city-states, however, were the tyrants, especially Dionysius I; they employed confiscations and direct taxes in order to defray their great military expenses. The second book of the *Oeconomica,* which tradition includes among the writings of Aristotle, cites a number of examples of the financial practices of tyrants and others. Although the work is not especially profound, it is nevertheless valuable as historical evidence. It dates probably from the time after Alexander's death, and may have been written before 306–305 B.C.

Increasingly materialistic, Greek life in the fourth century was nevertheless distinguished by intellectual achievements of the very highest order. In Plato and Aristotle the Greeks produced two men whose work will endure as long as men live on this planet. In every direction one can see new life stirring, in the fourth century rhetoric, in historiography, in the exact sciences, in medicine, and certainly no less in the plastic arts. Even technology is marked by notable inventions, although most of them are employed for warfare.

Isocrates (436–338) is a prime example of a man for whom intellectual and political life were not yet separate compartments. He became famous for his formal orations and, in his last years, for the great manifestos that he addressed to Philip II of Macedon. Isocrates was unquestionably an Athenian patriot, but he was able to see beyond Attica's borders and recognized that Greece could progress only if she were able to export her surplus population. To where? He was thinking, in particular, of the military conquest of Asia Minor in a war against Persia, a war in which the Greeks' leader should be the Macedonian King. Isocrates did not live to see the realization of his plan, but his works were an effective preparation for the coming of a new age. His attitude toward Athenian democracy was something else. He did not like the rule of the masses, and it is no accident that during all his life he played no role in the Athenian Assembly. In Athens, he attracted a crowd of pupils from all parts of the Greek world. They included, among others, the Greek historians Theopompus of Chios and Ephorus of Cyme. Isocrates had a weakness for rulers. He addressed pamphlets to Nicocles, King of Salamis on Cyprus, which form a kind of ancient "Mirror of Princes." He also maintained close relations with Dionysius I of Syracuse, Jason of Pherae, and Philip II of Macedon. The glorification of rulers ran contrary to the maxims of Athenian democracy, but Isocrates never had serious difficulties in his native city; this is a sign of the high regard in which he was held by his fellow citizens.

A man of an entirely different stamp was his younger contemporary, Demosthenes (384–322 B.C.). To read his political orations is to be struck by the intense fervor and the unique passion that permeated this man. He outshone all rivals in the art of moving people in the ekklesia; Demosthenes, with his unmatched powers of persuasion, over and over again imposed his will on the spellbound citizens of Athens. He was not overly nice in his choice of means; to achieve results with the farmers and artisans of the Assembly required broad strokes of the orator's brush, even at the cost of truth. Of his power as an orator, there can be no serious doubt. His policies as a statesman are another matter; they led Athens straight to the catastrophic defeat of Chaeronea (338). For many classicists, Demosthenes is not only the master orator but also the supreme statesman, the greatest Athens had produced since Pericles. The learned Arnold Schaefer, to whom we owe an indispensable book about Demosthenes (*Demosthenes und Seine Zeit,* 2nd ed., 3 vols., 1885–1887), makes the entire history of the fourth century revolve around his great hero. Even Werner Jaeger, in his book *Demosthenes* (1939), endeavored to turn the great orator into a great statesman as well.

Certainly Demosthenes was an arresting personality, and it is not surprising that practical politicians, from Niebuhr to Clemenceau, have come under his spell. Yet Demosthenes was lacking in a quality indispensable to every genuine statesman. Having once taken his stand against Macedonia and King Philip, he was unable to change his views with changing

273

circumstances. What his politics lacked was the element of conciliation, without which any policy is doomed to failure in the long run. Worse, Demosthenes, by carrying the political antagonism between Athens and Macedonia onto the cultural plane, deepened the gulf between Macedonia and Greece in a critical hour and made it ultimately unbridgeable.

Demosthenes had a rival in Athens with whom he carried on the bitterest conflict for twenty years. This was Aeschines, who was naturally gifted in all the qualities of a good orator. He had a pleasant voice and a winning manner, he was fearless, and he had a gift for improvisation which outshone that of Demosthenes. He was born in humble circumstances, and worked at first as a government scribe and an actor; a wealthy marriage gave him the independence he needed to become an orator. At the age of forty-four—he was six years older than Demosthenes—he was a member of the Athenian embassy sent, under the leadership of Philocrates, to King Philip II in Pella. From that time on he was a staunch adherent of Philip II, and a no less resolute opponent of Demosthenes. The speeches of Aeschines that have been preserved—only three in all—are formally of the highest quality; they have both verbal elegance and the power to convince. But his talents did not save him from ruin. In 330 he was defeated in the "crown case" by his enemy Demosthenes, and had to go into exile. He died in Samos, nearly seventy-five years old, without having been reinstated in his native city.

There were many orators active in Athens in the fourth century: Hyperides, Hegisippus, Lycurgus, Phocion, Demades, and Deinarchus (who had been born in Corinth). Unquestionably the most important of these was Hyperides, a contemporary of Aeschines and a pupil of Plato and Isocrates. He acquired a sizable fortune as an advocate, and entered politics on the side of Demosthenes. He was the talk of Athens, not only for his brilliant speeches but also for his weakness for the opposite sex. It is characteristic that he wrote a speech in defense of the hetaera Phryne, who had been accused of atheism. The trial, which took place probably after 350, appears to have ended in Phryne's acquittal.

The fifth century had been the golden age of Attic tragedy

and the Old Comedy. None of the great tragedians had lived to see the beginning of the fourth century, and of the comic poets, Aristophanes alone was still alive in 400 B.C. Our scanty knowledge of the drama of the fourth century is due to the popularity of Euripides; soon after the turn of the century, in other words after his death, his plays came to dominate the Athenian stage. His contemporaries had grudged him victories; posterity gave him immortality. But the fourth century was still prolific of dramatic works. The Athenian Astydamas is supposed to have written no less than 240 tragedies and satyr plays; Carcinus of Athens is said to have written 160; and there are only the two most productive of the fourth-century poets.

In the last two decades of the century the plays of Menander introduced the "bourgeois comedy." This New Comedy, wholly disengaged from the political, portrayed purely human problems, as is confirmed by the recently discovered play *Dyskolos,* found on a papyrus now in Geneva. Between Aristophanes and Menander stands the so-called Middle Comedy, of which we know little apart from a number of playwrights' names. But from the titles of their plays and from the scanty fragments, it would appear that political allusions and political plots were still present in their work to some degree. The Middle Comedy was a drama of transition; it spans the time between the end of the Peloponnesian War and the appearance of Menander. The most important external change is the discontinuance not only of the *parabasis* but also of the choral songs, which were still obligatory in the comedy of Aristophanes.

It was during this same period that a large number of theaters were built in Greece. One of the most beautiful is the theater of Epidaurus, built by the great architect Polyclitus the younger, who also built the famous circular edifice in Epidaurus known as the Tholos. It is possible, however, that the theater of Epidaurus was not built until the third century. The beginnings of the Athenian Theater of Dionysus date from the fourth century, as do also the theaters in Pella (Macedonia), Syracuse, and Halicarnassus.

In 373–372, the famous Delphic Temple of Apollo burned

down. It was replaced by a new temple which was completed only after long years of work. The progress of construction was supervised by a commission, the *naopoioi,* or "Temple-builders"; the lists of members of this commission and of the states they represent give us an approximate picture of the shifting balance of power in the Delphic Amphictyony in the middle of the fourth century. The new temple was completed about 320 B.C., on the foundations of the old preclassical Temple of Apollo; architecturally, it was an anachronism in terms of the buildings then going up in the rest of Greece. This is probably to be attributed to the conservatism of the Delphic priests. The excavation of the temple in modern times has left many questions unanswered. We are still curious, for example, about where the Pythia issued oracles. Was it in the interior of the temple? Where did the faithful wait? Where did one cast the lots which were another way of receiving oracles? To these questions there are still no answers. Delphi had, in any case, lost none of its importance during the fourth century; many states still sought its friendship, and many were granted the privilege of *promantia,* or priority in putting questions to the oracle. Among the states so privileged was tiny Skiathos along with its colonists (Bengtson, *Staatsvertraege,* No. 295).

One of the great wonders of the world, however, was the huge sepulcher that the Dynast Mausolus of Caria (d. 353) erected for himself in Halicarnassus, on the Asia Minor coast. It was completed after his death by his sister Artemisia. We find here an architecture that already anticipates certain features of the Hellenistic Age. The most important sculptors of the day—Praxiteles and Scopas among them—worked on the figures of the *Mausoleum,* as it was called after the ruler who made it his eternal home. Other outstanding constructions in Asia Minor were the Temple of Artemis in Ephesus, and the shrine of Athena Polias in the little town of Priene; the latter was dedicated by Alexander in the year 334. The splendid Temple of Apollo at Didyma near Miletus, on the other hand, seems not to have been begun before the year 300.

On the whole, the artists, sculptors, and painters of the

fourth century found a wide demand for their work, at home and abroad. Since most of the originals have been lost, we can form an impression of their talents only by means of late copies of their works. The greatest sculptors were Praxiteles of Athens, Scopas of Paros, and Lysippus of Sicyon, of whom the last-named became famous for his bronze figures. Lysippus, like the painter Apelles, repeatedly portrayed Alexander the Great.

It cannot be said, then, that the fourth century was a period of retrogression in art. In fact quite the opposite is true. The various local schools, especially those in the Peloponnese (Argos, Sicyon) developed a rich tradition of their own, providing Greek art with many new masterworks. It is immediately obvious, however, that it is no longer the gods but humans—specifically, beautiful humans—whom the sculptors portray. Even portraits of the gods display human features. The distance between the divine and the human has been contracted. This is the art of an age that more and more often pays divine honor to its great men.

Greek science developed, in the fourth century, above all under the impetus of the great philosophical schools at Athens, the Academy and the Lyceum. Their pupils spread their influence to all the known world. But the science of medicine developed independently on lines of its own, with its centers in the great schools for physicians, as in Cos and Cnidus. Cos was the seat of the school of Hippocrates, which was continued after his death by his sons and his son-in-law. The Cnidian school produced a great medical name in Eudoxus, who became more famous, however, as a natural scientist, astronomer, and mathematician. One of the major health centers of continental Greece was Epidaurus, with its Temple of Asclepius, god of healing. Invalids from the entire Greek world sought cures here, through divine dreams that came as they slept in the porticoes of the temple (incubation). We have a number of inscriptions offering thanks for miraculous cures; these are of great value, not only as evidence for the history of medicine in the fourth and third centuries B.C., but also as documents of social history. Among these "miracles" are a

277

few that are obvious cases of hysterical cures. Here is one example: "A boy, mute. This boy came into the temple because of his voice. When he had made the preliminary sacrifice and fulfilled all the usages, the servitor who brings the fire for the god, looking at the father of the mute boy, calls on him to pledge himself to make an offering of thanks within one year after he has received that for which he has come. Then the mute boy suddenly cried out: 'I pledge myself!' The father started and called on him to say it once more. The boy repeated it. Thenceforth he was well."

Epidaurus treated an enormous number of pilgrims. Among the patients were some personalities known to history, such as Andromache (or Troas), the wife of King Arybbas of Epirus. The Attic orator Aeschines was also in Epidaurus, as it seems.

The fourth century was an age of personal rule. Xenophon and Isocrates glorified kings and tyrants; they looked to them for a solution to the difficulties that bedeviled Greece. It is not surprising, then, to see some of these princes receiving, even demanding, godlike honors from their subjects. Thus Clearchus, the tyrant of Heraclea in Pontus, who had once been a pupil of Plato, gave himself out to be the son of Zeus. He wore a purple garment and a golden crown, carried in his hand a scepter or a "thunderbolt," and had the golden eagle of Zeus borne before him. His face was painted red (a parallel to the Roman *triumphator,* who painted his face and hands with dye). The Syracusan physician Menecrates signed his letters "Menecrates Zeus." He dressed himself as Zeus and had a number of prominent followers who likewise added the names of gods to their personal names. Menecrates is said to have been in some connection with Agesilaus (d. 361), as well as with Alexarchus, brother of Cassander and the reputed founder of the city of Uranopolis on the Chalcidice (after 316 B.C.). Menecrates is clearly a pathological case; this did not prevent many Greeks from coming under his spell. We shall better understand the divine kingship instituted by Alexander and his successors if we keep these instances in mind.

Viewed as a whole, the fourth century was a time of

278

transition; the classical civilization of the fifth century is still in being, to a considerable degree, but new trends now first take shape which will dominate the Hellenistic age. The decisive turning point is reached about the year 360 B.C. With the battle of Mantinea (362) the period of the Greek hegemonies came to an end. In 359, Philip II ascended the throne of Macedonia. But the pace of Greek cultural activity did not slacken; Athens was still the intellectual center of the old world, but other points on the map of the Greek world were eager to emulate her. Athenian culture spread rapidly; the Attic dialect was understood everywhere that Greeks lived. Philip II made it the official language of Macedonian administration, even though he was politically at odds with Athens. Ctesias of Cnidus, in Asia Minor, who resided for some time at the Persian court as a physician, already employed the Attic dialect in his literary work soon after 400 B.C.: his *Persika* is written not in Ionic but in Attic. The conquest of the world by Greek culture would be inconceivable without the unifying bond of a common language. The *Koine* dialect of the Hellenistic age, which emerged from the Attic, provided this universal language. It was the language in which the Greek mind expressed itself until the early years of the Roman Empire. And, even then, the new fashions in literary style looked not forward but backward—to the Attic of the fifth and fourth centuries B.C.

14

The Rise of Macedonia Under King Philip II (359–336 B.C.)

The greatest personality in the ancient world, during the quarter-century between 360 and 336, was the Macedonian King Philip II, son of Amyntas. Philip made Macedonia the leading nation in Europe. He laid down the foundations on which his son Alexander erected a world empire that superseded that of Persia. The power of the Persians was replaced by the dominion of the Macedonians, and the years around 360 B.C. mark a turning point in history. Ernest Kornemann was fully justified in choosing this as the starting point for his great *Weltgeschichte des Mittelmeerraumes von Philipp II von Makedonien bis Muhammed*. For Kornemann, Philip of Macedon stands at the beginning of a new era of world history, which continues through all the remainder of antiquity and concludes only with the assault of the Arabs.

There were, in fact, crucial changes taking place both in Persia and in Macedonia about the year 360. In 359–358, the Great King Artaxerxes II Mnemon died, after reigning for almost forty-five years. He was succeeded by his son Artaxerxes III Ochus (359–358 to 338), who, in contrast to his ineffectual father, was a vigorous ruler who took firm hold of the reins of government. Within a short time he had put the rebellious empire in order. Shortly before, in 360, the Thracian dynast Cotys had died. In 359, the Macedonian

280

King Perdiccas III lost his life in battle against the Illyrians. His son, Amyntas, was a small boy who, at such a difficult time, could not effectively rule a restive kingdom. What was to become of Macedonia? How was the country to defend itself against its foreign enemies? What form would its relations take with its newly powerful neighbor to the east, the Persian Empire? These were questions to which no optimistic answer could be given.

In Greece, too, the situation was extremely fluid. The battle of Mantinea (362) and the death of Epaminondas marked the end of the Greek hegemonies. Boeotia had fallen back to the level of the other, more or less unimportant Greek states. Sparta had received a crippling blow with the loss of Messenia. Only Athens, as leader of the Second Attic Maritime League, was—to outward appearances—still a power to command respect. But the confederacy's member states had been long dissatisfied with Athenian rule, which had broken the promises made at the founding of the alliance. A few years later (357), the so-called Social (meaning "Allied") War broke out; in 355, peace was made on terms that withdrew all the more important members from the confederation, and the Athenian state became a second-rate power.

Under Artaxerxes II, the Achaemenid Empire had suffered considerable losses and a sharp diminution in prestige. The great revolt of the satraps had shaken Persian rule in much of Asia Minor. The Great King's attempts to reconquer rebellious Egypt had failed. These internal difficulties explain the Persian Empire's inaction when faced with the Greek confusion of the years between the King's Peace and the battle of Mantinea. The King's son, the future Artaxerxes III Ochus, had, shortly before succeeding to the throne, captured the Egyptian King Tachos. (Tachos had undertaken an attack upon Syria; for Egypt, the regions of Syria and Palestine exercised an irresistible attraction; the cedars of Lebanon, for instance, were indispensable in treeless Egypt. Then, on ascending the throne, Artaxerxes III swept the entire empire of his enemies. He moved against the western satraps Orontes of Mysia and Artabazus of Phrygia. Orontes submitted, and

Artabazus crossed over to Macedonian territory. The Athenians seemed about to commit their fleet to the support of Artabazus, but the Great King deterred them with threats of retaliation. Artaxerxes III was a party to the peace treaty that ended the Social War. In Syria, Phoenicia, and Cyprus, also, battles had to be fought and won (see pp. 281, 350f.). Ultimately Artaxerxes was able to subdue Egypt once and for all in the winter of 343–342 (see p. 292 f.). This was the greatest success the Persians had achieved in many decades. It reestablished the empire's prestige in the world; if the internal strength of the Persian Empire was, for the most part, considerably overrated in the years that followed, this can be attributed to the resounding success of Persian arms in the Land of the Nile.

For the rest, however, Artaxerxes III Ochus was a typical Oriental ruler. His reign was filled with harem intrigues. He had a reputation as a grim despot, devoted to the arts of cruelty and cunning. But the centrifugal forces in his empire often left him no other choice. By whatever means, he gave the Persian Empire respect and new prestige, both at home and abroad. An unattractive figure, perhaps, but he preserved the majesty of his crown; a bad man, but a good king.

The heart of the Macedonian land is the region watered by the rivers Haliacmon and Axius. The original Macedonian state developed in the districts of Elimea and Orestis. It was from this area that the Macedonians gradually expanded to the north and east, putting themselves in possession of the entire country between Thessaly and the lower Strymon (the modern Struma). When the Macedonians descended to the sea we do not know, but it cannot have been earlier than about 700 B.C. No historical information has been preserved from this period; the list of the early kings of Macedonia, in particular, is a late fiction. We are on somewhat surer ground only when we reach the reign of Amyntas I, who reigned in the second half of the sixth century B.C.

Equally obscure is the origin of the Macedonian people. This question is as open today as it was over 2,000 years ago. Like the question of the nationality of the Dacians, it has been a subject of discussion among ancient historians for many generations. It is by no means a purely academic problem. If the Macedonians were not Greeks, then the battle of Chaeronea (338) would mark the end of Greek history, as was actually assumed by the great majority of nineteenth-century scholars, in particular Niebuhr, Grote, and Ernst Curtius. These historians were, however, deceived. With good reason; the science of comparative linguistics—which is decisive for this question—had, in their time, not yet pointed to a clear solution. Today, thanks particularly to the linguistic researches of Otto Hoffmann (*Die Makedonen*, 1906), we know that Macedonian names—especially of persons, but also of places and months—show that Macedonian is almost certainly a Greek dialect, most closely related to Thessalian (Aeolic). The isolation of the Macedonians from their Hellenic cousins— an isolation extending over many centuries—easily explains a number of peculiarities in the Macedonian language, for which no parallels are to be found in the other Greek dialects. Johann Gustav Droysen was right in regarding the Macedonians as Greeks; the history of the Macedonian people is a part of Greek history.

Most of the Macedonian rulers before Philip II remain little more than shadows to us. Amyntas I is said to have been on friendly terms with Peisistratus and his family. We find ourselves in the clear light of recorded history only with Alexander I Philhellene, in the first half of the fifth century. This ruler was admitted to the Olympic Games in a personal capacity. In other words he was regarded, like his house, as Greek. The explanation for this is surprising: the Macedonian Royal House of the Argeadae traced its origin back to Heracles, which legitimized it in the eyes of the Greeks. Alexander I was an active admirer of Greek culture; he had contact with Pindar, and Herodotus and Hellanicus stayed in his court. The King's court was at that time in Aegae, a lofty fortress in well-watered country. It was, in all likelihood, Alexander I Philhellene who created the famous Macedonian cavalry force, the *hetairoi*, as well as the infantry phalanx of the *pezhetairoi*. He thereby gave the plebeian infantry the honorable name of "King's Companions." The date at which these *pezhetairoi* were established has always been debated by historians. Besides Alexander I Philhellene, the names of Archelaus, Alexander II (whose short reign lasted only from 370 to 369/368) and especially Philip II have been linked with their creation.

It was King Archelaus (413–399) who transferred the royal residence from Aegae to Pella. Archelaus, who fought his way to the throne, was the kingdom's first great organizer. He built roads and fortresses, improved the army's equipment, and raised the economic level of the country by opening it to trade with the neighboring states. He may have divided lower Macedonia into a number of administrative districts named after urban centers, which also served as mobilization districts for the army. They continued in existence as long as there was an independent Macedonia. He also intervened in Thessalian affairs, foreshadowing the policy of Philip II. His work of internal reorganization was made all the more difficult by the opposition of the vassal princes, principally the rulers of Lyncestis and Elimiotis.

Archelaus was also a great friend of Greek culture, constantly welcoming Greek poets as his guests at his court in Pella. Euripides wrote and produced the *Bacchae* here, and glorified the King in his drama *Archelaus,* which refers to the history of the founding of the Macedonian dynasty. He is also supposed to have invited Socrates to come to Macedonia. Festivals were instituted by the King in the city of Dion on Olympus with poetical and gymnastic contests on the Greek models. After his death—reputedly at the hands of one of his followers on a hunt—Macedonia again fell victim to internal disorders. The period 399 to 359 is marked for the most part by very short reigns; the sole exception is Amyntas III (393–370), who found a place in history by his relations with the Chalcidian League and with Athens. But Macedonia had no real role to play in international affairs at this time.

The great change begins with the regency of Philip II, son of Amyntas III, born in 383. Philip was almost the same age as Demosthenes, who was to be his great adversary. Of great moment in his development was a stay in Thebes, where he went as a hostage at the age of fifteen. There, he came to know the great generals Epaminondas and Pelopidas, who remained his heroes as long as he lived. Philip was twenty-four years old when, in 359, he became regent for his minor nephew Amyntas, the son of Perdiccas III (365–359).

Macedonia was in dire straits; her neighbors were sweeping across her borders; there were several pretenders to the throne; confusion was universal. Philip showed his capabilities from the very first. He not only calmed his country's foreign enemies (partly by payments of money, to be sure), but also disposed of the pretenders, including the most dangerous, Argaeus, who had obtained the support of the Athenians. Philip was able to conclude a tolerable peace with Athens, by formally renouncing the Macedonian claim to Amphipolis. Athens, for her part, promised to deliver the city of Pydna to Philip in compensation for Amphipolis—a clause which was the root of future conflict. There was still a score to settle with the Illyrians, Macedonia's old enemies in the west. Philip was victorious in a great battle; and in the peace treaty that followed, the Illyrians had to cede their border districts on Lake Ochrid to Macedonia. The vassal principalities of Lyncestis and Orestis were abolished, their rulers having proved politically unreliable. It is not known when Philip was proclaimed King of Macedonia, though it was very likely before 354. In any case, his accession was a well-deserved honor for an uncommonly energetic and talented man. Amyntas, the nephew, was cast aside, for which he repaid his uncle with bitter hatred: Alexander finally simply killed him.

The Macedonian Kingdom was a military state. The King was, at the same time, supreme commander, priest and judge. His status, vis-a-vis the nobility, was that of *primus inter pares*. Because of his personal credit with the army, which he led with great bravery, Philip in the course of time acquired increased influence and power. In addition, he knew how to attract more and more of the nobility to his cause. He provided them with land and appointed them *hetairoi* (King's Companions). This group, reminiscent of Achilles' Myrmidons, contained in addition to Macedonians many men of Greek blood. They were bound to the ruler by special loyalties and revered him as their benefactor.

That the King, through his influence with sections of the nobility and army, became practically independent of the Macedonian state, and that the foreign wars, in particular, are to be regarded as the King's private undertakings, is a quite unfounded assumption which has been made by some modern scholars. Documentary proofs of its untenability were already known before this theory was advanced (e.g., one inscription of 392 containing the treaty between Amyntas III and the Chalcidian League; see p. 218). The opposite is correct: the ties between king and people were nowhere stronger than in Macedonia. The nucleus of the army under Philip consisted of the *pezhetairoi,* who were divided into a number of regiments (*taxeis*) armed with very long *sarissai* (thrusting lances); the solid wall they formed was the terror of their enemies, even the Romans, as late as the battle of Pydna. Philip adopted the tactic of the slanted infantry line from Epaminondas, and added the employment of cavalry on either flank as needed. Philip, with his keen political vision, could not fail to see that the landlocked Macedonian state had to find access to the sea. Without it, Macedonia would be perpetually dependent on the maritime powers, especially the Chalcidian League and Athens. This meant inevitable conflict with both these powers, and Athens had already been weakened by her defeats in the Social War (357–355). But without Greek civilization and the assistance of individual Greeks, it would be impossible to build a genuine state in Macedonia. Philip never lost sight of this, in the thick of all his wars against the Greeks.

The expansion of Macedonia under Philip II took place with a rapidity and purposefulness that astound the historian of today. The first phase covers a span of only four years, from 357 to 354 B.C. During this time, Philip not only succeeded in taking possession of the city of Amphipolis (357) but also conquered Pydna (357–356), Potidaea, and finally Methone (354). At the siege of Methone, Philip was struck by an arrow and lost the sight of one eye. These successes reveal the military efficiency and the diplomatic adroitness of the Macedonian king. Thus, during the siege of Amphipolis —the city was absolutely vital to his plans—he was able to hoodwink the Athenians entirely, assuring them that he merely intended to conquer this important entrepôt for *them*. With the most important Greek power in the north, the Chalcidian League, Philip was able to remain on good terms for the time being; a treaty of friendship and alliance dating from the year 357–356 gives evidence of this (Bengtson, *Staatsvertraege*, No. 308). This treaty shows evidence of the collaboration of the Delphic Oracle, with which Philip already had the best of relations.

Naturally, the progress of the Macedonians aroused the Athenians, who saw their position in Thrace threatened by Philip. The Athenians' urgent diplomatic efforts have left traces in a number of treaties, concluded in the years 357 to 355 with several dynasts in the north. Among the new allies of Athens were the Thracian princes Berisades, Amadocus, and Cersobleptes; the three kings Cetriporis of Thrace, Lyppeius of Paeonia, and Grabus of Illyria; and the Thracian city of Neapolis (Bengtson, *Staatsvertraege,* Nos. 303, 309, 312). But all of this was in vain: greatly hindered by the Social War, the Athenians were not in a position to appear in the north in force. The days when Athens could fight on many fronts were over; her citizens were no longer willing to assume the burdens of long and strenuous military service.

In the year 354, Philip controlled territories extending from the northern boundary of Thessaly to the river Nestus. Only the Chalcidian League continued to be independent; Philip had even granted to it the city of Potidaea, which he had wrested from the Athenians. By this time, the King's goal was clear. For Macedonia, an unurbanized land, the newly won Greek towns were of inestimable value as centers of Hellenic culture. Equally valuable was the conquest of the lands to the north and east with their militant population; in the armies of Alexander and the Diadochi we still find Paeonians, Illyrians, and Thracians from these regions. In this period, too, the city of Philippi was founded, the first city, so far as we know, to be named after a ruler. Philippi was the former Crenides, situated not far from the rich gold mines of Mount Pangaeus, which were exploited by Philip. Philip literally made history with this gold; many politicians took bribes from him, and Philip once said that no citadel was so high and steep that a donkey laden with gold could not find its way in.

Meanwhile, a war had broken out in Hellas which involved nearly all the states of the Greek mainland. This was the so-called Third Sacred War (356–346). The Phocians were opposed by a coalition of the other Greeks under the leadership of the Boeotians and the Thessalians. Like the other sacred wars, this was fought over a violation of the rights of the Delphic Amphictyony. The Phocians had troubled the Boeotians before this; they were extraordinarily obstinate, and they controlled the lines of communication between Thebes and Thessaly. They now dropped out of the Boeotian League. The Boeotians could not tolerate this. They saw to it that a number of the Phocian leaders were indicted before the Amphictyonic Council and condemned for religious desecration (356). The Phocians refused to pay the fines, and war was on. From time immemorial, incidents in the Delphic Amphictyony had had far-reaching effects, since all Greek states were represented in the association. An added factor was the central location of the temple of Delphi. It is significant for the impotence of the rest of Greece that the Phocians, at first, had no trouble in holding their ground against their enemies. Their leaders Philomelus and Onomarchus seized the Delphic sanctuary and minted its treasures into coins to pay their mercenaries. This forced loan from the Delphic shrine awoke a storm of indignation in Greece, although the Phocians had only done what other Greek states were always doing in emergencies.

The Phocians were a backward, poor people of central Greece, of no previous prominence whatever; their success reflects the complete impotence of the other Greek states, including the Boeotians. The Boeotians, in any case, had plunged into the confusion of the Persian satraps' revolts, sending an army under Pammenes to Asia Minor to aid Artabazus (353). Philip II was called in against the Phocians by the Thessalian princes, the Aleuadae, but was not equal to the mercenary army of Onomarchus; the Phocians were able to boast two decisive victories over him (353). This year marks the zenith of Phocian power, which now even encroached on Thessaly. But the very next year, in the battle of the Crokus field—probably in the vicinity of Pagasae in Thessaly —the Macedonians and Thessalians decisively defeated the Phocians. Onomarchus and 6,000 of his mercenaries fell in the battle. Philip is said to have had 3,000 prisoners cast into the sea as temple robbers—an unprecedented punishment, reminiscent of the repression of the German Peasants' Revolt. But when Philip attempted to invade Greece—doubtless to see to a proper settlement in Delphi—he found the pass at Thermopylae barred. The Phocians' allies, Sparta and Athens among them, had mobilized. Athens, which had been on the side of the Phocians since 356, had sent its entire hoplite levy to Thermopylae. Philip had no wish to engage his army in a life-or-death struggle; it was still too early for a decisive conflict with the Greeks. So he turned back (summer, 352). Phocis, and with it the Greek international order, had been saved from the power of Philip—for the present.

The second phase of Macedonian expansion opened with the year 352. Toward the end of the year, perhaps not until 351, Philip undertook a campaign in Thrace. Thrace extended from the Nestus River to the Black Sea; here Philip found very serious competitors, the Athenians, who at that time were reestablishing their rule in the Thracian Chersonese (Gallipoli). Thrace was an important market for Athenian goods, which were shipped into the interior either by the overland route or up the rivers, especially the Tonzus. Rich profits were drawn from Thracian trade, not only by Athens but by Thasos, the Greek cities on the western shore of the Black Sea, and Byzantium. The Greeks therefore regarded Philip's advance into this distant land as a severe threat to their interests. But Philip, after 352, was firmly in league with the Thracian princes Cersobleptes and Amadocus. The Athenians, and the Greeks generally, could only watch and wonder.

Philip's encroachment on the territory of the Chalcidian League was still more disquieting. The Macedonian conquered and destroyed Aristotle's birthplace Stagira (350 or at the latest 349–348); he then turned his forces against Olynthus, the administrative center of the Chalcidian League. He claimed that the Chalcidians had refused to surrender Philip's half-brother, who had fled to them as a refugee, and he used this as a pretext for war. Philip's attack on the Chalcidians was greeted by a wave of indignation throughout Greece. This feeling was heightened by Demosthenes in his three Olynthiac Orations. But the Athenians were not in a position to lend effective aid to their Chalcidian allies, especially since they had difficulties on their own doorstep, in Euboea; Philip had succeeded in inducing the cities of that island, with the exception of Carystus, to defect from Athens (349–348). To read the Olynthiac Orations of Demosthenes is to feel something of the impotence of the Athenian state, whose vital interests were being leached away by Philip, one by one. Olynthus fell to the Macedonians in 348, and the site was completely destroyed. Excavations conducted by a team of archaeologists from Johns Hopkins University under D. M. Robinson have succeeded in unearthing a part of the perished city. They afford us a vivid view of the life of a Greek city of the fourth century B.C. The Olynthians scattered over the entire Greek world, forming a restive element that time and again agitated against Philip, especially in Athens.

Failure in the Olynthian War gave point to the program of the peace party in Athens. Even Demosthenes could not resist the prevailing mood. In 346, after long-drawn-out negotiations, the Peace of Philocrates was concluded. It was named after the political leader who had headed the Athenians' embassy to Macedonia. Both Demosthenes and Aeschines were also members of that embassy, and from now on Aeschines appears as a convinced friend and partisan of Philip's. The negotiations revolved mainly around the question of whether

Phocis and the small Thessalian island of Halus were to be covered by the treaty; Philip wanted to keep a free hand against both. Athens could not very well abandon the Phocians, and so Philip acquiesced in the end. This was no great concession, as Philip still had the duty of defeating the Phocians, who continued to resist; on the other hand, the treaty's provisions against piracy were important for every Greek state, a bright spot in an age when common interests were so seldom considered, let alone pursued.

The Peace of Philocrates (Bengtson, *Staatsvertraege,* No. 329) brought no peace to the war of the Athenian orators, who used it as a debating point; the opposing points of view can be seen in Demosthenes' oration *De falsa legatione* of 343 B.C., and in Aeschines' *Against Ctesiphon,* delivered in 330 B.C. These should tell us much about the negotiations, but the statements of both orators are to be viewed with skepticism, as each speaks for his own cause, and neither is particularly concerned with the truth.

While the second Athenian embassy was still in Pella, in 346, Philip II undertook a lightning campaign against Thrace, forcing the Thracian Prince Cersobleptes into submission. He made short work of the Phocians as well. He forced their leader Phalaecus to capitulate, and gave the Phocian mercenaries safe-conduct to the Peloponnese (346). The Athenians, who had passed an unequivocal decree against the Phocian temple-robbers, nevertheless refused to collaborate with Philip against them. But the Third Sacred War was now ended, and the emissaries of the Greek states gathered in Delphi to confer about the reorganization of the Amphictyony. The Phocians were now excluded from the Delphic Associations, and were obliged to restore the pillaged temple treasures at the rate of sixty talents a year. These repayments, however, did not begin until 343. Phocis was moreover demilitarized, and its inhabitants required to settle in unwalled villages. Most important, however, was the fact that Philip now received the two votes of the Phocians. He had, in other words, become a member of the Delphic Amphictyony, naturally only in his personal capacity as a descendant of Heracles—but in practice this

291

meant that henceforth the King of Macedonia had an important voice in the affairs of the Amphictyony. There was a difference, too, in that Philip's status in Delphi was that of an individual person, whereas the eleven other delegations represented Greek states. This was a profound novelty that heralded the coming of a new era. At the Delphic Congress a general peace (*koine eirene*) was finally declared (in 346) which was to be binding on all members of the Amphictyony. This was a new King's Peace; but the king was a Greek, and not a Persian.

Philip's successes nevertheless alarmed many Greeks. There was acute tension in Athens between Macedonia's friends and Philip's enemies. When Philip solemnly presided over the Pythia at Delphi that autumn, Athens sent on emissaries to the games, which Philip correctly took as a personal affront. Athens backed down before the implied threats of the King and apologized; Demosthenes had to take it upon himself to convince the Athenian people that a war against Philip was impossible at that time. The real leader of the Athenian state, however, was not Demosthenes but Eubulus, who had made a name for himself in the field of finance. If Athens had recovered to some extent from the unhappy consequences of the Social War, it was thanks to Eubulus, not Demosthenes.

The years that followed were filled with toil and danger for Philip. He was severely wounded during the campaign against the Illyrians in 344, and Isocrates, in his concern, addressed a letter to him, asking him not to expose himself again to such chances, but to think rather of his great task, the war against Persia. Thessaly was given a new organization in the same year; a decarchy, or rule of ten, which was transformed into a tetrarchy, or rule of four, not quite two years later. The decarchy perhaps indicates a league of the ten most important states of Thessaly; the tetrarchy probably signifies the division of Thessaly into four regions; in any case, Philip had himself elected archon of all Thessaly, and effectively ruled the country.

By far the most important political event of these years, however, was the reconquest of Egypt by the Persian King

Artaxerxes III Ochus in the winter of 343–342. The preceding summer, Macedonia and Persia had already come to an understanding and concluded a friendship and nonaggression pact. These events clearly show a shift in the center of gravity of world politics; the two great powers come to an understanding, while Greece moves more and more toward the periphery of international affairs.

A very interesting document tells us something of political conditions in Athens. It is a letter to King Philip which Speusippus, the Head of the Platonic Academy, wrote in 342. This communication, which has been handed down to posterity among the letters of the Socratics, was subjected to a searching historical and philological examination by E. Bickermann and J. Sykntris, who have pronounced it genuine. Speusippus, whose pro-Macedonian sentiments are perfectly evident in the letter, recommends a certain Antipater of Magnesia to Philip. The writer has nothing good to say of Isocrates, whom he reproaches for having ignored Philip's benefactions to the Greeks. Speusippus attempts to buttress Philip's claims to Amphipolis and Olynthus with the mythological arguments so popular at that time (one can imagine that Philip's seizure of Olynthus had been the burden of much anti-Macedonian propaganda). The date of Speusippus' letter can be established conclusively by the author's mention, at the end of his letter, of the shortage of papyrus which the Persian King has caused by his conquest of Egypt. Speusippus rendered the Macedonian King an invaluable service through this letter; there were men everywhere in Greece who had once been pupils of the Platonic Academy; if their support could be gained for Philip, this could mean a great deal. But the friends of Macedon in Athens were not a unified group or party. Speusippus did not hesitate to blacken the image of his competitor Isocrates—the same Isocrates who in his pamphlets, especially in the *Philippus,* had welcomed the Macedonian as the future leader of a national war against Persia. In 342, Isocrates began work of the *Panathenaicus,* a pamphlet in which the unification of Greece under Philip was again recommended. It was published in 339, when Athens' war against Philip had already begun.

Modern historians, particularly German historians, have been reproached for writing the history of Greece in Philip's time entirely from a Macedonian point of view. There is certainly some justice in this. J. G. Droysen's remarkable early work (1833) opened the way to an entirely new view of Greek history in the Hellenistic age, by focusing attention on Alexander as a political creator and cultural pioneer. But it was impossible to extol Alexander without taking his father into account. K. J. Beloch rated the father even higher than the son, whose genius he acknowledged. Indeed, Philip had real qualities of brilliance. He was a highly gifted statesman and military commander. He knew how to arouse enthusiasm in his troops; he knew how to charm men's minds and hearts when he thought it profitable to win them. His contemporaries were well aware of his eminence. The historian Theopompus —whom Speusippus described as a frosty soul—called Philip the greatest man that Europe (i.e., the Balkan peninsula) had yet produced.

Philip was indeed very much the Balkan prince. His private life hardly met the standard of Greek middle-class morality. Besides his two legitimate queens, Olympias and Cleopatra the daughter of Attalus, we know no less than four other women by whom Philip had children. Olympias left the King when he married Cleopatra, and gave her the status of legitimate queen. Olympias took her son Alexander with her into exile, to her home in Epirus. Aphrodite and Dionysus were Philip's ruling gods; the life he led with his companions (*hetairoi*) was the scandal of the age, as we can still read in Theopompus (fr. 224, 225). But none of this really counted. Philip was politically and militarily superior, he was quicker and bolder in his strategy, more ruthless in the pursuit of his goals, craftier and more deceptive in diplomatic intrigue than any Greek. While Athens talked, Philip acted; the cumbersome institutions of the Greek polis could no longer produce the energy needed to stop him. Demosthenes, in the *First Philippic,* urged the Greeks to form an expeditionary corps, attack Philip in his own country, and no longer leave the initiative to the King of Macedon. Strategically sound advice certainly, but if the Athenian citizens continued to evade military service, the best strategic planning was a waste of time.

In 342 Philip began the final subjugation of Thrace. The war was another of Philip's outright acts of aggression; he claimed to be fighting in defense of the Greek cities under pressure from the Thracians, but everyone knew this was a pretext. Before Philip crossed the Nestus he had come to an understanding with the Getae and their King Cothelas, who held the land between the Balkan Mountains and the Danube. Philip was quite thorough in Thrace, where the fighting lasted into the year 341. Colonies were established, cities were founded, and many people from Macedonia settled in them; some doubtful elements of the kingdom's population were put out of harm's way by this means. A Macedonian was appointed governor (strategos) of Thrace, in imitation of Persian imperial administration. The concept of a subject country whose inhabitants are obliged to render military service and pay tribute, and over whom a governor exercises jurisdiction as the conqueror's representative, had no precedent in the previous history of Greece and Macedonia. But Philip had to ignore precedent. If he really wanted to control the extensive land between the Nestus and the Black Sea, whose princes, Cersobleptes and Teres, had been deposed, he had to do something quite new. He was building an empire; Persia provided a convenient model. It would be incorrect to say that Thrace had now come into Philip's personal possession; on the contrary, it was a Macedonian province, annexed to the kingdom, the first and the most important that Philip created.

Meanwhile, the Macedonian King had continued his activity in Greece. He had opened negotiations with the Aetolians in 342, at which time he seems to have promised them the important harbor of Naupactus on the Gulf of Corinth. He also sent a detachment of troops to Eretria on Euboea, as a support to the Macedonian cause there. Still more important were Philip's connections with the dynast Hermias of Atarneus. Hermias controlled the Troad, the gateway to Asia; in a future war with Persia, his attitude could be crucial. He appears to have placed his territory at Philip's disposal as a bridgehead in Asia Minor (342?). Not unnaturally, the Persian King commissioned Mentor of Rhodes to do away with Hermias. The Troad would remain in Persian hands, and with it the control of the Hellespont.

Since 343 tension between Macedonia and Athens had steadily increased. Demosthenes was certainly to blame for part of this. The interests of the two states collided on the island of Euboea and on the Thracian Chersonese (Gallipoli). The two states had been within inches of open war in 341, over a dispute between the city of Cardia and Attic cleruchs; in this case the Athenians were at fault. Everywhere in Greece the Athenians were working to get the better of the Macedonians. In 343, a number of Peloponnesian states—among them Argos, Messene, and Megalopolis—had concluded an alliance with Philip; a year later, Demosthenes won over the same states, along with Achaea and Arcadia, to an alliance with Athens. The Peloponnesians were clearly attempting to ensure themselves on both sides (Bengtson, *Staatsvertraege,* No. 337).

Demosthenes was everywhere at once. He made an arduous journey to incite the Illyrians and the Thracians (summer-fall 342). He succeeded in forcing the Macedonians off the island of Euboea; the cities of Chalcis and Eretria entered into an alliance with Athens, and finally a Eurobean League was formed, thanks largely to the work of Callias of Chalcis (Bengtson, *Staatsvertraege,* Nos. 339, 340, 342). But Demosthenes' greatest success was the founding of the Hellenic League in February or March of 340. In outward appearance, it was an imposing collection of states: Euboea, Acarnania, Achaea, Corinth, Megara, Leucas, and Corcyra. All had united in a treaty of friendship and mutual assistance. The basis of the treaty was, once again, a general peace (*koine eirene*), this time under the leadership of Athens. The allies pledged themselves to pay enrollment fees, and some of them were also to provide troops. When, on the sixteenth day of Anthesterion of the year 340, the League was constituted in Athens, Demosthenes was honored as its father. His energy had brought it into being, or so it seemed. But everyone in

Greece knew that it was only fear of Philip that had brought the allies together. Thebes, the most important state in central Greece, still kept aloof from the League; of necessity, the most important goal of the new alliance was to bring the Thebans into its ranks.

The machinery of war stirred into motion as Philip led his army against the city of Perinthus on the Propontis (Sea of Marmora). It was a very considerable force, equipped with a good many siege engines, that Philip had led against the Greek city. To invest Perinthus by sea as well, Philip needed his fleet; to bring it through the straits, he had to march overland to secure the Thracian Chersonese. Philip frankly conceded this violation of Athenian territory in a letter to Athens, which is to be found in the corpus of Demosthenes' orations (No. XII); the outbreak of war between Athens and Macedonia was thereby delayed. Perinthus received aid not only from neighboring Byzantium, but from the satrap Arsites, whose satrapy was situated on the opposite shore. Even Philip's new siege machines failed against the walls of Perinthus. A surprise attack on Byzantium also failed. But Philip seized the Athenian grain fleet, gathering at the entrance of the Bosporus for the voyage to Athens. A total of 230 ships of the greatest value fell into his hands; Philip was probably not unaware of the consequences of this. And, in fact, Athens declared war on Philip, in September or October of 340.

Plainly this was not Philip's but Demosthenes' war. The Athenian had been restlessly and unremittingly active against Philip for years: in his speeches—particularly the oration on the Chersonese, and also the *Third* and *Fourth Philippics*—he had courted the neutrals' favor and proposed an understanding with Persia. Demosthenes was no friend of the Persian King, and it has not been proved that he let himself be bribed with Persian gold. The circumstances seem to have left him no other choice; the tensions between Macedonia and Persia over the death of Hermias of Atarneus seemed to confirm the soundness of his policy.

But the real question was whether Athens was in any position to conduct this war effectively, and whether she had any hope of winning it. The question was not asked; the stele on which the text of the Peace of Philocrates was inscribed had already been overturned in the autumn of 340; the city was in the grip of a war fever that Demosthenes and his friends did everything in their power to inflame. The great orator was now a great war leader; he had himself elected Superintendent of the Fleet, and the first operations at sea were carried off successfully. The Athenian fleet under Chares freed Byzantium from Philip's naval siege; the King continued to press the city, but its greatest danger was over. At sea Philip was no match for Athens. On land, however, he could do as he liked; in 339, he even undertook an expedition against the Scythians which kept him far from the Greek theater of war for several months. The Scythian expedition probably served to secure his country's northern boundary, which had been overrun time and again by barbarian peoples. Tribal migrations were already taking place in the area between the lower Danube and the Balkan Mountains in Philip's time. The coming of the Celts, whom Alexander was to meet on the lower Danube, was already sending tremors through southeastern Europe.

When Philip returned to Pella from Scythia in the late summer of 339, the situation in Greece had changed completely. About a year before, in February, 339, the so-called Fourth Sacred War had broken out, in which Athens was again involved. The Locrians of the little state of Amphissa, not far from Delphi, had laid charges against the Athenians in the Council of the Delphic Amphictyony; Athens had rededicated two golden shields in the Temple of Delphi during the Third Sacred War, when the temple had not yet been reconsecrated. The shields, mementoes of the battle of Plataea, bore the inscription: "The Athenians, from the spoils of the Medes and the Thebans, when they fought together against the Greeks." In whose interest, F. R. Wüst has asked, was the outbreak of an Amphictyonic War at just this time? The answer is very likely to be: Philip of Macedonia. In any case Philip had trapped the Athenians into making a counter accusation: the people of Amphissa were cultivating accursed soil at Cirrha. The Amphictyonic Council, in pursuance of this, sent a party to Cirrha, which the Locrians of Amphissa attacked. Athens was now vindicated; Thebes, however, felt itself bound to protect Amphissa. Again it was to Philip's advantage that Thebes and Athens should fall out. Machiavellian diplomacy? The details are very complicated and difficult to unravel. The result, however, was that the Council of the Amphictyony, at its session in the fall of 339, invited Philip to assume the leadership of a Sacred War as hegemon of the Amphictyonic League.

The time had now come for action. With lightning speed, bypassing Thermopylae by way of Heraclea Trachinia and Cytinium, Philip entered the Cephisus valley and seized the town of Elatea. Not only Thebes but Athens, too, were now threatened by a Macedonian army within a few days' march. But Demosthenes again spoiled Philip's plans; as a result of his diplomacy, Thebes concluded an alliance against Philip with Athens (Bengtson, *Staatsvertraege,* No. 345). Athens was willing to make great concessions. The supreme command of the land forces was to be entirely in the hands of Thebes; the command at sea was to alternate between the two states. In addition, Athens assumed two thirds, Thebes only one third of the war costs. Philip could do nothing about it; allied forces rapidly blocked the roads from Elatea, preventing him from advancing further toward either Thebes or Amphissa. The winter of 339–338, apart from a few unimportant engagements, was given over to intense diplomatic activity by both sides, the Epicnemidian Locrians and the Phocians siding with Macedonia, the Peloponnesian states remaining neutral.

Unhappily the Greek allies determined from the beginning on a defensive strategy. They barred the Cephisus valley and placed a mercenary army under Chares across the road to Amphissa. Philip roundly defeated the mercenaries; he opened negotiations with Thebes once more; once more they collapsed on the intervention of Demosthenes. But Philip had now taken Naupactus, and so controlled the entry into the Gulf of Corinth; at any moment he might threaten the allied rear by sea; the allies, not without hesitation, resolved to risk a decisive battle.

It was fought on August 2, 338, near Chaeronea in the

Cephisus valley, and ended in a total defeat of the Greeks. The Greek dispositions had been well chosen. The plain was about one and two-thirds miles wide; the Greek battle line extended across it from Mount Thurium to the bank of the Cephisus River. The allies thus blocked not only the vital road to Thebes but also the road that branched off near Chaeronea and ran over the Cerata Pass. It is not clear why the Greeks did not extend their right wing across the river as far as Mount Acontium. On the Macedonian side, the crucial role was assigned to the cavalry, led by Alexander. The cavalry advanced on the left; the Macedonian right wing under Philip drew back. This was a tactical retreat: Philip's aim was to break the Greeks' battle line, and in this he was entirely successful. When the Thebans—the famous "Sacred Band" fighting on their right wing—had been routed by Alexander, Philip went over to the attack. The Athenians, now pressed on two sides, suffered heavy losses. Their retreat turned into a flight over the Cerata Pass. Philip could have destroyed the entire Hellenic army. He did not; he purposely refrained from sending out the cavalry to hunt down the fleeing Greeks. Like Bismarck after the battle of Koeniggraetz, Philip had a higher goal in view. It was the unification of Greece, to follow him in a great war on the Persian Empire.

The Macedonian victory at Chaeronea is one of the great turning points in Greek history. The armies of the Greek states had been overwhelmed by superior power. The rise of the monarchy, and its triumph over the city-state, was now under way. The Greek polis, inseparably linked with the great achievements of the human spirit, had been unable to defend itself on the field of battle against the monarchy of the north. Greece lay open to seizure by the Macedonians. What would be her fate: was she to become a Macedonian province, as Thessaly had a few years before? Actually the King had no such intentions. Through the mediation of Demades, who had become a Macedonian prisoner of war at Chaeronea, he opened peace negotiations with Athens. Before a single Macedonian soldier had set foot on Attic soil, the Athenians capitulated. The Maritime League was dissolved, but Athens retained suzerainty over the important cleruchies of Lemnos, Imbros, Skyros, and Samos, and continued to hold Delos. Possession of the Thracian Chersonese (Gallipoli) was transferred to Philip. The fate of Thebes was substantially worse. She sank to the status of a second- or third-class power. She had nothing more to do with leadership of the Boeotian League. One provision that was especially painful to Thebes was the return of Oropus to Athens; her resentment was to reopen the question in later years. Through the city of Athens there passed a general sigh of relief, for worse things had been expected of Philip. Demosthenes, who had left Athens, soon returned, and in the winter delivered the memorial oration for the flower of Athenian youth that had fallen at Chaeronea.

Philip's true greatness is shown in the reorganization of Greece which he directed in the winter of 338–337. After an autumn expedition into the Peloponnese, in which Philip confined Sparta to her original territory, the emissaries of all the Greek states (with the exception of Sparta) assembled in Corinth at Philip's invitation. There they agreed to found a general Hellenic federation that is known to history as the Corinthian League. The basis was, once again, a general peace (*koine eirene*). All constitutional changes by means of force were prohibited. Freedom and autonomy of the individual states were guaranteed; only Thebes, Chalcis, and Corinth were to have Macedonian garrisons. Each state, in proportion to its military capability, was to send a fixed number of representatives to the League Council (Synhedrion), which met in Corinth. A complete list of the members of the Corinthian League would be helpful, but this has reached us only in a very fragmentary condition. It does show that, in addition to many poleis, tribal states also belonged to the League. The Synhedrion was responsible for decisions of war and peace, for setting the quotas for the League army contingents, and for the assessment of League contributions. It also fixed penalties for violations of the League treaty. Philip was the hegemon (protector) of the League; an offensive and defensive alliance in perpetuity was signed between him and its members. This alliance was the prerequisite for the declaration of war against Persia. It was proclaimed as a war of revenge for the destruction of the Greek shrines by Xerxes in 480, events of almost a century and a half before. The League army's commander was to be Philip, who bore the title of *strategos autokrator* (commander with plenary powers).

Such was the unification of Greece brought about by Philip. The Greeks were overjoyed by it. The Greek states remained free and autonomous in name, but there was no doubt that in fact they all had to bow to Philip's commands. Monarchy had won an unmistakable victory over the city-state. From now on the King of Macedonia wielded his scepter over Greece as well. This clear loss was accompanied, however, by a considerable gain. Philip and his deputies on the League Council effectively saw to the maintenance of the peace and order that had been so lacking in Greece. Was the price the Greeks had to pay for peace and prosperity too high? But a further benefit must be weighed in the balance; following the counsels of Isocrates (who had died a few months earlier at the age of nearly 100), Philip had given the Greeks a national goal: the war against Persia.

The moment could not have been better chosen when, in the spring of 338, the Macedonian vanguard under Parmenio and Attalus crossed the Hellespont. From 338 to 336 the Persian Empire had been rent by struggles for the succession of the throne (see pp. 351–52); in Asia Minor, Mentor of Rhodes had died suddenly; Greek cities such as Cyzicus and Ephesus, and even Pixodarus, the satrap of Caria, were prepared to collaborate with Macedonia. But an event that no one could have foreseen changed the expectations of the world. In 336, while celebrating the marriage of his daughter to King Alexander of Epirus, Philip was murdered in the theater of Aegae in Macedonia. He was only 46 years old. The assassin, Pausanias, is said to have acted from personal motives, but it is possible that he was a tool of the rejected Olympias and of certain Macedonian nobles.

15

Alexander and the Conquest of the Persian Empire (336–323 B.C.)

"The name Alexander signifies the end of one world epoch and the beginning of another." These words of Johann Gustav Droysen may stand at the beginning of the story of the great Macedonian, who in his short thirty-three years of life literally changed the face of the world. He has not always found favor with posterity. The historian B. G. Niebuhr saw him as an ancient analogue to Napoleon; he called Alexander "a mountebank and bandit in the grand style." In our own day F. Schachermeyr has stressed the dark side of his character, writing (as did Niebuhr) under the indelible impression of contemporary experience.

We face an enigmatic personality in the young Macedonian king. In him the most extreme antitheses meet: an invincible, completely indefatigable will; a boyish enthusiasm for the heroes of the Homeric age, acquired from his tutor Aristotle; masculine joy in battle and in victory; a loyal concern for wounded comrades and the survivors of the fallen. But Alexander also harbors a literally consuming rage, that can move him to the total and blind destruction of faithful followers and comrades.

A mind at war with itself; where do the opposing forces come from? The dark side, it has been suggested, was inherited from his mother Olympias, the proud Epirote princess whose passion, especially for revenge, knew neither bounds nor moderation. We do not know if this is so. One thing alone appears certain: between father and son there was little love lost. Alexander was preeminently the son of his mother; like her, he saw in his father's weakness for other women, in his marriage to the young Cleopatra above all, a grave insult to the honor of the queen, and therefore to himself.

Nearly 2,300 years have passed since Alexander's death. To draw a picture of his personality, of his aspirations and his deeds, we must rely on almost equally ancient sources. The writings of those who took pen in hand while Alexander was still alive have been lost, except for fragmentary remains. But their accounts are of the very highest value, especially the work of the later King Ptolemy I of Egypt. The Greek Arrian of Nicomedia, writing in the latter part of the second century A.D., produced a work on Alexander's expedition called *The Anabasis of Alexander,* in which, for the first time, an attempt was made to separate the contemporary from the later sources. Another skein of the Alexandrian tradition is the History of Alexander (*Historiae Alexandri Magni*) by the rhetorician Quintus Curtius Rufus, probably also from the early Roman Imperial period. It is based to a large extent on what is known as the Alexander Vulgate, a literary tradition stemming from Cleitarchus, who wrote about 310 B.C.

This Vulgate later joins the broad stream of the Alexander Romance, a fictional treatment of Alexander's career extant in many versions and in many languages. The Alexander Romance is of considerable interest for ancient and medieval cultural history, but not for the history of Alexander. Why have we so little in the way of trustworthy evidence? Alexander's contemporaries had little understanding of his greatness and uniqueness, as little as contemporary Romans had of the greatness of Caesar. Also, Alexander in his lifetime never found a historian worthy to record his accomplishments. Greek historiography capitulated before the overwhelming phenomenon of Alexander the Great. It had no scale by which he might be measured.

Allegedly, Alexander was born during that night of the year 356 in which the Treaty of Artemis at Ephesus was set on fire by the publicity-seeking Herostratus. But this is probably only a "fable of simultaneity," of which there are many examples in ancient and modern times. At the early age of sixteen, Alexander was temporarily appointed regent of the kingdom by his father (340–339). At that time he founded the first city to be named after him, Alexandropolis in Thrace. He proved his quality as a commander at the age of eighteen, in the battle of Chaeronea. He had just turned twenty when he ascended the throne after his father's violent death in 336. He was already a completely developed man of independent judgment and of outstanding abilities. He had ideas of his own, and knew how to translate them into action. He also had the good fortune to find loyal aides. There was the elderly Antipater, whom Alexander, on crossing to Asia, left behind as regent of Macedonia and as his deputy to the Corinthian League. Among his father's generals the most valuable was Parmenio, a wise and prudent soldier who always gave his sovereign sound advice. That Alexander was often of another opinion is to be traced to the two men's difference in temperament, rather than to their differences in age.

The young king faced extraordinary difficulties at the beginning of his reign. The princely House of Lyncestis, Amyntas the son of Perdiccas, Attalus the new father-in-law of Philip—all stood against Alexander. If Philip's tried and proven generals, especially Antipater, had not come out for Alexander, history might have taken another course. Alexander acted with lightning speed. Attalus was eliminated. The Macedonian people's sympathies were won through tax exemptions. In Thessaly, Alexander was recognized as archon, the Amphictyonic Council transferred the leadership of Hellas to him, and the Synhedrion of Corinth appointed him to succeed his father as commander of the Panhellenic League's army against Persia. Alexander's measures, for their staggering speed, showed a sure instinct for political possibilities, and an undeviating consistency of aim to which Attalus, for example, fell as a sacrifice. Where would he turn now? To the most immediate threat, the northern barbarians, against whom he led an expedition in 335. His route took him across the Nestus River, then—possibly by way of the Shipka Pass—over the Haemus (the Balkan range) into the country of the Triballi. He even crossed the lower Danube, perhaps in the vicinity of Silistria. On his return march Alexander received news of the defection of the Illyrian King Cleitus, whose territory, centered on Pelion, south of Lake Ohrid, touched on the western border of Macedonia. Again, Alexander struck down his enemies without difficulty, but a complete victory was prevented by alarming news from Greece.

Philip's death had touched off great unrest among the Hellenes. Now a rumor spread that Alexander had died on the Illyrian expedition. First to revolt were the Thebans, who had every reason to be discontent with Macedonian rule. The Macedonian garrison in Thebes was besieged on the Cadmea; it was likely that other Greek cities, especially Athens, would side with the Thebans. Once again Alexander moved with terrifying speed. He broke off the Illyrian war and, entering Greece by way of Thessaly, suddenly appeared before the gates of Thebes. The inhabitants were not prepared to yield, and took up arms; the city was stormed by the Macedonians (we are told that Perdiccas opened the battle on his own initiative and against the King's command). Many terrible scenes marked the fall of Thebes. Sentence was passed by the members of the Synhedrion of the Corinthian League: all of Thebes was destroyed except the citadel (Alexander also spared the house of the poet Pindar); the Thebans were sold into slavery, and the city's territory was divided among the neighboring Boeotians.

This Draconic punishment was, as we have said, ordered not by Alexander but by the Greeks. In Diodorus' highly interesting report (XVII, 9 ff.), which is probably to be traced ultimately to Cleitarchus, the Panhellenic nature of the decision is stressed. This is nothing but propaganda, however; the destruction of Thebes was a piece of brutal power-politics. Alexander, impatient to begin war against Persia, meant to break the spirit of resistance in Hellas to protect his master plan.

The year was 334; the King was ready for his conquest. What was the situation in the Persian Empire? Two years earlier, in 336, Darius III, of a collateral line of the Achaemenid House, had ascended the throne of his ancestors. The all-powerful eunuch Bagoas had chosen him to be Great King. Darius III, surnamed Codomannus, was then forty-five years old. His first act was to force Bagoas to swallow poison.

Although Darius had distinguished himself before his accession to the throne in fighting the wild Cadusians, he was basically a rather mediocre prince. No credence should be given to other tradition (of Quintus Curtius Rufus) which makes him Alexander's peer in battle. The Achaemenid Empire, still imposing to the outward eyes, was by now a colossus with feet of clay. The empire's ruling race, the Persians, had long since lost the energies that had won them a world under Cyrus and Oarius I. Their original character had been weakened by affluence, by the influence of Oriental, especially Babylonian, civilization; power was slipping from their grasp.

Alexander seized it, in an incredible campaign that took him from the Hellespont to the Punjab, and which raises the question of the degree to which the King foresaw his plan of conquest as a whole. Did the entire campaign follow an overall strategic plan? Was it at least planned section by section? Or did Alexander follow his intuition, improvising as he went along, as success led him further and further into the depths of Asia? Alexander more or less improvised. The answer is not difficult. Only the plan of the campaign in Asia Minor shows a daring conception that must have been the result of careful preparation.

The great advantage began with the crossing of the Hellespont in the spring of 334. Nominally the war was an undertaking of the Corinthian League, but the preponderance of Macedonian troops showed the world it was Alexander's war. The Macedonians provided 30,000 men and 5,000 cavalry; Greece sent out only 7,000 foot and 600 horse under Alexander's banners. The Macedonian character of the army was unmistakable. Similarly the strategic direction of the war lay entirely in the hands of Alexander and his staff. Before setting foot on Asian soil, Alexander, standing on his ship, hurled a lance into the shore, taking symbolic possession of the new continent. The entire crossing had been marked by mythological and epic symbolism. On the European side of the strait Alexander had offered sacrifice at the shrine of Protesilaus in Elaeus; on the eastern side he made sacrifice to Poseidon and the other deities of the sea in the "Harbor of the Achaeans." In the Temple of Athena at Ilium he exchanged his own arms for those preserved there as relics of the heroes of the Trojan War. On the plain of the Scamander he celebrated the memory of Achilles and Ajax with feasting and sacrifice.

The Persians were not entirely unprepared. The governors of the immediately threatened satrapies—Hellespontine Phrygia, Greater Phrygia, Lydia, and Cappadocia—had gathered their forces together on the Propontis. They were joined by a contingent of Greek mercenaries under the command of the Rhodian Memnon. Memnon was the only one of the Persian generals who had a plan of action of any merit. It called for avoiding open battle with Alexander, but withdrawing before him, laying waste the land in his path; meanwhile the war could be carried directly to Greece, where an appeal to anti-Macedonian sentiment would raise willing allies. Alexander, his lines of communication endangered, might have been trapped in Asia—but the satraps would have none of it. They demanded a battle, and they got it.

The battle on the Granicus, fought in May or June of 334, was decided essentially by the Macedonian cavalry. Alexander himself had a decisive share in the victory. The Persian satraps helped; they committed grave tactical errors that doomed their hopes. The Greek mercenaries on the Persian side suffered heavy losses. By a dedication to Athena, the protectress of Athens, Alexander emphasized the Panhellenic character of the victory. But at the same time, he installed a Macedonian officer named Calas as satrap of Hellespontine Phrygia. This was the first sign that Alexander regarded himself as the legal successor to the Great King of Persia in the provinces he was taking from him by force.

No more battles were fought in Asia Minor; the land lay open to the Macedonians. Only in a few cities did the garrisons, mainly Greek mercenaries, continue to offer resistance. Sardis, the old capital of the Lydian Empire, fell to Alexander without a struggle. A series of Greek cities on the coast opened their gates to him; the oligarchs installed by the Persians were driven out and democracy reestablished, for example, in Ephesus. The Greek mercenaries in Miletus put up stronger resistance; Halicarnassus, where Memnon himself was in command, could be taken only after a long siege. Even then, two strongholds still remained in the hands of the Persians.

For the Greeks of Asia Minor, Alexander came as the liberator from the Persian yoke, and all of the cities acknowledged their gratitude to him. Since Alexander was the commander of the Corinthian League, it might have been assumed that these cities would be fitted in some way into the Panhellenic organization. This was, however, not the case. These cities of Asia Minor became part of Alexander's own empire. In what way, precisely, is not known; probably there was too little time to clarify the constitutional relationship between the King and the cities; there was a war to be won.

In Miletus, Alexander had given orders to send the Greek fleet home; now everything was to be staked on a single card; he would win on land, or not at all. He took a considerable risk; Persian superiority at sea was now overwhelming; a Persian naval attack against Greece in the Straits could cut the army's supply lines and the King's communications with Macedonia. The tireless Memnon, in fact, succeeded in taking Chios and large parts of Lesbos, among other places in the Aegean. But his sudden death at the siege of Mytilene freed Alexander and Antipater, Alexander's regent in Europe, from anxiety. That these fears were not unfounded is shown by the Persians' occupation of the strategic island of Tenedos, off the coast of the Troad. But meanwhile Alexander's operations in Asia Minor had achieved their goal; he had possession of the coasts.

The news of Memnon's death reached Alexander in the spring of 333, as he was preparing to march eastward from Gordium. It was one of the great strokes of luck that so often marked his life. He had already accepted the homage of the Carian Princess Ada, who had adopted him as her son in accordance with Carian custom. He had also won the cities of the Xanthus valley, and had moved on by way of Phaselis to Side and thence to Pisidia and Greater Phrygia. There he had established winter quarters in the ancient capital of Gordium on the Sangarius River. The story of Alexander's cutting of the Gordian knot is not necessarily true; it may belong to legend rather than history. With his first victory, the Alexander of legend had already begun to take the place of the real Alexander. The Greek historian Callisthenes, nephew of Aristotle, contributed to this heavily.

When Alexander left Gordium, the strategic situation had altered, and greatly to the King's advantage. Darius III had recalled the Persian fleet from Greek waters, which meant an end to the plan of bringing Greece to revolt. This was a fateful decision for the Persian Empire; it meant that Darius had renounced an initiative of his own, and would let the course of future operations be dictated by Alexander.

By way of Ancyra (Ankara) and Tyana, Alexander marched on to Tarsus. The crossing of the Taurus Mountains gave him no great difficulty, for Persian resistance was weak. At Tarsus he fell dangerously ill after bathing in the freezing Cydnus River, but he was saved by his physician Phillippus. The conquest of Asia Minor could be regarded as completed; the plan that once had been proclaimed by Isocrates had been carried out. Meanwhile, however, the Persian King had had many months, time to mobilize the great resources of the eastern regions of his empire. He was now prepared to fight a battle that would decide the war.

The battle was fought in November, 333, on the Syrian coastal plain, near the little town of Issus, not far from the modern Alexandretta. The battle had a unique background; the opposing armies had taken different roads and marched past each other, with the result that Darius was in Alexander's rear. After crossing the Amanus Mountains, the Persians had appeared at Issus, where no one had expected them. Here they did not hesitate to massacre the sick and wounded Macedonians who had been left behind.

At Issus, then, the two armies faced each other in the wrong directions. The Persians' right wing and the Macedonians' left wing rested on the sea. The core of the Persian force was a phalanx of Greek mercenaries, no less than 30,-000 of them, as we are told. The decisive role, however, had been assigned to the Persian cavalry, whose task was to attack along the seashore and overrun the Macedonian left wing. In addition, the Persians had sent a small detachment forward on their left wing across the Pinarus River, with orders to take the Macedonian in the right flank.

Alexander's dispositions decided the battle. In order to strengthen his left wing he had stationed the whole of his Thessalian cavalry there; on the right wing, he himself led his cavalry (*hetairoi*) in the decisive thrust against the Persians. Alexander's attack routed the Persian left wing, but left a gap in the Macedonian center; the Persians' Greek mercenaries rushed into it. Alexander had to hurry to the relief of his hard-pressed center to restore the situation. The Macedonian left was also under heavy pressure from superior enemy forces. But the Persian King, seeing the general disarray of his army, lost his nerve and took flight. This was the beginning of the end, for there was no holding the Persians in line once their King had fled. Only the Greek mercenaries continued to hold their ranks, so that at least some of them were able to get to safety. The Persian camp fell into Macedonian hands, and the mother, wife, and two daughters of the Great King fell prisoner to Alexander. Alexander's chivalrous treatment of these women is universally known.

Alexander's plan is obvious from the further course of the campaign; it involved the taking of the Phoenician coastal cities. Alexander did not think of pursuing the fleeing Persian King; he held unswervingly to his original design of occupying the coasts of the Persian Empire. Aradus, Byblus, and Sidon went over to Alexander's side without a struggle. Only Tyre—most powerful of the Phoenician cities, mother of Carthage—refused to submit. Tyre would not allow the King to offer a sacrifice to the Tyrian god Melkart within her walls, because only the city's prince was permitted to do so. So once again decision was left to the sword.

The siege of Tyre lasted a full seven months. It was the "new city," situated on an island over half a mile from the mainland, that was laid under siege. With untold difficulty Alexander had a causeway built from the mainland out to the island, and along this causeway the siege machines were brought up within range of the city walls. With the support of a fleet from the other Phoenician cities and from Cyprus, Alexander succeeded in blockading the city until a breach had been made in the wall. A horrible massacre now followed in the city. The surviving inhabitants, said to have numbered 30,000, were sold into slavery. The siege and the fall of Tyre paralleled the siege of Carthage in the Third Punic War, and the siege of Jerusalem by Vespasian and Titus. In all three cases a Semitic population tirelessly defied an enemy superior in strength, and perished only after a determined struggle.

Even before the fall of Tyre the Great King had made an offer of peace to Alexander; but the Macedonian had rejected it out of hand. Darius had been prepared to cede to Alexander all of his territory west of the Euphrates. But even then Alexander aspired to the conquest of the whole Persian Empire. It was not like Alexander to limit his ambitions. It is idle to speculate whether Darius' offer could have been the basis of a workable peace. Alexander was not interested in peace.

From Tyre, Alexander's forces moved straight toward Egypt, but there was long resistance to be overcome in Gaza. Finally, after two months, the city fell, and the road to the Nile was opened. Alexander did not enter Jerusalem.

What did Alexander want in Egypt? Did the prestige of the land of the Pharaohs and its age-old civilization draw him there? Not entirely. Egypt was a rich grainland that had brought the Persian kings enormous revenue. Only a few years earlier, in 343–342, it had been reconquered by Artaxerxes III Ochus, and its people were by no means loyal to the Persians. This cannot have been unknown to Alexander; he must also have known that the country lay before him without any adequate defense. From the border fortress of Pelusium the Macedonian continued to Memphis, the ancient capital, where the priests placed upon his head the double crown of

Upper and Lower Egypt. From there he sailed down the Nile; in the beginning of 331, near the westernmost (Canopic) mouth of the Nile, between Lake Mareotis, fed by the river, and the Mediterranean Sea, he founded the city of Alexandria. The site was brilliantly chosen; Alexandria combined the advantages of a first-class harbor and an excellent inland waterway. Within a few decades, the city rose to become, along with Carthage, the leading commercial center in the Mediterranean. The destruction of Tyre had made the founding of Alexandria a positive necessity.

From Alexandria the conqueror's route led to Paratonium on the border of Cyrenaica, and thence through the desert to the oasis of Siwa and the shrine of the god Ammon. There has been endless discussion of, and speculation about, this march to the oasis of Ammon. Like so many things in the life of Alexander, this clearly sprang from quite irrational drives: it was *pothos,* a longing for the indefinable, that led the King to the desert shrine. What took place in the temple we do not know; Alexander entered it alone. But the priest of the god had already hailed him as "Son of Ammon." The echo of this greeting was heard through all the world, as far as Greece and Ionia, for this title raised Alexander far above the Macedonian national kingship, far above his position as commander of the Panhellenic League; a new role was in the making. Indeed a new period in the life and work of Alexander dates from this solemn hour in the sanctuary of Ammon.

Alexander now reorganized the Egyptian administration. The country was entrusted to two Egyptians, Doloaspis and Petitis, as heads of the civil administration; military government was placed in the hands of two Macedonians, of whom one was responsible for Upper and the other Lower Egypt. In addition, two special border commands were created, called Libya and Arabia; these were entrusted to Apollonius and to Cleomenes, a Greek from Naucratis. In all this Alexander showed a cautious realism, taking care to keep military power in the hands of his own men. This organization, by the way, was adopted by the Ptolemaic kings of Egypt as the basis of their administrative system.

313

By the spring of 331, when Alexander left Egypt, he had given Darius almost a year and a half's time to mobilize the resources of his empire. And yet the Persians had not made the slightest effort to disrupt Alexander's lines of communication with Europe. On the contrary, they awaited him beyond the Tigris in Mesopotamia, near the town of Gaugamela (Tel Comel), about twenty-one miles northeast of present-day Mosul. Here, on October 1, 331, was fought the battle that decided the fate of the Achaemenid Empire. It can be precisely dated by a lunar eclipse recorded as taking place eleven days before the battle.

Again Darius had numerical superiority over Alexander; the Persian had also carefully reconnoitered the terrain, and had it leveled for the use of his scythed chariots. His line of battle was considerably longer than that of the Macedonians. This prompted Alexander to a countermeasure. He backed both wings of his army with special detachments, whose orders were to wheel to the side or to the rear if necessary, and there defend the army's flanks or rear against envelopment. The center of the two armies was occupied by the Persian King's Greek mercenaries on the one side and the bulk of the Macedonian infantry on the other.

Again, as at the battle of Issus, the Persian right wing gained ground. Under the command of Mazaeus they pressed as far forward as the Macedonian camp. But once more the battle was decided on the Persian center. When Alexander cut through the opposing formation with his cavalry (*hetairoi*), Darius lost his nerve for the second time and fled the field. B. G. Niebuhr maintained that Alexander's victories over the Persians, significant as they may have been, ought not to be overrated. Of the troops opposing the Macedonians, only the Greek mercenaries were their match by European standards; all the others were Orientals, above all the Great King himself.

Darius withdrew over the Kurdish Mountains, while Alexander moved, by way of Arbela, southward into Babylonia. The Persian governor of this province was Mazaeus, who had distinguished himself at Gaugamela. He surrendered the city of Babylon to the victor, who confirmed him in his office as satrap, though two Macedonians were placed at his side, one as military commander, the other as treasurer. Alexander remained about a month in Babylonia. He offered sacrifice to Bel-Marduk and gave orders for the restoration of the god's great temple, destroyed by Xerxes.

The conqueror now turned toward the Persian royal residences: Susa, Persepolis, and Ecbatana. He met resistance only among the Uxians and at the Persian Gates (Tang-i-Rashkan). Here the enemy position was held by Ariobarzanes, satrap of Persia, whom Alexander was able to overcome only by treachery. The satrap himself escaped to Darius, and was later received by Alexander with honors. Craterus had distinguished himself in the fighting; he emerges more and more as one of the most capable officers in Alexander's army. Susa surrendered without a fight, and the Macedonians found 40,000 silver talents and 9,000 minted darics in its treasuries, an enormous sum that testifies to the unimaginable wealth of the Persian kings. Persepolis, the majestic palace of the Achaemenid kings, adorned with huge and magnificent buildings by Darius I and Xerxes, likewise fell to Alexander without a blow given or received.

Alexander had characterized the war against the Persians as a war of revenge; here in Persepolis that war was ended by a symbolic act. It was Alexander himself who threw the first torch into the Palace of Xerxes; the glories of Persepolis went up in flames, and the destruction of the Greek shrines was avenged. Alexander acted here out of conscious policy and on emotional impulse, as a tradition going back to Cleitarchus has it: according to that tradition, Alexander, somewhat the worse for celebration, and instigated by the hetaera Thais, laid the Palace of Xerxes in ashes. In Persepolis, as in Pasargadae, enormous treasures fell into his hands.

In Pasargadae, Alexander visited the grave of Cyrus the Great, which he had restored by his engineer Aristobulus. Alexander arrived in Ecbatana (Hamadan) too late to catch the fleeing Darius. Here he discharged the Greek contingents of his army. The campaign that he had conducted as strategos

315

of the Corinthian League was thereby declared at an end. From now on, Alexander fought for his own interest. Not all of the Greeks returned to their homeland; many of them preferred to continue serving with Alexander as mercenaries. As the army went on to Ecbatana, it became clear that they had a long road still ahead of them. Darius still lived; he was hurrying along the great Royal Road to Rhagae, and on through the Caspian Gates toward the outer Iranian lands. In a relentless pursuit that spared neither men nor horses, Alexander overtook him near Hecatompylus—but only as a corpse. The satrap of Bactria, Bessus, had taken the Great King with him as a prisoner and finally had him put to death, so that he would not fall alive into Macedonian hands.

The death of the last ruler of the Achaemenid House was one of the decisive moments in Alexander's life. From now on he regarded himself as Darius' lawful successor, and as such had the murdered king interred in Persepolis with full honors. Alexander now held himself to be the legitimate ruler of all the peoples of the Persian Empire. As such he meant to fulfill all his obligations; the first was vengeance on the regicide Bessus.

Alexander's new role inevitably influenced his relationship with both Persians and Macedonians. From this time on an increasing number of Persian nobles took leading positions in the administration of the satrapies; in most cases, the King showed great skill in his appointments. Alexander's army, too, was greatly altered. The greater its distance from the Macedonian homeland, the longer its supply lines grew. To replace casualties in his army he soon had to fall back on Iranian troops, who were, however, organized into their own detachments with the army. Even Alexander would not have dared to incorporate Iranians into the Macedonian regiments, for his countrymen felt themselves to be conquerors and far superior to the Persians. This was to present Alexander with grave problems as time went on.

The pursuit of the Bactrian satrap Bessus took Alexander into Outer Iran. His campaign there lasted from the fall of 330 into the year 327. The fighting in the Iranian highlands was the hardest that Alexander encountered in all his life. The Iranians made a magnificently stubborn fight of it; their courage was heightened by religious fanaticism. Moreover, Alexander and his Macedonians were entering completely unknown regions. Their march took them through Afghanistan to the river Helmand (Etymandrus) in the south, thence to the Hindu Kush (Paropamisus), through the region of Bokhara and Western Turkestan to the Syr-Darya (Jaxartes), and from there to India. This was not only a military achievement of the first order, it was a journey of discovery, introducing the Greeks and Macedonians to an entirely new world.

The Greeks' ideas of the geography of these lands had been entirely inadequate before Alexander's time; in part, they had been positively fantastic. The Hellenes thought that the Jaxartes was the upper course of the Tanais (Don), which empties into the Sea of Azov. The Paropamisus or Hindu Kush they considered to be a continuation of the Caucasus range. Alexander and his Macedonians did not have the slightest idea of where they really were. But, thanks to the work of their "bematists," or human pedometers, their marches through the length and breadth of these lands laid a new foundation for geographical knowledge of central Asia. The data were utilized and exploited by the great geographer and polymath Eratosthenes of Cyrene (ca. 285–205 B.C.)

The direction of Alexander's march was also influenced by various chance events. He originally intended to seek out Bessus directly in his Bactrian satrapy, traveling by way of the northern parts of the satrapy of Areia. The satrap of Areia, Satibarzanes, had at first submitted to Alexander, but now defected to Bessus. Alexander pursued the satrap as far as Artacoana, then crossed Drangiana (which bordered it on the south) as far as the Helmand. Only then did he continue the march to Bactria, proceeding in a northeasterly direction to the Hindu Kush. The crossing of this mountain chain, eternally covered with snow, was a magnificent achievement for Alexander and his army; Hannibal's celebrated crossing of the Alps pales by comparison.

Meanwhile, Bessus had left his capital, Bactria, and fled

317

northward to the neighboring satrapy of Sogdiana. The broad current of the Oxus (Amu-Darya) lay between him and Alexander. But even this river was no decisive obstacle to Alexander's progress. The river was crossed, probably at Kilif; the infantry was carried across on sheepskins stuffed with rushes; the cavalry had to swim across, leading their horses by the reins. Bessus eventually found himself deserted by his followers; he was captured by Ptolemy, the later King of Egypt. Alexander dealt with the Persian cruelly; after cutting off his nose and ears, he sent him to Ecbatana; there, in the old Median capital, Bessus was executed, probably by impaling. Alexander obviously felt justified in carrying out the savage penal law of the Achaemenids; for him, Bessus was not an enemy but a regicide.

Passing through Maracanda (Samarkand) Alexander marched to the Jaxartes (Syr-Darya). Here another city named after Alexander was founded, Alexandria Eschata ("the outermost"). It is the modern city of Leninabad. Alexander's expedition in northeastern Iran was marked by the founding of a whole series of new cities, some of which were to have a great future—for example, Alexandria in Areia (Herat) and Alexandria in Arachosia (Kandahar). The founding of these cities was dictated, for the most part, by military considerations. The cities, however, were settled not only by soldiers but also by Greek civilians who had followed Alexander's army. Thus fragments of Greek culture and Greek life were transplanted to Iran and Turkestan, by the Macedonian conquest.

Bessus had perished; but Alexander now had a more dangerous adversary, Spitamenes, a Bactrian, who raised the region of Sogdiana in revolt against the King. Alexander was unable to capture him, but the Scythians beyond the Jaxartes, the Massagetae, to whom Spitamenes had fled, cut off his head and sent it to Alexander as a gift. This was another stroke of luck for Alexander, for Spitamenes had offered stubborn resistance in Bactria for more than a year. The daughter of Spitamenes, Apame, was wedded to Seleucus in 324, in Susa. No fewer than three cities bore her name (Apamea). She was the ancestress of the Seleucid family, which ruled over large parts of the Near East for about 250 years after Alexander's death.

Meanwhile, the year 327 had begun, and there was still resistance against Alexander in the northeastern border provinces of the Achaemenid Empire. By a brilliant feat of mountaineering, 300 Macedonians forced the craggy stronghold of Ariamazes near Nautaca to capitulate. Among the Iranian prisoners taken was the daughter of Oxyartes, Roxana, one of the few women to whom Alexander was ever deeply attracted. The wedding took place according to Iranian ritual, with the newly wedded couple eating a loaf of bread that had been cut in two with a sword. The common consumption of a loaf of bread is said to be the custom at weddings in Turkestan to this day.

Since the death of Darius III, Alexander had increasingly adopted the rituals and traditions of the Persian monarchy. Many Macedonians, especially those who had been close to his father Philip, were absolutely unable to approve this course. This explains three important incidents that cast dark shadows on Alexander's character. During his stay in Drangiana a conspiracy was uncovered against Alexander's life. It had been known to Philotas, the son of Parmenio, who had, however, not reported it. The assembly of the Macedonian army met as a court; Philotas (who was commander of the royal squadron of the mounted *hetairoi*) was condemned to death. Such was the sentence of the court; it is almost certain that it was actually the will of the King.

There is no question that a far more serious execution was carried out at Alexander's direct command. Parmenio, Philotas' father, was to die. The order was carried by racing camel to Ecbatana. Alexander was in a great hurry; he had to prevent the news of Philotas' execution from reaching Media first. Parmenio's death was nothing less than the bad conscience of the King. There is no political excuse that might cover it.

The third incident occurred in Maracanda in the fall of 328. After a night's drinking a violent interchange took place between Alexander and Cleitus, who had once saved the King's life on the Granicus. Cleitus' insults snapped the self-control of the King. He seized the javelin of a guardsman and ran his friend through—an emotional act that no one regretted more than Alexander himself. Cleitus had been his foster-brother.

Callisthenes, the nephew of Aristotle, also ran afoul of Alexander. The historian refused to perform the *proskynesis* —that is, to prostrate himself before the King in the Persian manner. On various occasions he spoke out against Alexander. Implicated in the "pages' conspiracy," Callisthenes was imprisoned and finally put to death, in India.

In the summer of 327, the Macedonian army descended to the plains of India. They were to remain there for two years. What motive took Alexander further into Asia is difficult to determine with any certainty. The romantic attraction of infinite distance, perhaps. Or he may have felt obligated, as successor to the Achaemenids, to conquer the Indian sub-continent, although only a part of it had belonged to the Empire of Darius I. The likeliest explanation is that Alexander, in his striving for world domination, was unwilling to forego the acquisition of India.

The expedition to India took Alexander and his Mace-donians into incredibly remote lands, including some where no European had ever set foot before. For the Macedonians, it was a totally strange world, whose people and places filled them with amazement. The religion and the customs of the Brahmans in particular fascinated Alexander. Tradition tells of conversations he is supposed to have had with the Indian gymnosophists, the monastic ascetics of Hinduism and Buddhism.

In eastern Iran, Alexander had opened contact with the Indian King Taxiles. The invasion route led through the Kabul valley, but it was only by storming the high mountain fortress of Aornus (Pir-sar) that the way into the plain of the Five Rivers was secured. At the Indus River a bridge had been prepared by advance detachments under Hephaestion and Perdiccas. Alexander led his great army of Macedonians, Greeks, and Iranians across into the Punjab. In Taxila, near the modern Rawalpindi, he was courteously received by King

Taxiles. Beyond the Hydaspes, however, lay the realm of another Indian King, Porus, Taxiles' enemy. Against this king, Alexander fought one more great pitched battle in the summer of 326. It is known to history as the battle of Porus or of the Hydaspes.

In its plan and execution the battle of the Hydaspes is a true mirror of Alexander's military genius. Unnoticed by his enemy, Alexander succeeded in crossing the rushing river. Passing from the forward march directly into the attack, the Macedonian King again decided the battle with his cavalry, which was superior to the enemy's. The Macedonians dealt with Porus' elephants by putting their mahouts out of action with arrows; the leaderless beasts blundered through their own ranks, spreading total confusion. Porus was wounded and taken prisoner, and Alexander treated him with all honors. Moving onward across the Acesines (Chenab) to the Hyphasis, Alexander met little opposition, except in the land of the Cathaeans; their city, Sangala, was taken by storm.

On the Acesines Alexander saw not only lotus plants but also crocodiles. He thought that he was in the country where the Nile has its source. He had no idea of the actual geography of India, and the natives had to tell him that the Acesines is a tributary of the Indus, and that the Indus empties not into the Mediterranean but into the ocean.

What more might he not discover? He was never to know. At the Hyphasis River (the modern Beas), his Macedonians refused to go on. The soldiers were exhausted by the continual rains; they feared the King would lead them on and on forever, into infinitely remote lands; their will was paralyzed by the endless distances of Asia. The King, for the first and only time in his life, had to yield. On the Hyphasis twelve great altars were erected, and the great army turned back to the Hydaspes.

An enormous fleet was constructed there, Alexander's principal officers outfitting the ships on the model of the Attic trierarchy. Command of the fleet was given to Nearchus, who had been a confidant of the King since his youth. The fleet sailed down the Hydaspes to the Acesines and on into the Indus. Two army detachments under Craterus and Hephaestion accompanied it on either side of the river. But there was still fighting to be done. Alexander was seriously wounded by an arrow in storming the city of the Malli, and was believed at first to be dead. His soldiers' joy was boundless when the rumor proved false. Nine months after setting sail on the river, Alexander's army reached the city of Pattala in the Indus Delta. This was in July, 325. India, or at least the Land of the Five Rivers, lay at Alexander's feet. The country was reorganized, its administration put partly into the hands of Macedonian governors, partly into those of Indian vassal princes. Alexander's sacrifice at the mouth of the Indus marked the symbolic conclusion of the conquest of the East.

At Pattala, Nearchus was commissioned to take the fleet and find a way to the mouth of the Euphrates. This was a highly dangerous voyage; knowledge of the coastal lands between India and Mesopotamia had long since been lost, after the voyage made by Scylax of Caryanda during the reign of Darius I. Nearchus' enterprise amounted to a new voyage of discovery.

While a part of Alexander's army, led by Craterus, returned to the west by way of Arachosia, Alexander set out on what was probably the most difficult part of his return march. He chose a route that led through the waterless waste of Gedrosia (Baluchistan). If Nearchus may be believed, Alexander knew precisely what awaited him here. But the example of his great models, Cyrus the Elder and the mythical Queen Semiramis, allowed him no rest; what they had done, he must outdo. Was the march really necessary? F. Hampl is convinced it was not, pointing to the enormous loss of life that it entailed. But the march through the Gedrosian desert ran parallel to the sea voyage of Nearchus. It was an inevitable pendant of the latter; that the King kept the more dangerous task for himself was entirely in character. In Carmania, in the vicinity of Hormuz, the King joined forces with Nearchus once more, and was overjoyed to learn that the fleet had survived the great voyage in good order.

Nearchus described the voyage in a work that is the basis for Arrian's *Indiké*. The narrative gives a splendid picture of the customs and manners of the coastal peoples of Baluchistan. Occasionally, it includes data on the flora and fauna. Nearchus' soldiers, for example, encountered whales for the first time, and tried to impress them by shouting and blowing trumpets. While Nearchus continued his voyage into the Persian Gulf, Alexander marched overland to Pasargadae, which he reached at the beginning of 324. He came as the lord of the entire Persian Empire; the lands from the Hellespont to the Hyphasis, from the Caucasus to Nubia, lay at his feet. As a commander and as an administrator he had accomplished things for which the world offered no precedent. Yet more was to be done.

Alexander had been absent in the East for six years; abuses had sprung up in the administration of his empire that hark back to the days of Achaemenid rule. The satraps of Persian blood, and even a few Macedonian satraps, had recruited mercenaries without troubling to consult their faraway King. This was now corrected and the culprits punished. One of the disobedient governors was Harpalus, whom Alexander had entrusted with the immense treasures stored in the palaces of the Persian kings. Harpalus had been a friend of Alexander's from his youth, yet Alexander's trust in him was utterly misplaced; he squandered the fortune that had been placed in his care. He fled from Alexander's wrath, sailed to Greece, and finally found a refuge in Athens. Harpalus is only one example of the corruption that had spread within Alexander's empire.

The last phase in the life of Alexander—a period of about a year and a half—reveals a decisive change in the King's character. Alexander no longer felt himself to be primarily a king of the Macedonians; he also saw himself as the Persian Great King and, more than that, ruler of the world. His plans were now measureless. He planned an expedition around the Arabian Peninsula; he considered the conquest of the entire western Mediterranean. These gigantic western plans of Alexander have been termed an invention of later authors (see S. S. Tarn, *Alexander the Great*), but this is not so. The

323

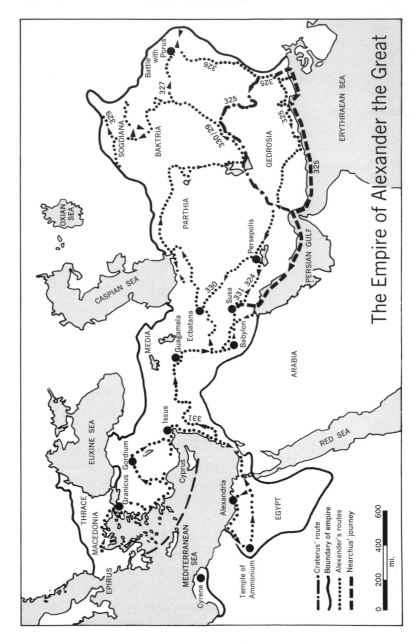

The Empire of Alexander the Great

324

western scheme appears in the *Hypomnemata* of Alexander, which go back to Eumenes of Cardia, the head of Alexander's chancellery. These designs were never carried out; after Alexander's death they were scrapped by the Assembly of the Macedonian army in Babylon.

Alexander wanted to make the Macedonians and the Persians joint rulers of the world. The fusion of these two peoples (of whose common Indo-European origin Alexander had, of course, not the slightest idea) was to be promoted by a mass marriage at Susa, where Alexander and his closest friends wedded Persian noblewomen. Alexander married Statira, a daugher of the last Great King. Hephaestion married her sister. Eighty other noble Macedonians wed daughters of Persian and Iranian families. No less than 10,000 Macedonians at that time received wedding presents from Alexander, having either already married Persian women or now wedding them at the mass marriage. Naturally there were many Macedonians who were unable (i.e., unwilling) to follow the King in this policy. Their anger and jealousy exploded in a mutiny at Opis on the Tigris in the summer of 324. When Alexander was about to dismiss a number of his veterans and send them back to Macedonia, the army demanded the discharge of all Macedonian soldiers, shouting and jeering at the King that he could take the field alone with his father Ammon. Alexander was furious. He had the ringleaders seized and executed out of hand. Then, in a bitter speech, he reminded the soldiers of what his father Philip and he himself had done to deserve well of the Macedonian people. Then he dismissed the entire army. When the soldiers saw that the King was in earnest about this, they had a change of heart and implored his pardon. In the Prayer of Opis, with which Alexander opened the great reconciliation banquet, the King implored the gods to grant harmony between Macedonians and Persians so that both nations might jointly rule his conquests. In other words, he held fast to his plan for a fusion of the two peoples. But a general fraternization of all the world's peoples was something that he never conceived, neither then nor at any other time in his life. There is no line to be drawn between Alexander and the ideas of human brotherhood of the French Revolution, although modern scholars have occasionally made the attempt.

Probably related to his plans for world conquest was his order for the repatriation of the Greek exiles. Alexander's directive was read aloud by his delegate, Nicanor of Stagira, at the Olympic Festival in the summer of 324. This decree (*diagramma*) of Alexander is hardly to be seen as arbitrary interference in Greek internal affairs. What Alexander sought was the internal pacification of Greece; this was of the greatest importance to his plans for the conquest of the western Mediterranean. Moreover Alexander, as Protector of the Corinthian League, considered himself fully justified in putting an end at last to the problem of the exiles. A second decree raises further difficulties: the King ordered the Greeks to pay divine honors to himself. In this he was certainly acting on Greek and not on Oriental precedent. For the Greeks, the man of great achievements was worthy to rise to the level of the gods. Lysander, the Spartan victor in the Peloponnesian War, had had divine honors paid him by the Samians. Alexander had achieved much more than Lysander, much more than any other mortal known to the Greeks. The Greeks consequently understood his demand. In Athens, even a man like Demosthenes had no objection to make against it. But the religious aspects cannot be separated from the political. If Alexander was a god for the Greeks, then not only did they owe him religious reverence (and indeed we read of the arrival of Greek sacred embassies in Babylon), but they also owed him political obedience; his rule was now given divine consecration. Alexander, gifted with a special charisma, had established the idea of Divine Kingship. A line of descent leads from Alexander to the Diadochi and the other Hellenistic divine kings, and thence to Rome, to Caesar and Augustus.

In the autumn of 324, Alexander's closest friend Hephaestion died in Ecbatana. The King's sorrow was boundless. He ordered a huge monument to the deceased built in Babylon. At the time of Alexander's own death it was still incomplete, and the Army Assembly ordered that work on it be stopped.

Alexander's last feat of arms that history reports was the subjugation of the wild Cossaeans in Susiana, in the winter of 324–323. He then returned to the city of Babylon. The Chaldean astrologers warned the King not to enter Babylon, but Alexander would not be diverted. He had chosen Babylon as the capital of his Asiatic Empire. Here he drew up detailed plans for the future. He was never to carry them out.

He had an enormous harbor laid out near Babylon, with provision made (including warehouses and magazines) for no less than 1,000 warships. Alexander had no idea of the size of the Arabian Peninsula— no more than anyone else of his time—but he had fixed on the idea of opening a sea route from the mouth of the Euphrates to Egypt. He had already sent out a few explorers, but none of them had reached their goal, as the distance proved insurmountable. Now Nearchus was to be sent, with an immense fleet. A few days before the great expedition was to depart, Alexander, returning from a drinking bout at the house of his friend Medius, fell seriously ill. For ten days and ten nights he wrestled with death. In the *Ephemerides,* the court journal, the course of the illness is recorded in all its details. From the fourth day on the fever never left him, he grew weaker and weaker, and his friends' desperate efforts to find a cure by consulting the god Serapis were in vain. Alexander died on the evening of the twenty-eighth day of Daïsios (according to the Macedonian calendar), which is June 10, 323, by the Julian calendar. Scholars, as a rule, assume the cause of death to have been malaria, though some suggest pneumonia, having its origin in the arrow wound that Alexander received in the battle with the Malli.

Alexander has shared the posthumous fate of so many great men in history. The value men set on him is, at least in part, dependent on the historical experiences of their own lives. We have only to think of the varying portraits that historians have drawn of men like Napoleon or Bismarck. We may well understand why historians of today have no laurels to award the Macedonian conqueror. War is always a misfortune, whatever its outcome. But if anyone has the right to be measured by the standards of his own time, it is Alexander. If a few

327

generations after his death there were Stoic philosophers who condemned aggressive war, these were *rarae aves,* of whom Alexander had never known. In Alexander's time, a conqueror was a hero par excellence. And Alexander was the greatest conqueror the world had ever seen. Antiquity held Alexander to be the greatest of all generals, and rightly so.

In the execution as well as the planning of his campaigns, whether against the barbarians on the Danube, the Greeks, or the Persians, Alexander showed extraordinary skill. He was a master not only of the set battle but also of guerrilla warfare, as he showed in his campaigns in northeastern Iran. His talent for improvisation was admirable, his tenacity was inflexible, as at the siege of Tyre. The verdict on Alexander as statesman is not so automatic: his plan for a fusion of nations was laudable, but was it feasible? That Alexander was many generations ahead of his time in this is certain; the Assembly of the Macedonian army in Babylon expressly abrogated these measures after his death. What might have become of them if the King had had a fairly long life, we cannot know.

The Macedonian-Persian community of nations remained only an ideal. This is insufficient grounds for condemning it. A world empire required the greatest possible rapprochement between its peoples, with their different races and cultures. The Macedonians were a hopeless minority in relation to the peoples of the Persian Empire. Alexander's empire represented a supranational political idea; he could not, when it came to carrying it out, shrink from its consequences.

The idea of the fusion of nations was more than a slogan; this is shown by Alexander's behavior toward the national groups in his empire. Whether he was dealing with Lydians, Carians, Egyptians, or Babylonians, Alexander displayed not only good will but also the greatest respect for their national and religious traditions. His religious tolerance in particular recalls the attitude of the great Persian kings. Here Alexander set new standards for his contemporaries; without him, the religious syncretism of the Hellenistic age and of the Roman Imperial period would have been unthinkable.

The King's achievements in the field of imperial administration had equally far-reaching effects. To be sure, he retained in principle the satrapy system of the Persian Empire; but frequently he set up Macedonian officers, either as *strategoi* or as *episkopoi* (supervisors), at the side of Persian or native civic governors; from this developed the later standard practice of separating civil and military administration. His appointment of special functionaries for finances was another innovation taken up by the Hellenistic monarchies of the Ptolemies and the Seleucids. His economic policy had dramatic results; by minting the gold and silver hoarded by the Achaemenids, Alexander injected enormous sums into the markets of the Near East and the Mediterranean; this measure, combined with the shift to the Attic standard of coinage, set the economy of his entire empire on a new foundation. Economic stagnation was now at an end, and an extraordinary degree of prosperity followed. Just before his fatal illness the King was overseeing the reconstruction of the Pallacottas Canal in Babylonia, further evidence of his efforts to restore Mesopotamia to her former economic well-being. These reforms, taken together, cannot be dismissed as accidental improvements. They give witness to the King's view that no state could exist without a healthy economy. The comparison of Alexander to Frederick the Great is absolutely justified in this respect.

It is clear that irrational forces played a role in the life of Alexander, but they could neither disturb nor alter the constructive design of his work. Here the facts speak for themselves; it is utterly wrong to assign his achievements solely to the luck that was his companion, as it was of so many great men. The political development of the Hellenistic empires cannot be imagined without the achievement of Alexander; no more can the emergence of a Hellenistic world civilization. But Alexander's impact was felt beyond the Hellenistic period, far into the time of the Roman Empire. The rise of Christianity and the spread of Islamic civilization presuppose the existence of Alexander's efforts. His life and his accomplishments lay at the root of much that is still alive today. That life has been a model for great men in all subsequent centuries, and no wonder. The originality of his thought, his intuitive grasp of

329

the possible and the necessary, the courage with which he carried out the most difficult enterprises with an adaptability that reflected genius, the fascination that his personality exercised on the men around him—these things reveal Alexander as a figure in the very first rank of history, a phenomenon for which the ages offer hardly any parallel. This man changed the world; he did not cease to do so with his early death.

For one thing, his march through Asia had changed the position of Greece, now on the periphery of world events. Alexander, as we have said, left his general Antipater behind in Macedonia as regent of the kingdom and strategos for Europe. It was no easy task that the loyal servant of the King accepted. Alexander himself was conscious of this; or so we assume from the fact that no less than 12,000 foot and 1,500 horse remained behind in Macedonia when the King crossed over to Asia. But Alexander constantly called for replacements; the number of troops in Macedonia fit for active service steadily declined.

All the more remarkable were Antipater's achievements. First he suppressed a rebellion in Thrace, in which the Macedonian governor (strategos) Memnon had taken part. Before completing the campaign in Thrace, he had to leave for Greece to intervene in the Peloponnese. Here the Macedonians had helped a number of tyrants to power, but all tyranny was odious to the Greeks. An Athenian inscription from 337–336 contains a law on tyrants introduced by a certain Eucrates; it appears that even in Athens men feared that a tyrannical rule might be established.

In the Spartan King Agis III, the Macedonians found a resolute opponent. He gathered behind him all the discontented states of the Peloponnese, among them Elis, Achaea, and a part of Arcadia. Argos, Messene, and Megalopolis, on the other hand, as enemies of Sparta, remained aloof. The issue was determined in the summer of 331 near Megalopolis. Here Antipater, with his Macedonians and troops of the Corinthian League, was victorious over Agis III, who died a soldier's death in battle. With that, the rebellion collapsed. News of the battle reached Alexander in 330. He is said to have called Antipater's victory a "battle of mice," in comparison with his own deeds in Asia; we may doubt this, for Antipater still had to deal with Greeks and not, like Alexander, with Orientals. The Synhedrion of Corinth asked Alexander to decide the fate of the rebellious Greeks. Possibly Sparta itself had to join the Corinthian League; she was in any case required to give Antipater fifty hostages.

Athens had wisely not taken part in the revolt. But the city's mood was anything but friendly to Alexander. In 330 the "case of the crown," postponed for years, was heard and judged. Demosthenes defeated his enemy (and the Macedonians' friend) Aeschines, who was sentenced to a fine of 1,000 drachmas. Also, after 324, Athens was outraged by the King's order for the return of the exiles. Demosthenes tried to obtain a postponement of this from the Macedonian authorities. But far more dangerous to Demosthenes were his actions in another connection; the great orator came to terms with Harpalus, who, as we have seen, had fled from Asia, and who now landed at the Piraeus in the summer of 324. It is an established fact that Demosthenes was one of the Athenians bribed by Harpalus; he was forced to admit to having received twenty talents. Demosthenes claimed that he had used the money for the people, for the theatrical fund (*theorika*), but this appears to be a mere excuse. At any rate, in the trial of those subverted by Harpalus, Demosthenes was sentenced to a heavy fine, and since he was unable to pay he was thrown into prison. He escaped to Troezen and later to Aegina (323). In 322, in the Temple of Calauria, Demosthenes met his destiny, taking his own life as Antipater's emissaries were about to seize him.

While Alexander was hurrying from victory to victory in Asia, the Greeks fell on hard times. There was a great famine that lasted five years, from 330 to 326. From this period dates an inscription from Cyrene listing shipments of grain from the city of Cyrene to the Greek mother country. Almost all the important Greek city-states are listed as recipients, with the exception of Sparta. Was there enough to eat in Sparta, or was Sparta purposely disregarded? If the latter, this reflects the consequences of the Spartan revolt against the Macedonians.

Also interesting is another inscription, according to which Athens sent an expedition under one Miltiades to the Adriatic in 325–324, to found a colony as a naval base against Etruscan pirates. The Etruscans—or Tyrrhenians, as they were called— had a formidable reputation for piracy, and preyed on Greek commerce both in the Adriatic and further west.

More or less the whole of Greece took part, actively or passively, in Alexander's march across Asia. Many Greeks served as mercenaries, some, too, as functionaries of the Macedonian King. Prestige accrued not only to those on the expedition but to their connections at home as well. Inscriptions from Olympia and Aegion in Achaea tell of a Cretan named Philonides who termed himself "foot-courier for King Alexander and Bematist (foot-measurer) of Asia"; Philonides, in other words, was one of Alexander's staff. Before that he was a courier in the Peloponnese, possibly in the service of the pro-Macedonian city of Sicyon. He is supposed to have covered the distance from Sicyon to Elis, about 150 kilometers, in a single day; unfortunately this is physically impossible. Men like Philonides not only acquired glory in Asia, they also acquired a sizable fortune—one more reason for the Greeks of the mother country to follow Alexander by the thousands. Alexander's march through Asia brought about a tremendous upheaval in the economic and social life of Greece; its full effects are to be seen in the Hellenistic period that followed his death. For a long time to come, Greece was to live in the shadow of Alexander.

16

Egypt and the Persian Empire

The reigns of Amasis and his son Psammetichus III, which brought the Saïte Dynasty to a close, were the last years of Egypt's independence.[1-3] By this time Egypt was all that Cambyses lacked—he had inherited [4] from his father Cyrus an empire comprising all the states of Asia. Amasis' attempt to protect himself through an alliance with Polycrates of Samos [5] proved useless; Phanes of Halicarnassus, a Greek general in the service of Amasis, turned traitor and went over to the Persian king. As Cambyses advanced on Egypt, Phanes supplied him with all the information he needed concerning the best routes across the Arabian desert and the best means of overcoming the Egyptian lines of defense. Abandoned even by Polycrates of Samos, Amasis found himself cut off while Cambyses struck up alliances with the Bedouins of the Arabian desert, whose camels, laden with skins of water, made it possible for the Persian army to cross the desert and reach Pelusium.

After the death of Amasis early in 525 B.C., it fell to his son and heir, Psammetichus III, to withstand the Persian offensive. The resistance organized by Psammetichus at Pelusium gave way, and the Egyptian army withdrew before Cambyses; a final attempt at resistance was defeated at Memphis, and Psammetichus was taken prisoner. Cambyses was master of Egypt where he remained until 522 B.C. With Cambyses begins the "First Persian Conquest" [6] (XXVII Dynasty), as it is usually called, which ended in 401 B.C. (?)

The Greek sources (Herodotus III, 27–38; Diodorus I, 46; Strabo XVII, 27; Plutarch, *De Iside et Osiride,* 44c) agree that Cambyses' reign was characterized by terror and impiety: he ordered the temples of the Egyptian deities sacked and burned, the gods derided and profaned, the sacred bull Apis killed, and the mummy of the Pharaoh Amasis burned. However, the primary Egyptian source, consisting of a stele from the Serapeum of Memphis,[7] does not agree with the Greek sources so far as the killing of Apis is concerned. The stele states that Apis was solemnly buried in the sixth year of Cambyses' reign (the date of the stele itself); the bull had been born in the twenty-seventh year of Amasis' reign. Moreover, the beautiful sarcophagus [8] used in this ceremony has been discovered in the Serapeum; it was a gift of Cambyses himself. Another stele,[9] also in the Serapeum, proves that the new incarnation of Apis, born in the sixth year of Cambyses' reign, which succeeded the bull mentioned above, could not have been killed by the king in a moment of rage, since it died in the fourth year of Darius' reign. Another primary source, especially useful for checking the dates of the tradition critical of Cambyses, is the inscription carved on the votive statue (known as the Vatican Naophoros) [10] of an important citizen of Saïs, Udzahorresne. This inscription is dated in the fourth year of Darius' reign—thus only a short time after the death of Cambyses himself.

Although Udzahorresne, as a member first of Cambyses' and then of Darius' court, could be suspected of flattering his Persian lords, nevertheless, the information he had inscribed on his statue could not have misrepresented the facts in any basic sense, given the recent nature of the events mentioned. In the inscription Udzahorresene admits that there was "great disorder" in Egypt upon the arrival of the "foreigners" who were quartered in the sanctuary of Neith at Saïs; but he adds that Cambyses intervened to protect the sanctuary, that he drove out the foreign troops, restored her revenues to the goddess, allowed the priests to resume their duties, reinstituted the ceremonies and processions, and came himself to venerate the goddess of Saïs. The damage done to Egyptian temples during the conquest of Egypt is also mentioned in an Aramaic document from Elephantine dated 408 B.C.[11] ("When Cambyses came to Egypt the temples of the Egyptian gods were all laid waste.")

It is undeniable that the invasion of Egypt by Cambyses involved some damage to the Egyptian temples, but Cambyses was not as much to blame as his rampaging soldiery. In addition to the misdeeds of the troops, the temples of Egypt suffered a curtailment of their income; Cambyses issued a decree limiting the incomes of all the temples of Egypt with the exception of three (of which only one, that of Memphis, has been identified with certainty). In this decree (which we know from a demotic document, the reverse side of Papyrus 215 in the Bibliothèque Nationale in Paris) [12] the numbers are not clearly legible, but it seems that the silver, beasts, birds, grain, and other produce due the temples in the time of the Pharaoh Amasis were calculated to be worth 376,400 *deben* and that this was the amount which Cambyses ordered "should not be given to the gods." If one considers—given that the reading of the figure is correct—that the value of the suppressed incomes surpassed that of the tribute paid by Egypt under Darius, one can interpret the suppression of the temple incomes as a precautionary measure considered advisable by Cambyses and intended to reduce the financial burden of the government.

Support of the temples had been a political necessity for the Saïte rulers, especially for Apries and Amasis. The first needed the backing of the priests to compensate for the failure of his foreign policy; the second, in order to reinforce his "usurper's" position.[13] Thus Cambyses' ruling can be considered as a matter of economy rather than a decision motivated by "impiety," all the more because the incomes for three temples were maintained; moreover, Cambyses did not interfere with the temple rites in the sanctuaries, and he did not forbid the priests to offer birds to the gods, although he stated in his decree that the priests had to "raise their own geese and offer them to their gods." These curtailments of their rights inspired unappeasable hatred in the Egyptain priests and undoubtedly provided the basis for the Egyptian tradition, extremely hostile to Cambyses, which was picked up and passed on by the Greeks.

The restoration of her incomes to the goddess of Saïs (which we are told of in Udzahorresne's inscription quoted earlier) was not a revocation of Cambyses' decree but a special measure, the result of the favor Udzahorresne enjoyed with the king. Cambyses had charged Udzahorresne to compose for him a series of titles in the style of the Pharaohs; in particular Cambyses wanted to present himself to the Egyptian people as the true heir of the Saïte Dynasty, who had come to Egypt to reclaim the throne which the usurper Amasis had taken from the legitimate sovereign, Apries.

There is a most significant legend which makes Cambyses the son of Apries' daughter (the three versions of the legend differ in their details but are identical in their essential meaning; see Herodotus I, 1–3; Athenaeus XIII, 10; Ctesias fragment 3P); and thus Cambyses was no foreign king, but a Pharaoh of the Saïte line. Herodotus' reference (III, 16) to the posthumous persecution of Amasis, whose mummy was burned by Cambyses, should be considered in this light; the Greek historian explains that this deed is as contrary to Persian religious beliefs (a devotee of Ahura-Mazda could not contaminate fire) as it is to the tenets of the Egyptian faith (according to which it was not lawful to burn corpses because an individual would be robbed of all chance for future life if his corpse was completely consumed). In reality Cambyses' action was in line with the Egyptian point of view; since he did not want to recognize Amasis as a legitimate Pharaoh, he saw to it that his memory was accursed in exactly the manner that he knew would be final and convincing to the Egyptian mentality.

The military expeditions to which Cambyses devoted himself immediately after the conquest of Egypt are further proof of his desire to play the role of an Egyptian sovereign by carrying out an Egyptain policy. (The expeditions against Carthage and the Lybian oases were not successful; the Napata expedition won nothing more than a biennial tribute [Herodotus III, 97–98] from northern Nubia, on the southern frontier of Egypt, which had been under the sovereignty of the Pharaohs for a very long time.) From a strictly Persian, and therefore distinctly Asiatic point of view, Cambyses had fulfilled the final goals of his policy with the conquest of the valley of the Nile. But he evidently went on to pursue the "African policy" which had been natural to his Saïte predecessors; he seems to have become involved in a political gambit which, if successful, could have foreshadowed the union of the central regions of the Achaemenid Empire in Asia with Africa, more precisely of Persia with Egypt.

It was not long before Cambyses had to face a reaction against his policies at home in the form of a revolt against the dynasty. The fact that revolt did not start in some province seeking its independence, but within the court itself, suggests that it was inspired by a reaction to his policies; the Magian Gaumata, claiming to be the legitimate heir of Cyrus, put forward his claims to the throne. Aroused from his dreams of African conquest, Cambyses hastened back to Persia, but died en route. In a passage that belongs within the tradition derogatory to Cambyses, Herodotus (III, 64–66) reports that he died from an accidental sword wound and that the mortal wound was at precisely the point in the thigh where Cambyses had struck the bull Apis.

Darius I (522–486 B.C.), the son of Hystaspes, satrap of Parthia, set about reestablishing order once he had had himself elected king. He got rid of Gaumata and energetically put down the revolts and usurpers' attempts to seize power which occurred in Asia, Susiana, Babylonia, Media, Armenia, and Hyrcania. After two years of warfare he was victorious. The intervention of the Great King became necessary in Egypt, too, to control leanings toward independence which had developed in Aryandes,[14] the satrap left there by Cambyses (Herodotus IV, 166–167; 200–203).

In the general reorganization of the provinces of the empire, the satrapy of Egypt (which Darius visited in 517 B.C.) ranked high; it was reckoned sixth among the twenty satrapies (Herodotus III, 89 ff.) into which the empire was divided. The annual tribute established for Egypt was 700 talents (Herodotus III, 91). Egypt was also obliged to support the Persian troops stationed at Memphis and the non-Persian auxiliaries serving with them. Egypt had to contribute 120,000 measures of grain and, in addition, the revenues from the fisheries of Lake Moeris—that is to say, 230 talents a year (Herodotus II, 149; III, 91).

Diodorus (I, 95) names Darius I as the sixth and last law-giver of Egypt; this reference is confirmed by a demotic document, the reverse of Papyrus 215 in the Bibliothèque Nationale in Paris [15] (the papyrus that tells of Cambyses' decree concerning the Egyptian temples), which states that in the third year of his reign Darius I sent his satrap in Egypt an order to assemble the wise men from among the warriors, priests, and scribes of Egypt so that they might draw up a record of the laws of the land as they had been practiced down to the forty-fourth year of Amasis' reign. The commission's labors lasted sixteen years, until the nineteenth year of Darius' reign. The laws thus compiled were inscribed on a papyrus in "Assyrian" script (Syrian-Aramaic) and in epistolary script (demotic). In ordering a copy of the corpus of Egyptian law in Aramaic, Darius clearly wanted to make the code available to government officials, and above all to the satrap, in the official language of the empire. Darius limited himself in his work to the laws of the country in force in the forty-fourth year of Amasis' rule—that is to say, at the end of Amasis' reign.

Darius' achievement was that of a compiler and codifier, not that of a legislator in the sense of an innovator; he ordered that modifications to Egyptian law resulting from the influence of Persian law be excluded.[16] Before Darius, Cambyses' decree mentioned earlier had disrupted the "temple law" in force under Amasis; Darius' legislative decree, together with his liberal measures concerning the Egyptian temples, added to his reputation as a lawgiver. Confirmation of this role can also be found in Diodorus (I, 95): part of Cambyses' impiety consisted in the way he flouted Egyptian law; Darius' legislative activity is described as an attempt to atone for these legal impieties.

We know from Udzahorresne's inscription that Darius

charged this important personage (who was also the king's physician) with the reestablishment of the "houses of life" [17] (that is, the educational institutions connected with the temples) "after the ruin," which may refer precisely to Cambyses' decree. Cambyses' successor judged that he could not do without the support of the priests if he wished to achieve a peaceful and lasting union of Egypt with his empire. His tolerant attitude (typical of his policy toward his provincial subjects), his recognition of the Egyptian religion, and the protection he gave the priesthood (the construction of the new temple at El Khargeh [18] and its endowment involved substantial sums) won him the favor of the priestly class and consequently that of the whole country. Nevertheless, Darius did not renounce the right to ratify the nomination of the priests (a royal right which had existed earlier in Egypt): a demotic document [19] dating from his reign records one of his decrees concerning the standards the satrap should adhere to in accepting or rejecting a priest for the post of *lesonis,* or administrative official of a temple.

Intending to increase the trade links between Egypt and the Persian Gulf, Darius I had a canal constructed across the Wadi Tumilat and the Bitter Lakes,[20] connecting the Nile at a point near Bubastis with the Red Sea. He thus completed a project which had been undertaken earlier by the Pharaoh Necho; Herodotus' references to this canal (II, 158; IV, 39) have been confirmed by the discovery in the Suez Canal Zone of three stelae with inscriptions in hieroglyphs and in cuneiform, the so-called Canal Stelae.[21]

Meanwhile the balance of power in the eastern Mediterranean world had been shaken. Athens had come to the aid of the Ionians of Asia Minor in their effort to throw off the Persian yoke; limited though the Athenian intervention was, it showed the Great King that Greece was his new rival. In 490 B.C. the Persians were defeated at Marathon by the Greeks. In 486 B.C., a little before the death of Darius I, Egypt rebelled; the insurrection has been interpreted as a direct consequence of Marathon, but an automatic reaction of this sort is difficult to accept; it seems more probable that it was a rebellion of the same type as that led by Aryandes, encouraged perhaps by a slackening of Persian authority while the Great King planned his revenge on the Greeks.

The revolt was put down by Xerxes (486–465/464 [14] B.C.), the son of Darius, with a campaign the year after his father's death (Herodotus VII, 7). Xerxes named his brother Achaemenes to the post of satrap of the Egyptian province. In the meantime the struggle between Greece and Persia continued to bring defeats for the Persian forces. The outcome of Xerxes' expedition against the Greeks is well known; Salamis, Plataea, Mycale, the liberation of Ionia, and the taking of Sestos on the Hellespont marked the course of the Persian defeat.

Xerxes I was succeeded by Artaxerxes I (465/464–425 B.C.). At the beginning of Artaxerxes' reign, Inaros (possibly a descendant of the Saïte royal family) led an insurrection in Egypt; the rebels succeeded in winning control of the Delta, but Memphis and Upper Egypt remained in Persian hands (this is borne out by several documents from Upper Egypt dated between the fifth and the tenth year of Artaxerxes' reign). Inaros asked for help from the Athenian fleet which was in the waters off Cyprus; his request was accepted; Achaemenes the satrap was defeated and killed at Papremis (Herodotus III, 12); and the Athenian ships sailed up the Nile as far as Memphis, where the Persian resistance was concentrated.

The Athenian intervention ended, however, in a defeat; in its turn the Greek fleet was surrounded near the island of Prosopitis by the Persian fleet commanded by Megabyzus, the satrap of Syria; after a long siege the few Greek survivors were forced to retreat to Cyrene. Another, smaller Athenian fleet, uninformed of the course of events, sailed up the Nile to aid the rebels and was wiped out. Megabyzus returned to Asia, leaving Arsames as satrap in Egypt. The rebel Inaros was taken prisoner and transported to Persia where he was crucified (454 B.C.).

In 449/448 B.C., with the peace of Callias, Athens undertook to adhere to a *modus vivendi* with Persia, which included a specific thirty-year agreement not to interfere with Persia's interests in Egypt or Cyprus. Calm was restored in Egypt, and there was no sign of a breach in the peace during the second part of Artaxerxes I's reign. Peace continued uninterrupted until the last years of the reign of his successor, Darius II (424–404 B.C.).

Between 411 and 408 B.C. there were signs of agitation in Asia Minor, in Media, and in Egypt; Aramaic documents [22] from the correspondence of the satrap Arsames, who was absent from Egypt during these years at the court in Susa, mention these troubles; it is not unlikely that Amyrtaeus, who initiated the sixty years of Egyptian independence following the first Persian domination, was already active in the Delta. Moreover, the violence which the Hebrews of the garrison at Elephantine suffered in 410 B.C., when their temple to Yahu (Yahweh) was destroyed [23] by the Egyptians, led by the priests of the god Khnum (and aided by the governor of Upper Egypt and the head of the garrison) may be not only a manifestation of religious intolerance; it may to a greater degree have political overtones.

Artaxerxes II (404–359/358 B.C.) was the last king of the "First Persian Conquest" of whom there is a record in Upper Egypt, at Elephantine; until the publication of a group of Aramaic papyri in the Brooklyn Museum,[24] it was believed that at the end of the reign of Darius II, Amyrtaeus controlled all Egypt; some of these papyri, however, show that Artaxerxes II was recognized as king in Upper Egypt during the first years of Amyrtaeus' reign, at least until December, 402.[25]

Before continuing our narrative of historical developments in the period following the XXVII Dynasty, let us briefly examine certain aspects of Egyptian life during this period, the general lines on which the country was organized as a satrapy, and some manifestations of Egyptian spiritual and artistic life in this epoch.[26]

The satrap, a member of the highest nobility and often a member of the Persian king's family,[27] was the representative of royal authority to his provincial subjects. He was the chief imperial administrator of Egypt and resided in the capital of the satrapy at Memphis. The chancellery of the satrapy at Memphis, an exact copy of the chancellery of the Great King at Susa, employed numerous functionaries and scribes, including Egyptian scribes for the documents and correspondence in the native language. In fact, whereas the official language of government for the entire Achaemenid Empire, naturally including Egypt, was Aramaic,[28] the satrap himself did not hesitate to use demotic Egyptian even in official correspondence with the people of the country (cf. the correspondence between Pherendates, satrap during the reign of Darius I, and the priests of Khnum at Elephantine[29]).

The traditional internal division of Egypt into districts or provinces, which had been in force in the preceding period, was maintained; this division was useful for both administrative and judicial purposes. In maintaining this framework the Persian government was true to its usual methods; the Persians seldom introduced innovations into the general organization of subject countries, limiting themselves to the substitution of Persian functionaries for local ones (and then not always, for there were Egyptians even in high posts).

It is interesting to note the growing influence, among the Persian officials, of the conquered country on its conquerors. The inscriptions[30] in Wadi Hammamat of two Persian brothers, Atiyawahi and Ariyawrate, are good illustrations of this increasing influence. The first was governor of the city of Coptos; in the earlier texts (the inscriptions cover the years 476–473 B.C.) he limited himself to mentioning the date and proper names, whereas in the later ones he added the image of the god of Coptos, Min, and in addition a brief invocation to the god. The second brother (whose inscriptions cover the years 461–449 B.C.) added, to Min, Horus and Isis of Coptos, and Amun-Re, the king of the gods; moreover, he assumed an Egyptian name, Gedhor (Greek: Tachos, Teos).

A governor (*fratarak,* in the Aramaic documents of the time) was in charge of every administrative district. Aramaic papyri found at Elephantine provide detailed information for one of these districts, the district of Tashetres, the southern province extending from Asswan to Hermonthis where the

342

province of Thebes began. Around 410–408 B.C. the *fratarak* for this district was the Persian Widrang, and his predecessor was Damadin. His residence was at Asswan; the "scribes of the district" and the *azdakaria* (Persian, from *azda*, "instrument," and *kar*, "make" or "do") were included in the administration of the province, probably within the chancellery of the *fratarak*. The lesser administrative entities, towns and cities, had their own governors, of inferior rank and responsible to the governor of the district.

The state treasury was at Memphis under the patronage of the god Ptah. The Egyptian Ptah-hotep (whose naophorous statue [31] is in the Brooklyn Museum and whose stele,[32] dated in the thirty-fourth year of Darius' reign, is in the Louvre) filled the important post of "head of the treasury" during the reign of Darius I. A large number of functionaries were employed by this branch of the government; every district had its "treasury" and "treasurers," its "treasury accountant," and its "treasury scribes" (in the Aramaic papyri of Elephantine, there even appears the expression "house of the king" as a synonym for "treasury"). Even the *pakhuta* [33] (mentioned with the "treasury scribes") were functionaries connected with the distribution of government pay to the army.

In the exercise of justice the satrap was the supreme authority (in the Rylands Egyptians Papyrus IX,[34] the satrap appears to have ordered imprisonment and the lash as punishment for wrongdoers, and it was to the satrap that a certain Peteesi, of El Hibeh, directed his petition requesting justice). Within each district the *fratarak* presided over the civil tribunal. From the Aramaic papyri of Elephantine,[35] which are almost our only source of information concerning the administration of justice, the nature of the courts, and judicial procedure, we can learn about these governor-judges—the "judges of the king," or district judges; the *tiftaya* (police functionaries, approximately); and the *guskaya* (informers, the "King's Ears" of Xenophon, *Cyropaedia*, VIII, 2, 10). Within military garrisons justice was the responsibility of the garrison commander; the Aramaic papyri of Elephantine also mention courts ("*segen* and judges") handling property suits in which members of the Hebrew military colony of Elephantine were involved.

The group of demotic documents on juridical subjects, dating from the Persian period, is our source concerning civil contract law in this period; [36] the law and the manner in which it was formulated show no break in continuity with the Saïte period. Certain elements of the law and its formulae are identical in Egyptian usage and in that of the Hebrew mercenaries of Elephantine (whose contacts with the Egyptian population began in any case before the Persian epoch, since they were first hired in the reign of Psammetichus II), and in some cases seem to derive from a common Neo-Babylonian source.[37]

The Achaemenid government kept a strong military force stationed in Egypt for the defense of the frontiers and for internal security. The Persians maintained border garrisons at Elephantine, at Daphnae, and at Marea for the defense of the South, the East and the West respectively, as in the days of the Saïte sovereigns (Herodotus II, 30). The Aramaic documents of the colony of Hebrew mercenaries stationed at Elephantine are indispensable for an understanding of the military organization of the period; from them we learn that a garrison (Aramaic *haila*) was divided into *degelin* or "standards," each bearing the name of its commander (who was always a Persian or a Babylonian); the *degel* was divided in turn into *mata* or "centuries." These, too, were named for their commander. Whereas the detachment of Hebrew mercenaries was based on the island of Elephantine (where the temple to Yahu was also located), the other Semitic military units (and perhaps some Egyptian ones as well) were stationed at Syene.

At Syene were the temples of Semitic deities such as Nabu, Banit of Syene, Bethel, and Malkat-Shemin.[38] There, too, were the headquarters of the *rab haila,* or commander of the garrison, protecting the southern frontier (who probably was in command of all the military detachments of Upper Egypt as far north as Memphis). Each month the mercenaries received money wages from the government and, in addition, a ration of grain and vegetables. Other units of Hebrews and perhaps of other Semitic peoples were stationed at Thebes and Abydos.

Memphis and its citadel, the "White Castle," were fortified (Herodotus III, 91), and the garrison included Hebrews along with colonies of other Semites;[39] Semitic mercenaries were employed in the dockyards of Memphis.[40] There were Semitic military units in the Delta: besides those at Daphnae, there were Hebrew mercenaries in the employ of the Egyptian government at Migdol (probably Pelusium);[41] at Tell Maskuta[42] there was a small group of Arabs who worshiped the goddess Ilat (han-Ilat).

The Persian government also used Egyptian soldiers. Egyptian troops participated, for example, in the Great King's expedition against Greece in 480 B.C. (Herodotus VII, 89; VIII, 17). There were Ionian and Carian troops in Cambyses' army when he conquered Egypt (Herodotus III, 1); the Persian army was as much a mosaic of various peoples as the Great King's empire itself; although they seldom rose to positions of command such as *rab haila* or *degelin* commanders, Caspians and Chorasmians served alongside Persians and Babylonians. In addition to the garrisons of foreign soldiers, Egypt of this period, especially the cities of Lower Egypt, swarmed with Persians, Babylonians, Semitic peoples, Cilicians, and Greeks, all earning their livings as merchants and craftsmen catering to the needs of the civilian population or the soldiers of the garrisons.

Various currencies, from the shekel to stater, were in circulation in Egypt (together with the metal bars known as *deben* or *kite,* which were valued according to their weight).[43] Documents show that various organized cults of foreign gods were also widespread in Egypt, and that the priests and temples of Nabu, Baal-Eshmun, Baal-Banit, Anat, Malkat-Shemin, and Ilat could be found more or less everywhere (with the exception of the god of the Hebrews, Yahweh, whose only temple was at Elephantine). On the other hand, foreigners in Egypt were willing to show an appreciation of the gods of the country whose guests they were; numerous *ex-votos*—stelae, vases, statuettes of gods (frequently of the bull Apis[44])—attest to their piety.

Without evident change or interruption the religious life of

345

the Egyptians continued as it had in the Saïte period, with its highly formalized temple rituals and its emphasis on magic; at the same time the cult of the various sacred animals continued to develop among the people.[45]

We have, from the period of Persian rule, an interesting example of the literature of the age, the *Instructions of Ankhsheshionky*,[46] written in demotic; in the tradition of Egyptian "wisdom literature," the author gives advice on the proper conduct of life to his son, epigrammatic in style and full of the sharp insight of popular proverbial wisdom.

Nor does the artistic life of Egypt in the XXVII Dynasty seem to show any essential changes or breaks with tradition. It should be noted, however, that during this period of foreign domination a true portrait, in the Western sense of the term, appears for the first time in Egyptian art,[47] although much of the sculpture keeps to the smooth idealism which was the dominant style in the Saïte period. Thus Egyptian portraiture had its beginning between the sixth and fifth centuries before Christ, and not under Greek influence in the Ptolemaic period. One of the best examples of portraiture is the naophorous statue of Psamtek-sa-Neit, now in the Cairo Museum.

A number of sculptures from this period show evidence of Persian influence in the dress of the figure (a long robe with sleeves of varying lengths, with an open V-neck, worn together with a full skirt draped and knotted in front);[48] the statues also wear bracelets and necklaces of Persian manufacture.[49] The naophorous statue of Udzahorresne in the Vatican Museum, mentioned earlier, belongs in this group, as do the statue of Ptah-hotep in the Brooklyn Museum, the statue of Henata in the Florence Museum, the statue of Psamtek-sa-Neit mentioned above in the Museum of Cairo, and that of Vahibra, also in the Cairo Museum.[50] Moreover, objects of Persian manufacture, made in Egypt by Persian craftsmen or imported from Persia, have been found in Egypt: seals and various other objects bearing cuneiform inscriptions, some sculptured heads of kings in the Persian style, lions and heads of lions carved in serpentine or alabaster of an Achaemenid type,[51] and vases which are surely the work of Persian artists.[52]

On the other hand, vases of Egyptian manufacture with hiero-glyphic and cuneiform inscriptions have been found in Susa. Egyptian laborers and architects took part in the construction of Darius I's palace in Persepolis; the strong influence of Egyptian art and architecture on Persian architecture is un-deniable.[53]

Such was the Egypt visited with great curiosity by Herodotus around 450 B.C.

With Amyrtaeus (405/404–400/399 B.C.) began the sixty years of native rule—the last of Egyptian independence—which covered three dynasties, the XXVIII, the XXIX, and the XXX.[54] Although she had recovered her autonomy, Egypt was still threatened by the Persians, who thought of Egypt as a rebellious province that had to be reconquered and punished. Thus every enemy of Persia became the natural friend of Egypt. The last three native Egyptian dynasties used this situation to maintain themselves in power, allying themselves with, or mutually supporting, other peoples of the Mediterranean basin.

Amyrtaeus, who may have been a descendant of the sovereigns of the XXVI Dynasty, is the only representative of the XXVIII Dynasty. Saïs was probably his capital. Thucydides mentions (VIII, 85, 99, 108, 109) that Amyrtaeus and the King of the Arabs allied themselves against the Phoenicians—a strategic move threatening regions still under the yoke of the Great King. This move was intended to forestall action by the Persians; however, the situation within Persia itself made such action unlikely at that moment. Amyrtaeus further increased his power by procuring ships and money, although he had to resort to treachery to do so: in 400 B.C. Tamos, an Egyptian from Memphis who had been governor of Cilicia under Cyrus, sought refuge with Amyrtaeus in Egypt together with his son, his fleet, and his treasure (Diodorus XXV, 19, 6). But instead of offering Tamos the protection he had sought, Amyrtaeus killed him and his son and seized their wealth.

Amyrtaeus' reign was brief, since by 399 B.C. he had already been dethroned (and possibly killed). A new dynasty followed, the XXIX, founded by Nepherites (400/399–395/ 394 B.C.), who came from Mendes in the Delta. During his reign the vicissitudes of Greco-Persian politics brought Sparta (which had been allied with Persia) into a friendly relationship with Egypt; in 395 the Pharaoh sent reinforcements to the Spartan fleet gathered at Rhodes. These reinforcements nevertheless fell into the hands of the Persians, under the command of the Athenian Conon.

Nepherites' successor, Achoris (394/393–382/381 B.C.) took an active part in Mediterranean politics, allying himself with Athens and entering into the league against the Persians, which united around Evagoras of Cyprus, the Pisidians and the Arabs of Palestine. Achoris sent fifty warships together with grain and money to Evagoras, who succeeded in defending Cyprus against Persia until 380 B.C. Achoris strengthened the Egyptian military forces with Greek mercenaries and made of Egypt a new maritime power. The numerous monuments of his reign are evidence of a strong economic revival; there are traces of his work as a builder in Upper and Lower Egypt.

His successor, Nepherites II, reigned only a few months and then was deposed by Nectanebo of Sebennytus (381/380– 364/363 B.C.), who founded the XXX Dynasty. (In the later years of Egypt, new and aggressive leaders always came from the Delta region, in part because they were in a better position to be active in the Mediterranean, in part because of the decadence of Upper Egypt.) The peace of Antialcidas (387/386 B.C.) had given Persia the freedom to attack Egypt. Chabrias, an Athenian leader who had in the past served Achoris, offered his help to Nectanebo, but Athens, at Persia's behest, recalled him from Egypt (379 B.C.) and sent her general Iphicrates to Persia, to serve in the Persian campaign against Egypt (Diodorus XV, 29, 4).

In 373 B.C. the Persian army, with an imposing naval and land force under the command of Pharnabazus, and accompanied by the Athenian Iphicrates, invaded Egypt at Pelusium. Nectanebo succeeded, however, in warding off this first attack with a defensive system of canals and barricades. The Persians then attacked the mouth of the Mendesian branch of the Nile. Pharnabazus then refused to follow Iphicrates' advice, to proceed rapidly to Memphis before the defense of the city could be organized. Meanwhile the Egyptians had succeeded in preparing defenses in the neighborhood of Mendes sufficiently to withstand the Persians, until the Nile, which was then in flood, rose far enough to force them to retreat. In the years that followed, every attempt to reconquer Egypt was hampered by conditions in the western provinces of the Achaemenid empire.

The reign of Nectanebo I was especially prosperous; the numerous monuments dating from his time attest to his energetic activities as a builder and to his desire to return to the style of the XXVI Dynasty—a tendency also evident in an archaizing taste in language, epigraphy, and sculpture (in sculpture a return to the classic tradition can be noted; the face is represented in the idealized Saïte style [55]).

The son of Nectanebo, Tachos (363/362–362/361 B.C.), set himself the ambitious project of reconquering Syria and Palestine. Going to the support of the rebels against Artaxerxes II, he organized a large fleet and a strong army. At his request Sparta sent a mercenary force headed by her king Agesilaus himself. Chabrias came from Athens to command the fleet. An expedition on this grand scale surpassed the resources of any Pharaoh of this period; Greek mercenaries were hired in numbers unprecedented in an Egyptian army, and the cost was very great. But Tachos succeeded in obtaining the necessary money by following the advice of Chabrias: the income of the priests was reduced to a tenth of what it had been, private citizens were induced to contribute all the precious metals in their possession (probably in the hope of gaining a high interest rate, whereas they were repaid in kind); construction and professional incomes were taxed.[56]

The Athenian's shrewd advice provided Tachos with the money he required and the army marched on Palestine, where Tachos was victorious in battle. However, his brother, whom he had left in Egypt as regent, betrayed him; at the same time his nephew, Nectanebo, abandoned him, deserting to Syria with the greater part of the Egyptian forces and Agesilaus and his troops. Tachos fled, seeking refuge with the Persian king in Susa, while Chabrias, who had tried to remain faithful to Tachos, returned to Athens. Meanwhile in Egypt a resident of Mendes (possibly a descendant of the ruling family of the XXIX Dynasty) had had himself proclaimed king and had gathered a large number of followers (Diodorus XV, 93, 2–6). The only course open to Nectanebo was to return to Egypt, but on doing so he was confronted by the usurper, who besieged him and Agesilaus in a city of the Delta. The Spartan force was more powerful, however, than that of the besiegers; Agesilaus succeeded in wiping out Nectanebo's enemies.

Nectanebo II ruled Egypt from 361/360–343 B.C.; numerous monuments and evidence of much building remain from his relatively prosperous reign. In 358 B.C. Egypt was threatened by a Persian invasion under the leadership of the prince Artaxerxes (accompanied perhaps by Tachos); little is known of this invasion, except that it failed. Another attempted invasion took place in 351 B.C., also under the command of Artaxerxes, now king (Artaxerxes III Ochus); no more is known of this attempt than of its predecessor, except that it, too, failed. From 349 to 346 B.C., while Syria and Cyprus rebelled against Persian domination, Nectanebo remained neutral, but in 346 B.C. he sent four thousand mercenaries to the king of Sidon, commanded by Mentor of Rhodes (Diodorus XVI, 42, 2), thus giving Artaxerxes an opportunity for the reconquest of Egypt.

By 343, Artaxerxes had reconquered Cyprus and Sidon; he could now turn his entire force against Egypt. Commanded by Bagoas, the Persians invaded at Pelusium. The Pharaoh's defenses were excellent, but the location of the Egyptian fortifications had been revealed to the Persians by Mentor of Rhodes, who had gone over to the Persian side and who was in command of a detachment of the invading army. This information made it possible for Bagoas to overcome the defenses of Pelusium; he then won the surrender of the cities of the Delta. Here, too, he was helped by the rivalry between Greeks and Egyptians. Meanwhile Nectanebo had remained in Memphis. When he learned that all of Lower Egypt was in the hands of the Persians, he gathered his valuables together and fled to Nubia (Diodorus XVI, 51, 1–2), probably seeking refuge with a prince of Northern Nubia, and hoping perhaps to be able to return to Egypt.[57]

We know nothing of the end of his life; later legends made him the father of Alexander the Great (Pseudo-Callisthenes). Possessed of magical powers, he was said to have assumed the appearance of the god Zeus-Ammon and made love to Olympias, Alexander's mother. This story satisfied the national pride of the Egyptians, since they could assert that the Persians had been driven out by an Egyptian!

In this fashion Egypt came once again under Persian sway, after sixty years of independence. This brief "Second Conquest," or XXXI Dynasty, ended in 332 B.C. It is likely that Artaxerxes treated Egypt harshly, considering her a rebellious province reconquered after long resistance. Greek authors (Plutarch, *De Iside et Osiride;* Alian, *Varia Historia,* VI, 8) charge Artaxerxes with a long list of impieties and acts of violence; he killed the bull Apis and dined with his companions on the flesh of the beast. (Most of the anecdotes, especially this concerning Apis—the traditional standard for judging the behavior of Persian monarchs in Egypt—are too similar to the accusations leveled against Cambyses to be trustworthy.) In place of the bull, Artaxerxes offered the Egyptians an ass to worship. He also killed the bull of Heliopolis, Mnevis, and the sacred ram of Mendes. He sacked the temples and destroyed the walls of the city. A stele of a later period, the "Stele of the Satrap," dated 312 B.C., claims that Artaxerxes confiscated territory belonging to the goddess of Buto.

Artaxerxes returned to Persia, leaving a certain Pherendates in Egypt as satrap (Diodorus XVI, 51, 3), but in 338 B.C. Artaxerxes was poisoned by Bagoas, who placed on the throne the king's younger son, Arses. In the summer of 336 B.C. Arses, too, was killed by Bagoas. From the end of 338 B.C. to 336 B.C. Egypt enjoyed a brief period of independence from Persia, under a king by the name of Khabbash.[58] Classical sources do not mention this dynasty, although a certain number of Egyptian monuments refer to it. The "Stele of the

Satrap," already mentioned, notes that in the second year of his reign Khabbash inspected the defenses of the Delta to see that they were ready to repel any Persian attack.

The origins of this king are obscure and have given rise to widely divergent theories—all based, however, on his name, which seems to be non-Egyptian—which make him an Arab, a rebellious satrap, a Libyan, or an Ethiopian. Perhaps the soundest of these theories is that which makes him a Nubian leader who had come into Egypt from the South. If this is true, the fact that Nectanebo II had taken refuge in Nubia may possibly have had something to do with the case.[59] All trace of Khabbash is lost in the second year of his reign. By 336 B.C., when Darius III Codomannus was placed on the throne by Bagoas after he had killed Arses, Egypt was once more under the control of the Achaemenid king. Meanwhile the ruin of the Persian Empire was at hand; in 334 B.C. Alexander the Great crossed the Hellespont and at the Granicus won his first victory over Persia. With the battle of Issus in 333 B.C. the western part of the empire was lost to Darius III. We know that a noble Egyptian, Semtantefnekhet of Heracleopolis, fought on the side of the Great King at Issus. His stele, known as the "Stele of Naples" (inscribed in the time of Alexander the Great [60]) records that he fought beside the Persian King against the Greeks, and that he escaped with his life and made his way through strange lands before he crossed the sea to return to Egypt.

At Issus, Sabaces, the satrap of Egypt, perished; after the battle the Macedonian Amyntas, who had gone over to the Persians, fled with a number of other officers and eight thousand men; from Cyprus they went to Pelusium. There Amyntas claimed to have been sent by Darius to to serve as satrap in place of Sabaces. He succeeded in crossing the Delta, and headed for Memphis. But Mazaces, the real satrap appointed to replace Sabaces, confronted Amyntas and murdered him and his followers. (Diodorus, XVII, 48, 2–5).

When, toward the end of 332 B.C., Alexander arrived in Pelusium, he was able to proceed in triumph as far as Memphis without encountering any opposition: Mazaces surrendered the country virtually without a struggle. Egypt ceased to be a part of the Achaemenid Empire, which was itself at an end, and became part of that of Alexander the Great. The Ptolemies inherited Egypt from Alexander, and the Romans received it in their turn.

17

Mesopotamia Under Persian Rule

In 612, Cyaxares the Mede destroyed Nineveh; in 539 Cyrus, seizing Babylon, brought to an end the last native Mesopotamian state. But the civilization that had emerged on Mesopotamian soil did not now disappear: more than five centuries were to pass before it finally did so. Babylon remained the center of an ancient nation, placed by the Persian conquest at the heart of the largest empire of antiquity. Now, more than ever before, unimaginably distant countries exchanged men and goods, ideas and religions: merchants, migrants, alien peoples transported by the Great King, drawn by Babylonia's brilliant past and by distant rumors of its charm and riches, came to swell and influence the native population of the Mesopotamian plain. Yet, the ancient Babylonian civilization held its own; its scientific and legal work went forward, for example, without a break. But men, gods, language, society as a whole, could no longer remain as they had been before; a new world was in the making, and the old civilization would slowly fade and blend into its new surroundings, leaving behind the best of its accomplishments as a legacy to later ages. An unusually rich fund of documentary evidence allows us to watch this transformation at work, with unusual clarity where many of its aspects are concerned.

The Neo-Babylonian (i.e., Chaldaean) period, from 627 to 539 B.C., has left us an astonishing wealth of texts of every kind; the Persian period, at least until about 400, is no less rich in its written remains. Texts surviving from the Persian period are numbered in the thousands; those deposited in our museums have yet to be fully catalogued; archaeological excavation keeps adding to our store, the latest large find having been made at Uruk (Warka), during the eighteenth campaign at that site: 205 economic tablets, dating from 550 to 489. We are, then, dealing with an immense amount of documentary evidence, of which scholars are able to make use only in part, and slowly, as publication proceeds piecemeal. There are some historical texts, but the great number of letters and contracts make our information on the Persian period largely economic and legal in nature. At Nippur, for example, the archaeologists discovered an archive of capital importance, that of a great business house, the House of Murashu, active toward the end of the fifth century B.C. in almost every phase of the economy. This is, of course, exceptional luck, but even under ordinary circumstances we can usually study, in some detail, the economic and social structure of Babylonia during more than two centuries, so rich is our written evidence for these aspects of the life of the age. Also, the great number of dated documents gives us hope of an eventual complete solution of the problems of chronology for this period. To all of this contemporary textual evidence, then, we add the results of archaeological exploration, and the narratives of the first Greeks to come into personal contact with this Eastern world (Herodotus, Xenophon, Ctesias); the result allows us to reconstitute a more accurate picture of the lives of these men than we can have for any other period of the ancient history of the Near East.

The fall of the Chaldaean Empire was hastened by the opposition that the actions of its last ruler aroused: King Nabonidus was the architect of its undoing. Treason played a prominent role in its defeat; Ugbaru, Governor of Gutium, the Persian officer who took Babylon, was actually a Babylonian official known to us from the days of Nebuchadnezzar, now gone over to the enemy. The transition from Chaldaean to Persian rule was painless; contemporaries were too delighted to be rid of Nabonidus to suspect that the world they knew might be coming to an end. All indications, after all, were to the contrary: Cyrus, on entering Babylon on the twenty-ninth of October, 529, assumed all the traditional titles of Babylonian royalty, confirmed all officials in their positions and put Ugbaru (Greek Gobryas) at their head. The enormous satrapy that he governed corresponded, geographically, to the Chaldaean Empire: it included all of Mesopotamia, Syria, Phoenicia, and Palestine; Cyrus' empire would, to the contemporary eye, have the appearance of a personal union between the empire of the Persians and the kingdom of Nebuchadnezzar. Cyrus took particular care to be enthroned at Babylon in due form: Cambyses, his son, acting as his proxy, took the hand of the god Marduk at the New Year (Akitu) festival, on March 27, 538; thenceforth Cyrus bore the titles of "King of Babylon and King of the Lands," thereby expressing the purely personal link that joined the Babylonian kingdom to Persia, rather than outright annexation by right of conquest.

Cyrus' first official acts showed the regard he had for his new subjects: he wisely reversed the religious policy of Nabonidus, winning the favor of the clergy and of devout laymen by the restoration of the old order; temples were restored, and divine services once more set in order; divine images and cult apparatus, brought to Babylon by Nabonidus, were returned to their original sanctuaries; the cities of Babylonia, the temples of Assyria, Gutium, and Elam, thus recovered their patron gods once more. Just as cleverly the supporters of the new government let it be seen that Cyrus, by his piety, by the blessing of the traditional gods shown in the series of striking successes that had marked his reign, was clearly the legitimate sovereign of the land: one may suspect the hand of the Babylonian priesthood in those texts that excoriate the memory of Nabonidus and hail Cyrus as the chosen of the gods, the ruler endowed with a divine mission. The people had, in fact, seen his troops enter Babylon without engaging in pillage of any kind; the *Babylonian Chronicle* notes, for the occasion, that "at the end of *Tashritu* [mid-October], the shield-bearers of Gutium guarded the gates of the Esagila [the temple of Marduk, abandoned by Nabonidus]; not one spear was brought near to Esagila, nor entered its sanctuary; not one ceremony was disturbed." To this chorus of praise was joined the voice, unexpectedly for us, of the prophets of Israel: Deutero-Isaiah hails Cyrus as "the anointed of the Lord"; about 538, the generous prince did for Jerusalem what he had done for the pagan temples of Mesopotamia: its cult objects were returned to it, and the foundations of a new temple laid down.

In Babylonia, the heartland of the new Persian Empire, Cyrus left his son Cambyses as a kind of viceroy: from his capital at Sippar, the young prince ruled the whole of Mesopotamia until 530, there serving his apprenticeship in the craft of kingship. When his father left for Turkestan to combat the Massagetae, Cambyses was singled out as the heir to the imperial throne by the title "King of Babylon." This was, as it turned out, a wise precaution: Cyrus was killed in battle in the summer of 530. From September on the Babylonian texts hail Cambyses, their own king, with the full imperial titulature: "King of Babylon and King of the Lands." But the new Persian sovereign did not long remain in Babylon; he set out on the conquest of Egypt, and died on the way back, in Palestine, where he received word of the rebellion of one Bardiya (Greek Smerdis), perhaps Cambyses' own brother. The Babylonians did not hesitate to recognize this new ruler in the spring of 522; but they did stick at accepting the usurper, Darius, and took up arms against him when he slew Bardiya in Media, on September 29, 522 B.C.

On October 3, 522, then, Babylon revolted; the sentiment of nationalism, so ably appeased by Cyrus and Cambyses, now ran unrestrained; the Chaldaean prince, Nebuchadnezzar, calling himself the son of Nabonidus, was hailed as king and seemed, for a time, a match for the luck of Darius. He won a victory over the Persian on December 13, 522; but only five days later he was defeated utterly and killed, at the battle of Zazana. On the twenty-second of that month the texts name Darius "King of Babylon and King of the Lands." The new sovereign was lenient in victory; next year, however, a new revolt broke out, with a new leader, Nebuchadnezzar V, he too claiming to be Nabonidus' son; hopes of an independent

Babylonian state rose once more. Unfortunately the new kingdom endured hardly ten weeks, from September to November of 521: the crack Persian army crushed the Babylonians under the inner ramparts of their capital; the King of Babylon was impaled, along with his partisans; the city was sacked, the royal tombs pillaged, the inner ramparts razed to the ground.

This, too, was relatively lenient punishment; Darius could easily have been far more harsh (as Xerxes was to be some forty years later). It is partly as a result of this clemency that, in spite of the wars and terrors of the years 522 and 521, Babylonia lived its life essentially undisturbed, in much the same fashion, from the conquest of Cyrus to the death of Darius in 486—i.e., for more than fifty years. Persian dominance was not openly exerted, its impact increased insensibly. It was only in the reign of Darius that there began the appointment of Iranians to official posts, a tendency that increased with time; Persians appeared side by side with Babylonians in the lower ranks of the administration, and even sat on the judicial bench, to assure the application and interpretation of the King's law. New royal taxes weighed heavily on Babylonia, as on all the satrapies of the empire, and a newly strict administration brought the life of the land more firmly under royal control. The misdeeds and fate of the corrupt Gimillu, servant of the Eanna temple of Uruk, are known from texts published a good many years ago. Here was a man who robbed the herds of his goddess, Ishtar, and engaged in a thousand peculations. A string of episodes that seem to come straight out of the pages of a picaresque novel show him escaping, with the aid of bribery, the arm of justice again and again between 538 and 534. Was this the efficiency of the new administration? In its defense we must note that Gimillu, in 520, was at long last called to answer for his misdeeds.

Babylon remained an imperial capital, of equal rank with Susa and Ecbatana. Within its walls Cyrus had received the homage of vassal rulers, "of all the kings who live in the palaces of the whole earth, from the Upper Sea to the Lower Sea, of all the kings of the West who dwell in tents." Darius lived at Babylon, occupying the palace of Nebuchadnezzar, where his (Darius') autobiography was found engraved on a stele. The Persian Empire had been divided into satrapies, but Babylon remained at the head of an administrative unit exceptional in its extent; Ushtanni, the satrap who resided there, was governor both of the satrapy of Babylonia-Assyria (the Ninth) and of the satrapy of Abar-Nahara (the Fifth)—that is, of the Trans-Euphratene lands, including Northwest Mesopotamia, Syria, Phoenicia, and Palestine. The two units together exactly equaled the empire of Nebuchadnezzar, now surviving in a different administrative dress.

The Persian Great Kings also borrowed from Babylonia their imperial architecture. They built a new palace in the city itself, between the palace of Nabopolassar and the old bed of the Euphrates, in that complex of royal constructions that its excavators named the *Südburg*. For this new palace, for the palace that Darius built at Susa, the Persians employed tried Babylonian architectural forms: the erection of vast terraces to serve as bases for the royal residences and, at Susa, the use of the traditional floor-plan of a great many small rooms opening on a series of courts, with enameled brick bas-relief friezes decorating the walls, figures of animals, flowers, or the soldiers of the royal guard, the "Immortals."

Xerxes, like the young Cambyses, served his apprenticeship as crown prince at Babylon; he lived in the part of the palace that was built between 498 and 496, probably the heart of the imperial palace that Darius had erected.

When Xerxes succeeded Darius on the throne, however, he put an end to the provincial policy of his predecessors; the special political status and geographical integrity enjoyed by the former great empires, Egypt and Babylonia, were now withdrawn; all the heterogeneous territories under Persian rule were to be treated alike, without regard to the prestige of their ancient civilizations. His reasons for this change escape us. Did Xerxes suppose the compromises of his forerunners no longer necessary, now that the empire was firmly established? It would seem so when we learn that, from 486 on (the year of his accession), he went out of his way to affirm the Iranian character of that empire by using the title "King of the Persians and the Medes, King of Babylon and the Lands." Or, on the other hand, did he see, in the reduction of the old kingdoms to mere provincial status, the only way of putting an end to violent Egyptian and Babylonian nationalism? In 485, Egyptian rebellion was severely repressed; then came Babylonia's turn. The chronology of these events is uncertain in the extreme: cuneiform letters and contracts carry date-formulae that tell us much, but for this period historians are far from agreement as to what this information means. Perhaps all the events of the Babylonian revolt and its repression took place in a single year; perhaps there were two revolts between 484 and 482, the second finally inspiring the Persian government to total repression.

There were two native kings raised to the throne of Babylonia, Bel-Shimanni and Shamash-Eriba, both reigning in 482, perhaps, or else perhaps in 484 and 482 respectively, but in either case for periods of no more than a few weeks each. What we do know is that in 482 the conquering Persians, led by Megabyzus, took their revenge unchecked. Many were the places that were reduced to rubble: Borsippa, for example, was probably destroyed entirely, for there is not a single document to be found there dated after that fateful year. Babylon itself survived, but with wounds visible for ages afterward; the second expedition to Greece was on foot, all possibility of revolt in the rear had to be snuffed out, and so a terrible example was made of the rebellious city and nation. First of all, Babylonia was reduced to the position of an ordinary satrapy. Its capital was pillaged, its walls once more dismantled; worse, the city was struck to the heart by the destruction of its sanctuaries: the Esagila and the great ziggurat of Etemenanki, the Biblical tower of Babel, were wrecked by Persian command. The sacred image of Marduk was melted down; the god's priests were arrested, and many slain. There could now never again be a King of Babylon; with the national god's idol gone, his cult could no longer be celebrated, including, and especially, the New Year's (Akitu) festival, wherein the King took the god's hand and annually received the rule of the land from its divine master. This meant that there could be no Babylonian Kingdom, not even a kingdom in personal union with the Persian Empire. This, then, was the end of the autonomy of Babylonia; the Persian Great King had, from now on, only one grade of subjects, all under the rule of an acknowledgedly Iranian overlord. The very memory of the Chaldaean Empire was erased from the map, as the supersatrapy once ruled from Babylon was broken up; Abar-Nahara, i.e., Northwest Mesopotamia and Syria-Palestine, now had its own governor and administration. Babylon had ceased to be a great capital; her political importance was at an end.

And yet Babylon was still, and was for long to remain, a great city—rich by reason of its economic life, strong in the number of its inhabitants, imposing for those of its monuments that Xerxes had not destroyed. The Persian kings, or members of the royal family, often resided there: Darius II, for example, before he succeeded to the throne, and at the end of his reign when he came there to die; Parysatis, daughter of Artaxerxes I and wife of Darius II, was sent to Babylon as an exile in 425, and Artaxerxes II was brought there after the battle of Cunaxa (September 3, 401) to be healed of his wounds. The Great Kings retained for their own use the Chaldaean royal palaces, and the extensions added by Darius; there, now entirely cut off from the city proper by the new bed of the Euphrates, they led the life of Persian grandees, establishing pleasure gardens with a pavilion in the royal precincts; Artaxerxes III, about 345, added an *apadana* to the palace of Darius.

It would be hard for us to know whether Persian rule was, from the reign of Xerxes onward, more harsh, more demanding of the subject. We might think we had reason to suppose so, considering the policy of that king and the smaller number of cuneiform documents that have come down to us from the late fifth century on. But it may be that Aramaic was now more often being used for the writing of documents on papyrus and parchment that had formerly been inscribed on clay tablets; and, of course, only the clay tablets would have survived to our own day. (Aramaic, written in a cursive alphabetic script, could be and almost always was written down in

361

ink on flexible and perishable materials: the angular cuneiform was invariably incised on clay.) The transactions of a firm like that of Murashu, at the end of the fifth century, may well indicate the possibilities for enrichment available to able financiers in this period. What else have we in the way of evidence? The testimony of Herodotus: to be read critically, of course, but with an eye to its consistency, which cannot fail to impress. It is, of course, difficult to credit him when he says that Babylonian families made all their daughters sacred prostitutes, or that they sold them at auction; but it is significant that he explains these curious customs as a result of the extreme poverty of most families, broken by the demands of the Persian administration. We cannot reasonably accept the figures he gives for the contributions drawn from Babylonia by the imperial government—we cannot, that is, accept them without suspicion—but they are some indication of how heavily the Persian demands weighed on the population of the province: a thousand talents a year in taxation, the upkeep of the Persian court and army for a third of each year by contributions in kind, and, or at least so he says, a bushel of silver every single day as the revenue of the satrap—the satrap who, at his subjects' expense, maintained 800 stallions and 16,000 mares in his private stables. No matter what the reliability of these figures, at least we can take it that the conquerors lived supremely well on the riches of their province, which the political mores of the empire allowed them to exploit almost at will.

From contemporary reports, from archaeological field work, we are able to form some idea of the geography and appearance of Mesopotamia in this age. Babylonia was the only area that was thickly settled and intensively cultivated—i.e., the plain between the sea and the point where the Tigris and Euphrates most closely approach each other. Assyria was not a desert, however; we do have the moving description of the ruins of Calah (modern Nimrud) and Nineveh by Xenophon, the very names of which had been forgotten when his band of mercenaries marched by. "The Greeks marched . . . to the River Tigris. There they found a great deserted city named

Larisa: formerly it had been inhabited by the Medes. The wall of this town was twenty-five feet thick and one hundred high; its circumference was two parasangs [about seven miles]. It was built of clay brick, on a stone foundation twenty feet high." Of Nineveh, Xenophon writes: "They marched . . . to a huge deserted fortification, near a town named Mespila [Akkadian *Mashpil* = 'deserted place'], formerly inhabited by the Medes. The foundation of the walls was made of a polished stone full of shells, fifty feet thick and fifty feet high. On top of this rose a brick wall, fifty feet thick and one hundred high. The circumference [of the whole] was six parasangs [about twenty-one miles]." (*Anabasis* 3.4. 6–7, 10.) But the city of Assur had not been abandoned; it was no longer a capital, but excavations have revealed evidence of human habitation there down to the Parthian conquest. There were many Assyrians dwelling throughout Mesopotamia, as we can tell by theophoric personal names, compounded with the name of their national god, Asshur.

The Greek mercenaries with whom Xenophon marched saw, on their way down the Euphrates from Thapsacus to Cunaxa, little but empty steppe, inhabited almost solely by wild animals, onagers, ostriches, and bustards. The Seleucid kings were later to establish, as part of their political and military system, cities scattered up and down the Middle Euphrates: Dura-Europus will be the best-known example. Babylonia, on the other hand, was still crammed with cities. Herodotus visited Babylon twenty or thirty years after the terrible punishment Xerxes had imposed on it, and still the city was impressive enough to move the father of history to assign to it the conventional epithets one applied to a great capital: "city of a hundred gates," for example, which the excavations show us cannot be taken literally. And yet there were immense areas of the city in ruins: some of the things Herodotus passes over in silence; other things that have been thought to be mistakes of his can, if read in this light, give us invaluable information about the state of the city. Herodotus, for instance, was unable to enter the palace quarter, cut off by the new course of the Euphrates from the rest of the city, an inaccessibility that the government turned to its advantage by quartering the Persian garrison there; this is why he does not mention the palaces of the Chaldaean kings, or that built by Darius, or the hanging gardens that the later Greek historians made so much of; he does mention the Ishtar Gate in the palace quarter, but he must have heard of it from the natives, he could not have seen it himself, which would explain his silence on the famous enameled-brick frescoes that adorned it. The inner city, however, he must have seen with his own eyes, particularly the temple of "Zeus Belus" (i.e., the Esagila), by which he understood the entire temple complex, including the great ziggurat. The complex as a whole was still an imposing monument in his time: Xerxes' depredations had not succeeded in wiping the huge step-tower off the face of the plain, but had sufficiently damaged it so that Herodotus was unable to give a very accurate account of it. He tells us that it was composed of eight (instead of seven) stories; this would be because the weathering of the upper stories, and the absence of sharp edges in this enormous mass of crumbled brick, slowly turning back into an amorphous hill of clay, made it impossible for him to tell one level from another—all the more reason why he could not have seen the small shrine that had once stood on the topmost storey; what he has to say about it is a tribute, not to his powers of observation, but to his informants' powers of imagination. Babylon no longer had her famous walls: Herodotus does not mention the outer wall; as for the inner wall, directly enclosing the city, which excavation has revealed as a double wall with several yards between its ramparts, he saw but one wall in his day; the dismantling under Darius and again under Xerxes, and the lack of repairs, had resulted in the crumbling of the tops of both walls, and the traveler had only the lower courses before his eyes; the fallen upper courses had filled the interval between the two, so that Herodotus saw but one, unusually wide, rampart. Excavation pretty well confirms this picture of a city still so impressive that Alexander was to make it the capital of his world empire, but steadily decaying year by year. In the heart of the city, in the residential quarter discovered at Merkes, archaeologists found very little new construction attributable to this period: old houses were generally kept in repair, but the number of empty house-lots increased continually; houses collapsed and were not reerected, and the inhabitants of the neighborhood used the lots as burial grounds; the number of these little cemeteries scattered among the dwelling-houses grew steadily during the two centuries of Persian rule.

Other cities, however, declined with more dramatic suddenness. We can study an example of this in the excavations at Ur. Under Nebuchadnezzar and Nabonidus the city had experienced a tremendous renewal of its fortunes, to which the great reconstructions of its sanctuaries bear witness. Cyrus, here as at Babylon, destroyed nothing; he even brought his enemy's projects to completion, simply removing the inscriptions that had sung the glories of Nabonidus. Under Cambyses and Darius the city reached the peak of its prosperity, and the greatest number of economic tablets we have from Ur date from the last twenty years of the sixth century. And then, irreversible decline. We need seek no explanation among the wars and revolts of the age; Ur simply suffered the consequences of that shift in the course of the Euphrates that was already noticeable in the Neo-Babylonian period. The network of canals was not kept in repair and dried up little by little; the city lost its port and its waterways, and the economic lifeblood of the land flowed elsewhere. New canals might have brought new life to the city, but Ur no longer justified them; her greatness was based solely on her geographical and commercial position, during the two millennia when the Persian Gulf and the Indian Ocean were more important avenues of trade with the East than the continental land routes. But the Persian conquest, in relatively short order, resulted in a new preeminence for the caravan routes across the Iranian Plateau. No longer the entrepôt of Oriental commerce, no longer the city where exotic goods were transshipped or stored, Ur saw not only its commerce but even its great lunar temples, on which Nabonidus had lavished a moon-worshiper's care, fall hopelessly into decay. The temples were gradually abandoned, their construction materials appropriated for private re-use;

365

private houses soon encroached on the soil of the sacred precincts; and when Alexander conquered Babylonia, Ur was no more than a miserable country town; the last text that has been found there dates from 316 B.C.

The richness of the Mesopotamian soil was proverbial; under Persian rule it continued to merit the world's envy. Assyria, ravaged by the wars of the late seventh century, was still populated but not prosperous, a second-rate region of no great account; but Babylonia was covered with a tight, complex network of irrigation canals, that ensured her agricultural fortune—or had ensured it up till now. Certain breakdowns in the canal system were apparent; the two great rivers had changed their courses; the irrigated lands were, to an ever increasing degree, salinated by minerals; these were problems that the men of this age were not always able to resolve. Negligence, destruction, waste of resources in unsettled times, caused irreparable damage to the irrigation system. In Babylon, the Euphrates had violently shifted its bed, breaking through quays and dikes north of the city and, sweeping out a broad curve, had cut the city in two; Ur had expired with its waterways. Excavation has revealed the gradual extension of urban building onto land formerly occupied by canals. Nevertheless, on the whole the country was still intensively cultivated and dotted with innumerable little villages and hamlets, or so we must suppose from the place-names mentioned on the tablets, many of which are compounded with personal names.

Agriculture and stock raising continued to provide the traditional products of the Babylonian soil: barley, dates, garlic, sesame, onions, and various other vegetables; the flesh and fleeces of the sheep and goat. Wood was sparse, as it always had been, and everything that required the use of fuel in its manufacture remained expensive, baked bricks being one example. Babylonia possessed vineyards and orchards, but it seems that grapes and figs were new crops, barely beginning their career in the country; the same seems to apply to flax, which was to spread to such a degree that Greek and Parthian Babylonia became one of the greatest centers of linen manufacture in the known world. Of all the crops nourished by the waters of the two rivers, the most lavishly cared for, and the most profitable, was certainly the date palm, a veritable factotum of a tree whose fruit, wood, leaves, and fibers all found useful employment. The palm was cultivated according to techniques that modern agronomists can only continue to pursue: the proper spacing of the trees, the utilization of the intervals between them for other crops, the mysteries of artificial fertilization, all were already known and assiduously practiced. The price for a palm orchard was, we shall not be surprised to hear, double that of a grain field of similar size.

Our information on the commercial life of the age is extremely disappointing: the archives of the business houses that we have at our disposal make no mention of long-range trade, and seem to take no interest in investment in commercial enterprises. Still, we do know that the Euphrates was sailed by innumerable cargo boats, some of which, according to Herodotus, went up to 150 tons burthen. The business houses, we must assume, were involved in an immense system of exchanges, even if their archives do not tell us so—collecting vast amounts of agricultural produce, which they then sold for cash, which in turn was handed over to the royal treasurers for rents and taxes, with the business house retaining enough to be able to lend out substantial sums at usurious rates of interest. Also, the relative abundance of metals (always imports in mineless Mesopotamia) attests the existence of long-range foreign trade with the distant sources of supply, a trade extensive enough to bring the price of metals down considerably, so great were the quantities imported.

The Persian period saw the introduction of important innovations in the social and economic order. Private property continued as before, but the practice of granting lands to collective groups, as remuneration for services rendered to the state, was extended to an unprecedented degree. The system bears more than one resemblance to that of feudal western Europe of the Middle Ages: vast landed properties were granted by the crown to soldiers and officials; in exchange for these "fiefs," families or even larger groups owed the king their services and a portion of the harvest. Soon enough, however, the crown preferred to accept, even demand, increased rents in kind in lieu of military service from men who spent their lives on their land-grants, although the language still retained the memory of the original nature of the grant: men spoke of "bow land," "horse land," or "chariot land," for the main object of these grants had been, at first, to assure the recruitment of the imperial armies. Certain documents show that the crown could still require of holders of such grants a kind of militia service; for example we know of a military call-up of 422, whose objective or assembly point was Uruk; also texts dealing with the division or transfer of these lands always note carefully the precise military and fiscal obligations that the new holders will have to fulfill.

But to the degree that changing needs and attitudes made men forget, little by little, the military service that many landholders owed the king, to the degree that officials and dignitaries, burdened by their duties, were unable to see to the farming of their grants themselves, the more acute business houses of Babylonia grew rich: taking over the management of the lands, paying the landholder a suitable rent, paying the crown the sums due to it by the original grant, the business houses were still able, by judicious exploitation of the lands under their direction, to ensure a healthy profit for themselves. Still their great prosperity is difficult to understand, unless we take into account the importance to the Mesopotamian economy of the introduction of a new financial element—coined money—and of the pressure of the crown's fiscal demands.

After 517 the Persian treasury issued the celebrated gold piece, the daric, the first imperial currency. There was also in existence a whole range of local currencies in silver, shekels coined by the Western satrapies, usually on the model of foreign coins but not adhering to any common standard between one satrapy and another. As there were local coinages, so also there were local measures, again in no particular agreement with each other: from Nebuchadnezzar on there had been an effort to popularize the "king's measure," which resulted in the acceptance by nearly all of Mesopotamia of a standard measure of capacity of about six gallons. But this official standard in no way eliminated the local measures, indeed the latter tended to come to the fore whenever the authority of the crown was weakened. In the same way the monetary standard of the empire was respected more or less; the various local coinages in silver (gold was reserved for the coins of the Great King) did, however, continue, offering no guarantee to speak of as to the weight or purity of their metal. The king's treasury was well aware of this: the archives of Persepolis make it perfectly clear that the treasurers would accept coined silver only according to its metallic weight; each coin fell into a classification according to the amount of alloy (white silver, medium silver [second rate], and base silver [third rate]), and the treasury refused to recognize face value, evaluating only according to the weight of pure silver involved.

The cash values given in our tablets must not delude us as to the real monetary situation in this age; prices, rents, salaries are cited in terms of silver shekels, but where there was actual payment in currency, the coins were valued by the metallic weight of each; or, alternatively, disburser and payee would agree as to what type of coinage was to serve as payment, so that the real values involved would be known in advance, and one could avoid the difficulties of weighing. For this reason we read expressions such as: "payable in silver of such and such quality, of this and that type." Most frequently, however, the cash citations are simply evaluations in terms of money of account; a salary, a rent, would be evaluated in silver, "payable with such and such a quantity of dates." In only one instance was cash payment obligatory for the payment of a portion of crown taxes.

Foreign coins, discovered in coin hoards here and there, should give us valuable indications of the volume of international trade, but do not. Greek coins, for example, are a sure witness to long-range trade and to the presence in Mesopotamia of Greek persons and products; but they tell us nothing as to the size of that trade: Greek coins were treated purely and simply as precious metal, in Mesopotamia, as raw material for melting and casting into ingots. A hoard found at Calah (Nimrud) or Nineveh, dating from the beginning of the fourth century, contained every kind of metallic object mixed together—vase handles, rings, Athenian coins, Aeginetan, Thracian, and Macedonian coins, all equally representing a reserve of raw metal that their owner might employ at will to fashion any metal object.

The economic life of Mesopotamia under Persian rule was marked by a constant rise in prices. It would be tedious to list, product by product, all the examples we have of this inflation, from the end of the Chaldaean period to the close of the fifth century: no class of foodstuffs, of raw materials, or of real property was exempt from it; the curious decrease in our documentation for the sale of houses and the increase in house rentals are probably to be attributed to it. The rise in prices might be explained as a function of the general destruction that accompanied the wars and rebellions of the age—except that, even if this played a considerable role in economic life, it could only have been an occasional one, an exacerbating factor in a general movement that continued for nearly two centuries. A more viable explanation would be the burden of taxation, in both cash and kind, making for shortages in goods and precious metal alike. Precious metals were relatively abundant at the beginning of the Persian period. By collecting it in taxation, and by issuing it again in coined form, the Persian government could have contributed greatly to the more rapid development of a monetary economy in the East; but quite the contrary, the crown hoarded gold and silver— the astonishment of Alexander's companions at the immense hoards that they discovered in every royal city is on record. At Susa alone, Alexander acquired 9,000 talents of coined gold (about 270 tons), but 40,000 talents of silver (about 1,200 tons) were found uselessly heaped up in piles of ingots. The draining-away and disappearance of precious metals were such that men found greater and greater difficulty in paying the cash portion of their taxes, to the extent that excessive cash borrowing was a general plague. Indebtedness, in fact, of every sort increased and multiplied, particularly on the part of taxpayers, which in turn sent the rates of interest sky high: the normal rate stood at about ten percent in Nebuchadnezzar's time, rose to twenty percent under Cyrus and Cambyses, and had reached forty to fifty percent by the end of the fifth century, as the Murashu archives inform us. Clearly there were those who saw, in a situation where the greed of the state was bleeding their countrymen white, an opportunity to make their own fortunes.

The late seventh century saw the appearance of private banks, growing up alongside the temples which, acting for ages past as deposit and lending institutions, were no longer capable of handling all the growing volume of financial business. The private banks at first engaged in credit operations, lending on security without interest at times, the income from the security (lands or slaves, for example) going to the creditor until the debt was paid in full; often the debtor proved unable to pay, and the creditor retained the security. The Egibi bank, active from the reign of Nebuchadnezzar until that of Darius I, issued loans of this kind. The credit system became more complex, and the profits of the banks grew step by step with their activities. In the fifth century the Murashu bank accumulated enormous profits, assuming an extremely complex role in the economy, to the proper functioning of which it became indispensable; a universal business house, it furnished food supplies and building materials to the temples; it made a specialty of taking charge of the land-grants of Persian dignitaries, putting them in order and paying both a rent to the landholder and his financial obligations to the crown. With immense quantities of land thus at its disposal, with considerable estates that it owned outright, the House of Murashu rented out land to countless peasants, drawing rent from all. One could borrow from the Murashu firm lands and herds, agricultural implements, and teams of traction animals; there was in fact next to nothing that one could *not* borrow from them; money, bricks, barley, dates, all were available—at a price. The capital of the House of Murashu was colossal; certain debt contracts on deposit in their archives testify to loans in amounts equal to 418 and 770 pounds of pure silver. War and vice were to Murashu and sons opportunities for profit; they bought up the booty seized by the Great King's armies on their campaigns, they rented prostitutes to procurers. The organization and distribution of irrigation water brought them immense gain, for whoever utilized their services in this matter owed them a quarter of the harvest. Rapacious profiteers they may seem to us, and no doubt were, ready to violate the legal order as we know from anecdotes of the thefts and violence committed by their agents in certain country villages; but this is not the entire story, for it ignores the economic usefulness of this all-pervading enterprise, doubtless not the only one of its kind. The House of Murashu and its competitors were solid credit institutions, and as such indispensable to the society they served; all the more so if we consider that these were the only institutions that could do what neither crown nor temple would or perhaps could do: when the Murashu firm took over the management of a great estate from its absentee proprietor, they brought to it unrivaled resources in men, material, and credit; they provided Babylonian agriculture with what we should nowadays call its infrastructure, for which, to be sure, they exacted a towering price, but in return assured the prosperity of their country's fields. The great estates of Babylonia required heavy investment and careful management, and the House of Murashu provided them: we know of one estate where it installed eighteen *nuriahs* (water-lifting devices), with seventy-two oxen to work them, to ensure the proper irrigation of the soil.

What we know of the structure of Babylonian society in the Persian period is not enough to give us a clear picture of all the elements involved. We do know, however, that the economic and social importance of the great temples had declined in favor of that of the business houses; we know that the condition of the lowly had hardly changed in relation to former ages, even if the conclusions drawn from the vocabulary of the time, especially as regards slaves, require revision. The great temples were still powerful forces in the country's economic life; they owned and managed vast estates, gave thousands of men their livelihood, provided credit to their dependents and kept huge herds, from which they often rented out beasts of burden.

372

The role of the business houses was, perhaps, of equal importance to that of the temples, until 403; but after that year, marked by the upheavals that accompanied the succession of Artaxerxes II to the imperial throne, we have not a single document attesting the activity of a large commercial firm; we might suppose that their records, from this point on, were written in Aramaic, on papyrus and parchment that have not survived the centuries. What seems more likely is that this absence of business documents is a witness to the slow economic decline of Mesopotamia, crushed by taxation perhaps, but in any case no longer a ready source of profit to the would-be Murashus and Egibis of the day. But the temples, diminished in importance though they had been, remained centers of economic activity. A sizable priestly aristocracy still existed, drawing enough of an income from the estates reserved for their support to make the buying and selling of these priestly prebends one of the transactions most frequently noted in our economic documents, from the latter part of the Persian period down to the time of Parthian rule. In the temples, too, the tradition of the Akkadian language and of the cuneiform script was maintained, while the more learned members of the priestly class devoted themselves to immense works of erudition and to mathematical astronomy. The activities of laymen in all these areas had certainly diminished, but we cannot suppose it had vanished, by the end of the Persian period, just because nearly every scrap of the written evidence, in Aramaic, has disappeared.

The life of the lower classes is barely known to us. Besides a large number of families who were dependents of the temples, and whom we may consider serfs, besides the considerable number who were feudatories in one sense or another of the Great King, holding their lands in tenure from the crown, there was an important class of men who were dependent on no one in particular, but of whom we cannot say precisely that they were free: small holders in the countryside, artisans and workmen in the towns, an itinerant mass of agricultural laborers, living meanly or dying miserably according to circumstance and chance. We assume the existence of this class, as we cannot demonstrate it from legal or economic documents that seldom speak of the poor. We can show that, at the beginning of the fifth century, an agricultural laborer was paid on the average a silver shekel per month; we can calculate, on the basis of the average price of provisions, that such a man might be able to afford six and a half bushels of barley, and about 132 pounds of dates, to feed himself and his family for a month. It is, of course, extremely probable that a man in this position was likely to be unemployed from time to time and lose his income altogether.

A confusion of vocabulary has tempted many to equate with the poorest of this class all the slaves mentioned in the texts, the *ardani* (plural of *ardu*); no doubt there were many slaves who were as badly off as the poorest freemen in terms of daily life, but *ardu* is not a term properly applied to slaves in the Western legal sense (i.e., in Roman law terms); the word means, rather, something that we may more justly translate "servant."

The Mesopotamian slave (*ardu*) properly speaking was always capable of owning land, using a seal (the symbol of legal personality), holding administrative office; the fact that he could be sold like an object never prevented him from engaging in activities that Roman law would never have allowed him. Persian law simply reinforced this: in a social hierarchy where every inferior referred to himself as the slave (*ardu*) of his superior, the satrap *vis-à-vis* the Great King, the minor official *vis-à-vis* his district chief, or, more common, the lowly servant of an almost equally lowly peasant *vis-à-vis* the master who had purchased him, in such a system "slavery" is not a sharply defined idea. The word could be applied to the status of every kind of dependent whose superior was able to employ constraint and violence to direct him, without thereby detracting from the possible social importance of the person so defined. Gimillu, "slave" of the Eanna temple at Uruk, was the author of no petty servile larcenies; he was an entrepreneur, supervising immense herds, directing vast estates, whose peculations were in proportion to his powers, and whom the authorities were able to bring to justice only after years of

374

flagrant theft. The House of Murashu had slaves in its service, but many of these *ardani* were trusted agents of their masters, business representatives in the fullest sense, and some of them had talent and luck enough to set up banking houses of their own, in which activity they were bound to their masters more by common interest than by any servile tie, of which the payment of a portion of their profits was perhaps a formal vestige.

Social classifications in Mesopotamia were therefore nothing if not complex: the ethnic composition of the population was no simpler. Personal and place names are our surest evidence for this: at the end of the sixth century we hear of villages of Persians, Tyrians, and Cimmerians; contracts furnish us with Egyptian, Sabaean, and Edomite names, alongside the more numerous Babylonian and Assyrian names; from 521 Persian names increase continually. It is clear, however, that the blending of nationalities on Mesopotamian soil was thorough and rapid; we soon read of men with Iranian names whose fathers had Babylonian names, and of the opposite with even greater frequency. The discovery, at Nippur, before the First World War, of the Murashu archives suddenly revealed a long list of Hebrew names, which witness to the great number of Jewish families remaining in Mesopotamia and to the prosperity of certain among them; they were to be found at Nippur, at Babylon, and in all the great urban centers. It may be that the ancestry of some of these families went back to the first Israelite exile of 721, in the time of the Assyrians. Those who followed the first wave, at the beginning of the sixth century in Nebuchadnezzar's reign, observed the counsel of Jeremiah (29:5–6): "Build houses and live in them; plant gardens and eat their produce . . . multiply there, and do not decrease." When the Edict of Cyrus was published in 538, only the contingents allotted from each family departed for the homeland; in 520 Zerubbabel brought 50,000 persons with him; in 458 Ezra was accompanied by only 5,000. The future role of the Jewish communities of the Babylonian diaspora is sufficient evidence for the numerical importance of those who remained "by the waters of Babylon."

The confrontation of the men of so many different nationalities, the importance of the Iranian element in the Babylonian population, could not have been without a deep effect on the intellectual and religious life of the land.

So great was the prestige, so enormous the antiquity, of Mesopotamian culture that the Persian conquerors had no thought of altering it to their taste, here on the soil that gave it birth. They rather came to it as pupils in many instances, borrowing Mesopotamian styles for the architecture and decoration of their vast imperial palaces. Even more important, Akkadian was given the status of an imperial language. In Cyrus' reign appear trilingual inscriptions, in Old Persian, Elamite, and Akkadian, a custom that was continued by his successors, the most famous example being the inscription of Darius on the rock of Behistun. The Old Persian language itself was written in a cuneiform script, adapted from that used for Akkadian, but so simplified that it employed only forty-three signs. Elamite, too, was written in cuneiform characters, its script peppered with Sumerian ideograms, its vocabulary as rich in Akkadian as in Persian loan-words. These were the official languages, employed in trilingual inscriptions down to the fourth century B.C. But errors of transcription began to appear more and more often in the Old Persian and Elamite texts. In ordinary life the decline of the three languages was even more marked. From the reign of Darius I on, no more texts in Old Persian appear on clay tablets; Elamite retained its hold somewhat longer: it was for long the administrative language at Persepolis, and down to the end of Xerxes' reign it was used enough to provide us with tens of thousands of Elamite tablets and fragments. After 460, however, it fell out of use. Akkadian was still commonly employed for administrative and legal texts down to about 400; the scribes wrote it poorly, ignoring flexions, and confusing cases, although we cannot precisely tell whether this is a sign of the popular ignorance of a dying language or of the popular development of a living one. What seems more probable is that Akkadian was going out of common use: so, at least, the decreasing number of documents on clay tablets would seem to indicate, as would the fact that its use was restricted more and more to the members of the priestly aristocracy—that is to say, to the most educated class—devoting itself, in the seclusion of the temples, to the preservation of the ancient national heritage.

Everywhere else—in Persepolis, at Susa, in Babylon itself—the use of Aramaic was gaining steadily; even the tablets bear Aramaic letters scratched in the clay (or, more usually, written on in ink), sometimes three lines' worth, digesting the tablet's contents to facilitate filing. The papyrus and parchment on which Aramaic is normally written have unfortunately vanished; but philologists have been able to trace the role this language played as the *lingua franca* of all western Asia. The everyday spoken language of Babylonia was either a much altered Akkadian or Aramaic; the written language was Aramaic, except for economic, legal, and administrative texts, which were written in a relatively correct Akkadian. Aramaic was always an intermediary stage in translation from one language to another: in administrative correspondence, for example, instructions given in Old Persian were translated and written down in Aramaic, sent to their destination, and there translated into whatever the local scribal language might be, Elamite at Susa, Akkadian at Babylonia. The need for simplification, the relative simplicity of Aramaic as compared to the older languages, soon made of the former the only language commonly spoken and written. Elamite and Old Persian might subsist, in much altered forms, as the spoken language of the people in the areas of their origin. The same may very well have occurred in the case of Akkadian, except that the latter, even when it had ceased to be an administrative language, remained the language of intellectual and spiritual culture, the language of the scribes, priests, scholars, and scientists, and the language of the jurists as well, in which legal documents would always be written when they dealt with members of a class still socially important, but ever more reduced in numbers.

What we know of the religious life of Babylonia reflects the condition of the country as the crossroads of western Asia, with all the diversity of men and cultures that this implied; but it also reflects the millennial persistence of the native Mesopotamian civilization. Theophoric personal names attest the presence of Iranian deities, such as Mithras and Baga, of Egyptian deities such as Isis and Harmachis, Aramaean deities like Shemesh, and so on; but wherever we have a case of religious syncretism, the Babylonian element usually outweighs the foreign: a man bears a name formed with that of Harmachis, but his son, perhaps born in Babylonia, will be named after the native god Nabu. The descendants of immigrant Iranians bear names referring to Babylonian gods; there are very few cases of men of Babylonian name giving their sons Iranian theophoric names. The temples never had anything to fear from the Persian conquest, with the exception of Xerxes' destruction of the Esagila at Babylon in 482; until Xerxes' time the conquerors maintained and repaired the sanctuaries of the ancient cities as a royal duty, after the manner of the Chaldaean kings. After Xerxes the royal generosity ran less freely, but we do know that Darius II, for example, contributed to the repair of certain buildings in the Eanna temple at Uruk, and that he was in all probability responsible for the construction of the temple archives from which thousands of texts have been recovered: this last building was of strikingly modern design, featuring an installation for the humidification of the atmosphere with running water, to preserve the clay tablets on file. Nabu at Borsippa, Enlil at Nippur, Anu and Ishtar at Uruk, Marduk (at least until 482) at Babylon—all of the most venerable gods and sanctuaries had the continuity of their phenomenally ancient worship assured. True, the temple of Nannar at Ur declined swiftly, but it did so as a result of the swift decline of its city from the end of the sixth century on. Other than the (politically motivated) destruction of the Esagila, then, the Persian kings do not appear to have done a single thing that might indicate hostility to the religion of their subjects, or an intention to uproot it. Their relative indifference, from Xerxes on, to the gods and sanctuaries of Mesopotamia is to be seen in the light of the general history of the Persian Empire: from the fifth century onward, the Great Kings paid less and less attention to the local sensibilities and traditions of the different parts of their empire, and Iranism has sometimes been suggested as the explanation of the conquerors' indifference to their subjects, and the increased harshness of an administration whose only purpose, by that time, was to drain the riches of the conquered lands into the Achaemenid treasure hoards.

Of all the peoples then inhabiting Mesopotamia, the Jews have exercised a special fascination on the attention and ingenuity of the learned. We have already alluded to their numerical importance in the population of the land and to their role in its economy. From the study of their personal names we can learn something of their religious attitudes as well. The reader of the Old Testament can discover that a number of the exiles took foreign theophoric names, formed with the designations of pagan gods. In 520 the grandson of King Jehoiachin, who led the second group of returning exiles to Jerusalem, bore the name of Zerubbabel; his principal aides had Persian names, Mordecai, Bilshan, and Bigvai; their predecessor, who had returned from exile in 538, was named Sheshbazzar, i.e., Shamash-apal-usur in Akkadian, a name formed with that of the Babylonian sun-god. The names to be found in the Murashu archives have considerably enlarged the material at our disposal: some of these names are also theophoric, formed with Akkadian divine names; a man with a name formed with that of Yahweh had a son whose name contained that of the Babylonian god Nabu, and his grandson's contained that of an Iranian god; a man with the name Bel-Yau (Yahweh is my Lord) was the ancestor of men with names formed with those of Marduk and Nabu, and so on. Are we to conclude, then, that many Jews in Babylonia were apostates to the religion of their fathers? That precisely this would from time to time occur would be inevitable; possibly it was even frequent; but the examples of Sheshbazzar and Zerubbabel, loyal servants of the God of the Fathers, should convince us that the mere possession of a pagan theophoric name need not indicate the apostasy of its bearer. Besides, many Jews in Babylonia took theophoric names popular in the land of their exile, but substituted for the name of the pagan deity that of

379

the God of Israel, in the forms El, Yeho, Yahu; a completely new name was created, Shabettai ("He of the Sabbath"), and the old name of Haggai was revived, referring to the traditional religious festivals, particularly the Feast of Tabernacles. In other words, the study of the personal names of the Babylonian Jews reveals unexpected evidence of the fidelity of many exiles to the religion of their homeland, and of the strength of the religious and nationalist response, in Mesopotamia, to the restoration of the sacred rites in Judah. None of which should surprise us, when we remember the role of the Mesopotamian Jews in the historical development of Judaism; it was they who edited the version of the sacred law proclaimed by Ezra at Jerusalem in 458; it was to their economic importance, their political influence, and the firmness of their faith that the repatriated Jews in Judah owed the men and money that their community required to subsist and to increase, as well as the royal benevolence without which the work of Nehemiah, after 445, would have proved impossible.

Conservative in language and religion, for all the foreigners who abounded in the land and brought to it their divinities and their speech, the civilization of Mesopotamia conserved as well the legal heritage of the land, the expression of a millennial concern for justice. The Persian period, like the centuries that preceded it, has left us documents that inform us of legal practice, with nothing to reveal the work of legislators and legal scholars. We are, however, able to conclude that the Persians preserved the juridical legacy of the past. Fragments of a copy of the Code of Hammurabi testify to the interest that this work continued to arouse, as do the formulae employed in the inscriptions of Cyrus and Darius I, whose phraseology is sometimes directly taken over from that of the great Code; legal historians have been able to trace the Code's juridical formulae through the different legal compilations of the ancient Near East, the last instance being that of the anti-demonic law promulgated in the reign of the Parthian King Mithridates I, in the late second century B.C.

Such was the reach of Babylonian law in terms of time, preserved by the legal conservatism of Mesopotamia; the organization of an empire as vast as that of the Persians, its administrative unity and the exchanges and contacts that this encouraged, afforded Babylonian law an opportunity for extension in terms of space. From the reign of Nebuchadnezzar to that of Darius I, Babylonian colonists were settled at Neirab near Aleppo, sixty miles from the Mediterranean; they formed close ties, matrimonial and commercial, with the local population; the texts from which we learn this show Babylonian law effectively outweighing the local juridical traditions, with contracts and engagements drawn up according to imported legal principles, in the very terms of the Babylonian formularies.

Changes there were in the law of Babylonia, inevitably, but they were extremely limited in nature and are hardly visible before 500. Various details in the formularies show modifications that are attributable to Iranian influence: for example, after the enumeration of the contractual clauses guaranteeing a lessee against various difficulties he might experience at the hands of the lessor, in the Persian period there is added to the usual formulae one making the lessor responsible to the court for warranty of the good condition of the leased object, even if this should be questioned by a third party. Of greater consequence, certainly, was the promulgation, after 519, of the King's law, the *data,* an Iranian term that now entered current usage; its content is unknown to us, but its existence is confirmed by contracts the texts of which contain the words: "according to the King's law." It is clear that the *data* was a collection of judicial precedents; we find it cited in connection with a toll, a sale of slaves, or a cash deposit. There were royal officials, no doubt, specifically charged with overseeing the application of the King's law in the courts; the two royal judges, for example, who sat with the judicial bench of Babylon, probably had this as their task.

To the past, again, Mesopotamia owed her extraordinary accomplishments in the sciences, a legacy to which the men of the Persian period were to add important contributions. Or, to be more exact, a specific class of men: the temples, less wealthy than they had been in former ages, more closely supervised by the Persian administration, were more than ever the milieus in which Mesopotamian culture was preserved. They were the last citadels of the Akkadian language, a scholars' language as it was fast becoming, but studied and written in the temples down to A.D. 75; there, for centuries, scribes continued to copy and recopy texts, religious, literary, and lexicographical, without which our knowledge of Sumero-Akkadian culture would be riddled with lacunae that we would not know how to fill. Fallen from their former economic primacy, the temples still retained enough capital to support, in every major city, a priestly aristocracy whose more gifted members, scribes and theologians in turn, were also the scientists of Babylonia.

We are unfortunately quite unable to determine the dates of the first important scientific discoveries made by these men. We know, for instance, that by about 500 the Babylonian astronomers had made a satisfactory calculation of the length of the solar year, without, however, troubling to translate this into a practical calendar for the use of ordinary men. Since the reign of Nabonassar, in 747, it had been known that nineteen solar years corresponded to nineteen lunar years, plus seven additional lunar months. There were centuries of indecision as to what method should be used for the intercalation of these seven months into the cycle of nineteen lunar years; even in the reigns of Cyrus and Cambyses, the priests of Babylon had to decide on each intercalation, and two of their letters inform us that their decisions were thereupon applied by all the temples of Babylonia. It was not until the fourth century B.C., in 383 or 367, that a standard system of intercalations was laid down.

In the course of the fifth century, the scholar-priests hit upon the idea of the zodiac, a mathematical abstraction that allowed them to improve the notation of their astronomical observations: sidereal events could already be located by reference to certain bright stars, it was an enormous step forward to be able to pinpoint them in terms of degrees within one of the signs of the zodiac. Without intending to, the astronomers had also given impetus to the development of a pseudoscience, horoscopic astrology, which was to become *the* principal science in the Greco-Roman world; in Babylonia, however, its beginnings were modest and its evolution slow: the first astrological horoscope based on observation of the planets, and on elucidation of their position with regard to the signs of the zodiac, dates from the year 410.

Various methods of astronomical calculation were perfected during these centuries, as were the tables for the periodic relations between the revolutions of the moon and those of the planets. Between about 500 and about 300, then, the Babylonian astronomers developed the techniques without which the rise of mathematical astronomy in the Hellenistic age would have been an impossibility: but just as we do not know the stages by which these discoveries were made, we do not know the names of those who made them. The Greeks and Romans have passed on to us certain traditions on this subject that a better understanding of the cuneiform texts now leads us to reject. The work of Naburiannus, for example, would be placed in the fifth century according to these traditions: this name has been thought to represent the Akkadian name Naburimmanu. To him is attributed one of the systems for determining the phases of the moon. Today the Akkadian reading of his name is thought uncertain; it has become impossible to attach any date to the work he is thought to have done, indeed it has become impossible to attribute any particular accomplishment to him at all. The identification of Cidenas, a contemporary of Artaxerxes, with a certain Kidinnu, who was the author of a series of astronomical tables, appears on the contrary to be well established. It is possible, as has been thought, that he was the discoverer of the precession of the equinoxes; but we have no reason to identify him as the inventor of a second system of determining the phases of the moon, a rival to the system to which the name of Naburimmanu has been attached. The tablets that report these discoveries to us may well be copies of older works, and the mention of the scribe's name tells us nothing of the real identity of the discoverer. It is, in fact, most probable that, as was the case with many literary, artistic, and scientific works, these discoveries were made by teams of investigators working jointly, and that our Greek and Latin authors, drawing on a tradition of whose origins and transmission we know absolutely nothing, had misunderstood their mysterious sources in attributing them to individual men.

On the first of October, 331, at Gaugamela in northern Assyria, Alexander the Great shattered the last army of the Great King. In the following weeks he seized control of Mesopotamia and entered the city of Babylon without resistance, either from its inhabitants or from its satrap Mazaeus. The victor was greeted with hymns, incense rose from the altars, and the streets were strewn with flowers. Alexander, grateful, already planning, perhaps, to make this the capital of his new empire, decreed the rebuilding of the city's temples, and the temple of Marduk before all. In what light did the Babylonians see their young conqueror? As the avenger of the crimes of Xerxes? As the hero who would restore the former glories of the holy city? As the man of destiny whose will would outweigh the apathy that had engulfed a people too ancient by millennia? Probably all these things at once.

The Babylonians thought, perhaps, that they were entering a new world, one that might be turned to their advantage. If so, time did not bear them out: two centuries of Greek rule made no fundamental change in their condition. What Babylonia had become since the late fifth century she was to remain: rich still, and for a long time after, but never to regain the prosperity that had been hers until the days of Darius I—an important province, by her position at the crossroads of the Near East and by the size of her population, but never to regain a political importance of the first rank. The composition of her population had been profoundly altered; the popularity of Aramaic, the superiority of the alphabetic script, were to continue to reduce the number of men who could still understand, and attempt to preserve, the cultural legacy of her endless past.

This was a dying civilization, but one too great and ancient to die a sudden death. During the difficult and obscure fourth century, Babylonia had put forth an effort sufficient to save, indeed to augment, the best of her heritage. She had achieved

384

a colossal labor of compilation, preserved her legal tradition, created new instruments of abstraction that were to serve as the foundation for mathematical astronomy. The Hellenistic age was to see the culmination of this work.

18

Palestinian Judaism in the Persian Period

The Book of Ezra says Cyrus the Great, in his first year (after his conquest of Babylon in 539), issued a decree permitting all the people of Yahweh in his dominions to go to Jerusalem and build the temple (1.1–4). Some 50,000 persons returned under the leadership of Zerubbabel, the governor of the Persian district of Judea (cf. Haggai 1.1), and of Joshua, the High Priest. They set up an altar, began regular offerings, and in the following year laid the foundations of the temple (Ezra 1.5–3.10). Ezra 4.4 f. dates these events about 537/536. This date is contradicted by the prophecies of Haggai, which declare that before the second year of Darius I (520) "not one stone was laid on another in the temple of Yahweh" (2.15, cf. 18). The list of returned exiles in Ezra 2 used discrepant sources (two genealogical, one territorial). The decree of Cyrus recurs in different form in 6.3 f. Therefore it came at least from tradition: had the author been inventing, he would have used the same invention in both places. However, the second form of the decree, in which Cyrus orders the building and grants funds for it, is hardly genuine, since the order was never carried out. The authenticity of the first decree is therefore also dubious. (Cyrus sent back some Mesopotamians to their homes [61] and may have done the same for the Judeans, but possibility is not proof.)

386

Though the details of the return of the exiles are thus obscure, the situation produced by their return can be reconstructed from indications afforded by earlier history. During the monarchies a conflict had gone on between those who believed Yahweh required the Israelites to worship him alone, and those who believed he might be worshiped together with other deities. The former (monolatrous) party is represented by the documents in the Old Testament, the latter (syncretistic) party had more popular following and usually controlled both government and temple. With the exile (587–539), the literate leadership of the monolatrous party was carried off to Babylonia. To the Babylonian period is plausibly attributed the development of several characteristics conspicuous in postexilic, but rare in preexilic, Judean material: extreme concern for "purity" (threatened by the surrounding world) and for circumcision and observance of the sabbath as distinctive signs of the true Jew; synagogue worship (prayer, praise, reading and exposition of the cult laws) as a center of communal life; a body of party literature—legal codes, histories, prophecies—presumably preserved in the synagogues and there expanded with psalms, prayers, and homiletic material, all shaped by the party position that the exclusive worship of Yahweh led to prosperity, the worship of other deities to disaster. As synagogues formed a network for assistance and encouragement, their theological reaction against the surrounding world became extreme. The prohibition of worshiping other deities led to denial of their existence, a motif that first becomes the dominant theme of a major work in the prophecies of "II Isaiah" (Is. 40–55), which heralded Cyrus' conquest of Babylon.

By contrast, the cult of Yahweh which survived in Judea was chiefly syncretistic. In 585 Ezekiel prophesied against the Judeans, "Thus saith the Lord Yahweh, 'You eat flesh with blood and lift up your eyes to your idols and shed blood; shall you then possess the land?'" (33.23 ff.). In the following century, "III Isaiah" (Is. 56–66) attacks those who "burn with lust among the oaks; . . . slay . . . children in the valleys"; pour libations and bring offerings to betyls, sacrifice on the mountains; practice ritual prostitution and worship idols; "sit in tombs and spend the night in secret places; . . . eat swine's flesh and broth of abominable things; . . . set a table for Fortune and fill mixed cups for Destiny"; etc. (57.1–10; 65.1–12). Consultation of *teraphim* (household deities) and worship of other gods continued to the time of the additions to Zechariah (10.2; 12.2). Palestinian archaeology yields a succession of syncretistic seals with Yahwist names on them, "Astarte" figurines, winged sun discs, etc., uninterrupted until the Hellenistic period.[62]

This syncretistic cult of Yahweh was not limited to Palestine. It was established in Damascus in the ninth century (II Kings 5.15 ff.; 8.8). In the eighth century it was carried to Mesopotamia,[63] in the seventh or sixth century to Egypt,[64] and with Nebuchadnezzar's exiles, to Babylon.[65] By the fifth century Malachi could declare that from the East to the West the name of Yahweh is great among the gentiles, and everywhere cakes and incense are offered to his names (1.11 f.). From this time on there are many traces of the worship of Yahweh by persons who worshiped other gods as well.[66] This syncretistic diaspora was in touch with the Palestinian centers of the cult;[67] mutual influence is presumable.

Members of the monolatrous party had more reason to return to Palestine than did the syncretists. The Deuteronomic code required sacrificial worship of Yahweh, but limited it to Jerusalem (12.4 ff.). Consequently the postexilic documents of the Old Testament (all from the monolatrous party) sometimes refer to the returned party members as "the returned exiles,"[68] and to the syncretistic population of Judea and the neighboring territories as "the people(s) of the land."[69] But there were occasional syncretists among the returned exiles;[70] and the monolatrous party won a small following from the local population (Ezra 6.21). Finally there was a third group: the priests of the Jerusalem temple had an economic interest in its preservation. Theologically they were adaptable: In the past they had cooperated in both Deuteronomic reform (II Kings 22.8 ff.) and syncretistic worship.[71] Their adaptability was probably strained by conflicts between the other parties.

388

Before the building of the temple there was no safety in the city because every man's hand was against his neighbor (Zech. 8.10).

Rebuilding was undertaken in the second year of Darius (520) by the Persian governor of Judea, Zerubbabel, and the High Priest Joshua, encouraged by the prophets Haggai and Zechariah.[72] Both prophets were of the monolatrous party. Since they saw in Zerubbabel the coming Messiah [73] (i.e., the "anointed" king whom Yahweh would send to save his people), he was presumably the party's leader. In Zechariah 6.9–15 [74] are the terms of an agreement between Zerubbabel and Joshua. Zerubbabel is to be crowned civil ruler and to rebuild the temple; Joshua is to be next him in rank and "a plan for peace shall be between them" (vs. 13)—i.e., they will respect each other's rights (evidence of previous disagreement). A contribution to the temple is to be made by members of Zerubbabel's following (returned exiles, vss. 10–11 and 14).

This agreement is also reflected by Zechariah 3 and Haggai 2.10–19. From these it appears that previously the High Priest Joshua and the sacrificial cult at the restored altar in Jerusalem had been attacked by the monolatrous party as "unclean." These attacks are to be dropped. The shift in the party line is excused by the prophet's vision of Yahweh's intervention to change Joshua's status. The High Priest is assured that if he will keep the law (as interpreted by the monolatrous party) he will be recognized as legal authority over the temple.

This agreement does not call for a purge of the cults of other gods. Evidently these were no longer officially practiced. The issue is now one of purity. Apparently the monolatrous party maintained that an idol was impure as a dead body.[75] Consequently priests who worshiped other gods in private, or who associated with worshipers of other gods, would themselves become impure and would render the offerings of the official cult impure and unacceptable to Yahweh. Hence the attacks on cult and High Priest as impure and the demand that the High Priest observe the law—i.e., the law of purity as the monolatrous party extended it. Since the priests were the authorities on purity and cult law, this demand shows an invasion of their domain. From now on the party conflicts in Jerusalem center on purity, and converts to the monolatrous party are described as "those who have separated themselves from the impurity of the peoples of the land," i.e., have accepted the party's purity law.[76]

The hortatory and apologetic tone of these oracles on the agreement between Zerubbabel and Joshua indicates that not all members of the monolatrous party approved the deal. There were different legal traditions within the party, as shown by the conflicting legal material it preserved—Deuteronomic and priestly elements, the legislation of Ezekiel, etc. As a further example, Haggai urged "all the people of the land" to help in rebuilding the temple (2.4), but when some proffered to help, Zerubbabel refused their offer (Ezra 4.1 ff.).

Here the editor of Ezra has confused matters by identifying "the people of the land" as the Samaritans of the north (4.2b and 4), a reflection of his own time (after Nehemiah).[77] But Zerubbabel's rebuilding of the temple was a Judean concern, and there is no evidence (save Ezra 4.2b) that the Samaritans noticed it. There is evidence of hostility between the Judeans and the monolatrous party in Jerusalem. "Zechariah's" breaking of the staff of union is said to signify the severance of Judah from Jerusalem.[78] The results of this break are foretold by Zechariah 12.2–10.[79] In the End, "the people of Judah will also be in the siege against Jerusalem," but Yahweh will open their eyes; they will say to themselves, "The dwellers of Jerusalem have prevailed against me through Yahweh of armies, their god"; and they will go over to the Jerusalemites and destroy the gentiles. Then Yahweh will give the victory to the Judeans first, but will protect the Jerusalemites and make the feeblest of them like David, and the house of David like a god.

The prominence this prophecy gives the house of David suggests the time of Zerubbabel, the last important figure of that house (I Chr. 3.19). And Zerubbabel's sudden disappearance from the evidence may explain why the prophecy, at the moment of triumph, concludes, "And I shall pour out on the house of David and the inhabitants of Jerusalem a spirit of compassion . . . and they shall look [back?] to him whom they pierced and shall mourn him as one mourns an only son." Perhaps Zerubbabel was assassinated by conspirators led by other members of the Davidic family. His messianic claims would have ruined them if he failed, and might have, if he had succeeded.

Zerubbabel's death probably led to the investigation by the officials of the Persian satrapy, reported in Ezra 5.3–6.13 (there was evidently no governor in the city at the time). The city council claimed the rebuilding had been authorized by Cyrus. A decree not only authorizing but subsidizing it was found in the imperial records (where some Judean in the secretariat may have planted it), and the temple was completed in the sixth year of Darius (516) with the help not merely of syncretistic Judeans, but of pagan officials (Ezra 6.13–15). From this time on, however, the Persian dossier on Jerusalem records attempted revolt.[80]

The period 515–458 B.C. seems to have been one of syncretist control. The denunciations of idolatry from III Isaiah and "Zechariah" probably belong here, as does the complaint in Zechariah 14.21 that there are "Canaanites" in the temple, perhaps a slur at priests born of marriages with neighboring Palestinians (cp. Ezra 9.1 f.). Malachi denounces marriage with gentiles and misinterpretation of the law by the priests. Malachi is "the last of the prophets," not because prophecy ceased, but because the monolatrous party did not wittingly preserve any later collections of prophecies.[81] It had all it needed for homiletic purposes, and further forecasts of the day of Yahweh (as the case of Zerubbabel had shown) were likely to lead to trouble with the Persian government.

However, the Persian government had troubles of its own. Early in the reign of Artaxerxes I Egypt revolted. The Athenians supported the revolt and seized Dor on the Palestinian coast, some sixty miles from Jerusalem, as a base on the way to Egypt.[82] If a city like Jerusalem were to revolt and call in the Athenians, Persian communications with Egypt would be cut, Egypt would be lost and Palestine might be. So the Persian court was anxious to please its Palestinian subjects. But it was misinformed by the monolatrous party as to affairs in Jerusalem. Therefore in 458 it sent to Jerusalem a Judean priest named Ezra,[83] who held the office of scribe in the Persian government and was now commissioned to carry out in Judea a legal reform which the government believed the people wanted.[84]

Ezra arrived in Jerusalem with a company of supporters, offerings to win over priesthood and populace, and a text he called "The Book of the Law of Moses" (not the completed Pentateuch, since it did not prescribe observance of the day of atonement).[85] He tried to make the introduction of the new law a public festival (Nehemiah 8.9 ff.), but its content made "all the people" weep. Among the causes of their grief was prohibition of marriage with non-Judeans. Ezra presently was "informed" that many such marriages had been contracted. He went into conspicuous mourning, attracted a crowd, moved them to tears by his eloquence, and forced the leaders of the people to swear to have the alien wives divorced, for the purification of Israel (Ezra 10.2 ff.). An assembly was called for the purpose; it set up a committee to investigate, and the committee produced a list of offenders (Ezra 10.9–44).

Here the text breaks off. What was done is not said. Most likely, Ezra was recalled by the Persian government. His divorce program must have caused trouble even beyond Judea. The alien wives were daughters of the gentry of the neighboring provinces, who added their complaints to those of the Judeans. Finally, perhaps Ezra tried to rebuild the wall of Jerusalem. Ezra 4.11–23 has a misplaced story of such an attempt, made in the reign of Artaxerxes and stopped by denunciation to the Persians. Whatever happened, the walls were not completed and the marriages were not dissolved. When Nehemiah arrived in the city, some fourteen years later, he found the one in ruins and the others in force.

Nehemiah [86] was a cupbearer of Artaxerxes I, who got permission to refortify Jerusalem. This was in 444. The Athenians had been driven out of Palestine, the Egyptian revolt had been suppressed, and Jerusalem seems to have been suffering from Bedouin raids (I Esdras 4.45, 50; Neh. 1.3). Thus the permission was justified by the circumstances. Nehemiah was of the monolatrous party; [87] therefore the gentry of the neighboring territories, remembering Ezra, were hostile to him as soon as he arrived (2.10, 19; 3.33), although (or rather, because) they had the closest relations with the upper classes of Jerusalem (6.17 ff.; 13.4 ff., 23 ff., 28). Their Jerusalem in-laws were probably even more hostile, which explains Nehemiah's secrecy as to his plans and the speed of his actions (2.11–18). As Persian governor he had the Persian garrison to support him (2.9; 4.10, 17; 5.10, 15 f.; 7.2; 13.19); but to carry through the reforms he wished, he would have to win over the populace which had hitherto sided with the syncretists.

Accordingly, as we know from his memoirs in the Old Testament, he began with the common interest—restoration of the city walls. The priesthood and gentry, compelled by public opinion, cooperated (3.1–32). The most his opponents in Judea dared attempt was a little passive resistance and circulation of defeatist verses. [88] They kept in touch with the outsiders (6.17 ff.), and these may have considered military action but did not dare risk it (4.2, 5 ff. et al.). To offset the burden imposed on the populace by the building (4.4; 5.18), Nehemiah next undertook the one Deuteronomic reform sure to be popular with the plebs—he compelled abolition of interest, release of property seized for debt, and remission of debts. This he did not by official order (as he might). Instead he made of it a great public scene in which he stood forth, against the money-lending gentry, as champion of the poor (5.7 ff.). Further, he remitted the taxes for the support of the governor, but entertained daily a hundred and fifty of the "Judeans" (probably heads of the local clans) and lesser officials. [89] And he strengthened the city by settling in it persons from the surrounding towns—presumably his supporters (7.4 f.). Here Nehemiah's memoirs break off. Elsewhere we hear of a celebration at the completion of the walls (Neh. 12), a collection of books concerning the kings and the prophets (II Macc. 2.13) and additional building on the temple. [90]

The memoirs are resumed after Nehemiah returned from a visit to the Persian court in 432. Evidently confident of support at Susa, [91] as well as popularity in Jerusalem, he now began his religious reforms. He first expelled from the temple an ally of the syncretist party, Tobias, governor of Ammon, who had been given his room there by the High Priest (13.4–9). Moreover, he had the room purified. Tobias' name and the name of his son Yehohanan (6.18) prove the family were worshipers of Yahweh. Nehemiah expelled him, not as a pagan, but as a syncretist. So we have here again the conflict with the priesthood over purity law. Nehemiah, a layman (6.10 f.), relying on the legal tradition of his party, has contradicted the High Priest on a question of purity.

Nehemiah next struck at the priesthood's control of the temple. He established the Levites in the temple and financed them by a ten percent tax on Judea's agricultural produce (13.10–14). The Levites were priests left unemployed by the destruction of the provincial holy places at the Babylonian conquest and by the refusal of the Jerusalem clergy to permit them to officiate in Jerusalem. Nehemiah, by securing their income, won for himself and his party a body of devoted and useful adherents. In the temple they could enforce on the priests the observance of his purity law; in the city they could help enforce the observance of the sabbath, hitherto neglected by the market people under the protection of, again, the local gentry (13.15–22).

With the Levites, his garrison, and his popular support, Nehemiah finally could attack the question of mixed marriages. By flogging and torture,[92] he made his opponents swear they would not henceforth permit such marriages, and he drove into exile a grandson of the High Priest who had married a daughter of Sanballat, the governor of Samaria, and other priests and Levites who had made similar marriages. Since priesthoods are usually split by factions, he probably had some priestly supporters, and he strengthened their hand by provisions for offerings to the temple (13.31).

Here again the reason for Nehemiah's action was the belief that, by marriage with syncretistic worshipers of Yahweh, the priests and so the cult would be rendered impure (13.29 f.). In this case the syncretism is certain. Sanballat gave Yahwist names to his sons Delaiah and Shelemiah,[93] but his own name testifies to the worship of Sin (the Mesopotamian moon god), and Delaiah and Shelemiah helped restore the temple at Elephantine in Egypt where a colony of Judean mercenaries worshiped Yahweh, Anat, and Bethel.[94]

With these events and a prayer, Nehemiah's memoirs end. They were written to defend his actions, which indicates that the opposition remained strong. How long he remained in power is unknown. He was not mentioned in a letter addressed to the Judean authorities in 411.[95] His conversion of the Jerusalem populace to the monolatrous party and his establishment of that party, represented by the Levites, in the temple, stopped the priesthood's drift toward syncretism. But for this, the monolatrous cult would have survived, if at all, as a diasporic religion, connected with Palestine only by tradition. The preservation of the territorial ties of Judaism, with their enormous historical consequences, was thus the work of Nehemiah.

Thus in Jerusalem the monolatrous cult had won. Official syncretism was now out of the question, and private syncretism was henceforth furtive. The conflict now was between Nehemiah's party, "the separatists," who disdained the local population, and the party of Nehemiah's opponents, "the assimilationists." On the separatist side were a few priests, most of the Levites, and the Jerusalem plebs; on the assimilationist side were most of the priests, the gentry, and possibly the Judean peasantry. Of these groups the gentry, the Levites, and the priests are represented by material in the Old Testament which reveals their characters and histories.

From the gentry come probably the worldly-wise collections of Proverbs (most of 22.17–31.31)[96] and certainly the remains of the original Job (3–27), dated in the fifth century by stylistic and theological relations to II Isaiah and by striking similarities to Greek tragedy, especially to *Prometheus Bound*.[97] Job's *hybris* led him to demand justice of God. The core of Ecclesiastes,[98] written a century later, ridiculed the human pretension to speculate on such subjects. The short stories Ruth, Jonah, Judith, and Tobit reflect assimilationist views and probably come from the gentry, as does the exquisite love poetry of the Song of Songs. All these are distinguished, as belletristic, from the national legends and histories, laws, and prophecies preserved by the monolatrous party. This belletristic material is evidence of an educated laity in touch with the culture of the surrounding world. Its literary products change with international fashion—gnomic verses in the sixth century, poetic drama in the fifth, philosophical reflection in the fourth (the similarity of Ecclesiastes to Epicurus has often been remarked), romantic short stories [99] and erotic poetry in the third and later. This same sequence of works shows the gentry coming to terms with Judaism. The earlier material in Proverbs, and Job 3–27, ignore Jewish ritual and tradition. Ecclesiastes, like many Greek philosophers, knows a popular piety which he practices but does not believe.[100] Ruth celebrates a marriage with a Moabite; Jonah represents the gentiles as instructed by Yahweh and rewarded for their obedience. But Ruth argues from the national legend (2.12; 4.11 etc.), and Jonah is concerned for the glory of the temple at Jerusalem (2.5). Judith and Tobit are meticulous Jews, but both works are defenses of the north Israelites, and Judith celebrates the conversion of an Ammonite (prohibited by Dt. 23.4; cf. Neh. 13.1). So the gentry held to their alliances with the neighboring peoples and accommodated not only themselves to Judaism, but Judaism to themselves.

Except for Proverbs,[101] these works from the gentry are original compositions, approximately datable and (save for interpolations) expressing consistently the opinions of individual authors. The literary remains of the Levites and the priests, on the other hand, are compilations of old and new material, reedited so often that their make-up is still disputed. This indicates their different *Sitz im Leben*.

From the Levites we have Chronicles-Ezra-Nehemiah, and Psalms, while concerning them we have a body of priestly material in Exodus, Leviticus, and Numbers.[102] In this the work of the Levites is referred to as "mounting the guard" (of the tent-temple) to protect it from impurity.[103] This military terminology and implication of police duty reflect Nehemiah's use of the Levites to enforce his purity and sabbath laws. Beside this they carry about the tent and its utensils, notably the "ark of the covenant." This reflects a Near Eastern practice of carrying in procession a sacred box which represented or housed a deity.[104] The Levitical priests of Jerusalem had thus carried the ark until the seventh century (II Chr. 35.3), and probably from Levitical tradition, the practice was taken over by the synagogue, the box now housing the divine law.[105] Apparently the Levites were active in the general substitution of synagogue service for sacrifice which about this time transformed the Palestinian cult of Yahweh. Hence Chronicles' homiletic material [106] and its representation of the Levites as mission teachers (II Chr. 17) and as interpreters of the law (cf. Nehemiah 8, a synagogue service).

In the temple the Levites attempted to perform some priestly functions but this the priests prevented.[107] Then they lost their their police power and gradually fused with the singers and gatekeepers.[108] Thus the "liturgical Levites" disappear in Chronicles,[109] and in the decree of Antiochus III the Levites have become the singers.[110] The importance of psalms in the synagogue and in Chronicles, as well as the Psalter, reflect this development. The concern of the Psalter for the poor probably reflects not only the poverty of the Levites themselves, but the policy of Nehemiah and the fact that the separatist party relied chiefly on the Jerusalem plebs. The heroes of their party history (Chronicles-Ezra-Nehemiah) are David, who established the Levites, and Nehemiah, who restored them.[111] In the Psalter the Levites produced perhaps the most influential work of Occidental literature—the one book of the Bible which is read in almost every Christian and Jewish service, the daily reading of the most private piety. More than three quarters of the Psalms deal with deliverance by Yahweh, usually from unspecified enemies. The historical identity (if any) of the enemies is a riddle.

By contrast with Levitic material, the priestly Pentateuch is surprisingly self-contradictory.[112] This reflects divisions within the priesthood, of which different members had been prominent in the syncretist and the monolatrous parties.[113] By exiling one contestant for the high priesthood, Nehemiah had helped another, presumably one who would follow the separatist party line and rely for support, after Nehemiah's demise, on the Levites and the plebs. Accordingly in 411, when the Judeans of Elephantine wrote to Jerusalem for help toward the rebuilding of their syncretistic temple, they got no reply from the High Priest Yehohanan.[114] The Levites were at the height of their power. They had the popular support won by Nehemiah; the priesthood was divided and the High Priest dependent on them; many assimilationists had been driven into exile; the new governor, a Persian,[115] would at first be cautious. Here we should date the Levites' attempt to take over priestly functions in the temple. The trouble caused by this attempt probably contributed to the Persian governor's decision to replace Yehohanan by his brother, most likely the brother who had married Sanballat's daughter and had the support of the Samaritan authorities who were friends of the governor. When his move was forestalled by murder of his candidate he revenged himself by a tax on the temple sacrifices. This and the scandal of the murder no doubt contributed to the separatist party's loss of power about the end of the fifth century. However, they still had strong support from the plebs, thanks not only to the memory of Nehemiah and to the Deuteronomic poor laws, but also to the Levites' popular teaching and preaching.

The assimilationists, on regaining control, used moderation. The Levites remained subordinates in the temple, but they remained. Chronicles and Psalms show they reconciled themselves to their priestly superiors. And the priests compiled a new edition of laws and attached legends, substantially the present Pentateuch, [116] which included material from both parties and won the allegiance of both.

Such a compilation, including codes with contradictory rules, presupposes harmonistic exegesis, or interpretation. The exegetes were primarily the priests, the authorities, by grace of the Great King, on questions of cult law. (Pentateuchal law is cult law, the rules to be observed by the worshipers of Yahweh; questions of civil and criminal law are touched only rarely.) However, the separatist party carried on its own exegetic tradition. Chronicles makes the Levites judges (perhaps

398

false) [117] and teachers of the law (II Chr. 17.7 ff.; 35.3, probably true). Relying on such party tradition, even a layman
might contradict a High Priest; Nehemiah had, the Maccabees,
the Essenes, the Pharisees, and the Christians would. This tradition of lay exegesis was to become one of the most important
characteristics of Judaism.

Turning to the text interpreted, the Levites were conciliated
by the inclusion (as an appendix) of their beloved Deuteronomic code with its many provisions on behalf of the poor.[118]
With this came the commandment that the law was to be
studied constantly (6.6 ff., foundation of rabbinic practice)
and the commandment to love Yahweh (6.5, the nexus between the legal and the mystical traditions). Another Deuteronomic element was the limitation of sacrifice to Jerusalem
(12.5 ff.) and the consequent permission of the slaughter of
domestic animals without sacrifice (12.15 ff.) The priests of
the rural shrines of Yahweh, opposing the limitation of sacrifice to Jerusalem, had compiled a counter code and had put
at the head of it (and this emphatic position indicates polemic
purpose) the old prohibition of slaughter without sacrifice.
This "holiness code," too, the priestly editors included in their
collection (Lev. 17–26).

The interests of the editors themselves [119] are represented
by the bulk of the laws: daily ritual and festivals, sacrifices,
tithes, vows and other sources of temple income, purity laws
(by extension, marriage laws). As a hereditary aristocracy,
they prized genealogies and added to the national legend a
framework of bogus ones.[120] Other additions reflect the increased power and pretensions to royalty of the High Priest [121]
(pretensions scarcely possible until the breakdown of Persian
provincial administration in the fourth century, culminating in
the satraps' revolt). Yet others represent the interests of the
assimilationist party: there is lenience toward old popular
rites and, at the same time, new elements, often of Babylonian inspiration, are introduced: every year the sins of the
people shall be laid on a goat to be sent from the temple into
the wilderness for Azazel.[122] There is much more friendliness
toward neighboring peoples.[123] Particularly important is the

development of a new legal concept, that of the "proselyte," the alien who has accepted the law, is subject to all its requirements and enjoys all its benefits. Subjection of resident aliens to the requirements of the cult law had begun with the holiness code,[124] but the privileges of the law (participation in the Israelites' sacrifices, atonement, and purification) were opened to them only now.[125] This made it possible for non-Judeans to be purified. Thus, immediately, the separatist party's objection to intermarriage as pollution was met; and remotely, in the later Hellenistic period, Judaism became a great proselytizing religion and so prepared the audience for Christianity. The immediate consequence proves the date of the legislation: Neither Ezra nor Nehemiah knew of the possibility that alien wives might become proselytes.

The success of the Pentateuch as a compromise code was climaxed by its acceptance in Samaria. To procure this (since the Samaritans must have had their own sacrificial cult of Yahweh), the Deuteronomic rules prohibiting sacrifice outside Jerusalem had to be "explained," but such exegesis had already been developed to reconcile the Deuteronomic with the holiness code. Samaritan acceptance of the Jerusalem code was motivated by political considerations. In the disintegrating empire of Artaxerxes II a Yahwist cult-union of the Judeans and Samaritans would form an important power. However, because of the popular following of the separatists in Judea, such a union could not be secure unless the Samaritans accepted the Jerusalem law. Acceptance was facilitated by the relationship of the ruling families of the two cities [126] and by the relationship of the populations. (Even the authors of Chronicles, when not writing polemic, carelessly referred to the northern Palestinians as "Israelites." [127]) Finally, the Pentateuch was largely composed of works embodying Israelite traditions common to both Samaria and Judea. Its acceptance at most revived some ailing customs, like observance of the sabbath (Neh. 13.15 ff.) and helped kill out others, like sacrificial worship at local shrines. (The local shrine could not compete with the local synagogue; prayer and praise were cheaper than sacrifice, cf. Strabo, *Geography,* 16.2.36.) Enforcement in Samaria was lax; syncretist names continued there to the time of Alexander.[128] From Jerusalem, too, we have several coins of this period bearing male heads and Athenian owls, and one bearing a deity, perhaps Yahweh, in Greek guise, seated on a winged throne and facing a Dionysiac mask.[129]

The political power formed by the new cult union (and indicated by the new coinage) probably allied with Egypt when Tachos, with Spartan support, invaded Palestine in 360.[130] The connection of the Jews with the Spartans may date from this time.[131] Artaxerxes III retook the city in the late 350s and exiled a good many of the anti-Persian party.[132] The books of the prophets, which were being collected about this time, have a rash of more or less interpolated passages denouncing alliance with Egypt *ex eventu*.[133] The change of parties in Jerusalem may have temporarily chilled relations with Samaria.[134] But this was transient. Within twenty years came Alexander and the collapse of Persian rule over Judea.

19

Syria Under the Persians

The history of Syria during the two centuries of Persian rule shows many blank spots. We can follow, principally from the Old Testament, and the documents preserved in it, the fortunes of the Jews under Persian domination, at least as far as religious matters are concerned (see p. 386 ff.); but only a few details of the history of Syria have come down to us, and these more or less by chance. By Syria we mean the territory extending from Poseideumn in the north to the Egyptian border. This is the Fifth *Nomos* (tribute district) of Herodotus, the land connecting Egypt and Mesopotamia; which from the earliest times played an important intermediary role in the history of the Near East.

The principal characteristic of Syria, in terms of geography, is its length; the country stretches for more than 420 miles from the mouth of the Orontes southward into the region below Gaza. Its width is much less, scarcely more than 150 miles at the country's widest point. The most important regions of Syria are as follows: In the north, there is the area between the Mediterranean and the middle Euphrates; this is Syria proper, known in the Hellenistic period as *Seleucis*. Next, to the south, is Coele Syria; the Greek name means "hollow Syria," and is probably a popular-etymological back-formation from an old indigenous name. Furthest south there is Palestine, which takes its name from the ancient Philistines. The coastal strip between Aradus in the north and Acco (the later

Ptolemais) in the south is occupied by the great Phoenician trading towns, of which Byblus, Sidon, and Tyre are the most important.

The demarcation of the different regions of Syria varies a good deal and in many cases is a matter of dispute. For example, the meaning of the term Coele Syria has undergone various changes in the course of time. Originally it signified a very much larger territory, more or less the whole of Syria excepting Phoenicia. In the Hellenistic period Commagene also belonged to Syria—i.e., the region between the Amanus Mountains, the eastern foothills of the Taurus, and the Euphrates. Until the end of the fifth century B.C., however, Commagene in all probability was part of the Persian vassal state of Cilicia. Of its fate in the fourth century nothing is known.

Syria's peoples were as varied as her regions. In the northern part of the Fifth Herodotean *Nomos* lived Aramaeans, who were also to be found in wide areas of Mesopotamia. They were related to the Biblical Canaanites. The population of Palestine was once Canaanite, but when the Israelite tribes occupied the country the Canaanites had had to give way; in many places they had melted into the Israelite population. The Phoenicians were Canaanites pure and simple, and retained the original Canaanite culture.

According to Herodotus, the Fifth *Nomos,* to which Cyprus belonged, had to pay the Persian King an annual tribute of 350 talents. Undoubtedly a large part of this sum was raised by the Phoenician trading cities. The caravan routes from central Asia ended in Phoenicia; and from there, carried on Phoenician ships, the products of Asia (largely metals and spices) and of Phoenicia itself (especially glass and purple dye) reached the entire world.

Soon after the collapse of the Neo-Babylonian (Chaldaean) Empire in 539, Syria had come under the power of the Persians (probably in 534). At first Syria and Phoenicia belonged to the great satrapy of *Babilu û Êbir-nâri* ("Babylonia and the land beyond the river," i.e., Syria). The satrapy proved to be too large to be administered efficiently; the satrap had his headquarters in the old royal city of Babylon, far from Syria.

403

It was decided to detach the territory west of the Euphrates. *Êbir-nâri* (in Aramaic: *Abar-Nahara*) became a separate province with its own satrap.

The satrap resided, it would appear, in the city of Tripolis. The Phoenician city-states were regarded more or less as allies, not as subjects of the Great King. In general the Persian central government did not interfere in their internal affairs. The remainder of Syria was divided into a number of small sub-satrapies (in Greek usually called "hyparchies"). Of these, Samaria, Idumaea, Moabitis, and Ammonitis are attested by the sources.

Abar-Nahara was the satrapy's name in Imperial Aramaic, the official language of Persian administration. Economically it was a highly productive unit. But it was probably not always easy to bring the many peoples of the country—differing in their origins, their history, their religion and, not least, in their economic interests—into a great viable political unit. The Persians, however, were extraordinarily tolerant, and the peoples of Syria received this tolerance, especially in matters of religion, with special gratitude. Although there were occasional revolts (mostly reflecting the Phoenician cities' nostalgia for independence), the Persian administration on the whole succeeded in gaining the Syrians' trust; Syria was integrated into the Empire, and the Persians were able to induce a certain feeling of imperial patriotism. The Syrians took justifiable pride in belonging to an Empire that for generations was a great world power, indeed the only world power of its time.

The Persian satraps put down roots in the country. Syria was governed by the family of Belesys. This family held large tracts of land in the satrapy. Xenophon mentions a castle and a game park belonging to the satrap in the vicinity of Aleppo (Xenophon, *Anabasis,* I, 4, 10). For the Great King, the special value of the Phoenician cities lay in their fleets, which took part in all the great imperial enterprises and, most of the time, with distinction. The Phoenicians fought against the Ionian fleet in the Ionian revolt. They played a decisive part in the battles of Artemisium and Salamis. They fought on the Eurymedon and in Egypt, where they helped defeat the Athenians near Memphis. In Egypt they fought under the command of Megabyzus, who was later appointed satrap of Abarnahara (454?).

Megabyzus was a grandson of the man of the same name who is mentioned as one of the aides of Darius I in the revolt against the Magus Gaumata, the false Smerdis. The grandson was a confidant of Xerxes and was also held in high honor by his successor, Artaxerxes I (465–464 to 424). In 448 he attempted, as satrap of Syria, to free himself from the rule of the Great King. In battle against the King he is said to have performed miracles of valor, but finally decided to reconcile himself with his sovereign. Incidentally, in his revolt he relied heavily on Greek mercenaries, who were valued everywhere in the empire for their military ability.

There is a famous archaeological monument of Phoenicia dating from the first half of the fifth century B.C. This is the sarcophagus of King Eshmunazar of Sidon. Carved from black basalt, it is what is called an anthropoid sarcophagus. It was found more than a hundred years ago, in 1855, in the vicinity of ancient Sidon, the modern town of Saida. It is an unmistakably Egyptianizing work of art. For the historian, however, its primary interest lies in its inscription in Phoenician, the most important part of which reads as follows:

> And furthermore the Lord of Kings gave us Dor and Jaffa, the splendid grain lands that lie in the plain of Sharon, in accordance with the mighty deeds that I did. And we added them to the territory of the country, so that they would belong forever to the Sidonians.

There is much to be said for the view that "mighty deeds" is a reference to the participation of the Phoenicians, especially the Sidonian ships, in the expedition of Xerxes against Hellas in 480.[135] Xerxes (according to the inscription) had as a result assigned to the King of Sidon the fertile fields of the plain of Sharon; this was a gift of particular value to the Sidonians, whose tiny hinterland was unable to feed the city's population. Whether the other Phoenician cities that took part in the war

405

against the Greeks, namely Tyre and Aradus, were similarly rewarded we do not know.

Even in the earlier part of the fifth century, Phoenician art already shows distinct Greek influences, alongside the usual Egyptian motifs. They are a sure sign of the presence of Greek artists in this ancient land. Both heads from the anthropoid sarcophagus of Sidon [136] show features of the contemporary Greek relief sculptor's art. Greek (probably Ionian) sculptors in the Orient are already producing works that contrast sharply with the art of the ancient Near East.

The wide extent of Phoenician trade is attested to by an Athenian decree honoring King Strato of Sidon that has been preserved by chance.[137] This king was roughly contemporary with Nicocles of Cyprus and Philip of Macedon. The Athenians formally conferred *proxenia* (public friendship) on Strato and his descendants; this status carried considerable privileges with it. In the honorary decree we read that the Athenian Council had *symbola* produced; these "diplomatic tokens" (*tesserae hospitales*) were customary in relations between friendly states and states bound to each other by treaties of mutual hospitality. Their function may be compared with that of signet rings (in fact, the Latin word *symbolum* means signet ring). The Athenian decree takes for granted the presence of emissaries traveling back and forth between the two cities.

The most important event in the history of Syria and Phoenicia in the fourth century was the rebellion of Tennes, King of Sidon, in 350 or 349 B.C. For this rebellion there is a comparatively full historical account in the *Universal History* of Diodorus (XVI, 41 ff.), who is able to give many particulars. The revolt evidently had a connection with the attack of Artaxerxes III Ochus on Egypt in 351 (?). What course this campaign in Egypt took cannot be known in detail; the only thing that is certain is that it ended in failure, and so provoked the defection of the great Phoenician trading city. The matter came to a head in the city of Tripolis, situated between Aradus and Byblus. Tripolis had three districts, each lying a stadium apart from the others; they were the quarters of the Aradians, the Sidonians, and the Tyrians.

It was in Tripolis that the Phoenician cities were accustomed to hold the meetings of their joint senate. The story goes that the Persian satraps and generals, who lived in the Sidonian quarter, treated the Sidonians with arrogance. Thus provoked, the Sidonians resolved on rebellion. They made alliance with the Egyptian King Nectanebo II, who had turned back the Persian attack. The rebels destroyed the royal park of the Great King near Sidon, and burned the supplies stored for the provisioning of the Persian cavalry. But the main objects of the Sidonians' rage were Persian officials, who were seized and handed over to the vengeance of the mob.

The Great King massed a considerable army in Babylonia and marched into Phoenicia, with the satraps Belesys of Syria and Mazaeus of Cilicia lending military support. Nectanebo II, for his part, sent 4,000 Greek mercenaries under the command of Mentor of Rhodes to Sidon's support. Mentor and the Phoenicians succeeded in defeating the Persian satraps, who were forced to evacuate much of Phoenicia. The situation was made worse for the Persians by the defection of nine Cypriote princes who made common cause with the Phoenicians. Thus the troubles spread. Even Cilicia and Judea were affected; Jews are said to have been forcibly resettled in Babylonia and in remote Hyrcania on the Caspian Sea. A Babylonian cuneiform tablet tells of prisoners from Sidon (Sidanu) who arrived in Babylon and Susa in October 345. But this date by no means marks the end of the Phoenician revolt.

The Persian King's own forces, when they came before Sidon, far outnumbered the defenders. This led the Sidonian King Tennes to enter into secret negotiations with Artaxerxes III Ochus. Mentor was also initiated into these plans. According to the story, Tennes is supposed to have betrayed 500 of Sidon's most eminent citizens into the Great King's hands. The city was thoroughly prepared to withstand a siege, but now through the treachery of its ruler fell into the power of the Persians. The Sidonians had already burned all their ships to prevent anyone from fleeing the city. When the Persians scaled the walls, and began to burn and loot in the closely packed city, many of the inhabitants together with their families plunged into the flames; no less than 40,000 are said to have lost their lives. But the Great King (so the story goes) was able to profit from the smoking ruins that had once been a proud maritime city: in the rubble was found a large quantity of gold and silver, melted down by the flames of Sidon.

However, the destruction of Sidon does not seem to have been as absolute as we would infer from Diodorus' account (XVI, 45, 5–6), for Sidon was soon inhabited again. The other Phoenician cities also reverted to Persian rule (probably in 344 or 343), though it was to be only for a relatively short time. When Alexander appeared in Syria in 333–332, after the battle of Issus, Sidon gave him a magnificent reception, while Tyre refused to receive the Macedonian within its walls. How Alexander broke the resistance of the Tyrians has been related above (p. 312 f.). Sidon received from Alexander a new king, Abdalonymus. As the name indicates, he was a Phoenician; perhaps this was the prince for whom the famous "Alexander Sarcophagus" was carved, although other names have been suggested by historians.

20

Arabia

"The Arabians were never subject to the Persians, but became their allies when they allowed Cambyses to march across their territory on his way to Egypt (in 525). For if the Arabs had not been well-disposed the Persians would not have been able to invade Egypt." So we read in Herodotus; he also tells us, elsewhere, that on the road to Egypt there was an entrepôt with trading establishments belonging to the King of the Arabs; in a third reference, he mentions that the Arabs were exempt from taxation.[138]

This situation had a history behind it. About the year 735 B.C. the King of Assur appointed one Idib'il governor of the tribes facing the Egyptian frontier and assigned to him fifteen (?) localities (the text is damaged at this point). Were these tribes the forefathers of the Arabs mentioned by Herodotus? Were they descendants of the early stratum of northern Arabs treated in Volume 4 of this series?

When Nehemiah arrived in Judea in 445, with a commission from the Persian court to establish this district as a province and to restore the city wall of Jerusalem, among those who hindered him was an Arab by the name of Geshem (Gashmu, Gusham). From Nehemiah 4.1 it appears that Geshem's tribe lived in the south—in other words, that it had pushed forward from Edom toward the western shore of the Dead Sea.

A fortunate find has been made in the Wadi Tumilat, an ancient point of entry into Egypt south of the coastal route, that gives us more definite information: two silver bowls of Persian workmanship dating from around 400 B.C. The inscription is in Aramaic: "Qainu, son of Geshem, King [or: and King?] of the Qedar." [139] He is probably to be considered not as the Biblical Geshem but as his grandson. In any case the two cannot be taken as unrelated. (One should not wonder at Nehemiah's mentioning Geshem's name without giving him this title, for he does the same with regard to the governor of Samaria.) Instead of "of the Qedar" (i.e., the tribe) the text could also be translated "of Kedar" (the place); the latter, however, was presumably the forerunner of the later and famous city of Petra.[140]

In the oasis of Taima' (Tema) in northwestern Arabia there stood until 1884 (when it was removed to the Louvre) a notable memorial of the overlordship that had once been Assur's and Babylon's and was at that time Persia's. On a stele dating from before 450 there is recounted in Aramaic the story of the god Salm's entry into the city in Assyrian garb and his reception among the city's gods; the inscription also states the revenues of his temple and confirms in his priestly office the son of an Egyptian who himself bears a Babylonian name.[141] Thus, Aramaic prevailed here just as it did in many other regions of the Persian Empire, as the official language of administration. In neighboring Dedan, there is also an Aramaic inscription, a so-called *sgraffito,* scratched into the rock. In addition there are *sgraffiti* and inscriptions from a few decades earlier, among them one on the grave of a king of Dedan, written in a later Dedan variant of the old North Arabian script. But peace did not long endure in Dedan. *Sgraffiti* from the vicinity of Taima' dating from the end of the fifth century tell of a war against Dedan and of a second war in the area nearby.[141] Concerned for its tributes and for the commerce of its subjects, the Persian government appears to have sent a *peha,* or governor, to Dedan at that time, if indeed it had not already done so. The office and the title later passed on to native magnates (cf. Volume 6).

Nagran, "the loveliest valley of the Peninsula," marked the northern boundary of South Arabia for about a millennium. In the villages of this oasis region, and to some extent also in the city of the same name, there dwelt a community called the Amir. We use the word "community" here instead of the usual word "tribe," which could mislead the reader. In the country-side the tribes comprised communes of peasants and herdsmen; in the cities, however, "tribe" designated the inhabitants of a quarter, divided in turn into clans and families. As the word is ordinarily understood, "tribes"—political communities of no-madic herdsmen, mostly camel herders—do not appear in South Arabia until the second century A.D. There were camels among the herds of the Amir and among those of their kindred only, in this area. From these and later indications it may be concluded that they delivered animals for the caravans that carried incense and myrrh to the north (Ghul II 433 ff.).

Two days' journey further to the south lay the oasis of Ragma with a city and many villages. It would be tempting to identify it with the Biblical Rama of Ezek'iel 27.22. Ragma and Nagran appear for the first time in a long inscription (R 3945) in which the Sabaean ruler, Karib'il Watar, writing toward the end of his life, in about 490, enumerates the con-quests that he has made for the honor of his god and the wel-fare of his land. Acting on the word of an oracle, Karib'il Watar had besieged the Minaean cities of Nashan and Nashq for three years until they surrendered. Nashq was added to Saba' on humiliating conditions. To the king of the Minaean city of Kamnah and to the king of Harim—a district that oc-cupied a special position between the Minaean and Sabaean cultures—conquered land was granted as a reward for remain-ing neutral. Now Karib'il took the field against Ragma and Nagran and defeated them. They lost thousands in dead, pris-oners and cattle (even if one or two zeros must be stricken, as often when dealing with passages in the Old Testament and in Assyrian royal inscriptions). Ragma was obliged to pay tribute.

Ma'in lay to the north and northwest of the three other king-doms of southern Arabia, Saba', Qataban, and Hadramaut. (Officially its name was "Ma'in and Yathil," the names of the capital and of the second largest city, although as we have already seen it comprised other cities as well. Even the inhabitants of the capital were called Ma'in, as were the people as a whole. The term "Minaeans," then, is used in this chapter in both these senses.) The country had suffered heavily under the Sabaeans, and remained the latter's vassal or ally until the end of the epoch under consideration.

Ma'in differed from the other kingdoms in the firm position of its monarchy and in its municipal constitution. It was also more dependent than the others upon trade, which increased after the founding of a commercial colony in Dedan, in the middle of the fourth century.[143] It served as a relay station for caravans and was fortified. Later a substation was established fifteen kilometers to the north in the oasis of Ḥigra (Egra, al-Ḥigr), where the route from Taima' joined the incense route.

The Minaeans also had colonies in South Arabia, at Ṣirwaḥ in Saba', in Timma', and in Shabwat (N 82), the latter two being respectively the capitals of Qataban and Ḥaḍramot (Ḥaḍramaut). In Timna' and especially in Dedan there are many examples of the influence of foreign culture on the colonists. The authorities in Dedan held the title of "The Two Presidents of the Colony and of the Minaeans of the Colony." Sabaeans, too, must have stopped there in peacetime for payment of a transit toll; this is indicated by Sabaeanisms on a famous inscription (R 3022). Otherwise they would have had to take the difficult shortcut through Yathrib (Medina) and via Khaibar and Taima' to the country east of the Jordan. All Minaean colonists (or rather their ancestors) came from Yathil and almost all had relatives there.

The earliest Minaean royal inscription [144] dates from the end of the fifth century B.C. It is reproduced here because it is unique; it is divided in three sections:

> (*First section*) 'Ammiyatha' Nabat, son of Abikarib and King of Ma'in, together with the Minaeans and Yathilians, lacerated his countenance and did penance before 'Athtar . . . , because he had removed documents of *certain men* from their temples in the city of Yathil, documents of the

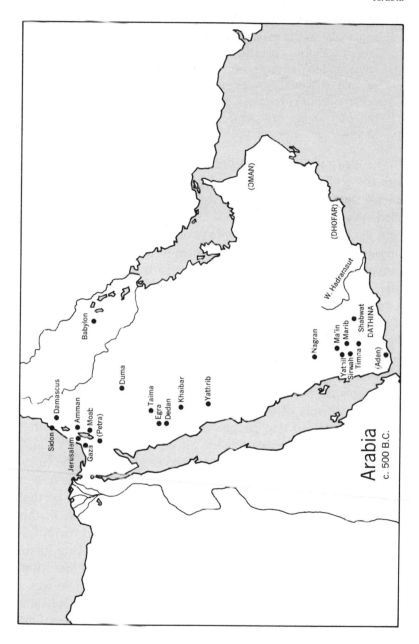

Arabia
c. 500 B.C.

Sidon
Damascus
Amman
Jerusalem Moab
Gaza (Petra)

Babylon

Duma

Taima
Egra
Dedan Khaibar
Yathrib

(OMAN)

(DHOFAR)

W. Hadramaut

Nagran
Ma'in
Marib Shabwat
Yathil DATHINA
Sirwah
Timna
('Aden)

413

Minaeans and of their *gifts* (*second section*) and because he had violated the proclaimed ordinance concerning the banklands of Yathil—in which ordinance he had placed the banklands under the protection of the gods of Ma'in and Yathil, so that it would not be inhabited (*third section*) and because *certain communes* have not troubled themselves about the *gifts* of the *Minaeans* for the lord (Ba'l) of Yathil, for 'Athtar . . . nor for the (other) gods of Ma'in and Yathil.

The lord (Ba'l) of Yathil mentioned at the end is identical with the god 'Athtar mentioned at the beginning. The "banklands" were fields artificially irrigated when the wadis were filled, twice a year, by the streams caused by the monsoon rains. Note that the passage speaks of "their temples," although only one is named. The curious formula appearing in the second section, "placed . . . under the protection of the gods," later constantly appears at the close of votive inscriptions. It is evidence of the Minaeans' and other Southern Arabs' dread of the curse protecting, among their neighbors, documents and the objects guaranteed by them from alteration. In the first and third sections the same occurrence is mentioned—namely, the King's having removed votive offerings together with the related documents from several temples, by agreement with the givers and the receivers of these offerings. To understand the sacrilege that the King had committed, we remind the reader that we have failed to explain why all Minaean colonists came from Yathil. That explanation is to be read between the lines. The rural surroundings of the city of Yathil could no longer produce food enough to feed its growing population, so that the surplus population had to seek a living elsewhere. In this situation the utilization of agriculturally useful land for building purposes was, in Yathil, strictly forbidden. The King, then, by granting an exception in return for a high remuneration, had violated his own ordinance. His reason for doing so was a state of emergency. The Sabaeans had waged a successful campaign in the South and were now preparing an undertaking against the North, so that Ma'in had to mobilize. This was certainly not the first time that the gods' rights had been violated under such circumstances. But this time the wrath of the gods was made manifest. The Minaeans and their allies were defeated. On the return march the Sabaeans besieged Yathil until they had seized all the crops, demolished the irrigation dams and stone sluices, and burned the sluice gates of the canals. It was for this reason that the King marched at the head of a procession of penitents in Yathil and Ma'in, going from temple to temple. Immediately this event was recorded in an inscription for men and gods alike. (The haste with which this was done explains the mistake noted above.) But one other question remains—i.e., the meaning of the reference in the first section to *certain men,* and in the third to *certain communes.* This was done to protect the individuals who had cooperated in the King's sacrilege from specific divine punishment, after they had endured the punishment visited on the community as a whole.

It was a praiseworthy duty for wealthy merchants, and in general for Minacans living abroad, to do something for their country, for example to undertake rebuilding of the fortifications of Ma'in and Yathil. Of course the natives, too—kings, heads of families, judges, priests—endowed similar constructions, usually temples, altars, and irrigation works. Even in the earliest inscription of this kind (R 2771; T 11), dating from about 370 B.C., there is a notice concerning a commercial journey made by the author of the inscription to Egypt, Gaza, and Syria/A'shur,[145] with a copy of an ancient protocol laying down the procedure to be followed in such public works: at the beginning of the inscription the author has to style himself and his family as loyal subjects of the King, which signifies that they have paid their taxes [146] and are not performing good works at public expense. The author then had to undertake and to fulfill a pledge of payment to the god, i.c., to the god's temple. He thereupon delivered to the temple—which functioned as a bank or, at that early date, rather as a barter clearing-house—an amount of crops considerably smaller than his royal harvest tax, and often a tenth of the tithe besides (the tithe on the produce of palm-groves?).[147] Meanwhile the construction proceeded, and was concluded with a sacrifice. Then the King and Council could grant to the donors immunity(?) [148]

and the right to hold office. The King also frequently bestowed land on the donors, a gift that meant expense and trouble for the recipient to begin with and returned gains only later on.

In the inscription mentioned above, the usual procedure was complicated by the fact that the principal donor, his cousins, and their fathers were all in debt to the gods, that is, to the temples. All of them therefore had to be declared free of debt by the Assembly of Ma'in and Yathil before they went before the King and Council.

In Saba' the caste of the Makrab appears to have come to power about the year 510 by a coup of some princes of the royal house under the leadership of Karib'il Watar. Its rule lasted about 200 years. Is "rule" the correct word? If the word is meant in the sense that the rule was exercised by a series of successive princes, this is probably true only for the second generation and one or another of the later generations. With three, presently four, family lines, each of which could offer at least one claimant to the throne at any given time, an orderly royal succession seems to have been impossible. But the land was extensive, and from the royal domains and the conquests of Karib'il the Makrab held so much landed property that the heads of the families were able to rule there without warring among themselves.

The empire that Karib'il had thrown together, in incessant campaigns, gradually withered away. About the year 400, Sumhu-'alay Yanaf [149] undertook a private campaign against the once-allied city of Qataban, as reported by his "intendant" (see below), full of pride at having equipped the troops. First a Makrab, then two of his relatives, seized the royal title. Together with three other princes, they waged a war against Qataban that lasted at least five years (R 3858 [150]). Then there followed a new Karib'il Watar, who did not rule in Marib, however, and therefore resided in Ṣirwaḥ.[151]

In place of the great conqueror had come a great builder, Yada"il Darih. He erected temples to the Sabaean national god Alamqah in Ṣirwaḥ and other places, but above all he built the huge oval wall encircling the Temple 'Auwam near Marib (possibly also the Temple itself?). The wall's eastern portion

416

has been examined only superficially, but the history of the erection of the western part can be followed with the aid of the inscriptions. At Yada"il's death the work was still incomplete. After a long interval an opening was made for the west entrance; after a somewhat shorter interval the western side was elevated, the mausoleum (*nṭà*) on the eastern side was built, and two great pillars (*mḥfd*) were set up before the main entrance. Between 350 and 330 the entire wall was completed, a platform (*mḥy'*) was prepared before the main entrance, and sixteen pillars, in two rows, were fixed into the platform. Before the west gate there were also two pillars. They were all used later in the construction of the entrance hall. Only the last row, erected by one of the three kings,[152] is still standing free. (Note the greater circumference of these pillars.) From the second building period on, those who were responsible for the construction of the temple wall were no longer the Makrab princes, but members of a newly rising class, the "intendants." These men administered the estates of the great princely landowners, and the city of Marib and the Temple 'Auwam.

Qataban was formerly limited to the basin of two wadis that run north and northeast from the South Arabian plateau into the desert. On the eastern wadi, which was settled at a very early date, lay the capital city of Timna', and upstream there were many sizable settlements. The country bordered on Saba' to the northwest, and on Ḥaḍramot to the northeast. Elsewhere it was surrounded by small, politically independent territories. They extended to the southwest as far as a point opposite the modern Aden; to the south they extended through the Datina (which has almost the same name today) to the Indian Ocean. In the southeast, Ausan thrust itself between Qataban and Ḥaḍramot. The capital of Ausan was Wasr (Wusr), and lay to the southeast of Timna', halfway between Timna' and the sea.

Toward the end of the sixth century, when the Sabaean Karib'il Watar began his march of conquest, if not even earlier, a warlike king arose in the land of Ausan. He loved to mock Karib'il, and was his equal in pugnacity and energy, but not in good sense. His initial base of operations was too small, though he endeavored to enlarge it. First he took from Ḥaḍramot the oasis of 'Abadan (near today's Niṣab or Anṣab) and then the oasis of the Wadi Gurdan (Jirdan), thus separating Ḥaḍramot from Qataban. He occupied a part of Qataban, probably the entire south. At the news that Karib'il was invading the south-western corner of Arabia, he made the two immediately threat-ened territories southwest of Qataban cede several towns to him and to his soldiers. Then he marched against the Sabaean, but lost the battle. Karib'il unsettled him with raids deep into the country at his rear. Ignoring the territories nearest him, Karib'il defeated the King of Ausan in Datina and before the gates of the latter's capital, "until he swept away . . . Ausan and its king." Then, in a second campaign, he fell with fire and sword on the territories that he had at first spared. It was a hard peace for the latter. Qataban and Ḥaḍramot got back the oases that had been seized from them. Everything that bor-dered directly or indirectly on Saba' was annexed by Karib'il, so that all that remained was a king without a country (R 3945).

The Sabaean military hegemony could not be maintained in the long run. Qataban allied itself with some of the subject states; the two Sabaean campaigns (see p. 411 and note 150) were unable to arrest the natural course of events. All these countries came gradually under the rule of Qataban, Ausan too, which soon after its conquest had again become inde-pendent. It is true that this situation appears first in the proto-col of a ruler of the first half of the second century B.C.[153] But this cannot be regarded as a *terminus ad quem,* for such a thing otherwise does not occur in the protocol. Down to about the year 350 four kings of Qataban are known, though their titles happen to be missing. Then there appear side by side a Makrab, son of the *last* ruler, and a king's son who is himself a king; then both appear on the same inscription.[154] The title of Makrab, then, appears to be a late borrowing from the Sabae-ans (to designate a prince not entitled to the throne?). Of similar origin seems to be the principle of the division of pow-ers, but only between two persons.

Ḥaḍramot was, and is, actually a wadi running parallel to

but remote from the coast of the Indian Ocean. The kingdom of the same name, however, extended on both sides of the valley, to the west and east. Its capital, Shabwat, lay near the border of Qataban. In language, education, and art, the land lagged behind others in South Arabia and was open to Sabaean influence, transmitted through a colony in Shabwat.[155] The incense country far to the east flourished under the protection of the kings of Ḥaḍramot.

On the maps the incense country bears the name Dhofar (Ẓafar), which properly signifies a city. Today the area belongs to Oman, although it is separated from the latter by a wide expanse of steppes and sandy desert. It is the only region of Arabia with tropical vegetation. On its coast grows the coconut palm (as Ibn Baṭṭūṭah reported as early as 1331).[156] The slopes of the high mountains enclosing the coastal plain are thickly wooded. A great waterfall descends from these heights, and in the rolling terrain of the high valleys there are fertile meadows. Near the watershed, where this paradise changes into desert plateaus of red sandstone, lies the zone of incense; [157] the zone of myrrh once extended from Ḥaḍramot to Qataban. Resins, incense, and myrrh all come from shrubs that grow to a man's height. Here, at the edge of the desert wastes, was the treasure that nourished the civilization of southern Arabia.

Conclusion

The two hundred years of Persian and Greek history from 520 to 323 B.C. mark the highest point in the cultural history of the ancient world. During this period, in the fifth century above all, Greek drama, art, and historiography touched heights that have never been equaled, much less surpassed by later generations of men.

These brilliant achievements are linked inseparably with the Greek institution of the *polis*—both city-state and community in one. Originating about 800 B.C. the polis, too, reached the peak of its development in the fifth century. The polis required the concentration of political life within extremely narrow geographical bounds; but it also showed a marked receptivity to cultural influences from every source. The city was the home of innumerable artists and thinkers, almost all of whom played their personal part in the political life of the community as good citizens. The polis was identical with its *politai*, its citizens, and this identity was at one and the same time its basic strength and weakness. The idea of self-government by free citizens was realized for the first time in the polis. It was against this background, drawing strength and inspiration from these institutions, that the Athenians in the Age of Pericles created, in politics and art, models for all mankind.

But the art of politics demands moderation, and this was something that many of the successors of Pericles were unable to practice. The greatness of Athens was destroyed by this; the stage was set for the downfall of Greece. Hubris had replaced restraint in many places in Greece, and the political ethics essential to any civilized people now withered away among the Greeks. The obvious example of this is the career of the daring —too daring—Alcibiades. From the end of the Peloponnesian War the Greek city-state was visibly and irreversibly ill; in the latter part of the fourth century, it was forced out of political existence by monarchy. Alexander had succeeded in conquering the Persian Empire, and erecting in the East an absolute monarchy that took its character from both Macedonian and Persian tradition; this was the shape of the future for the Greek world.

The Persian Empire, too, was a civilized state with an excellent administrative system, based on feudal ties. In the structure of the state and in the composition of society, loyalty between lords and vassals played a decisive role. These ethical ties must never be overlooked, for they give the life of the Persians its essential content. The Northeast Iranians' bitter resistance to Alexander shows that these were no empty obligations. The foreign peoples of the Persian Empire—Babylonians, Phoenicians, Lydians, Egyptians, Jews, and others—were allowed to cultivate all their own peculiar national gifts, and they gratefully acknowledged the opportunity. But the Persian Empire, like the Greek city-state, began to stagnate for lack of fresh energies and new ideas. This condition became clearly visible under Artaxerxes II Mnemon (404 to 359–358); the Persian state was about to meet its destiny.

What of the fates and lives of men as individuals—Greeks, Persians, and others—who lived within the spheres of influence of the two nations? Were they able to lead a life that fulfilled their capabilities? As far as the Greeks of the classical period are concerned, it is clear that they were. To live according to one's own will, according to one's own definition of the good life—this was the Greek idea of liberty. The Greeks made sacrifices in defense of this in the Persian War, but these sacrifices brought their own reward. Countless Greeks were able to develop their gifts to the fullest, and many of them made imperishable contributions to politics, art, and science as a result.

The Age of Pericles was a golden age not only for Athens and its citizens, but also for many other people in the Greek world. But we learn little about the lower classes of the Greek people; and the same, with minor exceptions, is true for the population of the Achaemenid Empire.

All of this was altered by the work of Alexander: not restricted, but expanded. His victory over the Persians opened a new world to the Greeks and Macedonians without depriving the defeated peoples of the liberty to live their own way. Independence and autonomy, the two pillars of the Greek city-state, were greatly limited to be sure; in the unequal struggle between the polis and the monarchy, royal government won decisively and permanently. But the great expanse of Alexander's empire, with its inexhaustible economic, military, and scientific opportunities, gave an entirely new aspect to the world of the Greeks. Greek culture and Greek life now had a dazzling new scope. The admirable achievements of the Greek city-states were crowned by the founding of Alexander's empire.

What the Greeks created in the age of the city-state was not done in vain. The monarchies of the East that emerged from Alexander's empire carried on their work: the Hellenistic culture that resulted was to transmit the Greek spirit to the Roman and the Christian world. Our ideas of humanism and humanity are still essentially Greek. While Western civilization endures, the Greek spirit will not cease to live, and work, and help to make us men.

Notes

Chapter 16

1. Dittenberger-Purgold, *Inschriften von Olympia,* No. 14 (Moretti, *Iscrizione agonistiche,* 1953, No. 13).
2. *Inscriptiones Graecae* I², 329.
3. For the recent literature on the subject see H. Bengtson, *Griechische Geschichte,* 2d ed., 1960, p. 279; refer also to H. Berve, "Dion," *Abhandlungen der Akademie . . . Mainz,* 10 (1956), pp. 7 ff.
4. For a general history of the Persians see A. T. Olmstead, *History of the Persian Empire,* Chicago, 1948.
5. General works on Egyptian history, with chapters on the late period: A. Wiedemann, *Aegyptische Geschichte* (Gotha, 1884); E. Drioton-J. Vandier, *L'Égypte* (Paris, 1962). For more detailed studies of the Saïte and Persian periods: A. Wiedemann, *Geschichte Aegyptens von Psammetich I bis auf Alexander der Grosse* (Leipzig, 1880); F. K. Kienitz, *Die politische Geschichte Aegptens vom 7. bis zum 4. Jahrhundert vor der Zeitwende* (Berlin, 1953).
6. For studies of Egypt during the Persian period: G. Posener, *La Première Domination Perse en Egypte* (Cairo, 1936); F. K. Kienitz, *op. cit.;* E. Bresciani, *La Satrapia d'Egitto* (Studi Classici e Orientali, VII) (Pisa, 1958), pp. 132 ff. For studies of the relations between Greece and Egypt: D. Mallet, *Les rapports des Grecs avec l'Egypte de la conquète de Cambyses (525) à celle d'Alexandre (332)* (Cairo, 1922); F. K. Kienitz, *op. cit.*
7. G. Posener, *op. cit.,* note 3; discussion on pp. 171 ff. concerning the behavior of Cambyses; also: A. Klasens, "Cambyses en Egypte," *Ex Oriente Lux* (1946), pp. 339 ff.

8. G. Posener, *op. cit.*, note 4.
9. *Ibid.*, note 5.
10. *Ibid.*, note 1; G. Botti-Romanelli, *Le Sculture del Museo Gregoriano greco-egizio* (Vatican City, 1951), p. 33, Plate 28.
11. A. E. Cowley, *Aramaic Papyri of the Fifth Century B.C.,* (Oxford, 1928), note 30 (13–14).
12. W. Spiegelberg, *Die sog. demotische Chronik des Pap. 215 der Bibliothèque National zu Paris* (Leipzig, 1914), pp. 32–33.
13. F. K. Kienitz, *op. cit.,* pp. 52–54.
14. *Ibid.,* p. 85.
15. W. Spiegelberg, *op. cit.,* pp. 30–32; E. Meyer, *Aegyptische Dokumente aus der Perserzeit,* Vol. II (Sitzungsbericht d. Preuss. Akademie d. Wissenschaften, 1915), pp. 304 ff.
16. As described by N. Reich, "The codification of the Egyptian Laws by Darius and the origin of the 'Demotic Chronicle,' " *Mizraim* I, 1933, pp. 78 ff. For another interpretation see E. Seidl, *Aegyptische Rechtsgeschichte der Saïten und Perserzeit* (1956), p. 60.
17. On the "houses of life" see H. Gardiner, "The House of Life," *Journal of Egyptian Archaeology,* 24 (1938), pp. 157 ff.
18. On the temple of El Khargeh, E. Winlock-Davies, *The Temple of Hibis in El Khargeh,* I, New York, 1941.
19. W. Spiegelberg, *Drei dem. Schreiben aus der Korrispondenz des Pherendates des Satrapen Darius I mit dem Chnum Priestern von Elephantine* (S. B. Berlin, 1928), pp. 604 ff.
20. G. Posener, *op. cit.,* pp. 180–181; F. K. Kienitz, *op. cit.,* p. 65.
21. G. Posener, *op. cit.,* notes 8, 9, and 10.
22. G. R. Driver, *Aramaic Documents of the Fifth Century B.C.* (Oxford, 1954), V, 6; VII, 1–4; VIII, 2.
23. On the Hebrew colony at Elephantine, the temple and its destruction, see E. G. Kraeling, *The Brooklyn Museum Aramaic Papyri* (New Haven, 1953), pp. 41 ff., pp. 100 ff.
24. *Ibid.*
25. *Ibid.,* p. 111.
26. See E. Bresciani, *La Satrapia d'Egitto, op. cit.*
27. The satrap possessed considerable wealth in Egypt which was managed by a *peqid,* who supplied the satrap with his

income: for this detail of the administration of the satrapy, see the documents for the satrap Arsames (454–404 B.C.) in G. R. Driver, *op. cit.*

28. H. H. Schaeder, *Iranische Beiträge*, I (1930), p. 202.
29. See note 15.
30. G. Posener, *op. cit.*, p. 178.
31. Published by J. D. Cooney, "The Portrait of an Egyptian Collaborator," *Bulletin of the Brooklyn Museum*, 15 (1953), pp. 1–16.
32. Published in *Recueil des Travaux*, 21 (1899), pp. 67–68.
33. Mentioned only in the Aramaic papyrus published by E. Bresciani: *"Papiri aramaici egiziani di epoca persiana* presso il Museo Civico di Padova," *Rivista degli Studi Orientali,* 35 (Rome, 1960), pp. 11 ff.
34. F. Griffith, *Catalogue of the demot. Papyri in the John Rylands Library,* III (1909), IX.
35. E. G. Kraeling, *op. cit.*, pp. 36–37.
36. E. Seidl, *Aegyptische Rechtsgeschichte der Saïten und Perserzeit,* 1956.
37. Fundamental to the argument: R. Yaron, *Introduction to the Law of the Aramaic Papyri* (Oxford, 1961), particularly pp. 114 ff.
38. On the Aramaic letters found at Western Hermopolis see M. Kamil, in the *Bulletin de l'Institut d'Égypte,* 28 (1947), p. 256.
39. E. Bresciani, *La Satrapia d'Egitto,* pp. 150–151.
40. On the shipyards: N. Aimé-Giron, *Textes araméens d'Égypte* (Cairo, 1931), pp. 12 ff.
41. E. Bresciani, *Papiri aramaici egiziani di epoca persiana,* 1.c.
42. J. J. Rabinowitz, "Aramaic Inscriptions of the Fifth Century B.C. from a North Arab Shrine in Egypt," *Journal of Near Eastern Studies* (1956), pp. 2 ff.
43. A. Segré, "Circolazione Tolemaica e Pretolemaica in Egitto," *Rivista Italiana di Numismatica* (1920), pp. 6 ff.; E. G. Kraeling, *op. cit.*, pp. 38–40.
44. See E. Bresciani, *La Satrapia d'Egitto,* pp. 177 ff. (archaeological appendix).
45. A. Erman, *Die Religion der Aegypter* [3] (Berlin, 1934). Ch. 19.
46. Published by S. R. K. Glanville, *The Instructions of Onchsheshonqy (Catalogue of Demotic Papyri in the British Mu-*

seum, Vol. II) (London, 1955); cf. S. Donadoni, *Storia della letteratura egiziana antica* (Milan, 1957), pp. 308–310.

47. For the most acute analysis of the subject: B. Von Bothmer and H. de Meulenaere, "Egyptian Sculpture of the Late Period," *The Brooklyn Museum* (1960), pp. 78–79, 81–82.

48. Cooney, *op. cit.,* p. 6.

49. The statue of Ptah-hotep in the Brooklyn Museum wears a necklace of the Persian type as does the statue (of which only the torso remains) described by G. Botti, "Busto di un dignitario della XXVII dinastia nel Museo Egizio di Firenze," *Bolletino d'arte del Min. Publ. Istruz.,* 2 (1956), pp. 1–3. The statute of Ptah-hotep and the statue of Ugiahor-resne in the Vatican Museum also wear Persian bracelets.

50. E. Bresciani, *La Satrapia d'Egitto* (archaeological appendix).

51. J. D. Cooney, "The Lions of Leontopolis," *Bulletin of the Brooklyn Museum,* 15 (1953), pp. 17 ff.; A. Roes, "Achae-menid Influence upon Egyptian and Nomad Art," *Artibus Asiae,* 15 (1952), pp. 21 ff.

52. A. Roes, *op. cit.,* p. 19.

53. G. Posener, *op. cit.,* p. 190, note 2. For the influence of Egyptian architecture on that of Persia, see Parrot-Chipiez, *Histoire de l'art dans l'Antiquité,* pp. 513, 885–887; Dieula-foy, *L'art antique de la Perse,* 5, 198.

54. F. K. Kienitz, *op. cit.,* pp. 76 ff. A demotic text, the so-called Demotic Chronicle (W. Spiegelberg, *op. cit.*) describes the last three dynasties in a prophetic manner. See Kienitz, *op. cit.,* pp. 136 ff.

55. B. Von Bothmer and H. de Meulenaere, *op. cit.,* pp. 95 ff.

56. The most recent and penetrating examination: E. Will, "Cha-brias et les finances de Tachos," *Revue des Etudes An-ciennes,* 62 (1960), pp. 254 ff.

57. F. K. Kienitz, *op. cit.,* p. 107

58. *Ibid.,* pp. 185 ff.

59. *Ibid.,* p. 189.

60. *Ibid.,* p. 111.

Chapter 18

61. ANET (J. B. Pritchard, *Ancient Near Eastern Texts* [2] Prince-ton, 1955), 316 a–b.

62. S. Cook, *The Religion of Ancient Palestine in the Light of*

Archaeology (London, 1930) (Schweich Lectures, 1925), pp. 41–71, esp. 57, 63, 70 and 82 f.; Y. Aharoni, "Excavations at Ramath Rahel," *Biblical Archaeologist,* 24 (1961), pp. 104 ff.

63. B. Maisler, "Gole Yisra'el be Gozan," *Yedi 'ot hahebrah ha'ibrit lehaqirat Erez Yisra'el,* 15 (1950), pp. 83 ff.

64. A. E. Cowley, *Aramaic Papyri of the Fifth Century B.C.* (Oxford, 1923) No. 30; E. G. Kraeling, *The Brooklyn Museum Aramaic Papyri* (New Haven, 1953), pp. 42 ff., 82 ff., 86. Jeremiah 44.15 ff.; Isaiah 19.19.

65. S. Daiches, *The Jews in Babylonia at the Time of Ezra and Nehemiah* (London, 1910), pp. 21 ff.; Ezekiel 14.1 ff; 20.31; Zechariah 5.5 ff.; Ezra 8.17 (?). In spite of Daiches' apologetics, the implications of the names are unmistakable.

66. E. Bickerman, "The Altars of Gentiles," *Revue internationale des droits de l'antiquité,* 3ᵉ série, 5 (1958), pp. 137 ff. Bickerman's contention that "Jews" did not participate in this worship is not convincing.

67. A. E. Cowley, *Papyri,* Nos. 30 and 31.

68. Ezra 4.1; 6.19 f.; 8.35 etc.; also simply "the exiles," 9.4; 10.6; Zech. 6.10. This and the following references are to the Hebrew Bible.

69. Neh. 10.31 f., cp. 13.25; Ezra 4.4; cf. 6.21 and Neh. 10.29. In preexilic documents the term meant simply "the citizen body," and this earlier use occasionally survived, cf. R. de Vaux, *Les Institutions de l'Ancien Testament,* 2d ed., 2 vols. (Paris, 1960–1961), Vol. I, p. 112.

70. E.g., Sheshbazzar's name (Ezra 1.8, etc.) testifies to at least his parents' worship of Sin or Shamash: W. Albright, *The Biblical Period from Abraham to Ezra* (New York, 1963), p. 86, vs. M. Noth, *Geschichte Israels,* 4th ed. (Göttingen, 1959), p. 279.

71. II Kings 23; Ezekiel 8. The things here reported could not have happened in the temple without the cooperation of the priesthood.

72. Zech. 9–14 are generally recognized to be spurious.

73. Haggai 2.23; Zech. 6.9 ff. (on which see below).

74. Text extremely corrupt. Basic is the commentary by J. Wellhausen, *Die Kleinen Propheten,* 3d ed. (Berlin, 1898), followed, with minor variations, by O. Eissfeldt, *Einleitung in das Alte Testament,* 2d ed. (Tübingen, 1956), p. 529; Noth, *Geschichte,* p. 282, etc.

75. *Mishnah, Abodah Zarah* 3.6 may show a survival.

76. Ezra 6.21; c. Nehemiah 10.29.

77. 4.2b is clearly polemic invention: The Samaritans were not the Assyrian importees of 200 years before. So too 4.9b–10, likewise based on II Kings 17.24–41. Another line of polemic appears in 9.1f. The editor has put Zerubbabel's rebuff in the reign of Cyrus to explain the "interruption" of the building from ca. 537 to 520, and collected after it hostile reports about the Judeans, down to the time of Artaxerxes (4.6–23). The "interruption" is an invention to reconcile the tradition of the return under Cyrus with the fact of the rebuilding under Darius.

78. Zech. 11.14 according to codices 62 and 147 of the Septuagint.

79. See J. Wellhausen, *Die Kleinen Propheten, ad loc.* Zech. 14.14 is probably a reminiscence of this passage. The statement in I Esdras 4.45 (text B), that the Judeans burned the temple, is probably textually corrupt, read "the Idumeans," cf. vs. 50.

80. Ezra 4.12, 15, 19. The revolts against the Babylonians, over two centuries earlier, would hardly have figured in Persian records; 4.15d and 20 are editorial.

81. Prophecy continued (Neh. 6.7, 9–14) and some later prophecies got into the canon as interpolations or as pseudonymous works, e.g., Jonah, Daniel.

82. F. Heichelheim, "Ezra's Palestine and Periclean Athens," *Zeitschrift für Religions und Geistesgeschichte,* 3 (1951), pp. 251 ff.

83. Ezra is perhaps the most controversial figure of the Old Testament. See W. Rudolph, *Esra und Nehemiah* (Tübingen, 1949). It is here assumed that the original story of Ezra is contained in (roughly) Ezra 7–8, Nehemiah 8, and Ezra 9–10; cf. Eissfeldt, *Einleitung,* pp. 676 ff.

84. For similar Persian reform of religious institutions in Egypt, see G. Posener, *La première domination perse en Egypte* (Cairo, 1936), p. 22; A. E. Cowley, *Papyri,* No. 21.

85. Nehemiah 8.2, 13 ff.; 9.1; cf. de Vaux, *Institutions* II, p. 419; M. Noth, *Geschichte,* pp. 302 ff.

86. At least Nehemiah 1–7.5a and 13.4–31 are parts of the genuine "memoirs" of Nehemiah; cf. O. Eissfeldt, *Einleitung,* p. 676.

87. Party support appears in 2.12; 5.8 ("We" are the diasporic Jews of the monolatrous party).
88. 3.5, 4.4. The passive resisters were of the gentry.
89. 5.14 ff. Note the absence of the gentry (*horim*) from the list of guests, cf. 5.7; 6.17, etc.
90. II Macc. 1.18; Isaiah 56.5; Sirach 49.13d; Neh. 2.8; cf. Ezra 6.14 (the temple not completed till the time of Artaxerxes).
91. Doubtless he had to earn this support by living down the record of Ezra and showing that a member of the monolatrous party could make himself a popular governor of Jerusalem and keep the city both tranquil and loyal.
92. 13.25 '*Akkeh* probably refers to flogging, not execution, since the hair-pulling follows it as something worse.
93. A. E. Cowley, *Papyri*, No. 30.
94. E. Kraeling, *Brooklyn Papyri*, pp. 82 ff., especially 88.
95. A. E. Cowley, *Papyri*, No. 30.
96. For the interpretation and dating of the works discussed in this paragraph, see the relevant passages in Eissfeldt, *Einleitung*, and R. Pfeiffer, *Introduction to the Old Testament*, 2d ed. (New York, 1953).
97. Discussed by H. Kallen, *The Book of Job as a Greek Tragedy* (New York, 1918). Neither in the case of Job nor in that of Ecclesiastes (below) is there reason to suppose any literary relationship between the similar works.
98. Now disfigured by innumerable pious interpolations.
99. On these, M. Braun, *History and Romance in Graeco-Oriental Literature* (Oxford, 1938).
100. Eccl. 7.16; 8.14 ff.; 9.7 f.
101. Proverbs in this, as in many respects, resembles the *corpus Theognideum*.
102. On the Levites the essential works are still W. von Baudissin, *Die Geschichte des alttestamentlichen Priesterthums* (Leipzig, 1889), and G. Hölscher, "Levi," *Paulys Real-Encyclopädie*, 12 (1925), cols. 2155 ff.
103. Num. 1.53; 18.3; cf. 4.3, 23, 30; 8.24, etc. W. von Baudissin, *Geschichte*, pp. 33 ff.
104. S. Cook, *Religion*, pp. 164 ff.
105. S. Cook, *Religion*, pp. 214 ff.; E. Goodenough, *Jewish Symbols in the Greco-Roman Period*, 9 vols. (to date) (New York, 1953 ff.), indices, s.v., Torah Shrine.
106. On this see G. von Rad, "Die levitische Predigt in den

Büchern der Chronik," *Festschrift Otto Procksch* (Leipzig, 1934), pp. 113 ff.

107. Numbers 16. The forgotten study of H. Vogelstein, *Der Kampf zwischen Priestern und Leviten* (Stettin, 1889), contains the most interesting attempt to organize historically the polemic and related passages of Chronicles and the priestly pentateuchal material. See also Pfeiffer, *Introduction,* pp. 264 and 795–801.

108. The stages of the fusion are traced by G. Hölscher, "Levi," 2185 ff.

109. H. Vogelstein, *Der Kampf zwischen Priestern und Leviten,* p. 84.

110. Josephus, *Antiquities,* 12.142.

111. W. Rudolph, *Chronikbücher* (Tübingen, 1955), VIII ff., also G. von Rad, *Das Geschichtsbild des chronistischen Werkes* (Stuttgart, 1930).

112. Cf., e.g., Ex. 20.24 and Dt. 12.4 ff.; Lev. 17.1 and Dt. 12.20 ff.; Ex. 21.7 and Dt. 15.12; Ex. 12.9 and Dt. 16.7; Dt. 14.22–29 and Num. 18.21–24; Lev. 10.14 and Dt. 18.3.

113. Monolatrous, Hilkiah (II Kings 22.8 ff.); Ezra. Snycretist, cf. above, note 11, later Joshua (Zech. 3.3 ff.), Eliashib (Neh. 13.4 ff., 28).

114. A. E. Cowley, *Papyri,* No. 30; Josephus, *Antiquities,* 11.297 ff. Yehohanan is Ioannes (Neh. 12.10 Yonathan; 12.22 Yohanan).

115. *Id.* (Bigvai-Bagoas).

116. The forms the compilation took in its earlier stages are disputed; with the accounts in O. Eissfeldt, *Einleitung,* and R. Pfeiffer, *Introduction;* cf. M. Noth, *Überlieferungsgeschichte des Pentateuch* (Stuttgart, 1948). The official form in the fourth century must have been that which the Samaritans and Jews now have in common.

117. H. Vogelstein, *Der Kampf zwischen Priestern und Leviten,* p. 70; W. von Baudissin, *Die Geschichte des alttestamentlichen Priesterthums,* p. 165.

118. The devotion of the Levites to Deuteronomy has been demonstrated by G. von Rad, *Das Geschichtsbild des chronistischen Werkes.*

119. On the priestly material in general see especially G. von Rad, *Die Priesterschrift im Hexateuch* (Berlin, 1934).

120. Cf. the similar fashion in Greece, represented by, e.g., Hecataeus of Miletus and Pherecydes.

121. R. de Vaux, *Institutions,* I, pp. 162, 175, 320; II, pp. 241, 267, 270 ff.
122. Id. II, pp. 415 ff.
123. G. von Rad, *Die Priesterschrift im Hexateuch,* pp. 21–28, on Gen. 17.1–27; 27.46; and 28.1–9.
124. Lev. 17.8–15; 18.26; 20.2; 22.18; 24.16; 25.47–54.
125. Ex. 12.43–50; Num. 9.14; 15.1–31.
126. Completion of the deal may have been celebrated by further family alliances, which helped Josephus to confuse events in the reigns of Artaxerxes I and III; cf. *Antiquities* 11.302 ff., F. Cross, "The Discovery of the Samaria Papyri," *Biblical Archaeologist,* 26 (1963), pp. 115 ff.
127. II Chr. 30.5, 25; 35.18. Zechariah still prophesied to "the house of Israel" as well as "the house of Judah" (8.13).
128. F. Cross, "The Discovery of the Samaria Papyri," p. 115.
129. E. Goodenough, *Jewish Symbols in the Greco-Roman Period,* Vol. I, 270 f. and III, Nos. 668–670.
130. Diodorus, *Bibliotheca Historica,* 15.92.2; Nepos, XII (Chabrias), 2.3; Plutarch, *Agesilaus,* 36 ff.
131. The letter in I Macc. 12.19 ff. is a fake, but the tradition was established before Maccabean times, II Macc. 5.9.
132. E. Schürer, *Geschichte des jüdischen Volkes im Zeitalter Jesu Christi,* 3d–4th eds., 3 vols. (Leipzig, 1901–1909), Vol. III, pp. 7 ff. E. Bickerman, *From Ezra to the Last of the Maccabees* (New York, 1962), pp. 11 f. and note 8, connects the capture with that of Sidon reflected by the Babylonian docket translated in S. Smith, *Babylonian Historical Texts* (London, 1924), pp. 148 f.
133. Is. 19; 20 (esp. 5f.); 30.1–5; 31.1–3, cf. 36.6, 9 and II Kgs. 18.21, 24; Jer. 2.18 f.; 24.9; 37.7; 42; 43; 44; 46; Ezek. 17.26 ff.; 29 (esp. 16); 30; 31; 32.
134. This may account for Josephus' location here of the building of the temple on Gerizim, *Ant.* 11.321 ff. (The temple made no legal difference; what the law forbade was sacrifice.)

Chapter 19

135. W. Galling, *Zeitschr. des Deutschen Palästina-Vereins,* 79 (1963), pp. 140 ff.
136. One head is today in the Ny Carlsberg Glyptothek in Copenhagen, the other (found at Sakkara) in Berlin: see W. Otto

(ed.), *Handbuch der Archäologie,* I, Tafelband, p. 197, 1 and 2.

137. Dittenberger *Sylloge Inscriptionum Graecarum,* I³, No. 185.

Chapter 20

138. Herodotus III, 88.4–5, 91. This geographical indication (to which we must add, of course, a hinterland of unknown extent) agrees with the position of Arabia among the conquered lands given in the royal inscription of Persepolis and Naksh-i-Rustam, from the time of Cambyses' successor Darius.

139. See, for example, W. F. Albright, "The Biblical Tribe of Massa' and Some Congeners . . . ," *Estratto da Studi Orientalistici in onore di Giorgio Levi della Vida,* I (Rome, 1956), p. 12, n. 4.

140. Compare Qedar in the lists of hierodules from Ma'in (see chapter on Arabia in the following volume of this series) with Agatharchides, §87.

141. M. Lidzbarski, *Handbuch der nordsemitischen Epigraphik* (Weimar, 1898; Hildesheim, 1962), I, p. 447, II, Tafel p. 27; G. A. Cooke, *A Text-Book of North-Semitic Subscriptions* (Oxford, 1903), p. 69; R. Dussaud, *La pénétration des Arabes en Syrie avant l'Islam* (Paris, 1955), p. 176.

142. On Dedan, see Werner Caskel, "Lihyan und Lihyanisch," *Arbeitsgemeinschaft für Forschung des Landes Nordrhein-Westfalen, Geisteswiss. Heft 4 (Abh.) (Köln-Opladen,* 1954), p. 37, in which, however, the dates must now be corrected; in addition, a second king has been discovered. For what follows, see A. van den Branden, *Les textes thamoudéens de Philby, 2 vols.* (Lyons, 1956), 266a, ac, ag (if the text has been correctly read).

143. A. Janssen and R. Savignac, *Mission archéologique en Arabie, mars-mai 1907. De Jérusalem au Hedjaz. Médaïn Saleh. II: El-' Ela, d' Hégra à Teima, Harrah de Tebouk* (Publ. de la Société française des fouilles archéologiques), Texte et Atlas (Paris 1909, 1914, appeared 1920), 324, pls. XCIV, CXXXVIII (erroneously given as Lihyanic: J. Pirenne, Paléographie des inscriptions sud-Arabes . . . , te. I (Brussels, 1956), p. 98 [hereafter cited as Pirenne, I]). This inscription should be attributed to the descendants of a family long settled on the spot, as its script is archaic.

144. *Répertoire d'épigraphie sémitique publié par la Commission du C.I.S.,* tes. V–VII, rédigés par G. Ryckmans (hereafter cited as R.), 2980 = A. Fakhry, *An Archeological Journey to Yemen,* 1, 2: G. Ryckmans, *Epigraphical Texts,* 3 (Cairo, 1951 1952), 14. J. Pirenne, I, 257–260, had the merit of recognizing that this inscription must be combined with R. 3943. I disagree, however, with the translations of both.

145. See Eduard Schwartz, *Philogogus,* 86 (1931), pp. 373–399.

146. Similarly Ghul, *BSOAS,* 22 (1959), p. 17. Mahmad 'Ali Ghul was the first (unknowingly) to break with the traditional view of this genre of sources, on the basis of his outstanding knowledge of the Koran and the Islamic legal tradition; since then, new texts and fragments have increased the material at our disposal. We can now add that all land not in the possession of the temples was royal land.

The traditional view of these inscriptions was that they indicated that donors *collected* (not paid) royal taxes: the erroneousness of this is shown by the fact that all, with one exception (R. 3022), were private persons, not officials. One must accept Conti Rossini's conclusion (see note 147, below) that donations in the amount of one tenth of a tithe of the harvest are involved. If the resulting sum seems inadequate to cover the cost of the relevant construction, we may bear in mind that, in this particular case, twelve persons other than the author of the inscription ("his men") are jointly concerned in the donation—i.e., there are thirteen tenths of a tithe available, not one tenth. We may also conclude, from the evidence mentioned above, that *far'* cannot mean "first fruits," as these would be too inconsiderable for anything as expensive as the financing of a construction; we must therefore take the term in its original sense of "harvest." Finally, the distinction between donation and recompense was previously misunderstood, so that the donors were thought to be local administrators, as indicated by their supposed responsibility for tax collection.

On the second of the privileges awarded donors (on the first, see note 148 below), it should be remarked that *sšr'* merely denotes the capacity to hold public office, as is obvious from his errors in the inscription R. 3022. The donors are, in this case, actually officials.

The first clause of the financial statement reads: *bkbwdt'ktrb'* . . . *'Attar/'hl/sbrr*—i.e. "by a vow [of payment], for which he remains responsible to 'Athtar." This responsibility could, however, be discharged by fulfillment of the remaining payments. If this were not done, the responsibility would descend from father to son; and if sons, too, proved unable to pay, as by reason of bad harvest or a loss in trade, then "the transaction will be extended" (as in the case given in the text, pp. 413–14). "Free and slave," at the end of the inscription, is merely a rhetorical collective term, and should not be translated literally.

147. *fr`* (R. 2774: *fr`hy*) *fr`s*, which, according to its form (so C. Conti Rossini, *Chrestomathia arabica meridionalis,* Rome, 1931, p. 220) as well as its sense would denote one tenth of a tithe.

148. *t'mn*. A privilege also common among the Sabaeans, as was that which follows; those granted it became *'mnhtn* once they were called to office (R. 3562).

149. Son of Yath'i'amar: compare A. Jamme, *Sabaean Inscriptions from Mahram Bilgîs (Mârib)* (Publications of the American Foundation for the Study of Man, Baltimore, 1962), 555 (hereafter cited as Ja.) with Pirenne I, Tableau généalogique: he is therefore not to be identified with the anonymous author of R. 3943, who (see Pirenne I, 148) is apparently one of the two builders of the southern sluice of the dam at Marib.

150. Yakrubmalik, although not named among the three Makrab princes in R. 3858 (he came of a different family), is shown by Ja. 550 to have taken part in this war, although not in person and only in terms of defensive measures. This is evident from the sometimes boastful, sometimes peevish language of his "intendant," who first maintained a military alert for three years, then had to lead a diversion against an unspecified place in enemy territory, from which, two years later, on the conclusion of the peace, he led his eighty men safely home. He received, by the way, his official thanks, not from his lord, but from the latter's son, although the father was still alive. Was this chance or custom? The same question applies to the case of a man with the same name who allowed his son to be adopted by the intendant.

151. *Corpus Inscriptionum Semiticarum,* pars quarta, t. I. III, 37 (Paris, 1889–1932), 37; *cf.* Pirenne, I, 191 f.

152. Ja. 552, 555, 557, 550, 551, p. 389, and the sketch on plate

C. "Sixteen columns" is not found in the inscriptions, but in 551: "all columns" (the last row), as in 550, for the next-to-the-last row. The translation given in the text before the South-Arabian words is based on the archaeological finds and the inscriptions. In this connection *mghbb* (sing., *maghabbat*, omitted in our text) is to be read "excavations" (for the pillars). Two excavations (556) for a single pillar (cf. 557) are comprehensible in terms of R. LeBaron Bowen and Frank P. Albright, *Archeological Discoveries in South Arabia* (Baltimore, 1958), p. 224, last paragraph.

153. Pirenne, I, 229.
154. *Ibid.,* 172 ff.
155. *Ibid.,* 148 f.; Beeston sees this otherwise.
156. *Voyages d'Ibn Batoutah,* 5th ed., Vol. 2 (Paris, 1949), p. 204.
157. Bertram Thomas, *Arabia Felix* (New York, 1932), pp. 36–105, 122.

Bibliography

A detailed guide to the ancient sources and to modern research publications is supplied in chapter bibliographies of H. Bengtson, *Griechische Geschichte von den Anfängen bis in die römische Kaiserzeit* (*Handbuch der Altertumswissenschaft* III, 4), 2d ed., Munich, 1960. See also the collection of Greek treaties, with commentary, in H. Bengtson, *Die Staatsvertraege der griechisch-römischen Welt von 700 bis 338 vor Christi,* Munich, 1962. A general bibliographical guide to the study of ancient history may be found in H. Bengtson, *Einführung in die alte Geschichte,* 4th ed., Munich, 1962, pp. 158 ff. See below, *Cambridge Ancient History,* for bibliographies in English.

GENERAL HISTORIES OF ANTIQUITY

The Cambridge Ancient History, ed. by J. B. Bury, S. A. Cook, F. E. Adcock, M. P. Charlesworth, N. H. Baynes. 12 vols. Cambridge, 1924–1939. See Vols. IV: *The Persian Empire and the West* (reprinted 1953); V: *Athens 478–401* (reprinted 1958); VI: *Macedon 401–301* (reprinted 1953). All volumes provide extensive bibliographies.

Historia Mundi: Ein Handbuch der Weltgeschichte in 10 Bänden, begründet v. F. Kern, hg. v. F. Valjavec. Vol. III (1954): *Der Aufstieg Europas.*

Histoire Générale des Civilisations, publ. sous la direction de Maurice Crouzet. Vol. I: *L'Orient et la Grèce antique,* by A. Aymard and J. Auboyer. 2d ed. Paris, 1957.

Meyer, E. *Geschichte des Altertums*. 5 vols. Stuttgart, 1884–1902. For the period covered in this book, see Vol. III, 3 (3d ed., edited by H. E. Stier, 1937); Vol. IV, 1 and 2; Vol. V (4th ed., edited by H. E. Stier, 1939, 1956, and 1958).

Rostovtzeff, M. *A History of the Ancient World*. 2 vols. Oxford, 1926–1927.

PERSIAN HISTORIES

Ghirshman, R. *Iran*. Harmondsworth, 1955 (new ed., 1964).

Junge, P. J. *Dareios I., König der Perser*. Leipzig, 1944.

Meyer, E. *Der Papyrusfund von Elephantine: Dokumente einer jüdischen Gemeinde aus der Perserzeit und das älteste erhaltene Buch der Weltliteratur*. Leipzig, 1912.

Nöldeke, T. *Aufsätze zur persischen Geschichte*. Leipzig, 1887.

Olmstead, A. T. *A History of the Persian Empire*. Chicago, 1948 (reprinted 1959).

Prašek, J. V. *Geschichte der Meder und Perser*. 2 vols. Gotha, 1906–1910.

Schaeder, H. H. *Das persische Weltreich*. Breslau, 1941.

GREEK HISTORY: GENERAL

Beloch, K. J. *Griechische Geschichte*. 4 vols., each in two parts. 2d ed. Strassburg-Berlin, 1912–1927. See Vols. I (end) through IV (beginning) for the period covered by the present book.

Bengtson, H. *Griechische Geschichte von den Anfängen bis in die römische Kaiserzeit*. 2d ed. Munich, 1960.

Berve, H. *Griechische Geschichte*. 2 vols. 2d ed. Freiburg i. Br. 1950/51 (Geschichte der führenden Völker, Vols. IV–V).

Bury, J. B. *A History of Greece to the Death of Alexander the Great*. 3d ed. London, 1951.

Busolt, G. *Griechische Geschichte bis zur Schlacht bei Chäroneia*. 3 vols. 2d ed. Gotha, 1893–1904. See Vols. II, III, 1 and 2. In spite of its title, the work covers only the period down to the end of the Peloponnesian War (404 B.C.).

De Sanctis, G. *Storia dei Greci dalle origini alla fine del secolo V*. 2 vols. Florence, 1961 (new ed.).

Glotz, G. *Histoire grecque*. 4 vols. Paris, 1938–1945 (Nouvelle édition, avec la collaboration de R. Cohen).

Wilcken, U. *Griechische Geschichte im Rahmen der Altertumsgeschichte*. 9th ed., edited by G. Klaffenbach. Munich, 1962.

GREEK HISTORY: PARTICULAR PERIODS

Bengtson, H. "Die griechische Polis bei Aeneas Tacticus," *Historia,* 11 (1962), pp. 458 ff.

Berve, H. *Das Alexanderreich auf prosopographischer Grundlage.* 2 vols. Munich, 1926.

Bickermann, E., and Sykutris, J. *Speusipps Brief an König Philipp.* Leipzig, 1928.

Burn, A. R. *Persia and the Greeks.* London, 1962.

Cloché, P. *La politique étrangère d'Athènes de 404 à 338 av. J.-C.* Paris, 1934.

Cook, J. M. *The Greeks in Ionia and the East.* London, 1962.

De Sanctis, G. *Pericle.* Milan-Messina, 1944.

Grundy, G. B. *The Great Persian War and Its Preliminaries.* London, 1901.

Henderson, B. W. *The Great War Between Athens and Sparta: A Companion to the Military History of Thucydides.* London, 1927.

Lévêque, P., and Vidal-Naquet, P. *Clisthène l'Athénien.* Paris, 1964.

Momigliano, A. *Filippo il Macedone.* Florence, 1934.

Mossé, C. *La fin de la démocratie athénienne.* Paris, 1962.

Nesselhauf, H. *Untersuchungen zur Geschichte der delisch-attischen Symmachie* (Klio-Beiheft 30). Leipzig, 1933.

Radet, G. *Alexandre le Grand.* 7th ed. Paris, 1950.

Stern, E. v. *Geschichte der spartanischen und thebanischen Hegemonie vom Königsfrieden bis zur Schlacht bei Mantineia.* Dorpat, 1884.

Stroheker, K. F. *Dionysios I: Gestalt und Geschichte des Tyrannen von Syrakus.* Wiesbaden, 1958.

Tarn, W. W. *Alexander the Great.* 2 vols. Cambridge, 1948.

Wade-Gery, H. T. "The Peace of Kallias," in his *Essays in Greek History.* Oxford, 1958, pp. 201 ff.

Wilcken, U. *Alexander der Grosse.* Leipzig, 1931.

Wüst, F. R. *Philipp II. von Makedonien und Griechenland in den Jahren von 346–338 v. Chr.* Munich, 1938.

CULTURAL HISTORY

Burckhardt, J. *Griechische Kulturgeschichte,* ed. by J. Oeri. 4 vols. Berlin, 1898–1902; now to be consulted in the German

Collected Works, Vols. VIII–XI, with an introduction by F. Stähelin.

Christensen, A. *Die Iranier,* in *Handbuch der Altertumswissenschaft,* III, 3, ed. by W. Otto. Munich, 1933.

Dodds, E. R. *The Greeks and the Irrational.* Berkeley–Los Angeles, 1951.

Ehrenberg, V. *The People of Aristophanes.* 2d ed. Oxford, 1951.

Jaeger, W. *Paideia: The Ideals of Greek Culture.* 3 vols. 2d ed. Oxford, 1945; reprint of Vol. I, 1965 (Eng. transl.).

Marrou, H. I. *A History of Education in Antiquity.* London, 1956 (Eng. transl.).

Osten, H. H. v.d. *Die Welt der Perser.* Stuttgart, 1956 (Grosse Kulturen der Frühzeit, Vol. 5).

Otto, W. *Kulturgeschichte des Altertums: Ein Überblick über neue Erscheinungen.* Munich, 1925.

CONSTITUTIONAL AND MILITARY HISTORY

Adcock, F. E. *The Greek and Macedonian Art of War.* Berkeley, 1957.

Barker, E. *Greek Political Theory: Plato and His Predecessors.* 4th ed. London, 1951.

Bengtson, H., in *Gnomon* (1937), pp. 113 ff. (on the Persian state).

Busolt, G. *Griechische Staatskunde.* 2 vols. (Vol. II jointly with H. Swoboda), in *Handbuch der Altertumswissenschaft,* IV 1, 1. Munich, 1920 and 1926.

Ehrenberg, V. *The Greek State.* Oxford, 1960 (Eng. ed.).

Glotz, G. *The Greek City and Its Institutions.* London, 1951 (Eng. transl.).

Hammond, M. *City State and World State in Greek and Roman Political Theory until Augustus.* Cambridge, Mass., 1951.

Jones, A. H. M. *Athenian Democracy.* Oxford, 1957.

Kromayer, J., and Veith, G. *Antike Schlachtfelder.* 4 vols. Berlin, 1903–1931 (with a *Schlachtenatlas zur antiken Kriegsgeschichte,* Leipzig, 1922 ff.).

——— *Heerwesen und Kriegführung der Griechen und Römer,* in *Handbuch der Altertumswissenschaft,* IV 3, 2. Munich, 1928.

Wilamowitz-Moellendorff, U. v. *Staat und Gesellschaft der Griechen* (Hinneberg, P., *Kultur der Gegenwart,* II, 4, 1). 2d ed. Leipzig-Berlin, 1923.

ECONOMIC HISTORY

Finley, M. I. (ed.) *Slavery in Classical Antiquity.* Cambridge, 1960.

Hasebroek, J. *Staat und Handel im alten Griechenland.* Tübingen, 1928.

Michell, H. *The Economics of Ancient Greece.* 2d ed. Cambridge, 1956.

Pöhlmann, R. v. *Geschichte der sozialen Frage und des Sozialismus in der antiken Welt.* 2 vols. 3d ed., edited by F. Oertel. Munich, 1925.

RELIGIOUS HISTORY

Nilsson, M. P. *Geschichte der griechischen Religion.* 2 vols., in *Handbuch der Altertumswissenschaft,* V, 2. 2d ed. Munich, 1955 and 1961.

Nyberg, H. S. *Die Religionen des alten Iran.* Leipzig, 1938 (Germ. transl. from the Swedish).

Rohde, E. *Psyche.* New York, 1925 (Eng. transl.).

Rose, H. J. *A Handbook of Greek Mythology.* 6th ed. 1958 (reprint), New York, 1959.

Weinreich, O. *Menekrates, Zeus und Salmoneus.* Stuttgart, 1933.

Zaehner, R. C. *The Dawn and Twilight of Zoroastrianism.* London, 1961.

SCIENCE AND PHILOSOPHY

Capelle, W. *Geschichte der Philosophie. Die griechische Philosophie von Thales bis Cicero,* in *Sammlung Goschen,* Vols. 857–859, 863. 2d ed. Berlin, 1953–1954.

Herzog, R. *Die Wunderheilungen von Epidauros.* Leipzig, 1931.

Jaeger, W. *Aristotle: Fundamentals of the History of his Development.* 2d ed. Oxford, 1934 (reprint, 1962).

Pohlenz, M. *Hippokrates und die Begründung der wissenschaftlichen Medizin.* Berlin, 1938.

Randall, H. J. *Aristotle.* New York, 1960.

Rehm, A., and Vogel, K. *Exakte Wissenschaften,* in Gercke-Norden, *Einleitung in die Altertumswissenschaft* II, 5. 4th ed. Leipzig-Berlin, 1933.

Sambursky, S. *The Physical World of the Greeks.* London, 1956.

Zeller, E. *Outlines of the History of Greek Philosophy.* 13th ed., revised by W. Nestle. London, 1931 (reprint, New York, 1955) (Eng. transl.).

LITERATURE AND ART

Beazley, J. D. *Attic Red-figured Vase Painters.* Oxford, 1942.
Bury, J. B. *The Ancient Greek Historians.* New York, 1958 (reprint).
Buschor, E. *Griechische Vasen.* Munich, 1940.
Carpenter, R. *Greek Sculpture.* Chicago, 1960.
Cook, R. M. *Greek Painted Pottery.* London, 1960.
Lesky, A. *Geschichte der griechischen Literatur.* 2d ed. Berne, 1963.
Lippold, G. *Die griechische Plastik,* in *Handbuch der Archäologie,* 5. Lieferung. Munich, 1950.
Rumpf, A. *Malerei und Zeichnung,* in *Handbuch der Archäologie,* 6. Lieferung. Munich, 1953.
Schmid, W. *Geschichte der griechischen Literatur,* Vol. I, 1–I, 5, in *Handbuch der Altertumswissenschaft* VII, 1. Munich, 1929–1948.
Schmidt, E. F. *Persepolis,* Vols. I and II. Chicago, 1953–1957.
Wycherly, R. E. *How the Greeks Built Cities.* 2d ed. London, 1962.

HISTORICAL ATLASES

Atlante storico, by M. Baratta, P. Fraccaro, L. Visintin. Novara. 1954.
Grosser Historischer Weltatlas des Bayerischen Schulbuchverlages, Teil I: *Vorgeschichte und Altertum* (with explanatory notes in a separate volume) by H. Bengtson and V. Milojčić. 3d ed. Munich, 1958.

EGYPT

Elgood, P. G. *Later Dynasties of Egypt.* Oxford, 1951.
Kienitz, F. K. *Die politische Geschichte Ägyptens vom 7. bis zum 4. Jahrhundert vor der Zeitwende.* Berlin, 1953.
Posener, G. *La première domination perse en Egypte: Recueil d'inscriptions hiéroglyphiques.* Cairo, 1936.

Wiedemann, A.   *Geschichte Ägyptens von Psammetich 1. bis auf Alexander den Grossen.* Leipzig, 1880.

MESOPOTAMIA

For the general history of the Persian Empire consult the following:
Cambridge Ancient History: Vol. IV: *The Persian Empire and the West.* Cambridge, 1953. Vol. VI: *Macedon* (401–301), Cambridge, 1953.

Olmstead, A. T.   *A history of the Persian Empire.* Chicago, 1948. Reprint, 1959.

Schaeder, H.   *Das persische Weltreich.* Breslau, 1941.

Among works that treat special aspects of Persian civilization, the following also deal with the history of Mesopotamia:

Cameron, G.   *Persepolis treasury tablets* (University of Chicago Oriental Institute Publications, 65). Chicago, 1948. See also his contribution to the work: C. Dentan, ed. *The Idea of History in the Ancient Near East.* New Haven, 1955.

Foucher, A.   *Les satrapies orientales de l'empire achéménide* (Compte rendu de l'Acad. des Inscr. et B.-Lettres). Paris, 1938, pp. 336 ff.

Leuze, O.   *Die Satrapieneinteilung in Syrien und im Zweistromlande von 520 bis 320.* Halle, 1935.

Schlumberger, D.   *L'argent grec dans l'empire achéménide.* Paris, 1953.

Documents for the history of Mesopotamia in the Persian period are numerous; they have been made the subject of publications spread over more than half a century. The latest of these publications is that of San Nicolò, M., and Petschow, H. *Babylonische Rechtsurkunden aus dem 6. Jahrhundert v. Chr.* Munich, 1960. (Includes bibliography of all the earlier publications.)

Also of very great importance is Cardascia, G. *Les archives des Murashu* (455–403), Paris 1951, in which numerous texts were translated for the first time, and provided with a rich historical, philological, and juridical commentary.

For a knowledge of some of the sites, consult the texts of Herodotus and Xenophon in the classical collections. Add the studies of:

Svend Pallis, "History of Babylon (538–93 B.C.)," in *Mélanges Pedersen,* pp. 275–294.

Wetzel, F. "Babylon zur Zeit Herodots," *Zeitschrift für Assyriologie,* N.F. 14 (1944), pp. 45–68.

The results of the archaeological excavations are to be found in the following volumes of the *Wissenschaftliche Veroffentlichung der Deutschen Orient-Gesellschaft:*

Koldewey, R. *Die Königsburgen von Babylon* (54 and 55). Leipzig, 1931–32.

Reuther, Oscar. *Die Innenstadt von Babylon* (47). Leipzig, 1926.

Wetzel, F., Schmidt, E., and Mallwitz, A. *Das Babylon der Spätzeit* (62). Berlin, 1957.

For the excavations at Ur, see Woolley, L. *The Neo-Babylonian and Persian periods.* London, 1962.

In the *Reallexikon der Assyriologie,* I, Berlin and Leipzig, 1932, consult the following articles: "Assur" (E. Unger) and "Babylon" (E. Unger).

The problems posed by the chronology of this period have called forth a considerable literature. We shall cite only the general study: Parker, R. A., and Dubberstein, W. H. *Babylonian chronology* (626 B.C.–A.D. 75). Providence, 1956 (a new edition has been announced).

See also the article, which clarifies the crisis in the reign of Xerxes by De Liagre Böhl, T. "Die babylonischen Prätendenten zur Zeit des Xerxes," *Bibliotheca Orientalis,* 19 (1962), pp. 110–114.

On aspects of Mesopotamian economic and social life, consult the works of:

Dubberstein, W. H. "Comparative Prices in Later Babylonia (625–400)," *American Journal of Semitic Languages and Literature,* 56 (1939), pp. 20–43.

Ebeling, E., the article "Bankhaus" in Vol. I of the *Reallexikon der Assyriologie.*

Porada, E. "Greek Coin Impressions from Ur," *Iraq,* 13 (1951), pp. 95–101.

Robinson, E. S. G. "A Silversmith's Hoard from Mesopotamia," *Iraq,* 12 (1950), pp. 44–51.

Weingort, S. *Das Haus Egibi in neubabylonischen Rechtsurkunden.* Berlin, 1939, pp. 57–64 (cf. the article by A. Ungnad in *Archiv für Orientforschung,* 14, pp. 57–64).

For the fate of the Israelites resettled in Mesopotamia, consult, aside from general histories of Israel, the works of:

Ebeling, E.   *Aus dem Leben der jüdischen Exulanten in Babylon.* 1914.

Sidersky.   "L'onomastique hébraique des tablettes de Nippur," *Revue des études juives,* 78 (1929), pp. 177–199.

For the history of law refer to the classic work of San Nicolò, M. *Beiträge zur Rechtsgeschichte im Bereich der keilschriftlichen Rechtsquellen.* Oslo, 1931.

For the history of science, refer to the bibliography given at the end of the chapter "Seleucid Mesopotamia" in Vol. VI of the present collection.

Finally, for an impression of the constant enrichment of our documentary evidence, consult, for example, Ungnad, A. "Neubabylonische Privaturkunden aus der Sammlung Amherst," *Archiv für Orientforschung,* 19 (1962), pp. 74–82, and the report given by J. J. A. Van Dijk on the texts discovered at Uruk (Warka) during the eighteenth campaign, in Volume 18 of *Vorläufige Berichte über die Ausgrabungen in Uruk/Warka* (Berlin, 1961), pp. 39–41.

PALESTINE

Cook, S.   *The Religion of Ancient Palestine in the Light of Archeology.* London, 1930 (Schweich Lectures, 1925).

De Vaux, R.   *Ancient Israel.* New York, 1961 (Eng. transl.).

Eissfeldt, O.   *Introduction to the Old Testament.* New York, 1965 (Eng. transl.).

Noth, M.   *The History of Israel.* 2d ed. London, 1960 (Eng. transl.).

Vogelstein, H.   *Der Kampf zwischen Priestern und Leviten.* Stettin, 1889

SYRIA

Galling, K.   *Studien zur Geschichte Israels im persischen Zeitalter.* Tübingen, 1964 (collected essays).

Leuze, O.   *Die Satrapieneinteilung in Syrien und im Zweistromlande von 520–320* (Schriften der Königsberger Gelehrten Gesellschaft 11, 4), Halle a.d.S., 1935 (*cf.* H. Bengtson, *Gnomon* [1937], pp. 113 ff.).

Otto, W.   *Beiträge zur Seleukidengeschichte* (Abh. Bayer. Akad. 34, 1), 1928, pp. 30 ff.: Ebir-nari, Koilesyrien und Seleukis.

ARABIA

Caskel, W.   *Lihyan und Lihyanisch* (Arbeitsgemeinschaft für

Forschung des Landes Nordrhein-Westfalen, Geisteswiss), Heft 4 (Abh.). Köln and Opladen, 1954.

Jamme, A. *Sabaean Inscriptions from Maḥram Bilqîs (Mârib)*. Publications of the American Foundation for the Study of Man, ed. by W. F. Albright, III. Baltimore, 1962.

LeBaron Bowen, R., and Albright, F. P. *Archaeological Discoveries in South Arabia,* with contributions by B. Segall, J. Ternbach, A. Jamme, H. Comfort, and G. W. Van Beek. Publications of the American Foundation for the Study of Man, ed. by W. F. Albright, II. Baltimore, 1958.

Nami, K. Y. *Nuqush khirbat Baraqish ʿala daumagmuʿat M. Tawfik.* 1, 2, 3. Cairo 1954, 1956, 1959 (Fisal min magallat kulligat al-adab, 1954, 1955, 1956).

Pirenne, J. *Paléographie des inscriptions sud-Arabes . . . , t. I . . .* (Verh. knkl. vlaamse Ac. . . . von Belgie, Kl. d. Letteren, nr. 26). Brussels, 1956.

Tawfik, M. *Les monuments de Ma' in . . .* (Arabic). (Publ. de l'Inst. Franç. d'Arch. orientale du Caire, Etudes sud-arabiques, t. I). Cairo, 1951.

PALESTINIAN JUDAISM IN THE
PERSIAN PERIOD

Sources

Charles, R., et al., eds. *The Apocrypha and Pseudepigrapha of the Old Testament.* 2 vols. Oxford, 1913.

Cowley, A. E. *Aramaic Papyri of the Fifth Century B.C.* Oxford, 1923.

Diodorus. *Bibliotheca Historica,* rec. F. Vogel and C. Fischer. 5 vols. Leipzig, 1888–1906.

Kraeling, E. *The Brooklyn Museum Aramaic Papyri.* New Haven, 1953.

The Mishnah, tr. H. Danby. Oxford, 1933.

Nepos. *Oeuvres,* ed. A. Guillemin. Paris, 1923.

The Old Testament.

Plutarch. *Vitae Parallelae,* iterum rec. C. Sintens. 5 vols. Leipzig, 1892–1895.

Posener, G. *La première domination perse en Egypte.* Cairo, 1936 (Bibliothèque d'étude . . . de l'Institut française d'archéologie orientale, XI).

Pritchard, J., ed. *Ancient Near Eastern Texts Relating to the Old Testament.* 2d ed. Princeton, 1955 (cited as ANET).

Smith, S. *Babylonian Historical Texts.* London, 1924.

Strabo. *Geographica,* rec. C. Müller and F. Dübner. 2 vols. Paris, 1853–1877.

SECONDARY BOOKS

Albright, W. *The Biblical Period from Abraham to Ezra.* New York, 1963.

Baudissin, W. von. *Die Geschichte des alttestamentlichen Priesterthums.* Leipzig, 1889.

Bickerman, E. *From Ezra to the Last of the Maccabees.* New York, 1962.

Braun, M. *History and Romance in Graeco-Oriental Literature.* Oxford, 1938.

Cook, S. *The Religion of Ancient Palestine in the Light of Archaeology.* London, 1930 (Schweich Lectures, 1925).

Daiches, S. *The Jews in Babylonia at the Time of Ezra and Nehemiah.* London, 1910 (Jews College Publications, 2).

Eissfeldt, O. *Einleitung in das Alte Testament,* 2d ed. Tübingen, 1956.

Goodenough, E. *Jewish Symbols in the Greco-Roman Period.* 9 vols. (to date). New York, 1953 ff. (Bollingen Series, XXXVII).

Kallen, H. *The Book of Job as a Greek Tragedy.* New York, 1963.

Noth, M. *Geschichte Israels.* 4th ed. Göttingen, 1959. *Überlieferungsgeschichte des Pentateuch.* Stuttgart, 1948.

Pfeiffer, R. *Introduction to the Old Testament.* 2d ed. New York, 1953.

Rad, G. von *Das Geschichtsbild des chronistischen Werkes.* Stuttgart, 1930 (Beiträge zur Wissenschaft vom A. und N.T. IV.3).
——— *Das Priesterschrift im Hexateuch.* Berlin, 1934 (Beiträge zur Wissenschaft vom A. und N.T. IV. 13).

Rudolph, W. *Chronikbücher.* Tübingen, 1955 (Handbuch zum Alten Testament).
——— *Esra und Nehemiah.* Tübingen, 1949 (Handbuch zum Alten Testament).

Schürer, E. *Geschichte des jüdischen Volkes im Zeitalter Jesu Christi.* 3–4 ed. 3 vols. Leipzig, 1901–1909.

de Vaux, R. *Les Institutions de l'Ancien Testament.* 2d ed. 2 vols. Paris, 1960–1961.

Vogelstein, H. *Der Kampf zwischen Priestern und Leviten.* Stettin, 1889.

Wellhausen, J. *Die Kleinen Propheten.* 3d ed. Berlin, 1898.

Articles

Aharoni, Y. "Excavations at Ramath Rahel." *Biblical Archaeologist,* 24 (1961), pp. 104 ff.

Bickerman, E. "The Altars of Gentiles." *Revue internationale des droits de l'antiquité.* 3ᵉ série. 5 (1958), pp. 137 ff.

Cross, F. "The Discovery of the Samaria Papyri." *Biblical Archaeologist,* 26 (1963), pp. 110 ff.

Heichelheim, F. "Ezra's Palestine and Periclean Athens." *Zeitschrift für Religions-und Geistesgeschichte,* 3 (1951), pp. 251 ff.

Hölscher, G. "Levi." *Paulys Real-Encyclopädie der classischen Altertumswissenschaft,* 12 (1925), pp. 2155 ff.

Maisler, B. "Golë Yisra'el beGozan." *Yedi 'ot hahebrah ha'ibrit lehaqirat 'erez Yisra'el,* 15 (1950), pp. 83 ff.

Rad, G. von "Die levitische Predigt in den Büchern der Chronik." *Festschrift Otto Procksch.* Leipzig, 1934.

Index

'Abadan (Nisab, Ansab), 418
Abar-Nahara, 359, 361, 404, 405
Abdalonymus, 408
Abdera, 103
Abrocomas, 266
Abu Simbel, 266
Abydos, 190, 211, 344
Academy, 76, 246, 253–54, 259, 277, 293
Acanthus, 175, 218
Acarnania, 95, 170, 173, 223, 224, 267, 296
Acco (Ptolemais), 402–03
Acesines (Chenab) River, 321
Achaea and Achaeans, 49, 93, 99, 164, 231, 235, 237, 296, 308, 330, 332
Achaemenes, 93, 340
Achaemenid Empire, 1–5, 8–10, 12–14, 71, 94, 281, 307, 314–16, 318–20, 323, 329, 337, 342, 344, 349, 352–53, 379, 423, *see also* Persian Empire
Achilles, 308
Achoris, 348
Acontium, Mount, 300
Acragus, 24, 66, 112, 196, 197, 199, 244
Acropolis, 28, 32, 51, 56, 76, 115,

117, 120, 121, 139, 151, 202
of Dionysius in Sicily, 200, 246
of Thebes (Cadmea), 219
Ada, 310
Aden, 417
Admetus, 75
Adria, 243
Adriatic Sea, 158–60, 243, 332
Aegae, 283, 302
Aegaleus, heights of, 59
Aegean, 1, 20–22, 27, 36, 43, 47, 63–65, 67, 72, 81, 90, 97, 100, 157, 162, 165, 167, 169, 181, 189, 209, 211, 218, 221, 223, 267, 309
Aegina and Aeginetans, 21, 35, 43, 49, 56–57, 91, 92, 99, 103, 111, 145, 162, 167, 253, 331, 370
Acgion, 332
Aegospotami, 193, 200, 206
Aeneas of Stymphalus, 264
Aeneas Tacitus, 263–66, 269
Aeschines of Sphettus, 150, 221, 269, 274, 278, 290, 291, 331
Aeschylus, 52, 66, 121–23
Aetna, 240
Aetolia and Aetolians, 173, 231, 295
Afghanistan, 317
Agariste, 84

Agathocles (son of Carcinus), 248
Agesilaus, 207, 208, 216–19, 224, 232, 235, 237, 264, 267, 278, 349–50
Agesipolis, 217, 218, 220
Agis I, 179, 183
Agis III, 330
Agriculture
    in Arabia, 414
    in Babylonia, 366–67, 372
    in Greece, 144
Ahuramazda (god), 15, 16, 18, 336
Aigikoreis, 33
Ajax, 308
Akerman, 133
Akitu festival (Babylonian New Year), 356, 360
Akkadian (language), 373, 376, 377, 379, 382
Alalia, 24
Alcetas, 224
Alcibiades, 116, 129, 135, 158, 178–83, 185, 188–92, 422
Alcidas, 170
Alcmaeonid family, 27–29, 42, 45, 48, 60, 84, 162
Aleppo, 381, 404
Aleuadae, 49, 289
Alexander (Molossian King), 249
Alexander I Philhellene (Macedonia), 60, 79, 283–84
Alexander III (the Great), 1, 2, 14, 134, 247, 249, 259, 260, 262, 263, 267, 268, 272, 276, 277, 280, 285, 294, 300, 303–32, 351–53, 364, 366, 370, 384, 401, 408, 422, 423
    armies of, 287
    divine kingship of, 278, 326
Alexander of Epirus, 302
Alexander of Pherae, 231, 234
Alexander Romance, 304
Alexander Vulgate, 304
Alexandretta, 310

Alexandria, 313
Alexandria Eschata, 318
Alexandria in Arachosia (Kandahar), 318
Alexandria in Areia (Herat), 318
Alexandropolis, 305
Alexarchus, 278
Alian, 351
Alpheus, 233
Amadocus, 287, 290
Amanus Mountains, 310, 403
Amasis, 151, 333–36, 338
Ambraciotes, 173
Amir, 411
Ammon (god), 313, 325, 351
Ammonitis and Ammonites, 396, 404
Amorges, 183, 187, 188
Amorgos, 106
Amphictyonic Council, 298–99, 305
Amphilochians, 173
Amphipolis, 155, 175–77, 181, 218, 226, 236, 251, 285–87, 293
Amphissa, 298–99
Amu-Darya River, 318
Amun-Re (god), 342
Amyclae, 232
Amyntas, 352
Amyntas (son of Perdiccas III), 281, 285, 305
Amyntas I, 282, 283
Amyntas III, 218, 259, 284, 286
Amyrtaeus, 95, 204, 341, 347
Anabasis, 204, 205
Anahita (god), 18
Anapus, 185
Anat (god), 345, 395
Anatolia, 5, 205, 206, 235
Anaxagoras of Clazomenae, 84–85, 107, 108, 131, 132, 160–61
Anaximander, 22
Ancona, 243
Ancyra (Ankara), 310
Andocides, 210

Andromache (Troas), 278
Andromachus of Tauromenium, 247
Andros, 60, 103
Annobal (Hannibal?), 236
Anshan, 5
Antheli, 54
Antialcidas, 212–13, 227
  Peace of (King's Peace), 1, 213, 215–17, 221, 222, 225, 227, 230–31, 239, 243, 244, 348
Antigone, 123
Antiochus III, 397
Antipater (general and regent under Alexander), 260, 305, 309, 330, 331
Antipater of Magnesia, 293
Antiphon of Rhamnus, 188
Antisthenes, 150, 263
Anu (god), 378
Aornus (Pir-sar), 320
Apame, 318
Apella, 161, 219
Apelles, 277
Apis (sacred bull), 334, 337, 345, 351
Apollo (god), 200
  Delian, 44, 70
  Delphic, 35, 50, 56, 60, 275–76
  Temple of (Didyma), 276
Apollocrates, 246
Apollonius, 313
Appollonia, 21, 218
Apries, 335, 336
Arabaya, 11
Arabia and Arabians, 313, 323, 327, 409–19
Arabian desert, 333
Arabs, 2, 51, 261, 280, 345, 348, 352, 409
  King of the, 347, 409
Arachosia, 11, 318, 322
Aradus and Aradians, 311, 402, 406
Arakha, 10
Aral Sea, 8, 23

Aramaeans, 403
Aramaic (language), 12, 338, 341–44, 361–62, 373, 377, 384, 410
Arbela, 314
Arcadia and Arcadians, 74, 146, 231, 235–38, 272, 296, 330
Arcadian League, 231, 233, 236–37
Archelaus, 284
Archidamian War, 70, 71, 156–57, 166, 169, 217
Archidamus, 166
Archidamus III, 248–49
Archilochus, 35
Architecture
  of the Achaemenid Empire, 14–16
  in Arabia, 416–17
  in Athens, 26, 89, 106, 109, 111, 115–18, see also Acropolis; Parthenon; Stoa Poikilé
  Delphic Temple of Apollo, 275–76
  in Egypt, 348–50
  of the Greeks, 3, 16
  Mausoleum in Halicarnassus, 276
  of the Persians, 3, 41, 347, 359, 376
  of temples, 276
  of theaters, 121, 275
Archons, 29, 33, 48, 83, 88
Archytas, 244
Areia, 317, 318
Areopagus, 33, 82–83, 87, 88, 122
Argadeis, 33
Argaeus, 285
Argeadae, Macedonian Royal House of the, 283
Arginusae, 193, 251, 253
Argos and Argives, 21, 35, 40, 49, 50, 73, 75, 90, 91, 95, 164, 178, 179, 182, 208–10, 212, 213, 235, 277, 296, 330
Argyronesi, 55
Aria, 11
Ariamazes, 319
Ariobarzanes (satrap of Persis), 315

Ariobarzanes of Phrygia, 234, 235
Aristagoras, 38–41
Aristides, 48, 59, 60, 70, 88, 136, 177
Aristippus (mercenary), 266
Aristippus of Cyrene, 263
Aristobulus, 315
Aristodemus, 24
Aristogeiton, 27
Aristomache, 241
Aristophanes, 124–26, 129, 162, 270, 275
Aristotle, 32, 70, 82–83, 87, 99, 130, 149, 189, 222, 253, 255, 258–63, 272, 290, 303, 310, 320
Ariyawrate (Gedhor, Tachos, Teos), 342
Armenia, 4, 5, 9, 11, 205, 337
Armies, see Hoplites; Military power
Armina, 11
Arrabeus, 176
Arrian of Nicomedia, 304, 323
Arsaces (Artaxerxes II), 204, 212, 266, 280, 281, 341, 349, 361, 373, 400, 422
Arsames, 340, 341
Arses, 351, 352
Arsites, 297
Art, 111, 272, 276–77, 422
    in Egypt, 346–47, 406
    in Greece, 406, 421
    in Phoenicia, 405, 406
    in Sicily, 196, 245, 246
    See also Architecture; Painting; Sculpture; Vases
Artabanus, 77
Artabazus, 281–82, 289
Artacoana, 317
Artaphernes, 32, 38, 41
Artaphernes (younger), 43
Artaxerxes I, 75, 77, 96, 186, 340–41, 361, 391, 392, 405
Artaxerxes II Mnemon (Arsaces), 204, 212, 266, 280, 281, 341, 349, 361, 373, 400, 422

Artaxerxes III Ochus, 280, 281–82, 293, 312, 350, 351, 361, 401, 406, 407
Artemis (goddess), 200
    Temple of (in Ephesus), 276
    treaty of, 305
Artemisia (sister of Mausolus), 276
Artemisia of Halicarnassus, 59
Artemisium, Cape, 53, 55, 57, 77, 133, 404
Artemon of Slazomenae, 106
Aryandes, 337, 340
Arybbas, 278
Asclepiads, 130
Asclepius, Temple of, 277
Asia Minor, 6, 11, 13, 22, 28, 34, 64, 72, 75, 83, 96, 100, 133, 157, 165, 167, 170, 187, 188, 192, 193, 203–04, 206–12, 235, 264, 267, 272, 276, 279, 281, 289, 296, 302, 307, 309–10, 339, 341
Asopus, plain of, 61
Aspasia, 90, 108, 150, 160–61, 169, 193
Aspendus, 211
Asrubal (Hasdrubal?), 236
Asshur (god), 363
Assinarus River, 185
Asos, 259, 261
Assur, 363, 410
    King of, 409
Assur-uballit, 5
Asswan, 342–43
Assyria and Assyrians, 4–5, 11, 13, 356, 359, 362, 363, 366, 375, 384, 410
Astrology, 383–84
Astronomy, 382–83, 385
Astyages (Ishtuwegu), 5
Astydamas, 275
Atarneus, 259, 264, 295
Athena (goddess), 119, 120, 308
    Temple of (Athens), 94
    Temple of (Illium), 308

Athena Chalcioecus, 74, 162
Athena Hygieia, 153
Athena, Pallas, 151
Athena Parthenos, 108, 117
Athena Polias, 276
Athenaeus, 336
Athenian Maritime League, see Attic Maritime League, Second; Delian-Attic Maritime League
Athenian wall, 64–65, 75, 98, 116–17, 165, 166, 168, 194, 209
Athens, 21, 35, 95–113, 144, 147, 209–10, 234, 268, 279, 339–40, 391, 406
  Carthage and, 198
  colonies (cleruchies) of, 78–79, 213, 236, 331
  commercial power of, 146
  democracy in, 26–33, 80, 82, 115, 148, 180, 188–93, 203, 211, 252, 268–70, 272, 273
  Macedonia and, 285, 287, 289–301, 331
  military service in, 140–42
  under oligarchy, 202–03
  Peloponnesian War and, 157–86, 188–94, 201, 210–11, 213
  Persian War and, 37, 39, 40, 42–51, 53, 56–66, 95
  rivalry of with Sparta, 69, 95, 97, 220, 233; see also Sparta
  theater of, 120–26, 273–75
  See also Athenian wall; Attic Maritime League, Second; Delian-Attic Maritime League; Demosthenes; Pericles
Athletics, 137–40
Athos, Mount, 43, 48
'Athtar (god), 412, 414
Athura, 11
Atiyawahi, 342
Atossa, 9
Attalus (father of Cleopatra), 294, 302, 305

Attic Greek (dialect), 20, 279
Attic Maritime League, Second, 221–24, 226, 235–36, 281, 300, see also Delian-Attic Maritime League
Attica, see Athens
Aulis, 207
Ausan, 417, 418
Autophradates, 210
'Auwam, Temple, 416–17
Axius River, 282
Azazel, 399
Azov, Sea of, 317

Baal, Banit (god), 345
Baal-Eshmun (god), 345
Babairu, 11
Babel, tower of, 360
Babilu û Eblr-nâri, 403
  King of, 8
Babylon, 326, 327, 354–61, 363–64, 375, 382, 384, 386–88, 410
Babylonia and Babylonians, 7, 9–11, 14, 37, 48, 133, 205, 266, 307, 314–15, 328, 329, 337, 345, 354–63, 366–68, 372, 377, 384, 399, 407, 410, 422, see also Neo-Babylonian Empire
Babylonian (language), 15
Bacchylides, 66, 134
Bactria, 11, 77, 316–18
Baga (god), 378
Bagoas, 307, 350–52
Ba'l (god), 414
Balkan Mountains, 295, 298, 306
Baluchistan, 322, 323
Banit of Syene (god), 344
Banking, 270–71, 371
Bardiya (Smerdis), 9, 15, 357, 405
Beas (Hyphasis) River, 321, 323
Bedouins, 333, 392
Behistun, 9, 10, 15, 376
Bel-Marduk (god), 8, 315
Bel-Shimanni, 360

Beloch, K. J., 65, 83, 88, 107, 148, 162, 294
Belesys (satrap of Syria), 407
Belesys, family of, 404
Bematists, 317, 332
Berisades, 287
Berve, H., 47, 246–47
Bessarabia, 23, 29
Bessus, 316–18
Bethel (god), 344, 395
Bible, 12, 14
Bickermann, E., 293
Bigvai, 379
Bilshan, 379
Bitter Lakes, 339
Black Sea, 21, 23, 39, 103, 133, 205, 212, 289, 295
Boeotia and Boeotians, 32, 61, 92, 97, 112, 118, 140, 144, 164, 166, 171, 175, 178, 179, 184, 207, 208, 212, 213, 215, 216, 220, 224–26, 229–38, 281, 288, 306
Boeotian League, 225, 227, 236, 288, 301
Bokhara, 317
Borsippa, 360, 378
Bosporus, 23, 39, 40, 96, 116, 118, 165, 211, 297
Bottiaeans, 218
Boule, 79, 86, 87
Brahmans, 320
Brasidas, 155, 158, 167, 175–77
Brea, 103
Brygae, 43
Brygus, 120
Bubastis, 339
Buchner, E., 221
Buddhism, 320
Burckhardt, Jakob, 125
Busolt, G., 43
Buto (goddess), 351
Byblus, 311, 403
Byzantium, 65, 73, 103, 106, 211, 221, 236, 289, 297, 298

Cadmea, 219, 220, 306
Cadusians, 307
Caere, 243
Calah (Nimrud), 362, 369
Calas, 308
Calauria, Temple of, 331
Caleacte, 196
Calendars, 130, 132–33, 382
Callias, peace of, 1, 64, 69, 96, 100–02, 154, 183, 221, 340
Callias (athlete), 139
Callias (son of Calliades), 107–09
Callias of Chalcis, 296
Callicratidas, 193
Callimachus, 44–45
Callipolis, 24
Callipus, 246
Callisthenes, 96, 260, 310, 320
  Pseudo-Callisthenes and, 351
Callistratus of Aphidnae, 224, 268, 270
Calydna, 59
Camarina, 24, 134, 172, 199, 244
Cambyses (father of Cyrus), 5
Cambyses (son of Cyrus), 8–9, 19, 39, 333–39, 345, 351, 356, 357, 359, 365, 371, 382, 409
Campania and Campanians, 24, 66, 197, 200, 243
Canaanites, 391, 403
Canal Stelae, 339
Capelle, W., 255
Cappadocia, 5, 11, 13, 235, 308
Carcinus of Athens, 275
Cardia, 296
Caria and Carians, 40, 41, 51, 55, 59, 104, 149, 183, 187, 188, 192, 210, 266, 276, 302, 310, 328, 345
Carmania, 322
Carrhae, battle of, 2
Carthage and Carthaginians, 24, 39, 49, 52, 65–66, 106, 116, 146,

180-81, 195-99, 209, 210, 236, 240, 241-47, 266-68, 311, 313, 336
  Athens and, 198
Carystus, 44, 72, 290
Casaubon, 263
Caspian Gates, 316
Caspian Sea, 8, 23, 407
Caspians, 51, 345
Cassander, 278
Catana, 182, 197, 240, 244
Catanzaro, Isthmus of, 243
Catapults, 241, 267-68
Cathaeans, 321
Caucasus Mountains, 317, 323
Caulonia, 242, 243
Celts, 243, 298
Ceos, 236
Cephala, Cape, 55
Cephallenia, 92, 164, 167, 177, 224
Cephalus (slave owner), 145
Cephalus (of Syracuse), 147
Cephisodorus, 149
Cephisodotus, 226
Cephisus River, 300
  valley of, 299, 300
Cerata Pass, 300
Cersobleptes, 287, 290, 291, 295
Cetriporis, 287
Chabrias, 224, 268, 348-50
Chaeronea, 97, 273, 283, 299-301, 305
Chalcedon, 211
Chalcidian League, 217-18, 284, 286, 287, 290
Chalcidians, 32, 98, 105, 160, 169, 172, 178, 179, 218, 290
Chalcidice, peninsula of, 21, 43, 48, 119, 158-59, 175-77, 181, 217, 219, 259, 278
Chalcis, 98, 101, 146, 260, 296, 301
Chaldean Empire and Chaldeans, 4, 7, 327, 354-56, 361, 364, 378, see also Babylonia and Baby-

Ionians; Neo-Babylonian Empire
Chares, 224, 267, 298, 299
Charidemus, 267
Cheirisophus, 205
Chelidonian Islands, 96
Chenab River, 321
Chersonese, 28-29, 42-43, 103, 191-93, 226, 236, 289, 296, 297, 301
Chios, 64, 70, 79, 106, 135, 142, 164, 187, 209, 221, 236, 309
  treaty with, 102
Chorasmia and Chorasmians, 11, 345
Choregia, 79, 114-15, 121
Christianity, 2, 329, 399, 400
Cidenas (Kidinnu), 383
Cilicia and Cilicians, 43, 345, 347, 403, 407
Cimmerians, 375
Cimon, 65, 72, 73, 76-80, 84, 95, 104, 106, 117, 123, 182
Cimonian Peace, 96
Cinadon, 205-06
Cirrha, 298-99
Cithaeron, heights of, 61
Citium, 95
Citizenship
  in Athens, 29, 87, 89-90, 234
  in Sicily, 200
City-states (*poleis, polis*), 20, 25, 66, 68, 85, 99, 148, 159, 165, 209, 210, 215, 216, 219, 231, 238, 247, 261-65, 268, 272, 294, 300, 301, 331, 421-23
Clazomenae, 22, 188, 211, 212
Cleander, 24
Cleandridas, 98
Clearchus, 266, 278
Cleisthenes, 27, 29-33, 39, 42, 84, 86, 189, 190
Cleitarchus, 306, 315
Cleitus, 319-20
Cleitus (Illyrian King), 396

Cleombrotus, 220, 224, 228
Cleomenes, 313
Cleomenes (Spartan King), 32
Cleon, 71, 89, 125, 158, 169–71, 174, 176–77, 180
Cleopatra (daughter of Attalus), 294, 304
Cleophon, 191, 193
Cleruchies (*klerouchia*), 98, 102–03, 145, 171, 194, 209, 213, 235, 236, 296, 301
Clothing
  in Greece, 114
  in Egypt, 346
Cnidus, 188, 207–09, 211, 277
Coele Syria, 402, 403
Coinage, 6, 7, 13–14, 41, 101–02, 113, 118, 271, 288, 329, 345, 368–70, 401
Coinage Law, 101–02
Colchis, 133, 149
Colonae, 73
Commagene, 403
Conon, 206–09, 213, 224, 226, 271, 348
Coptos (city), 342
Coptos (god), 342
Corcyra (Corfu), 21, 75, 112, 114, 159–60, 164, 172, 174, 177, 224, 227, 296
Corinth, Gulf of, 91, 93, 99, 169–70, 295, 299
Corinth, Isthmus of, 50, 56
Corinth and Corinthians, 21, 91, 99, 105, 111–12, 114, 142, 145, 158–62, 164, 165, 172, 173, 177, 178, 193, 197, 208–11, 213, 247, 248, 267, 274, 296, 301, 305, 307, 316, 331
Corinthian League, 63, 301, 305, 306, 309, 326, 330, 331
Corinthian War, 224, 244, 271
Coronea, 97, 208, 219, 267
Corsica, 24, 243

Coryphasium, peninsula of, 174
Cos, 207, 209, 277
Cossaeans, 327
Cothelas, 295
Cotys, 280
Council of the Five Hundred, 30, 83, 189–91, 300
Council of the Four Hundred, 30, 190
Craterus, 315, 322
Crathis River, 24
Cratinus, 84, 108, 124, 125
Crenides, 288
Creon, 123
Cresilas, 84
Crete and Cretans, 50, 146, 267
Crimisus River, 247
Critias, 128, 202
Croesus, 6, 35, 50
Crokus field, battle of, 289
Chronicles, 396–98
Croton, 22, 24, 35, 39, 49, 242, 244
Ctesias, 51, 59, 94, 279, 336, 355
Cunaxa, 363
  battle of, 205, 361
Cuneiform writing, 12–13, 16, 339, 346, 347, 361–62, 373, 376
Curtius, Ernst, 283
Cyaneic Cliffs, 96
Cyaxares the Mede, 5, 6, 354
Cyclades, 44, 191
Cylon, 161
Cyme (Cumae), 24, 66, 197
Cyndus River, 310
Cynosarges, Gymnasium of, 46
Cynuria, 21, 35
Cyprus and Cypriotes (Cyprians), 40, 49, 65, 93, 95, 109, 186, 206, 207, 209, 212, 282, 312, 340, 341, 348, 350, 352, 403, 407
Cyrenaica, 8, 313
Cyrene, 49, 133, 134, 146, 331
  Doric, 94, 340

Cyrus the Great, 1, 4-9, 11, 14, 19, 307, 315, 322, 337, 347, 354, 356-58, 371, 375, 376, 380, 382, 386, 387, 391
Cyrus the Younger, 190, 204-06, 267
Cythera, 175, 191
Cytinium, 299
Cyzicus, 190, 197, 302

Damadin, 343
Damascus, 388
Damon, 84
Danube River, 23, 28, 295, 298, 306, 328
Daphnae, 344, 345
Daphnaeus, 197
Dardanelles, 21, 39, 40
Darics, 14, 315, 368
Darius (son of Xerxes), 75
Darius I, 3, 9-11, 13-19, 22, 23, 27-29, 41-43, 48, 118, 315, 320, 322, 334, 335, 337-40, 342, 343, 347, 357-59, 361, 364, 365, 371, 376, 380, 381, 384, 386, 391, 405
Darius II Ochus, 186-87, 192, 204, 341, 361, 378
Darius III Codomannus, 1, 307, 310, 312, 314-16, 319, 352
Dascyleum, 187, 192, 208
Datames of Cappadocia, 235
Datina, 417, 418
Datis, 43, 44
David, 390, 397
Dead Sea, 409
Decelea, 125, 183, 191, 193
Decelean War, 157
Dedan, 410, 412
Deinarchus, 274
Deinomenids, 195
Delaiah, 394-95
Delian-Attic Maritime League, 65, 69-72, 76-81, 89, 90, 92, 94, 97, 101-04, 106, 110, 111, 158, 160-62, 168, 176, 181, 186, 202, 209, 211, 215, 221-23, 227, *see also* Attic Maritime League, Second
Delium, 175, 230, 251
Delos, 44, 70, 94, 113, 152, 301
Delphi, 56, 60, 97, 113, 118, 119, 149, 152, 161, 177, 200, 230, 234, 271, 275-76, 288, 289, 291, 292, 298
Delphic Amphictyony, 64, 92, 276, 288, 291-92, 298-99
Demades, 274, 300
Democracy, 74, 92, 102, 235, 262, 269, 309
    in Athens, 26-33, 48, 80, 82, 148, 180, 188-93, 203, 211, 252, 268-70, 272, 273
    in Sicily, 195-96, 248
    in Sparta, 158
Demophantus, 191
Demosthenes, 170, 173-74, 184, 185, 267, 269, 273-74, 284, 290-92, 294, 296-99, 301, 326, 331
Dercylidas, 206
Dhofar (Zafar), 419
Diadochi, 1, 101, 262, 287, 326
Diagoras of Melos, 128
Diaitai, 88-89, 115, 191
Didyma, 276
Dieitrephes, 184
Dienelt, K., 100
Dio Chrysostom, 118
Diocles, 248
Diodorus, 95, 222, 226, 248, 306, 334, 338, 347, 348, 350-52, 406, 408
Diogenes of Sinope, 263
Dion, 246, 247, 257
Dion (city), 284
Dionysia, Greater, 120, 121, 123
Dionysus (god), 120
Dionysus, Theater of, 121, 122, 275

Dionysius I, 195, 199, 200, 209, 219, 225–27, 234, 240–45, 248, 253, 268, 272, 273
Dionysius II, 245–47
Dionysius of Phocaea, 40–42
Dioscuri (gods), 200
Dipaea, 74
Dittenberger, Wilhelm, 236
Dnieper River, 133
Doloaspis, 313
Dolopes, 71
Don River, 317
Dor, 391, 405
Doris and Dorians, 91, 97, 99, 130, 172, 183
Doris (wife of Dionysius I), 241
Doriscus, 51
Drabescus, 78
Drama, 3, 26, 67, 88, 108, 120–26, 129, 245, 260, 274–75, 396, 421
Drangiana, 11, 317, 319
Droysen, Johann Gustav, 283, 294, 303
Dryopes, 72
Ducetius, 196–97
Dura-Europus, 363
Durazzo (Dyrrhachium), 21, 159
Duris Vase, 135

Eanna Temple, 358, 374, 378
Ecbatana, 8, 9, 13, 315–16, 318, 319, 326, 358
Ecclesiastes, 395, 396
Edom and Edomites, 375, 409
Edones of Thrace, 42
Education
  in Egypt, 339
  in Greece, 126–30, 135–37, 143, 253
  Plato on, 256–58, 265
  Socrates on, 252
Egibi bank, 371, 373
Egypt and Egyptians, 5, 11, 12, 14, 20, 25, 37, 39, 51, 112, 146, 167, 204, 266, 281, 282, 292, 293, 312–14, 327, 328, 357, 359, 388, 391, 392, 295, 401, 402, 407–08, 409, 410
  Athenian expeditions to, 91, 93–95, 109, 186
  Herodotus' visit to, 133
  Persian Empire in, 8–9, 332–53
Eion, 71, 76, 155
Eirene (goddess), 226
Ekklesia (People's Assembly), 85–87, 107, 273
El Hibeh, 343
El Khargeh, 339
Elaeus, 308
Elam, 9, 11, 356
Elamite (language), 12, 15, 376, 377
Elatea, 299
Elea (Velia), 25, 242
Elephantine, 12, 133, 335, 341–45, 395, 398
Eleusis, 118, 183, 203
  Mysteries of, 152–53, 181, 182
Elimea, 282
Elimiotis, 284
Elis and Eleans, 74, 118, 167, 178, 179, 182, 220, 230, 236–37, 330, 332
Elleporus River, 242
Elpinice, 77, 80
Elymians, 195, 199
Empedocles of Acragas, 105, 196
Enlil (god), 378
Epaminondas, 148, 216, 227–39, 281, 285, 286
Ephesus, 22, 75, 207, 276, 302, 305, 309
Ephialtes (battle of Thermopylae), 54
Ephialtes (son of Sophonides), 79, 80, 82–85, 88, 90, 122n
Ephors, 73, 74, 140, 219
Ephorus of Cyme, 51, 237, 273
Epicharmus, 66

Epicurus, 396
Epidamnus, 159
Epidaurus, 91, 121, 233, 275, 277–78
Epipolae, plateau of, 240–41
Epirus, 75, 219, 223, 278, 294, 302
Epistates, 86–87
Eratosthenes of Cyrene, 317
Erechtheis, 99
Erechtheum, 114, 147
Eretria, 40, 44, 98, 145, 295, 296
Erythrae, 78–79, 102, 170, 187, 264
Esagila, 356–57, 360, 364, 378
Eshmunazar, 405
Essenes, 399
Etemenanki, ziggurat of, 360
Eteocarpathus, 209
Ethiopia and Ethiopians, 51, 167, 352
Etruria and Etruscans, 23–25, 39, 66, 105, 243, 332
Etymandrus River, 317
Euboea, 32, 44, 53–55, 72, 97–98, 103, 141, 145, 146, 184, 187, 190, 207, 260, 290, 295, 296
Eubulus, 270, 292
Eucleides, 203
Eucrates, 169
Eucrates (author of law on tyrants), 330
Eudoxus, 277
Eumenes of Cardia, 325
Eupatrids, 32
Euphrates River, 5, 8, 13, 312, 322, 327, 359, 361–63, 365–67, 402–04
Eupolis, 84, 107, 125
Euripides, 122–24, 127, 134–35, 150, 275, 284
Euripus, 55, 184
Eurobean League, 296–97
Eurotas, 232, 233
Euryalus, 185, 241
Eurybiades, 53, 57

Eurymedon, 72, 73, 78, 80, 90, 91, 404
Eurymedon (strategos), 170, 172, 174
Euthymus, 139
Evagoras, 206, 209, 348
Ezekiel, 390, 411
Ezra, 375, 380, 386, 388, 390, 392, 393, 396, 399

Festivals, 115, 119, 120
Fischer, General E. von, 51
Fleets, *see* Maritime power
Food, 114, 212, 269
Fravartish (Phraortes), 9
Freedom, 19, 67–68, 423
    Ionian revolt and, 39
    of speech, 108, 122, 269

Galen, 130
Gallipoli, 103, 193, 289, 296, 301
Gandhara, 11
Gargaphia spring, 61
Gaugamela (Tel Comel), 314, 384
Gaumata, 9, 337, 405
Gaza, 312, 402
Gedhor, 342
Gedrosia (Baluchistan), 322
Gela, 24, 112, 172, 175, 199, 244
Geleontes, 33
Gelon, 66, 242
Georgios, 57
Geshem (Gashmu, Gusham), 409–10
Getae, 295
Gimillu, 358, 374
Gobryas (Gubaru, Ugbaru), 7, 355, 356
Gordian knot, 310
Gordium, 309, 310
Gorgias of Leontini, 126, 127, 134, 172, 196, 225
Grabus of Illyria, 287

Granicus, 319
  battle of, 308, 352
Great Kings, *see specific names*
Greek (language), Attic dialect, 20, 279
Gregor, 101
Grote, George, 283
Grotefend, 16
Gubaru (Gobryas, Ugbaru), 7, 355, 356
Gutium, 7, 355, 356
Gylippus, 183, 184
Gytheum, 92

Habron, 93
Hadramaut (Hadramot), 411, 417–19
Haemus, 306
Haggai, 380, 389, 390
Hagios, 57
Haliacmon River, 282
Haliartes, 208
Halicarnassus, 59, 188, 211, 275, 276, 309
Halicyae, 173
Halus, 52, 291
Halycus River, 243
Halys River, 5, 35
Hamadan, 315
Hammurabi, Code of, 380
Hampl, F., 322
Hannibal, 197, 236, 245
Harahuwati, 11
Haraiwa, 11
Harim, 411
Harmachis (god), 378
Harmodius, 27–28
Harpagus, 7
Harpalus (Greek), 51
Harpalus (Macedonian), 323, 331
Harran, 5
Hasebroek, 147
Hazarapatish (chiliarch), 12

Hebrews (Jews), 341, 344, 345, 375, 386–402, 407, 422
Hecateus, 22
Hecatomnus, 210
Hecatompylus, 316
Hegesipyle, 76
Hegisippus, 274
Heliaia (popular court), 87, 88, 101
Heliopolis, 351
Hellanicus, 283
Hellenic League, 60, 64, 69, 296
Hellenistic Age, 245, 261, 277, 279, 294, 328, 385, 402
Hellenotamiai (League Treasurers), 104, 107, 170
Hellespont, 22, 40, 43, 51, 59, 60, 64, 103, 104, 122, 146, 165, 170, 190, 191, 211, 212, 226, 296, 302, 307, 323, 340, 352
Helmand (Etymandrus) River, 317
Helots, 74, 112, 140, 142, 148, 162, 178, 205–06, 232
  Messenian, 74, 78, 93, 232
Henata, 346
Hephaestion, 320, 322, 325, 326
Hephaestus (god), 117
Hera, Temple of, 118
Heraclea, 173, 175, 278
Heraclea Minoa, 244
Heraclea Trachinia, 299
Heracleides (rival of Dion), 246
Heracleides of Mylasa, 55
Heracles, 283, 291
Heraclitus, 22
Herat, 318
Herbessus, 200
Herippidas, 267
Hermae, 27, 116, 181
Hermae, Hall of the, 76
Hermes (god), 181
Hermias of Atarneus, 259, 264, 295–97
Hermippus, 108, 145–46
Hermocrates, 175, 197, 199

Hermonthis, 342
Herodotus, 3, 4, 10, 11, 13, 18, 22,
    37 38, 43 45, 47, 51, 52, 56, 60,
    61, 63, 64, 71, 105, 133, 134,
    151, 156, 197, 283, 334, 336–40,
    344, 345, 347, 355, 362–64, 367,
    402, 403, 409
Herostratus, 305
Hesiod, 35, 136
Hicetas of Leontini, 247
Hieron, 66
Higra (Egra, al-Higr), 412
Himera, 24, 66, 116, 172, 183, 195,
    197, 199, 242
Himeras River, 243
Himilco, 242
Hindu Kush (Paropamisus), 317
Hinduism, 320
Hipparchus (son of Charmus), 42,
    48
Hipparchus (son of Peisistratus), 21,
    26–28
Hipparinus, 197, 241, 246
Hippias, 21, 26 29, 43, 44
Hippias of Elis, 126, 128, 129
Hippocrates (brother of Cleisthe-
    nes), 84
Hippocrates (father of Megacles),
    48
Hippocrates (Sicilian tyrant), 24
Hippocrates of Cos, 130–31, 133,
    149, 152, 277
    Oath of, 131
Hippodamus of Miletus, 105, 117,
    131–32, 255
Hipponax, 22
Hipponium, 243
Histiaea (Oreos), 98, 103
Histiaeus, 38, 42
Historiography, 3, 22, 67, 105, 155–
    56, 272, 304, 421
Hoffmann, Otto, 283
Homer, 20, 34, 118, 135–37, 303
Hopletes, 33

Hoplites, 224, 251
    Athenian, 45, 141, 164, 165, 167,
        169, 170, 174, 175, 177, 182,
        184, 211
    Greek, 46, 60, 205
    Sicilian, 200
    Spartan, 140, 164, 174–75
Hormuz, 322
Horus (god), 342
Hug, 263
Hundred Years' Treaty, 173
Huwarazmiya, 11
Huza, 11
Hydaspes, 321
Hyperbolus, 179, 180
Hyperides, 274
Hyphasis (Beas) River, 321, 323
Hypomeiones, 205
Hyrcania, 9, 186, 337, 407
Hystaspes, 9, 77, 337

Iapygians, 197
Iasus, 188
Iberians, 243
Ictinus, 117, 118
Idib'il, 409
Idumaea, 404
Ilat (han-Ilat, goddess), 345
Illyria and Illyrians, 149, 218, 243,
    281, 285, 287, 292, 297, 306
Imbros, 40, 194, 209, 212, 301
Inaros, 93, 340
India, 2, 7, 12, 51, 317, 320–22
Indian Ocean, 365, 417, 419
Indus River, 320–22
Inscriptions, 19, 27, 346, 347, 380
    of Behistun, 9–11, 15–16, 376
    about Chalcidian League, 217, 286
    in Dedan, 410
    about Erechtheis, 99
    about Erythrae, 78–79
    Greek, 116, 199, 203, 220, 222,
        231, 264, 332
    in the Hall of the Hermae, 76

Inscriptions (*Continued*)
  of Karib'il Watar, 411
  about Makrab kings, 418
  Minean, 412–15
  about miraculous cures, 277–78
  at Naksh-i-Rustam, 10, 15, 16, 18
  in oasis of Taima' (Tema), 410
  at Persepolis, 18
  Persian, 3, 10, 13
  about Plataea, 298
  about public works (Arabian),
    415–16
  Sabaeanisms in, 412
  on Stele of Naples, 352
  at Susa, 15, 41
  at Troezen, 56
  about tyrants, 330
  of the Vatican Naophoros, 334
  in Wadi Hammamat, 342
Ionia and Ionians, 6, 7, 11, 14, 22, 23,
    25, 49, 51, 55, 57, 63, 64, 67,
    75, 79, 96, 97, 104, 111, 114,
    118, 145, 187, 188, 191, 206,
    210, 339, 340, 345, 406
  dialect of, 130, 134, 279
  revolt of, 19, 29, 36, 38–44,
    404
Ionian Sea, 21, 134, 164, 165, 167,
    177, 213, 223, 224, 232
Ionian War, 155, 157
Ionic alphabet, 203
Iphicrates, 211, 224, 266, 267, 348–
    49
Iranian Plateau, 365
Iran and Iranians, 1–7, 9, 316–20,
    325, 328, 358, 359, 361, 375,
    376, 378, 379, 381, 422
Isagoras, 32
Isaiah, 387, 395
Ishtar (goddess), 358, 378
Ishtar Gate, 364
Ishtuwegu (Astyages), 5
Isis (goddess), 342, 378
Ismenias, 219, 234

Isocrates, 96, 202, 216, 221, 227,
    272–74, 278, 292, 293, 302, 310
Isonomia (equality of citizens before
    the law), 29, 33–34, 39
Israel and Israelites, 392, 400, 403
Issa, island of (Lissa/Vis), 243
Issus, 310–11, 314, 352, 408
Italiote League, 242–43
Italy, 20, 22–25, 34, 35, 49, 104–05,
    112, 134, 140, 146, 157, 172,
    173, 177, 182, 196, 197, 229,
    240, 242–44, 246, 248–49, 253
Ithome, Mount, 80, 232

Jaeger, Werner, 227, 260, 261,
    273
Jaffa, 405
Jason of Pherae, 216, 222, 225–26,
    230, 273
Jaxartes, 317, 318
Jehoiachin, 379
Jerusalem, 312, 379, 380, 388–95,
    397–401
  Temple of, 8, 357, 386
  walls of, 392, 393, 409
Jews, *see* Hebrews
Jezireh, 11
Job, 395, 396
Jonah, 395, 396
Jordan River, 412
Joshua, 386, 389, 390
Judaism, 395, 396, 399–400
Judea and Judeans, 386–95, 398,
    400, 401, 407, 409
Judith, 395, 396
Justinian I, 254

Kabul valley, 320
Kamnah, 411
Kandahar, 318
Karib'il Watar, 411, 416–18
Kedar, 410
Khabbash, 351–52
Khaibar, 412

Khnum (god), 341
  priests of, 341, 342
Khshathrapuvan, *see* Satraps and
  satrapies
Khshathrita, 9
Kidinnu (Cidenas), 383
Kalif, 318
King's Peace (of Delphic Congress),
  292
King's Peace (Peace of Antialcidas),
  1, 213, 215-17, 221, 222, 225,
  227, 230-31, 239, 243, 244, 348
Koester, August, 53
Kornemann, Ernst, 3, 280
Kuh-i-Rahmat, 15
Kurdish Mountains, 314
Kusiya, 11

Lacedaemon and Lacedaemonians,
  21, 40, 52, 61, 72, 73, 80, 91,
  92, 100, 134, 140, 142, 144, 146,
  148, 162, 165, 168, 174, 178–
  80, 187, 201, 203, 216–19, 222,
  224, 225, 229-31, 267
Laches, 172, 173
Laconia, 231
Lacrates, 266
Lade, 40
Lakiadae, 77
Lamachus, 181
Lampsacus, 75, 103, 193
Language, 128, 354
  in Egypt, 338, 342, 349
  of Greek world, 20, 34, 134, 203,
    279
  of Macedonian administration,
    279
  of Persian Empire, 12–13, 338,
    342, 373, 376–77, 410
Larisa, 363
Larymna, 236
Lasus of Hermione, 27
Laurium, Mount, 49, 113, 145, 184
Lebanon, 281

Lechacum, 211
Leipsyhydrion, 28
Leitourgiai (public works), 114–15,
  271
Lemnos, 40, 194, 209, 212, 301
Lenaea, 121, 123
Lenaean Festival, 245
Leninabad, 318
Leonidas, 53–56, 61
Leontiades, 219, 220
Leontini, 24, 105, 108, 160, 172,
  180, 199, 240, 244
Leotychides, 63
Lepanto, 170
Lephtari Rock, 53
Lesbos, 41, 64, 70, 106, 142, 164,
  170–71, 187, 188, 191, 193,
  207, 209, 211, 309
Leucimne, Cape, 159
Leukothea, Temple of (Pyrgi), 243
Leuctra, 229-31, 238
Levites, 394–99
Liar kings, 10, 15, 19
Libya and Libyans, 11, 20, 93, 133,
  167, 197, 313, 336, 352
Lindos, 103
Lipari Islands, 173
Lissa/Vis (Island of Issa), 243
Lissus, 243
Literature
  in Egypt, 346
  See also Drama; Poetry
Livy, 168
Locri, 241–44, 246
Locri Epizephyrii, 134, 139, 172, 182
Locris and Locrians, 53, 92, 97, 164,
  208, 236, 267, 298–99
Lucania and Lucanians, 139, 242,
  249
Lyceum (*Peripatos*, Peripatetic
  School), 259–60, 263, 277
Lycia and Lycians, 40, 133
Lycomid, 42
Lycophron of Pherae, 225

Lycurgus, 270, 274
Lydia and Lydians, 5–7, 13, 22, 35, 40, 149, 210, 308, 309, 328, 422
Lygdamos of Naxos, 26–27
Lyncestis, 176, 284, 285
House of, 305
Lyppeius of Paeonia, 287
Lysander, 192–94, 200–03, 205, 207, 208, 268, 326
Lysias, 147–48
Lysicles, 169
Lysippus of Sicyon, 277
Lysis the Pythagorean, 229

Maccabees, 399
Macedonia and Macedonians, 1, 52, 60, 75, 78–80, 113, 124, 134, 140, 146, 158, 160, 165, 167, 175, 176, 179, 217–19, 224, 227, 231, 233, 236, 239, 258–60, 262, 273–74, 279, 370, 422, 423
under Alexander the Great, 303–32
Athens and, 285, 287, 289–301, 331
people of, 282–83, 325
under Philip II, 280–302
Mada, 11
Maeander, 22
Maeander River, 40, 75
Magi, 18
Magnesia (city), 75
Magnesia Peninsula, 53
Magus, 9, 337
Ma'in (Ma'in and Yathil) and Minaeans, 411–12, 414–16
Maka, 11
Makrab, 416–18
Malachi, 388, 391
Malea, Cape, 267
Malkat-Shemin (god), 344, 345
Malli, 322, 327
Mandane, Princess, 5
Mandonium, 249

Mandrocles of Samos, 23, 118
Mantinea, 178, 179, 217, 237–39, 264
battle of, 215, 237–39, 279, 281
Maracanda (Samarkand), 318, 319
Marathon, battle of, 30, 37, 44–46, 119, 122, 339
Mardonius, 43, 59–63, 65
Marduk (god), 7, 356, 360, 378, 379, 384
Marea, 344
Mareotis, Lake, 313
Marib, 416, 417
Marinatos, Spyros, 54
Maritime power, 8
of Athens, 21, 49, 51, 53, 56, 65, 92–93, 95, 102, 142, 144, 164, 166, 169–70, 172, 173, 182, 184–86, 189, 193, 194, 201, 215, 226–27, 234, see also Attic Maritime League, Second; Delian-Attic Maritime League
of Corinth, 112
of Egypt, 348
of Greece, 56–57, 64
of Ionia, 40
of Macedonia, 286
of Persia, 41, 43, 47, 51–52, 57, 207, 208
of Sparta, 142, 164, 170, 211, 212
of Syracuse, 212, 241, 243
of Thebes, 236
Markos of Catana, 247
Marmora, Sea of (Propontis), 22, 28, 40, 297
Massagetae (Massagetes), 8, 318, 357
Makrab, Massilia (Marseilles), 25, 105
Mathematics, 22, 277
Mathieu, 227
Mausolus of Caria, 276
Mazaces, 352
Mazaeus, 314–15, 384

Mazaeus of Cilicia, 407

Media and Medes, 5, 9, 10, 11, 51, 298, 318, 319, 337, 341, 357, 360, 363, *see also* Persia and Persians

Medicine, 130, 259, 272, 277

Medism, 47, 74, 81

Medius, 327

Megabyzus, 77, 94, 340, 360

Megabyzus (satrap of Abar-Nahara), 405

Megacles (father of Cleisthenes), 29

Megacles (son of Hippocrates), 48

Megalopolis, 233, 238, 296, 330

Megara, 21, 50, 91, 97–99, 141, 142, 145, 148, 161, 164, 165, 167, 175, 178, 296

Melian dialogue, 156, 180

Melissus, 106

Melkart (god), 311

Melos, 129, 180

Memnon (Rhodian), 266–67, 308, 309

Memnon (Macedonian), 330

Memphis, 93, 94, 312, 333–35, 338, 340–45, 349, 350, 352

Menander, 275

Mende, 103, 119, 218

Mendes, 348–51

Mendesian Cape, 94

Menecrates, 278

Mentor of Rhodes, 259, 266, 296, 302, 350, 407

Mercenaries, 2, 14, 21, 146, 184, 188, 195, 197, 200, 204–05, 211, 216, 224, 227, 235, 241, 243–45, 249, 264–68, 288, 289, 291, 299, 308, 309, 311, 314, 315, 323, 332, 344, 345, 348–50, 362, 363, 395, 405, 407

Markes, 364

Mespila, 363

Messana (Messina), 134, 172, 173, 196, 199, 242, 244, 247

Messapians, 197, 249

Messene, 232, 233, 296, 330

Messenia and Messenians, 20–21, 74, 78, 80, 92, 119, 148, 173–74, 232, 234, 235, 238, 281

Messina, Straits of, 105, 165, 183, 243

Mesopotamia, 5, 7, 314, 356, 357, 359, 361–63, 366–70, 373–76, 378–80, 386, 388, 402, 403, *see also* Babylonia and Babylonians

Methana peninsula, 174

Methone, 92, 167, 236, 286

Methymna, 170, 171

Meton, 132

Meyer, Eduard, 10, 23, 43, 51, 67, 157, 179–80

Migdol, 345

Miletus and Milesians, 6, 22, 38, 39–42, 101, 106, 111, 145, 187, 204, 276, 309

Military power

of Assyria, 5

of Athens, 30, 45, 60, 104, 287

of Babylonia, 7

of Boeotia, 230, 232

of Egypt, 349

of the Greeks, 62, 140–44, 267–68, 307

of Macedonia, 283–84, 286, 307, 314

of Media, 5

of Persia, 2, 7, 9, 11, 12, 41, 43, 45, 48, 51–52, 94, 314, 344–45, 358

of Phocis, 289, 291

of Sparta, 34, 49, 60, 78, 164, 219

of Thebes, 230

Miltiades (elder), 28

Miltiades (founder of Adriatic colony, 325–324 B.C.), 332

Miltiades (younger), 28–29, 42–47, 76

Min (god), 342

Mithridates I, 380
Mithras (god), 18, 378
Mnemon, *see* Artaxerxes II Mnemon
Mnevis, 351
Moabitis and Moabites, 396, 404
Moeris, Lake, 12, 338
Molos and Molossians, 54, 75, 219, 224
Money, *see* Coinage
Mordecai, 379
Moses, The Book of the Law of (Pentateuch), 392, 397–400
Mosul, 314
Motya, 66, 199, 241
Mudraya, 11
Müller, Gerhard, 258
Munychia, hill of, 28, 202
Murashu, House of, 355, 362, 371–73, 375, 379
Music, 135, 137
Mycale, Mount, 41
    battle of, 63, 72, 84, 340
Mycalessus, 184
Myron, 119
Myronides, 92
Mysia, 281
Mytilene, 170–71, 209, 259, 309
Myus, 75

Nabonassar, 382
Nabonidus, 7, 355–57, 365
Nabopolassar, palace of, 359
Nabu (god), 8, 344, 345, 378, 379
Naburiannus (Naburimmanu), 383
Nagran, 411
Naksh-i-Rustam, 10, 15, 16, 18
Nannar (god), 378
Napata expedition, 336
Nashan, 41
Nashq, 411
Nasos, 200
Nationalism and patriotism, 34, 36, 39, 50, 80, 165, 215, 216, 267,
302, 328, 351, 357, 360, 380, 396, 399, 404, 422
Naucratis, 25, 39
Naupactus, 93, 99, 119, 170, 295, 299
Nautaca, 319
Navarino, 174
Naxos, 24, 26, 38, 44, 70, 72, 75, 103, 224, 240
Neapolis (Naples), 197
Neapolis (Thrace), 287
Nearchus, 321–23, 327
Nebuchadnezzar, 355–57, 359, 365, 368, 370, 371, 375, 381, 388
Nebuchadnezzar V, 357
Nectanebo I (of Sebennytus), 348–49
Nectanebo II (nephew of Tachos), 349–52, 407
Nehavend, battle of, 2
Nehemiah, 380, 390, 392–400, 409–10
Neirab, 381
Neith, sanctuary of, 334
Nemean brook, battle of, 208
Neo-Babylonian Empire (Chaldean), 4, 5, 7, 344, 354, 365, 403, *see also* Chaldean Empire and Chaldeans
Neodamodai, 205, 206
Nepherites I, 348
Nepherites II, 348
Nestus River, 287, 289, 295, 306
New Persian (Sassanian) Empire, 2
Nicanor of Stagira, 268, 326
Nicias (son of Niceratus), 149, 151–53, 167, 169, 170, 175–77, 179–83, 158–86
Nicias, Peace of, 125, 177, 178
Nicocles of Cyprus, 273, 406
Nicomachus, 259
Nicostratus, 172
Niebuhr, B. G., 283, 303, 314
Niebuhr, Carsten, 15–16

Nike of Paeonius, 119
Nile River, 94, 133, 313, 321, 339, 340, 349
Nile Valley, 9, 12, 337
Nilsson, 151–53
Nimrud (Calah), 362, 369
Nineveh, 4, 5, 354, 362, 363, 369
Nippur, 355, 375, 378
Nisaea, 97, 98, 175
Nobility
  in Athens, 29
  in Ionia, 39
  in Persia, 9
Notium, 192
Nubia, 8, 11, 266, 323, 336, 351, 352

Oarius I, 307
Ochus, see Darius II
Ohrid, Lake, 285, 306
Odeon, 117, 122
Oenobius, 155
Oenoe, 91
Oenophyta, 91, 92
Oeta, Mount, 173
Oetaea, 92
Olbia, 133
Olmstead, A. T., 52
Olorus, 154
Olympia, 20, 24, 108, 113, 118, 119, 134–35, 139, 236–37, 268, 272, 332
Olympias, 294, 302, 304, 351
Olympic Festival, 268, 326
Olympic Games, 127, 128, 134, 237, 283
Olympus, 52, 284
Olynthiac Orations, 290
Olynthus, 217, 218, 220, 290, 293
Oman, 419
Oncken, Wilhelm, 261
Onomacritus, 27
Onomarchus, 288, 289
Ophis River, 217

Opis, 325
Opus, 53
Oracles, 27, 151
  Delphic, 28, 35, 50–51, 56, 139, 151, 275 76, 287
Orchomenus, 97, 236
Oreos, 103
Orestis, 282, 285
Oroetes, 19, 22
Orontes, 281
Orontes River, 402
Oropus, 227, 301
Orphics, 22, 27
Ortygia, 200, 247
Ostia, 75
Ostracism, 30, 32, 48, 106, 139, 179
  in Sicily (petalismos), 195–96
Oxus (Amu-Darya) River, 318
Oxyartes, 319

Paches, 170–71
Pactolus, 7
Paeonians, 287
Pagae, 91, 97, 98
Pagasae, 146, 289
Painting, 91, 118–19, 276 77
Palestine and Palestinians, 281, 348, 349, 356, 357, 359, 361, 388, 391, 392, 395, 397, 400–03
Palici, 196
Palikoi, 196
Pallacottas Canal, 329
Pallas Athena (goddess), 151
Pammenes, 289
Pamphylia, 72, 211
Panathenaea, 115, 120
Pandosia, 249
Pangaeum (Pangaeus), Mount, 21, 113, 288
Panhellenes, 35
Panhellenic (Olympic) Games, 127, 128, 134, 237, 283
Panhellenic Peace Congress, 100
Panionion, 40, 41

Panormus (Palermo), 66, 199, 241, 242
Paphlagonians, 146
Papremis, 93, 340
Paratonium, 313
Parmenio, 302, 305, 319
Parnes, Mount, 202
Paros, 47, 103, 112, 224
Paropamisus, 317
Parthenon, 117, 118, 193
Parthia and Parthians, 2, 7, 9, 11, 337, 363, 366, 373
Parthian Arsacid Empire, 2
Parysatis, 361
Pasargadae, 5, 9, 14, 315, 323
Pasion (banker), 270, 271
Pasion (mercenary), 266
Pattala, 322
Patzer, H., 157
Pausanias, 61–63, 65–67, 73, 74, 162, 232
Pausanias (assassin of Philip II), 302
Pausanias (Spartan King), 193, 203, 208
Pederasty, 150
Peisander, 207
Peisianax, 76
Peisistradids, House of, 21, 26–28, 43
Peisistratus, 21, 26, 28, 29, 44, 122, 283
Pelion, 306
Pella, 259, 275, 284, 291, 298
Pellene, 233
Pelopidas, 213, 229, 230, 233, 234, 285
Peloponnese and Peloponnesians, 49, 52, 73, 75, 80, 159, 162, 164–66, 168, 170–71, 173–79, 183, 188, 190, 193, 197, 201, 203, 205, 206, 215, 217, 219, 220, 224, 231, 235–37, 266, 277, 291, 296, 299, 301, 330, 332

Peloponnesian League, 21, 28, 32, 34, 61, 69, 71, 90, 91, 98, 100, 142, 158, 161, 164, 170, 217, 218, 220, 226
    Athens as member in, 194
Peloponnesian Wars, 1, 71, 82, 91, 101, 103–05, 107–09, 115, 117, 121, 122, 124, 141, 142, 144, 145, 148, 154, 156–94, 201, 204, 210, 212, 251, 275, 326, 422
    Athens and, 157–86, 188–94, 201, 210–11, 213
Pelusium, 312, 333, 345, 348, 350, 352
Pentecontaetia, 122, 144, 154, 155
Pentakosiomedimnoi, 33, 83
Pentateuch, 392, 397–400
Perdiccas (Macedonian general), 320
Perdiccas II, 146, 160, 167, 176, 179
Perdiccas III, 281, 285, 305
Periander, 160
Pericles, 37, 79, 80, 82, 84–90, 92, 93, 95–102, 104–12, 116–17, 125, 131, 132, 141, 145, 149, 153, 157, 158, 160–62, 166–69, 175, 177, 178, 180, 193, 221, 255, 273
    Age of, 3, 82, 112, 116, 133, 135, 421, 423
Pericles (son of Pericles), 193
Perinthus, siege of, 268, 297
Perioeci, 205–06, 232
Perrhaebia, 52
Persepolis (Persai), 10, 12–16, 18, 315, 316, 347, 369, 376, 377
Persia and Persian Empire, 1, 3–8, 19–23, 37–41, 51, 75, 94, 96, 106, 133, 154, 165, 186–89, 201, 203–06, 212–13, 215, 216, 221, 222, 226–27, 230–31, 234, 235, 238–39, 259, 272, 282, 292–93, 295–97, 300, 302, 305, 328, 329, 359, 361, 422

Alexander's conquest of, 262, 280, 306–27, 422

Athens and, 32

in Egypt, 8, 39, 292–93, 333–39

Sparta's treaty with, 125, 156, 157, 187–89, 206, 212

Persian Gulf, 323, 339, 365

Persian, Old (language), 15, 376, 377

Persian Wars, 20, 36–37, 64, 68, 80, 90, 95–96, 123, 145, 151, 233

Persis, 5, 11, 315

Peteesi, 343

Petitis, 313

Petra, 410

Phaenarete, 251

Phalaecus, 291

Phaleas of Chalcedon, 255

Phalerum, Bay of, 44, 46, 57, 59

Phalinus of Zacynthus, 266

Phanes of Halicarnassus, 333

Pharisees, 399

Pharnabazus, 187, 192, 206–08, 348–49

Pharsalus, 225

Phaselis, 72, 102, 310

Phayllus of Croton, 49, 138

Pherae, 216, 222, 225

Pherendates, 342, 351

Phidias, 108–09, 117–19, 161

Phigalia, 168

Philaids, 76

Philip II, 1, 233, 258, 259, 268, 272–74, 279, 280, 284–302, 325, 406

Philippi, 288

Philippus of Opus, 257

Philiscus of Abydos, 234

Philistines, 402

Philistus, 197, 243, 246

Phillipus (physician to Alexander), 310

Philocrates, 274

Peace of, 290–91, 298

Philomelus, 288

Philonides, 332

Philosophy

Greek, 3, 126–30, 150, 196, 246, 250–66, 277, 328

in Old Testament, 396

Philotas, 319

Philus, 217, 264

Phocaean settlement, 25, 39

Phocaea, 41

Phocian Wall, 54

Phocion, 274

Phocis and Phocians, 53, 54, 61, 92, 97, 164, 228, 229, 231, 271, 288, 289, 291, 299

Phoebidas, 219

Phoenicia and Phoenicians, 8, 41, 51, 57, 72, 94, 146, 206, 207, 282, 311–12, 347, 356, 359, 403–08, 422

Phormio, 107, 169–70

Phraortes (Fravartish), 9

Phrygia, 234, 235, 281, 308, 310, Hellespontine, 308

Phryne, 274

Phrynichus (Athenian oligarch), 190

Phrynichus (playwright), 42

Phyle, fortress of, 202

Phyrigia, 146

Pinarus River, 311

Pindar, 66, 134, 283, 306

Pir-sar, 320

Piraeus, 42, 98, 112, 115–17, 131, 165, 167, 172, 193, 194, 202, 209, 221, 331

Pisa, 237

Pisidia and Pisidians, 310, 348

Pissuthnes, 106, 187

Pixodarus, 302

Plataea and Plataeans, 44, 65, 66, 67, 72, 73, 133, 227

battle of, 61–63, 154, 232, 298, 340

night attack on, 154, 155, 166

siege of, 171–72

Plato, 126, 128–30, 132, 149, 202, 244, 246–47, 250, 253–62, 265–66, 272, 274, 278
Pleistarchus, 61
Pleistoanax, 98, 176
Plemmyrion, 184
Pliny, 118
Plutarch, 75, 84, 88, 95, 100, 102, 180, 334, 351
Plynteriai, 191
Pnyx, 132
Po River, 25
    Delta of, 243
Poetry, 22, 105, 134, 150, 152, 395, 396
    in Athens, 27, 77, 107, 121, 125
    in Syracuse, 66
Pöhlmann, Robert von, 258
Poleis, see City-states
Polybius, 243
Polycleitus of Argos, 119
Polyclitus, 275
Polycrates of Samos, 8, 22, 27, 34, 151, 333
Polygnotus of Thasos, 118–19
Polymnis, 229
Pontus, 112, 278
Population, 112
Porus, 321
Poseideumn, 402
Poseidon (god), 119, 162, 200, 308
    Temple of, 118
Poseidonia (Paestum), 242
Postal system, 13
Potidaea, 21, 158, 160, 162, 167, 169, 236, 251, 286, 287
Pratinus of Phlius, 27
Praxiteles of Athens, 276, 277
Priene, 63, 276
Procles, 173
Prodicus of Ceos, 126, 218
Propontis (Sea of Marmora), 22, 28, 40, 297, 308
Propylaea, 117

Prosopitis, 94, 340
Protagoras of Abdera, 105, 126, 128, 129
Protesilaus, Shrine of, 308
Proverbs, 395, 396
Proxenus, 266
Prytaneum, 115
Prytany, 86–87, 115
Psalms, 396–98
Psammetichus III, 8, 90, 333, 344
Psamtek-sa-Neit, 346
Psyttaleia, 57, 59
Ptah (god), 343
Ptah-hotep, 343, 346
Pteria, 6
Ptolemies, 329, 352
Ptolemy (regent of Macedonia), 233
Ptolemy I (Egypt), 304, 318
Punjab, 307, 320
Putiya, 11
Pydna, 236, 285, 286
Pylos, 71, 191
Pylos, Bay of, 174–76
Pyrgi, 243
Pyrrhus, 249
Pythagoras and Pythagoreans, 22, 230, 246, 253, 255
Pythia, 35, 276, 292
Pythian Games, 230, 260
Pythocleides, 84

Qainu, 410
Qataban, 411, 412, 416–19
Qedar, 410
Quintus Curtius Rufus, 304, 307

Ragma, 411
Rama, 411
Ramses II, 266
Rawalpindi, 320
Red Sea, 339
Religion, 67, 128
    of the Arabians, 414–16
    of the Babylonians, 7, 377–78

Delphic Amphictyony and, 64
of the Egyptians, 345–46
festivals and, 120
of the Greeks, 20, 33, 34, 60, 143, 150–53, *see also* Oracles
of the Hebrews, 341, 379–80, 386–402
of the Mesopotamians, 354, 356
of the Orphics, 27, 258
of the Persians, 7–9, 16, 18
Plato and, 258
of Pythagoras, 22
in Sicily, 196
Socrates and, 251
theater and, 88
tolerance in, 8, 19, 328, 334, 338–39, 341, 378, 404
Rhagae, 316
Rhegium, 105, 108, 160, 172, 181, 182, 196, 240, 242, 243, 246
Rhium, Strait of, 93, 170
Rhodes, 70, 146, 188, 207–09, 236, 259, 267, 296, 348
Roads, 13
in Macedonia, 284
Robert, Louis, 143
Robinson, D. M., 290
Rohde, Erwin, 139–40
Roman Empire, 279, 304, 328, 329
Rome and Romans, 168, 240, 243, 244, 249, 286, 326, 353, 423
Roxana, 319
Royal Road, 13
Russia, 20, 34, 37, 40, 103, 133
Rüstow, Alexander, 68
Ruth, 395, 396

Saba' and Sabaeans, 375, 411, 412, 415–18
Sabaces, 352
Sacred War, Second, 97
Sacred War, Third, 271, 288, 291, 298
Sacred War, Fourth, 298

Saïs, 334, 347
goddess of, 334, 336
Saïte Dynasty, 333, 335–37, 340, 344, 346, 349
Saka, 11
Salamis, Gulf of, 56–57
Salamis, Island of, 21, 133, 183
battle of, 1, 37, 42, 56–60, 66, 67, 72, 76, 122, 154, 340, 404
Salamis, Cyprus, 95, 206, 273
Salm (god), 410
Samaria and Samaritans, 390, 394, 398, 400, 401, 404
Samarkand, 318
Samnites, 197, 249
Samos and Samians, 8, 22, 27, 34, 41, 64, 70, 94, 105–07, 109, 118, 188, 189, 191, 200, 201, 211, 235, 274, 301, 326
Samothrace, 211
Sanballat, 394, 398
Sanctis, De, 112
Sangala, 321
Sangarius River, 310
Sarcophagi, 405, 408
Sardis and Sardinians, 6, 11–13, 19, 22, 24, 32, 38, 40, 51, 187, 192, 204, 207, 210, 212, 309
Saronic Gulf, 35, 55, 91, 111, 167
Sassanian Empire, 2
Sassanids, 2
Satibarzanes, 317
Satraps and satrapies, 10–13, 39, *see also specific names*
Sattagydia, 11
Scamander, plain of, 308
Schachermeyr, F., 45, 303
Schaefer, Arnold, 273
Schwartz, Eduard, 157
Science, 422
Babylonian, 382
Greek, 25, 277
Mesopotamian, 354
Scillus, 220

Scione, 176
Scipio Africanus Major, 245
Scopas of Paros, 276, 277
Scylax of Caryanda, 322
Scylletium, Gulf of, 243
Sculpture, 67, 118–19, 152, 276–77, 346, 349
Scyllias of Scione, 54
Scythia and Scythians, 11, 23, 37, 133, 149, 298, 318
Scythian campaign of Darius, 22, 23, 27, 28, 39
Segesta, 93, 105, 173, 180, 181, 195, 241
Seleucids, 2, 7, 319, 329, 363
Seleucis, 402
Seleucus, 318
Selinus, 24, 172, 181, 195–97, 199
Semiramis, 322
Semtantefnekhet of Heracleopolis, 352
Seneca, 250
Sepeia, Battle of, 21, 49
Sepias, Cape, 53
Serapeum of Memphis, 334
Serapis (god), 327
Serdaeans, 24
Sestos, 64, 211, 340
Shabwat, 412, 419
Shamash-Eriba, 360
Sharon, plain of, 405
Shekel (shiklu, siglos), 14, 345, 368, 369
Shelemiah, 394–95
Shemesh (god), 378
Sheshbazzar, 379
Shipka Pass, 306
Sicanians, 199, 241
Sicels, 24, 196–97, 199, 200, 240, 242, see also Sicily and Siciliotes
Sicily and Siciliotes, 20, 42, 49, 65–66, 93, 106, 112, 114, 116, 125, 133, 134, 157, 195–200, 209, 210, 215, 234, 240–48, 267

expeditions to, 157, 172–73 175, 180–87, 195, 197, 242, 267
Plato in, 246–47, 253, 254, 257
See also Sicels
Sicyon, 142, 164, 233, 277, 332
Side, 310
Sidon (Saida) and Sidonions, 311 350, 403, 405, 406–08
Sigeum, 21, 28, 122–23
Silistria, 306
Simonides, 66
Sin (god), 395
Sippar, 357
Sirwah, 412, 416
Sitalces, 146, 167
Sithonia peninsula, 176
Siwa, oasis of, 313
Skaptehyle, 155
Skiathos, 53, 276
Skudra, 11
Skyros, 71, 194, 209, 212, 301
Slavery, 59, 148–49, 171, 180, 184, 200, 232, 262, 306, 312, 371, 372, 374–75, 381, see also Helots
Smerdis (Bardiya), 9, 15, 357, 405
Social War, 270, 281, 286, 287, 292
Socrates, 108, 125, 126, 129, 135, 144–45, 150, 181, 250–53, 255, 258, 263, 284
Socrates of Achaea, 266
Sogdiana, 11, 318
Sogdianus, 186
Soleis, 66
Soli, 40
Solon, 21, 86, 87, 112, 113, 136, 143, 144, 225
Solus, 199
Sophainetus of Stymphalus, 205, 266
Sophism and sophists, 114, 123, 126–29, 134, 156, 172, 178, 225, 251
Sophocles, 107, 122, 123, 174
Sophonides, 82

Sophroniscus, 251
Sosis, 266
Sostratides, 174
Sparta, 27, 28, 35, 40, 105, 150, 217
   20, 227–35, 237–38, 264, 270,
   281
   Argos and, 91, 95
   Athens and, 32, 50, 66, 69–81, 95,
      97–100, 104, 116, 125, 154, 158,
      200, 220, 222–23, 233, 235,
      289
   athletics in, 138
   in Corinthian League, 331
   in Corinthian War, 201–13
   education in, 129, 256–57
   Egypt and, 348–50, 401
   Helots and, 21, 148, 232
   Macedonia and, 330
   military service in, 140–42
   money in, 113
   in Peloponnesian League, 21, 34,
      90–92
   Peloponnesian War and, 1, 158–
      68, 170–80, 182–83, 187–90,
      192–94
   Persia and, 1, 43–44, 49, 52, 54,
      61–66, 125, 156, 157, 187–89,
      206, 212, 215, 227, 233, 234,
      289, 301, 348
   population of, 112
   in Sicily, 200
   Thebes and, 230–31, 237–38
Spartolus, 169
Spercheius, 54
Speusippus, 293, 294
Sphacteria, 71, 174
Sphodrias, 220
Spina, 25, 105, 243
Spitamenes, 318
Stagira, 175, 259, 290
Statira, 325
Stephanus, 220
Stesagoras, 28
Stier, Hans Erich, 34, 90

Stoa, Poikilé (Painted Portico), 76,
   91, 118–19
Stoicism, 328
Strabo, 334, 400
Strato of Sidon, 406
Stratos, 170
Struthas, 210–12
Strymon (Struma), 51, 71, 78, 103,
   155, 282
Sumerian ideograms, 376
Sumhu-ʻalay Yanaf, 416
Sunum, Cape, 118
Susa, 10, 13, 15, 38, 41, 133, 187,
   212, 213, 234, 315, 318, 325,
   341, 342, 347, 350, 358, 359,
   370, 377, 393
Susiana, 327, 337
Swoboda, H., 79
Sybaris and Sybarites, 24, 35, 39,
   104, 242
Sybota Islands, 160, 172
Syene, 344
Sykntris, J., 293
Syloson, 22–23
Synhedrion (League Council), 301–
   02, 305, 306, 331
Syr-Darya (Jaxartes), 317, 318
Syracuse and Syracusans, 24, 66,
   112, 113, 116, 146–48, 152,
   172, 173, 175, 180, 182–85, 188,
   195–200, 209, 234, 240–48, 275,
   278
Syria, 8, 9, 146, 266, 281, 282, 310,
   340, 349, 350, 356, 359, 361,
   402
   under the Persians, 402–08

Tachos, 281, 349–50, 401
Taenaron, 162
Taima' (Tema), oasis of, 410, 412
Tamos, 347
Tanagra, 184
   battle of, 77, 92, 116
Tanais (Don) River, 317

Tang-i-Rashkan, 315
Taras, 105, 114, 159, 182, 244, 249
Tarentines, 197
Tarn, S. S., 323
Tarsus, 310
Tashetres, 342–43
Tatagus, 11
Tauromenium, 242, 244, 247
Taurus Mountains, 310, 403
Taxes, 9, 41, 71, 115–16, 170, 209,
    225, 271, 272, 305, 349, 358,
    362, 367, 369, 370, 373, 393,
    394, 398, 409, 415
Taxila, 320
Taxiles, 320–21
Taygetus, 232
Tegea and Tegeans, 62, 73–74, 178,
    208, 237, 238
Telecleides, 84, 108
Teleutias, 218
Tell Maskuta, 345
Temesa, 139
Tempe Pass, 52, 133
Tenedos, 309
Tennes, 406
Teres, 295
Thais, 315
Thapsacus, 363
Thasos, 21, 35, 43, 49, 70, 75, 77–
    80, 92, 103, 112, 190, 201, 211,
    289
Theater, see Drama
Thebes (Egypt), 342, 344
Thebes and Thebans, 53, 55, 61–63,
    92, 155, 166, 172, 184, 208, 210,
    213, 219–21, 223–31, 233–37,
    285, 288, 297–301, 306, see also
    Boeotia and Boeotians
Themistocles, 42–43, 47–49, 51, 53,
    55–57, 60, 64, 66, 67, 70, 73–
    76, 80, 83, 122, 142
Theognis, 50
Theophrastus, 153
Theophrastus of Eresus, 260, 263

Theopompus of Chios, 96, 273, 294
Theramenes, 190–91, 193, 202
Thermae, 248
Thermopylae, 52–57, 133, 173, 289,
    299
Theron, 66
Theseum, 76, 117
Theseus, 71, 76
Thespiae, 227
Thespians, 52, 55
Thespis of Icaria, 26
Thessaly and Thessalians, 52, 53,
    133, 140, 144, 148, 173, 175,
    219, 222, 225–26, 230, 231, 233–
    34, 266, 267, 283, 288, 289, 311
    Athens and, 91, 95, 165
    as Hippias' allies, 28
    Macedonia in, 284, 287, 289, 292,
        300, 305, 306
    Persia and, 49, 59, 216, 282
Thessalus (son of Cimon), 182
Thibron, 206, 211
Thirty Tyrants, 148, 202–03
Thirty Years' Peace, 99, 100, 104,
    145, 154, 159, 161, 162, 166
Tholos, 86, 275
Thrace, 11, 21, 23, 27, 28, 40, 42–44,
    49, 64, 76, 78, 96, 103, 104,
    113, 146, 149, 155, 160, 165,
    167, 175–76, 184, 191–93, 208,
    223, 226, 236, 280, 287, 289,
    296, 297, 301, 305, 330, 370
    Macedonia in, 289–91, 295
Thrasybulus of Collytus, 221
Thrasybulus of Steiria, 202, 211–12,
    221
Thucydides (historian), 75, 96, 107,
    120, 134, 142, 150, 154–58,
    162, 167, 171, 176, 177, 180,
    184, 185, 187, 188, 347
Thucydides (son of Melesias), 102,
    106, 109, 139
Thurii, 104–05, 117, 126, 131, 133,
    147, 159, 182, 242

Thurium, Mount, 300
Thyrea, 167
Tigris River, 5, 13, 41, 314, 325, 362
Timaeus, 199, 247
Timosthenes, 65, 69
Timna', 412, 417
Timocrates, 208
Timocreon of Ialysus, 70
Timoleon, 247–48
Timotheus (son of Conon), 224, 226–27, 235, 236, 266–68
Tiribazus, 210, 212
Tissaphernes, 187–89, 192, 204, 206–07, 266
Tithraustes, 207
Tobias, 394
Tobit, 395, 396
Tolmides, 92–93, 97
Tonzus River, 289
Torone, 176, 236
Toynbee, Arnold J., 68
Trachis, plain of, 54
Trade
    Arabian, 409, 412
    Athenian, 103, 105, 112–13, 145–47, 159, 162, 236, 289
    Babylonian, 7, 365, 367
    Greek, 24, 39, 40, 202, 210, 216, 332, 369
    Ionian, 39
    Macedonian, 236, 284
    money in, 14, 113, 369
    Peloponnesian, 175
    of Persian Empire, 339
    Phoenician, 403, 406
    Sicilian, 196
    Thracian, 289
Traeis, 242
Trapezus, 205
Treasuries
    of Athena, 109–10
    of Athena Polias, 109
    of Delian League, 70, 94
    in Egypt, 343

of Macedonia, 323
of Persia (ganzaka), 12, 14, 15, 368, 379
Treitschke, Heinrich von, 261
Triballi, 306
Triphylia, 236
Tripolis, 404, 406, 407
Troad, 73, 133, 259, 295, 296, 309
Troezen, 56, 98, 136, 174, 233, 331
Troy and Trojans, 119, 308
Turkestan, 317–19, 357
Tyana, 310
Tyndaris, 242, 244
Tyranny, 26–27, 262, 272, 278
    in Athens, 21, 26–30, 42, 115, 202
    in Corinth, 159
    in Erythrae, 79
    in Ionia, 38
    in Sicily, 24, 66, 195–96, 199–200, 244–45, 247–48, 254
    in Thessaly, 225
    of the Thirty Tyrants, 148, 202–03
Tyre and Tyrians, 311–13, 328, 375, 403, 406, 408
Tyrrhenian Sea, 243
Tyrrhenians, see Etruria and Etruscans

Udzahorresne, 334, 336, 338–39, 346
Ugbaru (Gobryas, Gubaru), 7, 355, 356
Ullrich, Franz Wolfgang, 156–57
Ur, 365–66, 378
Uranopolis, 278
Uruk (Warka), 355, 358, 368, 374, 378
Ushtanni, 359
Uxians, 315

Vahibra, 346
Vases
    Egyptian, 346–47
    Greek, 24, 119–20, 135

Vatican Naophoros, 334, 346
Veith, Lt.-Col. Georg, 62
Velia (Elea), 25, 242
Vogt, J., 149

Wadi Gurdan (Jirdan), 418
Wadi Hammamat, 342
Wadi Tumilat, 339, 410
Wasr (Wusr), 417
Widrang, 343
Wilamowitz, Ulrich von, 143–44, 221
Women, 87, 149–50, 256, 362
Wüst, F. R., 298

Xanthippus, 60, 64, 84
Xanthus valley, 310
Xennias, 266
Xenophanes, 66, 127
Xenophon, 6, 146, 187, 192, 194,
    205, 207, 209, 212, 216, 219,
    223, 226, 229, 238, 253, 264,
    266, 267, 270, 278, 343, 355,
    362–63, 404
Xerxes, 1, 14, 18, 48–49, 51–52, 54–
    55, 57, 75, 77, 84, 93, 122, 207,
    302, 315, 340, 358, 359, 361,
    363, 364, 376, 378, 405
Xerxes II, 186

Yada"il Darih, 416–17
Yahweh (Yahu), 341, 344, 345,
    379–80, 386–91, 394–401
Yathil, 411–12, 414–16
Yathrib (Medina), 412
Yauna, 11
Yehohanan, 394, 398

Zacynthus, 92, 164, 174, 177, 226
Zagros Mountains, 4, 14
Zarathustra (Zoroaster), 18, 19
Zazana, 357
Zechariah, 388–9
Zeno of Elea, 25, 84
Zerubbabel, 375, 379, 386, 389–91
Zeus (god), 50, 200, 278, 351
    Olympian, 248
Zeus, Temple of, 118
Zranka, 11

NOTE ON EDITOR AND CONTRIBUTORS

HERMANN BENGTSON, who wrote a large portion of this volume and who is also its editor, is a professor of Ancient History at the University of Munich. He was formerly associated with the University of Tübingen and has written and edited several books on Greek history.

EDDA BRESCIANI, author of the chapter on Egypt, is a professor of Egyptology at the University of Pisa and has participated in several archaeological expeditions.

WERNER CASKEL, who wrote the chapter on Arabia, is a professor of Oriental Studies at the University of Cologne and a member of the German Archaeological Institute.

MAURICE MEULEAU, author of the chapter on Mesopotamia, is an assistant professor at the College of Arts and Sciences of the University of Paris-Nanterre.

MORTON SMITH, who wrote the chapter on Palestine, has been associated with Columbia University since 1957. He is now a professor of History there.